The New South and the "New Competition"

The New South and the "New Competition"

Trade Association Development in the Southern Pine Industry

James E. Fickle

Published for the Forest History Society

by the

University of Illinois Press

Urbana Chicago London

Publication of this book was supported by grants from
Memphis State University and the Forest History Society.

Library of Congress Cataloging in Publication Data

Fickle, James E.   1939-
  The New South and the "new competition."

Includes bibliographical references and index.
1. Southern Pine Association—History. I. Title.
HD9757.A2F5   381'.4567406'075   80-12420
ISBN 0-252-00788-3

Contents

Contents

Acknowledgments

It is virtually impossible to identify all of the people who assist in the production of a book. However, several were especially helpful at critical times in the development of this project. First and foremost was Professor John L. Loos of Louisiana State University, who suggested the topic and offered both expert guidance and genuine interest. The staffs of the archives at the University of Houston, the University of Texas, Stephen F. Austin State University, the University of Mississippi, and the National Archives went above and beyond the call of duty to provide the materials I needed. Special recognition should be given to the late V. L. Bedsole, Elsa B. Meier, Marcelle F. Schertz, and W. Stone Miller of the Department of Archives at Louisiana State University in Baton Rouge. Charles East of Baton Rouge and Richard Wentworth of the University of Illinois Press provided interest and encouragement at crucial points. Professors Archie P. McDonald and Robert S. Maxwell of Stephen F. Austin State University and Judy McDonald of Nacogdoches, Texas, made it possible for me to spend valuable time researching in East Texas. Bob Maxwell also shared his vast knowledge of the southern lumber industry and examined the manuscript at various stages. Professor George T. Morgan, Jr., of the University of Houston provided valuable assistance. Dr. E. Berkeley Tompkins of Washington, D.C., Carolyn and Don Short of Baton Rouge, and Sarah Dunlap Jackson of the National Historical Publications and Records Commission provided hospitality and expertise. The staffs of the Southern Pine Association and the Southern Forest Products Association gave assistance whenever it was requested.

Acknowledgments

Mrs. Dorothea Martin, in particular, provided greater impetus for completion of the project than she will ever know. Herbert C. Berckes and Stanley P. Deas of New Orleans, former chief executive officers of the Southern Pine Association, kindly agreed to be interviewed, and Professor Charles W. Crawford of the Memphis State University Oral History Office helped to make this possible. Professors Anne Trotter and John H. DeBerry of the Memphis State History Department read the manuscript during its early preparation, and Professor Aaron M. Boom helped secure and facilitate various research and travel grants. Profesors F. Jack Hurley and Donald W. Ellis read portions of the manuscript in later stages, and Mrs. Sidney B. Daniel and her staff of the Memphis State Stenographic Services Department typed and retyped it in various forms. Mrs. Crystal Stallings Smith edited the final version for the University of Illinois Press. Harold K. Steen and Ron Fahl of the Forest History Society offered their encouragement, and the society has generously undertaken co-publication of the book. Memphis State University supported the last phases of the project because of the personal interest of former president Billy M. Jones. My wife, Marian, and children, Valerie, Steven, and Ashley, have been unswervingly supportive, and my parents have provided the best and most loving kind of encouragement--they cared enough to read the manuscript!

Memphis, April, 1980   James E. Fickle

Introduction

The story of the "New South" and the desire of its leaders for industrialization is well known. However, in dealing with this subject students have virtually ignored the lumber industry, which was in some ways representative of the entire "New South" experience. It combined leadership from both North and South and depended heavily upon imported northern capital, and its leaders were loudly "southern" while dealing closely with Yankee financial interests. The industry retained many aspects of the old plantation type of economic organization and represented, throughout much of its history, characteristics of the "Frontier South." The history of lumbering is in many ways not only typical of industry in general in the late-nineteenth-century "New South," but also of southern industrial history in more recent times.[1]

The development of the southern lumber industry is, however, of more than regional importance. It represents one phase, and an extremely important one, of the development of a major national industry. The southern lumber industry's history is a significant part of the story of World War I, the Great Depression, World War II, the U. S. conservation movement, the age of corporate mergers, and the movement for product standardization through voluntary industry organizations.

The study of trade associations[2] is another neglected aspect of American economic and business history. Textbook authors say that these organizations have been important in our nation's economic development, yet rarely do they deem it necessary even to explain what they are.[3] Failure to devote adequate textbook coverage to them is largely due to the lack of detailed information about such organizations and the resulting paucity of studies dealing with specific associations.

Trade associations were of central importance in the ideas of those early twentieth-century American businessmen and governmental leaders who advocated the "new competition" approach of Arthur Jerome Eddy.[4] Featuring economic planning, government-business cooperation, and the free exchange of prices and production information among supposed competitors, the "new competition" represented a significant departure from more traditional American antitrust attitudes. In Eddy's scheme, self-governing trade associations would be permitted to regulate business ethics, eliminate wasteful competition, and deal with societal problems--all under the loose supervision or with the cooperation of federal authorities. Heavy trade association involvement in World War I mobilization helped to popularize the concepts of national economic planning and industrial self-government, which were seen again during the course of the National Recovery Administration experiences, World War II mobilization, and the Korean War.[5] Trade associations in the southern pine industry, particularly the Southern Pine Association, were deeply involved in and are representative of these trends and experiences.

The shortage of studies of southern lumbering and its trade associations is not entirely the fault of historians. For many years industry members were extremely tight-lipped. In many cases lumbermen were unaware of or disinterested in their roles within a broad historical perspective. Their papers and records were often unavailable and were sometimes intentionally destroyed. Frequently lumbermen nurtured an obsessive distrust of professional writers. Only within the last few years have associations and industry members opened their records and papers to scholars.

In studying trade associations it is impossible to separate an organization from its industry; thus this work is the story of both associations and the southern pine industry. The research upon which it is based has led the author to conclude that developments in the industry and associations are typical of general tendencies on the southern and national economic scenes. The problems faced --wars, depressions, transportation, quality standards, conservation, and labor--were those of the South and the nation generally. The Southern Pine Association became the industry's leading trade association. Whether or not the SPA was successful in many areas can be debated, and in some cases it is even difficult to determine the criteria of success. However, in one important way it was very successful--it survived in an industry traditionally characterized by extreme individualism, factionalism, and dissension. The southern pine industry's experiences provide both new outlooks on many aspects of American history and a case study of trade association development and activities in an important southern industry operating on the national level.

NOTES TO INTRODUCTION

1. It is interesting that C. Vann Woodward in Origins of the New South, 1877-1913 (Baton Rouge: Louisiana State University Press, 1951), pp. 309-10, cites lumber manufacturing as one of those industries which "bulked large in the vaunted industrialization of the New South," yet in this large volume he devotes parts of only about five pages to it. George Brown Tindall, The Emergence of the New South, 1913-1945 (Baton Rouge: Louisiana State University Press, 1967), does little better. In this massive book the southern lumber industry is mentioned on only about twenty pages. Gerald Nash's 1966 statement that "southern lumbering is a subject that is still not exhausted" as a field for study remains valid today. Gerald D. Nash, "Research Oportunities in the Economic History of the South after 1880," Journal of Southern History, XXXII (Aug., 1966), 314.

2. According to Joseph F. Bradley, The Role of Trade Associations and Professional Business Societies in America (University Park: Pennsylvania State University Press, 1965), p. 4, there are many synonymous words which can replace the phrase trade association, including board, congress, council, federation, foundation, institute, league, and society.

3. For example, of four well-known textbooks dealing with American economic history, two do not even mention trade associations, and one, while referring to such organizations on three occasions, does not bother to tell what they are. Gerald Gunderson, A New Economic History

of America (New York: McGraw-Hill, 1976); Robert L. Heilbroner and Aaron Singer, The Economic Transformation of America (New York: Harcourt Brace Jovanovich, 1977); Harry N. Scheiber, Harold G. Vatter, and Harold Underwood Faulkner, American Economic History (New York: Harper and Row, 1976); and W. Elliot Brownlee, Dynamics of Ascent: A History of the American Economy (New York: Alfred A Knopf, 1974).

4. Arthur Jerome Eddy, The New Competition (New York and London: D. Appleton, 1912).

5. Ellis W. Hawley, The New Deal and the Problem of Monopoly: A Study in Economic Ambivalence (Princeton, N.J.: Princeton University Press, 1966), pp. 8-16.

1

The Industry and
Its Early Associations

Forests have strongly affected the American people's destiny since the earliest times. As impediments and attractions they had an influence on patterns of settlement and development that is hard to overemphasize. During the colonial period, settlers began to utilize the forest commercially, and the first timber products were dispatched from Virginia in 1608 by Captain John Smith, who sought to substitute other valuables for the gold which the Jamestown colony failed to produce.[1] Several communities claim the first sawmill; records of the Virginia Company indicate that mills were built in Jamestown in 1608.

The southern lumber industry started in coastal areas and spread inland irregularly, with activities concentrated along waterways. Sawed lumber was scarce in the South despite the abundance of timber, and in the early nineteenth century small steam-powered mills sprang up to serve local needs. According to tradition, the first steam mill was established in New Orleans in 1803 and was shortly destroyed by a mob of men who earned their living by pitsawing.[2] The first Texas mill was established at the junction of Buffaloe Bayou and Braes Bayou in the southeast corner of the state about 1830.[3] In Mississippi, Andrew Brown, a Scotch immigrant, took over a mill at "Natchez-under-the-Hill" in 1828, and by the Civil War he had built a thriving cypress lumber manufacturing business.[4] By the 1850s the vicinity around St. Tammany Parish in Louisiana on the north shore of Lake Pontchartrain had about forty sawmills.[5] The fledgling industry attracted native Southerners, Northerners, and people from

other lands, and by the eve of the Civil War it was
solidly established, although it served primarily local
needs. By 1860 lumber was, for example, the largest
industry in Mississippi.[6] The war temporarily disrupted
southern lumbering, but the attention it focused upon the
region, plus the cutting-out of timber in the Great Lakes
states and the development of Dixie's railroads, provided
a springboard for exploitation of southern forests on a
scale previously only imagined.[7]

The story of southern lumbering's growth after the
Civil War is intertwined with Reconstruction and the rise
of the "New South." The industry's development was based
on exploitation, idealism, foresight, and extremely short-
sighted greed in various combinations. The existence of
vast amounts of available public land in the South and the
cutting-out of the Great Lakes states' properties of large
companies that had theretofore scorned yellow pine spurred
this development.[8] C. Vann Woodward says that changes in
federal land policies in the South illustrate a transition
in northern policy from "the missionary and political to
the economic and exploitative phase."[9]

On the eve of the Civil War, the five southern public-
land states--Alabama, Arkansas, Florida, Louisiana, and
Mississippi--had 47 million federally owned acres. This
was about one-third of their land area, and most of it was
unfit for agricultural settlement and covered with heavy
stands of cypress and yellow pine. This forest cover was
regarded primarily as an obstacle to settlement and
development, except by mill owners along the waterways,
and part of it had been open to entry for many years at
$1.25 an acre. Following the adoption of the Graduation
Act in 1854, it was available for as little as twelve and
one-fourth cents an acre, depending upon how long it had
been on the market.[10]

After the Civil War, administration of the South's
vast public lands became an intricate part of Reconstruction. Radical Reconstruction leaders hoped to reserve the
lands for people of undoubted loyalty and for the
freedmen. George W. Julian, an abolitionist congressman
from Indiana, and chairman of the House committee on
public lands, took the lead in shaping land policy in the
South. Through his efforts and an almost strictly
Republican vote, the Southern Homestead Act was passed in
1866. This measure ended cash sales in the five southern
states, reserved public lands for homesteaders, limited
grants to eighty acres, and excluded ex-Confederates from

homesteading privileges. Julian hoped to overhaul the land laws of the entire nation, but he was defeated by railroad, lumber, and speculative interests.[11]

The end of Reconstruction brought a growing demand to open southern timber for exploitation by both Northerners and Southerners. Southerners claimed that most public lands in the South were unfit for agricultural purposes and of little use for the freedmen. The timberlands had not contributed to either the federal government's coffers or the development of the southern economy, and they were being illegally stripped by lumber interests which developed after the Civil War.[12] According to Paul W. Gates, "by 1876 the southern land question had ceased to be confused with reconstruction issues and had become a problem in land economics and business policy."[13]

Opposition to repeal of the Southern Homestead Act was based upon a desire to prevent concentrated ownership of the lands. After a long fight, the repeal effort came to a head in 1876. Congressman William S. Holman of Indiana led the struggle against repeal, but he was overwhelmed by a nearly unanimous South with significant northern support. Unlike Julian in the earlier effort, Holman did not enjoy the aid of radical reconstructionists. Although representatives of northern and western lumbering states tended to support Holman, they were somewhat divided because many of their constituents were cutting out and waiting eagerly for the opening of southern lands. The land reform movement had not gained sufficient force to be significant in the fight.[14]

The Southern Homestead Act was repealed in 1876. The repeal removed all limitations upon public land transactions in the five southern states and legalized private sales. It placed no limit upon the size of purchases and directed that the lands be offered at public sale as soon as practicable. Land was offered to the highest bidder at public auction and, if not sold, could be purchased later at a minimum price of $1.25 an acre. The minimum price became standard for virgin timberland, and the law proved unusually favorable to large-scale land speculators. During the following twelve years, vast tracts of valuable forest land were purchased by speculators at bargain prices.[15]

Exploitation of southern public lands during the late 1870s and 1880s was carried out largely by timber speculators who preceded actual lumbermen, although some lumber operators were involved. Homesteading was no longer so much the work of claimants employed by lumber companies, as it had been from 1866 to 1876 when the amount of land that could be entered was restricted, but the practice undoubtedly continued, with smaller operators now the primary culprits.[16] In the 1800s, for example, the Blacksher Brothers, operators of a mill on Juniper Creek near Brewton, Alabama, bought timberland from homesteaders at the rate of three sacks of corn, three sides of bacon, a ten-pound caddy of tobacco, one barrel of flour, and forty pounds of coffee for each forty acres of virgin longleaf pine timber. When the timber was especially good, the Blackshers might throw in an extra sack of corn and ten pounds of coffee.[17]

Timber speculation was significant in all southern states, but most heavily concentrated in Louisiana and Mississippi. Both Northerners and Southerners were involved, but domination fell into Yankee hands. Northern speculators and lumber companies sent "timber cruisers" into the South to examine the forest resources. They returned with glowing reports of miles of virgin timber that could be easily logged and purchased dirt cheap from the federal and state governments. Excitement and speculative fever became so great that the Illinois Central Railroad ran a series of special trains into the southern piney woods for would-be purchasers.[18]

Big purchasers of the early period included a group of Chicago capitalists who bought 195,804 acres in Louisiana and subsequently sold much of their holding to the Long-Bell interests.[19] The largest purchaser in Alabama and Florida was Daniel F. Sullivan, an English immigrant characterized as the "timber and lumber king of Florida" and a "sort of Gulf Coast Jay Gould in the timber business." Sullivan controlled some 250,000 acres in the two states, 150,000 of which had been bought directly from the federal government. At the time of his death in 1885, it was reported that Sullivan virtually controlled the port city of Pensacola and its transportation facilities and that he was moving toward a similar position in Mobile. His personal fortune was estimated at $1 million in bonds and cash plus land and lumber businesses.[20] Sullivan's wealth, although certainly out of the ordinary, indicates the size of the interests encountered in the southern lumber industry. Men of enormous wealth were not uncommon. Large buyers during the 1800s included several families that figure significantly in the development of the Southern Pine Association. Many lumbering families intermarried and sent younger sons and associates into the South to manage their interests. Some of these men settled permanently in the region and became fiercely loyal to the South, and even somewhat provincial.[21] Large purchasers from both North and South established firms which remained important southern pine producers well into the twentieth century. One of these was Delos A. Blodgett of Grand Rapids, Michigan, who cut out in that area and bought 126,238 acres of pine land in Mississippi and over a half million acres in Louisiana.[22]

Other large purchasers included Henry J. Lutcher, the son of a German immigrant, and G. Bedell Moore, who jointly owned a lumber mill in Williamsport, Pennsylvania, and large operations throughout western Pennsylvania. Their timber supply began to dwindle in the 1870s, and Lutcher went to look at timber in the Great Lakes states. After visiting Michigan and Wisconsin, however, he heard of enormous forests in Dixie and went South, riding for weeks on horseback through the forests of southwest Louisiana and southeast Texas. Despite a local banker's warning that he was buying valueless land that could not be cultivated, Lutcher bought thousands of acres of virgin timber. Some was obtained from local farmers who were eager to sell. The partnership eventually purchased 500,000 acres of pine and cypress in Louisiana, some at only fifty cents an acre. In 1877 Lutcher and Moore moved to Orange, Texas, and constructed the first big sawmill in the state, with a capacity of 80,000 to 100,000 board feet per day. Until the turn of the century the Lutcher and Moore firm was the largest in the Texas-Louisiana area, and the two men were referred to as the "lumber kings of the world" and "giants of the South." By 1890 no lumbermen in the South and few in the North could match the output of Lutcher and Moore's operations.[23] Blodgett, Lutcher, and Moore all played leading roles in southern lumber trade associations.

Other interests bought timber from state and local governments and individual sources. They were often encouraged by local citizens to bring capital into the South. One Tennessean said, "As for these investments of Northern capital, the South is glad to have it come. We welcome the skilled lumberman with the noisy mill."[24] Phelps Dodge and Company of New York experienced its greatest expansion in lumbering during Reconstruction, with its post-Civil War operations concentrated in Texas and particularly in Georgia. In 1868 it organized the

Georgia Land and Lumber Company, which was honored by Georgians with a county and several towns named after members of the combine. The holdings of William E. Dodge and his Georgia Land and Lumber Company in the south-central Georgia counties of Dodge, Laurens, Pulaski, Telfair, and Montgomery comprised some 300,000 acres of virgin pine timber.[25]

The southern states displayed remarkable eagerness to give away their landed heritage. In Mississippi the state legislature passed an act in 1882 that exempted new industries from taxation for ten years after starting operations. Eight years later, George and Silas Gardiner, large lumber operators of Clinton, Iowa, came South to inspect timber resources because of a shortage of white pine in their area. With their brother-in-law, George Eastman, they purchased 16,000 acres of land around Laurel, Mississippi, from John Kamper for four dollars per acre. Kamper was amused by the Yankee purchasers' gullibility.[26]

Lumbermen acquired and exploited the southern forests with a vengeance. A syndicate headed by Hamilton Disston of Philadelphia bought 4 million acres at twenty-five cents an acre from the state of Florida in 1881. Lutcher and Moore purchased the timber on sixteen sections of school land in Newton and Sabine counties in Texas for $32,347, and John Henry Kirby obtained 7,000 acres of school land timber in Jasper County, Texas, for $30,187. In Mississippi Alcorn Agricultural and Mechanical College sold 23,040 acres for $85,000 to five companies, including the J. J. Newman Lumber Company of Hattiesburg and Delos A. Blodgett of Grand Rapids, Michigan.[27] Other large sales were made by railroads and, increasingly, by the original speculative purchasers. In 1905 James J. Hill of the Great Northern remarked that one acre of timber was more valuable to a railroad than forty of agricultural land.[28]

As exploitation of southern timber went on, it was increasingly common for large lumber interests to acquire stumpage from several sources, and as competition became heated, prices and tempers rose. In a single decade around the turn of the century the price of some southern pine acreage rose from $1.25 to $60.00 an acre.[29] The Long-Bell Lumber Company's 203,000 acres in Louisiana's Calcasieu Valley were bought from nineteen different individuals or groups who had claimed the lands between 1880 and 1888. The Industrial Lumber Company of Elizabeth,

Louisiana, bought 58,320 acres from fourteen different sources. The Calcasieu Pine Company and Southern Lumber Company obtained 46,760 acres from three groups. Lutcher and Moore acquired an additional 12,000 acres from second parties, and the Central Coal and Coke Company of Kansas City similarly purchased 76,300 acres.[30] The tendency to buy from several sources and the consequent bidding for timber form part of the background of trade associations in the southern pine industry. This competition caused much of the tension and conflict that kept associations from acting effectively.

The concentration of southern land in the hands of northern investors and companies by the late 1880s aroused the spector of a "lumber trust." This fitted in with the growing fear of monopolies and trusts which were regarded as threats to traditional American practices and values. The southern pine industry was frequently charged with monopolistic practices and those and similar charges resulted in an investigation of the entire lumber industry by the United States Bureau of Corporations, which issued its report in 1913-14.[31] In the southern states, legitimate homesteading after 1876 resulted in the establishment of numerous small and productive farms. The failure of land speculators to enrich Dixie prompted a reconsideration of public land policies by many Southerners. They now wanted to eliminate large-scale sales of their lands and reserve them for still more new farms. Through the efforts of southern congressmen, anti-monopolists, and conservationists, the movement to shut down large-scale speculation began in 1888, and the next three years brought the end of cash sales and baronial purchases of public lands.[32]

The bonanza period of southern timber buying had seen many huge purchases by companies that remained significant. However, they were unable to keep out numerous competitors, and the industry was characterized by the presence of producers of all degrees of size, skill, and performance. Although there were intricately interwoven relationships between companies, an effective lumber trust was beyond the far-flung and highly volatile industry's grasp.[33]

Areas of settlement in the South created further divisions. Sawmill men from the Great Lake states tended to move south along two separate paths. Some settled east of the Mississippi River in Alabama, Mississippi, and Eastern Louisiana. Others located west of the river in

Missouri and then filtered down into Arkansas, western Louisiana, and Texas. These groups became distinct factions within the industry, with frequent outbreaks of animosity centering around disputes over freight rates. West-of-the-river interests tended to build up chains of from six to a dozen sawmills. Their ranks included many of the industry's big names, among them Samuel H. and Robert Fullerton, who invested in Louisiana in 1894 and later extended their operations to Arkansas, William Buchanan and John Henry Kirby, R. A. Long of Long-Bell, Captain J. B. White of Kansas City's Exchange Sawmills, and the Frost, Dierks, and Pickering interests.[34]

By the late nineteenth century, then, the southern lumber industry was firmly established and had developed characteristics which shaped its trade associations. The industry featured large concentrated landholdings dominated by northern interests but richly sprinkled with Southerners. It was characterized by highly competitive producers who scrapped heatedly and colorfully over timber acquisitions and sales. It was divided into regions, the most significant being east and west of the Mississippi River. Finally, the industry was led by men who were caught up in ruthless competition which increasingly seemed unnecessary and wasteful. The story of trade association development would largely be that of the forces of planning and cooperation trying to overcome intense provincialism, diversity, and animosity. The Southern Pine Association and its predecessors emerged from this background.

The term trade association has been defined and redefined, but while the emphasis and phraseology may change, most definitions boil down to the following factors. Trade associations are generally organizations of competitors in a single industry banded together to present a united front. Structural forms vary as a result of governmental policy, but most pursue roughly similar goals. Usual activities include representing the industry before governmental bodies, establishing ethical standards, developing quality and grading regulations, conducting public relations and advertising work, compiling accurate statistics, and attempting to solve specific problems in areas such as transportation or competition with other industries. The emphasis may vary, but these are the general concerns of trade associations.[35] In the background of many trade associations there is a history of hostility to organized labor and of attempts to

8

influence or control production and prices. The prevalence of such activities has been widely disputed, but there has been sufficient evidence to attract the interest of Congress and various governmental investigatory bodies on numerous occasions.[36]

American associations in the antebellum period were organized on a very small scale in terms of geography and membership. They tended to be impermanent for a variety of reasons, ranging from the economic philosophy of the age to the fact that the American economy of the time was dominantly agricultural.[37] However, the Civil War was the springboard for a tremendous acceleration in American industialization[38] and with it, despite the antipathy of most Americans, came the beginnings, on a local or regional level, of trade associations. These organizations were dedicated basically to a defense of their members against the harmful effects of intense and ruthless competition, and they attempted to bring stability into the chaotic economic environment.[39]

However, it was the twentieth century, after the federal antitrust statutes had been defined and the place of trade associations within the legal structure tentatively established, that brought real growth in the number, size, strength, and influence of American trade associations. Credit afforded the associations for their part in the World War I defense effort by government officials, including Bernard Baruch, and the favorable attitude of Herbert Hoover and the U. S. Department of Commerce in the 1920s ushered in the real development of American trade associations.[40] This growth in their stature and respectability culminated in recognition by the national government and the architects of the first New Deal, who built the National Industrial Recovery Act's codes of fair competition and standards around the framework provided by the nation's trade associations.[41]

With the sudden end of the NRA in 1935 and the advent of the "trust-busting" phase of the second New Deal, trade associations lost their favorable position with government, and they moved into a period fraught with the tensions and pressures of ambivalent governmental attitudes. The growth of corporate mergers made the future of trade associations rather uncertain, and even valuable service in World War II and the Korean War did not solve their problems. In fact, the wars began a period in which these trends were accelerated and intensified. The position of the lumber industry and its trade associations, and the

The New South and the "New Competition"

Southern Pine Association and its region in particular, was representative of the national situation throughout these periods.

The origins of lumber trade associations are difficult to trace because of a tendency to guard records from outside eyes, the secretive rise and abrupt expiration of some organizations, and the slowness of industry leaders and professional scholars to realize the historical importance of the associations. Many organizations' files have simply disappeared, and only in recent years have the industry and the scholarly community taken steps to guarantee that a similar fate does not befall the remaining records of trade associations and organizations. Fortunately, the files of some companies are now available to scholars, and through a study of the materials they received as members of industry organizations, one can construct a sketchy, although generally accurate picture of some early organizations in the southern pine lumber industry.

The structure, emphasis, and functions of associations in the lumber industry have differed widely, but all have dealt with similar problems. Most originated around one or more of the following areas of concern: production, prices, quality standards, labor problems, and transportation. Activities in advertising, technology, government relations, safety, and other matters have also been undertaken, but they have generally come later or have been definitely secondary concerns. Statistical work has been common and fundamental to other association activities.

Trade association development in the lumber industry was part of the maturation process. As lumbering grew and became national, the need for organizations to deal with problems of scale became obvious, although not always heeded. The very conditions which produced organizations often served to undermine their existence. For example, lumbering has always been one of the few large American industries which approximate the classical concept of competition. It has numerous firms and entry into the industry, particularly for the small producer, is relatively easy.[42] Furthermore, those who have engaged in the lumber business have often been extreme individualists, men whose families followed the industry's migration and succeeded "because of sheer hard work, ingenuity, and often ruthlessness."[43] This extreme individualism and the nature of local markets meant that in the industry's early days each millowner produced lumber according to his own taste or that of his immediate customers. There was no real attempt at standardization. However, as they grew and began to serve wider markets, and as transportation and communications improved, the mills had to compete with companies in distant locations. Consumers began to demand uniform standards as distribution through wholesalers and retail lumber yards became more common.[44] From this background came attempts to bring order into the industry by establishing manufacturing or grading standards and to eliminate cutthroat competition by agreements on production and prices. The early stages of this effort were hampered by the producers' extreme individualism and their distrust of one another. Frequently, they would not abide by agreements, and their organizations tended to be very loose and unstable.[45]

One of the earliest organizational attempts was in the South. During the early 1850s millmen in southern Mississippi formed the Bayou Bernard Lumber Company, which attempted to fix prices while eliminating the middleman and competition among mills serving New Orleans. After a few months, it disintegrated, a victim of rising prices and the competition of other lumber-producing and -marketing areas. The Bayou Bernard Lumber Company was thus a prototype not only in objectives, but also in its failure.[46] Another early attempt to organize was made by thirty-six manufacturers along the Susquehanna River in Pennsylvania. In 1873, they united to standardize products, collect and disseminate statistical information, and establish ethical standards.[47]

Numerous other cooperative efforts in the 1870s blossomed and quickly withered away. The National Association of Lumbermen, created in 1874 to control production and fight the post-Panic of 1873 price decline, proved powerless because of limited support.[48] In 1881, a trade journal editorial discussed the association under the heading "Another Association Fiasco," saying that "the lumber trade is rapidly building for itself a national reputation as the parent of commercial organizations that never amount to anything. There seems to be a fatality about lumber organizations that insures for them an early and ignominious dissolution."[49]

Passage of the Sherman Antitrust Act in 1890 was a watershed in lumber trade association development nationally and in the South. The Sherman Act clearly prohibited practices which characterized many early associations and channeled them toward refining at least their external objectives and activities. While not regarded as effective, the Sherman Act did coincide with forces within the trade association movement itself. As a result, associations became more businesslike, with paid professional or semiprofessional staffs, permanent facilities, and a more dignified and professional demeanor.[50] Many of the discredited attempts at production control and price-fixing were continued, but the new organizations attempted to create a more favorable impression for their industry. By the end of the 1890s, the various lumber areas were organized into regional associations. The process was capped by the formation of the National Lumber Manufacturers' Association, an organization of affiliated regional groups, in 1902.[51]

The first relatively successful trade association in the lumber industry was the Mississippi Valley Lumbermen's Association. It grew out of the Northwestern Lumber Manufacturers' Association that was organized in 1881 in an attempt to curtail production and combat falling prices.[52] The MVLA was founded on September 1, 1891, and members of the Weyerhaeuser lumber empire were active in its creation. The organizers frankly admitted that the raison d'etre of the association was to establish "more nearly uniform prices." The MVLA set up committees to deal with grading, price lists, and railroad rates. Building upon the earlier work of the Northwestern Lumber Manufacturers' Association, it began to formulate grading rules, which were finally adopted in 1895. The association's attempts to control prices brought legal difficulties shortly after its organization. The MVLA was tried before a federal district court in St. Paul in 1892 on charges of price-fixing in violation of the Sherman Antitrust Act. It escaped without damage from this experience, but the resultant interest among the citizenry brought the matter to the attention of the Minnesota legislature, which investigated lumber prices in 1893 and paid special attention to the association's price list, which they felt could have been used for illegitimate regulation of prices. Nothing came of this investigation, but it was typical of the interest and activities aroused by trade association endeavors to influence the market. The episode was a harbinger of the public search for a "lumber trust" that continually harassed the industry well into the twentieth century.[53] In 1906 the Mississippi Valley Lumbermen's Association was consolidated with the

Wisconsin Valley Lumbermen's Association, organized in 1893, to form the Northern Pine Manufacturers' Association.[54] The MVLA provided the first trade association experience for John E. Rhodes, who became the original secretary-manager of the Southern Pine Association.

Regional trade association organization in the southern lumber industry began about the same time as in the Great Lakes states. As the years wore on, there would be a good deal of cross-fertilization between the two areas. Frequently, the same companies were active in both regions and many who became influential in southern organizations had received their associational baptisms in the Great Lakes states. The background and motives of associations in both areas were virtually identical. The Southern Pine Association can be traced back to several subregional groups of the 1880s, which by the end of the decade, had united into a single organization representing much of the South.

The driving force behind the most direct early antecedent of the SPA was Captain J. B. White, manager of the Grandin, Missouri, plant of the Missouri Lumber and Mining Company. White was first in a line of great Missouri lumbermen who dominated the southern lumber industry and its associations well into the twentieth century. The captain was already a leading figure when he called the first meeting of yellow pine manufacturers in June, 1883, at Poplar Bluff, Missouri. White represented the seventh generation of a lumbering family which had gradually moved westward from lumbering origins in New York and New England.

Mostly lumbermen from Arkansas and Missouri attended the meeting at Poplar Bluff, and the general consensus was that grading rules for yellow pine were urgently needed. The lumbermen were equally convinced of the need for uniform prices. Later White called a meeting at Little Rock that was well attended by manufacturers from the two states. At this meeting the lumbermen formed the Missouri and Arkansas Lumber Association, with White serving as president. However, the first southern action toward grading lumber was not taken until a meeting in Texarkana during January, 1886, which was attended by seventy-five operators.[55]

During the same period, East Texas and western Louisiana manufacturers began to organize trade associations through which they "exchanged production data, comparative price lists, and privately circulated lists of malcontent or undesirable workmen. The operators also cooperated on political and legislative action and agreed on common labor and wage policies.[56] During the 1880s, manufacturers from the Sabine River area organized the Texas and Louisiana Lumbermen's Association. By 1883, twenty-six mills in the Sabine area were making reports to the association, and it eventually expanded to cover all of Texas and Louisiana.[57] The organization finally became known as the Texas and Louisiana Lumber Manufacturers' Association. Headquarters were in Beaumont, and R. E. Kelley served as secretary. The organization solicited reports from its members with their monthly mill cut and stock on hand. It circulated tables showing this information, listing the mills covered, and making comparisons with the same period for the preceding year.[58]

Two of the organization's primary activities were establishing price lists and curtailing output during periods of overproduction. The lists were reasonably effective.[59] The association attempted to keep members in line, and they were requested to report all cases of price cutting to the secretary for investigation.[60] The association's correspondence indicates that its members apparently took this admonition seriously.[61] The Texas and Louisiana Lumber Manufacturers' Association also tried with varying success to curtail output in the industry. In these endeavors it sought with some success to enlist the support of non-member mills.[62]

In 1897 the association attempted to cooperate with mills and associations in Arkansas, Missouri, and Mississippi to form an organization called the Yellow Pine Exchange. This body was designed to "reduce the cost of manufacture, regulate output, formulate price lists, supply statistical information and to consider more efficient means of marketing." There were to be directors from each state, a pledge of honor, and a money deposit to enforce adherence to the agreement. The organization's prospectus noted that publicity concerning the exchange's affairs was to be "prohibited."[63]

Mississippi producers and their neighbors in Alabama and Georgia were experiencing the same difficulties as their western and northern counterparts. In 1888, lumbermen from those three states met in Meridian and attempted to establish uniform prices. A Mississippian urged the cooperation of all lumbermen, asserted that they could prevent ruinous competition in prices, and warned that other industries were uniting to promote their own interests.

14

The Mississippi producer said he deplored a system "that allowed the ignorant customer to fix the price of a commodity."[64] Two years later, representatives of several local and subregional associations united to form the Southern Lumber Manufacturers' Association. This was the first truly regional southern lumber trade association and the first direct predecessor of the Southern Pine Association.

The nucleus of the Southern Lumber Manufacturers' Association was the old Missouri and Arkansas Lumber Association, organized in 1890, which had developed into the Missouri, Arkansas, and Texas association. The organization admitted manufacturers of all kinds of lumber, although producers of yellow or southern pine dominated. Its membership came from practically the entire South except the Atlantic Coast states. Separate organizations in the Carolinas, Virginia, Georgia, and Florida were later absorbed into pan-regional organizations. Producers catering to the export market and hardwood manufacturers took little part in the association.[65]

The Southern Lumber Manufacturers' Association membership came principally from Missouri, Arkansas, and Mississippi. The first slate of officers included persons of past and future significance. Captain J. B. White was president, and the organization's first secretary was J. H. Trump of Little Rock. One of his successors was George K. Smith, the leader of several southern pine industry trade organizations before the Southern Pine Association's formation. The Southern Lumber Manufacturers' Association immediately adopted grading rules in 1890, but the grades differed from those of the Texas and Louisiana Lumber Manufacturers' Association. Manufacturers in the two associations reached a compromise in 1899, and the Texas and Louisiana producers became affiliated with the Southern Lumber Manufacturers' Association.[66]

The Lumber Trade Journal praised the compromise between the two areas and stated that the main tasks then confronting the organization were "attainment of uniform grading all over the South, and the establishment of a statistical department which shall be complete and accurate."[67] This was a euphemism meaning that the association should gather accurate materials upon which comprehensive price-fixing and curtailment agreements could be established. In truth, the association began cranking out price lists and suggestions when it was organized. An estimated fifty-two price lists were issued from its

headquarters in St. Louis between 1890 and 1905.[68]
Efforts to control prices and regulate production were
continuous. During 1896, for example, there were frequent
meetings and notices concerning these matters. In the
last half of the year, members were told there would be
meetings at which "the question of horizontal curtailment
of output will be presented" and that "an effort will be
made to arrange for curtailment of output for the next six
months."[69]

Attempts to influence the market were not limited to
subscribers. The association appealed to non-members for
information concerning their output and stocks in order to
make its statistics more reliable.[70] In 1898, it
attempted to draw up an agreement with white pine manufacturers that called for the selection of enough inspectors
to visit all mills in the association and bring their
grades to a rigidly enforced uniform standard. The association also wanted to form a committee to establish
prices for the members and formulated a "gentleman's
agreement" at a yellow pine manufacturers' meeting in St.
Louis on November 16, 1898, to adhere to the standardized
prices.[71] Captain J. B. White said the agreement would
bring "a new era in the prosperity of the Yellow Pine
Industry" and "a closer affiliation and friendship with
the Assocation of White Pine Manufacturers of the
North."[72] Early in 1899 forty-one of the larger manufacturers agreed to support a price list established in
January of that year.[73] The association's efforts to
regulate production and prices also led it to work for the
establishment of a Yellow Pine Clearing House Association
to "report the movement of Yellow Pine into consumption
each week, and give to all its members an adequate idea of
the volume of business, and its relation to the producing
and consuming capacity."[74]

The association's emphasis upon prices and production
was evident during its entire existence. During its formative period in the early 1890s, the SLMA urged members
to curtail production and adhere closely to the price list
promulgated by its committee on values. As late as June,
1904, near the end of its existence under the Southern
Lumber Manufacturer's Association name, it held an extraordinary meeting. Some 70 to 80 percent of the southern
pine manufacturers in Mississippi, Arkansas, Louisiana,
and Texas agreed to reduce output by one-third for two
months. This was to be accomplished by eliminating night
operations, shortening the work week, or reducing the
working day. These measures were credited with

drastically curtailing production, and R. A. Long, a
dominant figure in the industry, said they had arrested
the downward price sprial and started a trend toward
increasing values. However, the turnaround was probably
due more to increased construction in major cities and a
rising price level in the overseas market than to production curtailment. The public blamed the generally rising
lumber prices from 1899 to 1906 on trade associations
rather than on general economic conditions. As a result,
in 1906 the Southern Lumber Manufacturers' Association
faced possible investigation and prosecution for issuing
price lists and engaging in other questionable activities.
On the advice of attorneys, the association replaced its
price list committee with a new market committee, which
was in turn abolished in October, 1906. From then on,
Secretary George K. Smith issued periodic market reports
based upon data supplied by some sixty correspondents.[75]

Despite its preoccupation with statistics and controlling prices and production, the Southern Lumber Manufacturers' Association set precedents in a wide variety of
other activities. It followed the example of the Mississippi Valley Lumber Association in grade marking and moved
toward the acceptance of its grading rules as industry
standards. The association established a bureau of uniform grades and inspection to regulate and enforce its
requirements. The bureau employed a chief inspector and
five assistants who visited members' mills at thirty- to
forty-day intervals and reported on the work of each
firm's graders to its management. The chief inspector
later served in the same capacity with both the Yellow
Pine and the Southern Pine associations. The difficulties
of effective cooperative action were evident in this
field, as well as in price and production control. On one
occasion, the association's secretary complained that an
investigation into claim adjustments in the industry
revealed a lack of uniformity in grading that was
"deplorable." His major complaint was that the producers
were "sweetening" the grades. Nevertheless, by the turn
of the century the association believed its grading and
inspection work was "gradually bringing the output of our
members to a uniform standard."[76]

The Southern Lumber Manufacturers' Association was
involved in a number of other fields common to modern
trade associations. It conducted advertising campaigns
which were financed through monthly assessments and special subscriptions.[77] It attempted to secure reduced

17

railroad rates for its producing areas and established a
"fully organized Freight Claim Bureau for the purpose of
handling over-charge railroad claims against various Railroad companies for the use of members only." Eventually,
it boasted a full-fledged rate and claim department.[78]
Indications of association interest in other areas
included the creation of committees on weights and insurance, campaign education, and a credit department. At the
very end of its existence under its old name, the association had a committee investigating the advisability of an
export department.[79] Despite these other activities, the
Southern Lumber Manufacturers' Association's main emphasis
continued to be on production control and regulation of
prices. Whether they deserved it or not, the SLMA and
other organizations were blamed for rising lumber prices
by many citizens, and by the end of 1905 antitrust sentiment in parts of the South was fairly strong. Possibly
because of this hostile climate of public opinion, the
manufacturers decided to drop the Southern Lumber
Manufacturers' Association name in favor of a new one.[80]
It was also true, however, that some members simply wanted
to adopt a name that would "indicate the fact that we
represent Southern Pine and not all Southern Lumber."[81]
At its annual meeting in 1906, the association changed its
name to Yellow Pine Manufacturers' Association. George K.
Smith continued as secretary, the headquarters stayed in
St. Louis, and the organization remained essentially the
same in membership and functions. It was the immediate
predecessor of the Southern Pine Association.[82]

Before discussing the activities of the Yellow Pine
Manufacturers' Association, however, we should examine the
activities of several other organizations which operated
concurrently. Together with the YPMA, they shaped the
background out of which the Southern Pine Association
emerged. The organizations which existed before and concurrently with the Yellow Pine Manufacturers' Association
fall into several categories. Some associations organized
on a local or limited regional basis operated outside the
areas of the Yellow Pine and Southern Pine associations'
main strength and early interest. They competed in fringe
areas for members and over matters of local importance,
such as freight rates, but nevertheless generally cooperated with the YPMA and the SPA and were eventually
absorbed into the Southern Pine Association. Other associations included local or subregional organizations
within the main areas of strength of the Yellow Pine

18

Manufacturers' Association and SPA, that competed head-on
with the bigger groups for membership and loyalties.
These groups were frequently created by one man or by a
small group who hoped to build their own empire. None of
their challenges were successful, but they cropped up
periodically and occasionally proved embarrassing or
annoying to the larger organizations because of their
attempts to seduce members and their charges that the
bigger associations were fronts for control of the entire
industry by the large operators.

A third group of associations included organizations
within the YPMA and SPA region which were generally organized on a local or subregional basis with objectives
complementary to those of the larger associations. The
YPMA and SPA worked closely with these bodies, which dealt
primarily with limited problems. Typical of these groups
were mill managers' associations concerned with production
and local management matters and organizations centered
around specific general problems such as transportation,
advertising, or labor. The only really significant challenges to the hegemony of the larger general associations
came from these supposedly cooperating and complementary
organizations.

Organizations in the first category, those eventually
absorbed into the Southern Pine Association, began in the
same period as the direct predecessors of the SPA, and the
desire to establish grading rules was largely responsible
for their formation. One of the first large meetings to
deal with grading standards was at Savannah, Georgia, on
February 14, 1883. This gathering, which was called the
Southern Lumber and Timber Convention, adopted a set of
rules for grading called the "Savannah Rules of 1883."
These rules, the first in the southern lumber industry,
were first applied by the Georgia Sawmill Association,
formed in May, 1889, with twenty-five members drawn from
Georgia and parts of South Carolina and Florida. In 1903,
the Georgia Sawmill Association became the Georgia
Interstate Sawmill Association, and by 1906 its membership
included about 150 mills with a combined annual production
of approximately 700 million board feet. On July 16 of
that year, the group's name was changed to Georgia-Florida
Sawmill Association in recognition of the fact that the
membership was almost evenly divided between manufacturers
from those two states. The Georgia-Florida Sawmill
Association was succeeded by the Florida Dense Long Leaf

Pine Manufacturers' Association, which was finally absorbed by the Southern Pine Association in 1927.[83]

North Carolina manufacturers were also drawn together by the need for uniform manufacturing standards, and in May, 1888, they formed the Carolina Pine Association, which immediately adopted grading rules. This organization was succeeded in 1889 by the North Carolina Pine Lumber Company, and the final organization to emerge in this area was the North Carolina Pine Association, which was formed in 1897 and finally taken over by the Southern Pine Association in 1931.[84] With the absorption of the Florida Dense Long Leaf Pine Manufacturers' Association and the North Carolina Pine Association by the SPA, the entire southern producing area was brought into one great regional organization.

There were numerous small associations of the second category which, although they were organized basically on a local level, tried on occasion to sap the strength of the larger groups. The general characteristics of these smaller bodies were exhibited by the Texas and Louisiana Saw Mill Association, which was organized in February, 1908, with a paid secretary and offices in Houston. This group stemmed from a meeting of "prominent mill men of East Texas" in Houston in November, 1907, that emphasized transportation problems. The meeting established a committee to draft a constitution and by-laws, and another session was held in Beaumont on November 30, with additional members joining. A final session was scheduled for February, 1908. In the meantime, a number of manufacturers from Louisiana expressed their desire to join the new organization. Invitations to the February meeting were issued to all mill men in the two states. The secretary of the association felt that "our first duty is to increase our membership list in order that the association may represent to the fullest, the lumber industry of Louisiana and Texas."[85]

The secretary's desire to extend the organization's membership was understandable, and he was quite willing for that extension to come at the expense of other organizations. In fact the Texas and Louisiana Saw Mill Association, like many other smaller groups, found it difficult to justify its existence to members belonging to the larger associations as well. In 1908, for example, a prominent Texas man resigned from the Texas and Louisiana association and wrote that the basic reason for his withdrawal was the fact that "we feel that our membership

in the Yellow Pine Manufacturers' Association is rendering
us practically all of the benefits that we could secure
from your Association."[86]   The Texas and Louisiana Saw
Mill Association's experiences were typical of those of
other small organizations struggling to survive in the
southern pine region.

The third category, cooperating specializing groups,
included a number of state and subregional associations,
such as the Mississippi Lumberman's Association, the
Mississippi Pine Association, the Alabama-West Florida
Association, the Southern Logging Association, and the
Lumbermen's Association of Texas, which was composed of
both manufacturers and retail dealers.[87]   A number of
similar associations were formed during the life of the
Southern Pine Association and its predecessors, but
perhaps the most colorful and significant of the specialized groups sprang into existence in 1906 just as the
SLMA was evolving into the Yellow Pine Manufacturers'
Association. Its interests and activities influenced the
development of both the YPMA and the Southern Pine
Association. The new organization, the Southern Lumber
Operators' Association, grew out of a background of labor
difficulties, which constantly plagued the southern pine
industry despite frequent statements from various company
and association spokesmen that theirs was and always had
been a peaceful industry. The SLOA was an employers'
association in the purest and simplest meaning of the
term. The only reason for its birth and continued
existence was to act as a vehicle of the southern lumber
operators' opposition to unionization. Unlike trade associations which develop relatively well-rounded and diverse
programs, the Southern Lumber Operators' Association never
wavered from its single obsessive purpose—the elimination of organized labor from the southern lumber region.

It is quite obvious that the SLOA and the YPMA were
closely related. Both were headquartered in St. Louis,
both pulled membership from virtually the same sources, at
times one man served on the paid staffs of both associations, and surviving records indicate that the two organizations consciously worked together. The Operators'
Association outlived the YPMA, and its relationship with
the Southern Pine Association was not as open, but it
seems clear that the groups cooperated in certain areas.
The Operators' Association performed a valuable service
for both of its companion organizations by allowing them
to keep their reputations from being sullied by open

involvement in labor conflicts. Thus, they could remain effective and maintain a respectable image in the community and with the government while their members attained their objectives in the labor field through the less-respectable Operators' Association.

A combination of generally poor economic conditions in the southern lumber industry and numerous employee grievances during the early twentieth century produced labor strife which culminated in the "Louisiana-Texas Lumber War" of 1911-12. The industry suffered from overproduction and great price fluctuations, and the usual manufacturer's response was to decrease his hours of operation to reduce labor costs. Employee unrest was stirred by this tactic, as well as by many long-standing grievances which included poor housing and conditions in the company towns, low wages, the use of company scrip, the convict lease system, and many other abuses.

The labor strife of the early twentieth century was directly responsible for the organization of the Southern Lumber Operators' Association in September, 1906. The leading force in its formation was C. B. Sweet, vice-president of the Long-Bell Lumber Company, whose operations were considered hotbeds of labor unrest. George K. Smith, secretary of the YPMA, served as treasurer.

The Operators' Association concentrated upon a single goal: "to resist any encroachment of organized labor." By the time of the "Louisiana-Texas Lumber War" in 1911-12, it had grown to include eighty-seven companies with mills in Arkansas, Texas, Louisiana, Alabama, Oklahoma, Florida, and Mississippi. There was a complete hierarchy of administrative officers and eleven district governing boards which were to deal with local and regional emergencies. The constitution provided for a Benefit Trust Fund, to which member mills contributed through assessments of their total production for the relief of plant owners whose facilities were closed because of labor difficulties. Members could be dismissed for only two reasons--nonpayment of assessments and failure to follow policies dictated by the association directors. Despite the chronic inability of lumbermen to work together in cooperative enterprises, in the most heated period of labor strife during the lumber war only one member was expelled because of failure to observe the requirements of membership.[88]

The details of the lumber war and its antecedents, once generally neglected by historians, have been recently chronicled in several excellent studies. The story is interesting because it involved attempts by the Brotherhood of Timber Workers to unite black and white workers in the struggle, because the colorful Industrial Workers of the World became involved, and because the conflict featured techniques ranging from the use of blacklists and other means of labor control to the employment of Burns and Pinkerton detectives by the operators. The struggle was violent, resulting in several deaths at the infamous Graybow Incident, and by early 1916, due to the unceasing pressure of the lumbermen, even the most dedicated unionists had to admit their organizations were dead. The Southern Lumber Operators' Association had triumphed over the workers, but it continued to keep a close eye on movements among the laborers.[89]

Despite the operators' success, however, it is obvious that the early twentieth century was a time of industrial turmoil in the pine woods, belying the oft-repeated boast that there was never any significant labor trouble in the industry. In fact, the birth of the industry's strongest organization, the Southern Pine Association, came directly on the heels of this great labor conflict, and its immediate and direct predecessor was intimately involved with the Southern Lumber Operators' Association and its struggles.

NOTES TO CHAPTER 1

1. Wesley Frank Craven, The Southern Colonies in the Seventeenth Century 1607-1689 (Baton Rouge: Louisiana State University Press, 1949), p. 69; Stanley Horn, This Fascinating Lumber Business (New York: Bobbs-Merrill, 1943), p. 18. See also Thomas D. Clark, "The Impact of the Timber Industry on the South," Mississippi Quarterly, XXV (Spring, 1972), 141-64.

2. Horn, Fascinating Lumber Business, pp. 100-101; John Hebron Moore, Andrew Brown and Cypress Lumbering in the Old Southwest (Baton Rouge: Louisiana State University Press, 1967), pp. 13-14, says that the mill was probably destroyed in 1806 by a fire which was not caused by arsonists.

The New South and the "New Competition"

3. Bill Doree, "Texas' First Steam-Powered Sawmill," Gulf Coast Lumberman, C (Apr. 1963), 13.

4. Moore, Andrew Brown, passim.

5. Henry Weston to S. W. Weston, Dec. 15, 1950, reproduced in "The History of the Weston Lumber Co.," unpublished manuscript in the possession of H. C. Berckes, New Orleans, La.

6. James H. McClendon, "The Development of Mississippi Agriculture: A Survey," Journal of Mississippi History, XIII (Apr., 1951), 81.

7. Around 1840, J. F. H. Claiborne traveled through the forests of south Mississippi and reported, "For twenty miles at a stretch you may ride through these ancient woods and see them as they have stood for countless years, untouched by the hand of man. The time must arrive when this vast forest will become a source of value. The smoke of the steam mill will rise from a thousand hills." John Francis Hamtramck Claiborne, "A Trip through the Piney Woods," Publications of the Mississippi Historical Society, IX (1906), 523.

8. Horn, Fascinating Lumber Business, p. 102.

9. C. Vann Woodward, Origins of the New South, 1877-1913 (Baton Rouge: Louisiana State University Press, 1951), p. 115.

10. Paul Wallace Gates, "Federal Land Policy in the South, 1866-1888," Journal of Southern History, VI (Aug., 1940), 304.

11. Gates, "Federal Land Policy," pp. 305-8; Woodward, Origins, pp. 115-16.

12. Gates, "Federal Land Policy," pp. 308-12; Nollie Hickman, Mississippi Harvest: Lumbering in the Longleaf Pine Belt, 1840-1915 University: University of Mississippi Press, 1962), pp. 69-71.

13. Gates, "Federal Land Policy," p. 311.

14. Ibid., pp. 311-13.

15. Ibid., pp. 311-14; Hickman, Mississippi Harvest, pp. 71-72.

16. Gates, "Federal Land Policy, pp. 314-15, 328.

17. Statement of W. T. Neal, President of T. R. Miller Mill Company, Brewton, Alabama, in "Proceedings of 26th Annual Meeting, Southern Pine Association, March 13-14, 1941, Proceedings of Meeting of Conservation Committee, March 13, 1941," Southern Pine Association Records, Box 9a (Louisiana State University Archives, Baton Rouge, Louisiana). Collection hereafter cited as SPA Records.

18. Gates, "Federal Land Policy," pp. 313-15; Horn, Fascinating Lumber Business, p. 102.

19. Gates, "Federal Land Policy," pp. 315-16.

20. Ibid., p. 321.

21. An example would be the Gardiners of Laurel, Mississippi's Eastman-Gardiner firm, who moved their families from the North. Jo Dent Hodge, "Lumbering in Laurel at the Turn of the Century" (M.A. thesis, University of Mississippi, 1966), p. 21.

22. Gates, "Federal Land Policy," p. 317.

23. Ibid., pp. 317-18; Robert S. Maxwell, "Lumbermen of the East Texas Frontier," Forest History, IX (Apr., 1965), p. 13.

24. Tradesman (Chattanooga), XIV (May 1, 1886), p. 16, cited in Woodward, Origins, p. 118.

25. Richard Lowitt, A Merchant Prince of the Nineteenth Century: William E. Dodge, (New York: Columbia, 1954), p. 264; Horn, Fascinating Lumber Business, p. 103.

26. Hodge, "Lumbering in Laurel," p. 13. The Eastman-Gardiner firm became a pillar of the southern lumber industry.

27. Gates, "Federal Land Policy," p. 326. When Congress created new states out of the public domain, it reserved to itself the management and disposal of the public lands within their borders. However, it granted land to the states for various purposes, among which was to aid in the development of public schools. Lands granted for this purpose were called school lands.

28. R. E. Appleman, "Timber Empire from the Public Domain," Mississippi Valley Historical Review, XXVI (Sept., 1939), p. 193.

29. Ibid.

30. Gates, "Federal Land Policy," pp. 323-24.

31. R. C. Fraunberger, "Lumber Trade Associations: Their Economic and Social Significance" (M.A. Thesis, Temple University, 1951), p. 21; Gates, "Federal Land Policy," p. 327; Ralph W. Hidy, Frank Ernest Hill, and Allan Nevins, Timber and Men: The Weyerhaeuser Story (New York: Macmillan, 1963), pp. 305-7.

32. Gates, "Federal Land Policy," pp. 327-30.

33. Hidy, Hill, and Nevins, Timber and Men, pp. 290, 301.

34. Horn, Fascinating Lumber Business, pp. 104-5.

35. For definitions of trade associations see Joseph F. Bradley, The Role of Trade Associations and Professional Business Societies in America (University Park: Pennsylvania State, 1965), pp. 4-5; George Cooper, "Trade Associations before 1900," American Trade Association Executives Journal, VI (Jan. 1954), 13; Joseph Henry Foth, Trade Associations: Their Services to Industry (New York: Ronald Press, 1930), p. 3; and Benjamin S. Kirsh and Harold Roland Shapiro, Trade Associations in Law and Business (New York: Central Book, 1938), p. 10.

36. Richard W. Gable, "Birth of an Employers' Association," Business History Review, XXXIII (Winter, 1959), 538; Corrine Lathrop Gilb, Hidden Hierarchies: The Professions and Government (New York and London: Harper

and Row, 1966), pp. 228-29; Minita Westcott, "History of Trade Associations," American Trade Association Executives Journal, VIII (Apr., 1956), 33. Trade associations are generally, however, differentiated from employers' associations, which concentrate almost entirely upon labor problems. See Foth, Trade Associations, p. 3, and Gable, "Birth of an Employers' Association," p. 538.

37. Bradley, Role of Trade Associations, pp. 19-22; Foth, Trade Associations, p. 4; Louis Galambos, Competition and Cooperation: The Emergence of a National Trade Association (Baltimore: Johns Hopkins, 1966), p. 7.

38. For differing interpretations of the impact of the Civil War on American industrialization see Ralph Andreano, ed., The Economic Impact of the American Civil War (Cambridge, Mass.: Schenkman, 1962).

39. Foth, Trade Associations, 10; Westcott, "History of Trade Associations," p. 33. During this period a number of national associations and large regional associations were formed, including the Carriage Builders' National Association in 1872, the American Paper and Pulp Association in 1878, the National Association of Brass Manufacturers in 1886, the National Wholesale Lumber Dealers' Association in 1894, the National Lumber Manufacturers' Association in 1902, and others. Bradley, Role of Trade Associations, p. 22.

40. Bradley, Role of Trade Associations, pp. 23-24; Cooper, "Trade Associations before 1900," p. 14; Foth; Trade Associations, pp. 4-5; Westcott, "History of Trade Associations," p. 35.

41. For an early study of the effectiveness of trade associations in curing the economic problems of various depressed industries see Simon N. Whitney, Trade Associations and Industrial Control (New York: Central Publishing, 1934).

42. Joseph Zaremba, Economics of the American Lumber Industry (New York: Speller & Sons, 1963), p. 7.

43. Vernon H. Jensen, Lumber and Labor, (New York and Toronto: Farrar and Rinehart, 1945), p. 24.

The New South and the "New Competition"

44. James Boyd, "Fifty Years in the Southern Pine Industry," Southern Lumberman, CXLIV (Dec., 1931), 65; A. S. Boisfontaine, "The Southern Pine Association in Retrospect: Seventeen Years of Trail Blazing in the Trade Association Field," Southern Lumberman, CXLIV (Dec., 1931), 109.

45. Fraunberger, "Lumber Trade Associations," pp. 11-12.

46. Hickman, Mississippi Harvest, p. 32.

47. Wilson Compton, "Lumber: An Old Industry and the New Competition," Harvard Business Review, X (Jan., 1932), 163.

48. Hidy, Hill, and Nevins, Timber and Men, 174.

49. C. W. Judson in Northwestern Lumbermen, XVIII (Jan. 7, 1881), 3; quoted in Fraunberger, "Lumber Trade Associations," p. 11.

50. Fraunberger, "Lumber Trade Associations," p. 13.

51. Compton, "Lumber: An Old Industry," p. 163.

52. Hidy, Hill, and Nevins, Timber and Men, p. 174.

53. Ibid., pp. 174-76. Hidy, Hill, and Nevins state that the Mississippi Valley Lumbermen's Association accomplished nothing measurable in influencing prices and that other associations in the white pine region were similarly unsuccessful. They attribute the general rise of white pine prices after 1897 to the higher duties on lumber imports imposed by the Dingley Tariff of 1897, a general upward trend in commodity prices, higher timber and logging costs, higher costs for supplies, and the growing scarcity of white pine.

54. Frank A. Connolly, "Lumber Organization Activity in the Half-Century," Southern Lumberman, CLXIV (Dec., 1931), 107.

55. Boyd, "Fifty Years," pp. 64-65; John M. Collier, The First Fifty Years of the Southern Pine Association, 1915-65 (New Orleans: Southern Pine Association, 1965), p. 35.

56. Robert S. Maxwell, "Lumbermen of the East Texas Frontier," p. 15.

57. Ruth Alice Allen, East Texas Lumber Workers: An Economic and Social Picture, 1870-1900 (Austin: University of Texas Press, 1961), p. 32.

58. There is an account of the association's organization and purposes in the Beaumont Journal (May 12, 1894), a copy of which is in the Alexamder Gilmer Collection, University of Texas Archives. The Journal, which Kelley edited, served as the official organ of the association. There are copies of these reports and tables in the Kurth Papers, Box 2 (Forest History Collections, Stephens F. Austin State University Library, Nacogdoches, Tex.). Collection hereafter cited as Kurth Papers.

59. R. E. Kelley to Members, Nov. 30, 1895, Kurth Papers, Box 2.

60. R. E. Kelley to Members, Dec. 12, 1895, Kurth Papers, Box 2.

61. R. E. Kelley to Angelina County Lumber Company, June 25, 1897, Kurth Papers, Box 6.

62. R. E. Kelley to Yellow Pine Manufacturers in Texas and Louisiana, May 14, 1896, and Kelley to Lumber Manufacturers of Texas and Louisiana, April 29, 1896, Kurth Papers, Box 6.

63. "Prospectus, The Yellow Pine Exchange, June 8, 1897," Kurth Papers, Box 6.

64. Hickman, Mississippi Harvest, p. 199.

65. George K. Smith to Members, Dec. 23, 1905, Kurth Papers, Box 84.

66. Boisfontaine, "Southern Pine Association in Retrospect," p. 109; Boyd, "Fifty Years," pp. 64-65; Collier, First Fifty Years, p. 36; Hickman, Mississippi Harvest, pp. 199-200. George K. Smith left his position with the Southern Lumber Manufacturers' Association at the end of February, 1897, and became associated with the Holladay-Klots Land and Lumber Company. He was succeeded

as secretary of the association by F. McCullam. Smith remained amenable to the wishes of the large southern pine interests and again became secretary of the association in 1898.

67. Boyd, "Fifty Years," p. 65.

68. Hickman, Mississippi Harvest, p. 200.

69. George K. Smith to Manufacturers of Yellow Pine, July 25, 1896, and Smith to Manufacturers, Aug. 1, 1896, Kurth Papers, Box 4. A circular from Smith calling for a special meeting in Memphis on November 18, 1896, advised that there would be "the Submission . . . of various plans for regulation of output, and betterment of prices."

70. George K. Smith to Manufacturers of Yellow Pine, June 29, 1901, Kurth Papers, Box 35.

71. "Agreement Formulated at Meeting of Yellow Pine Manufacturers Held November 16, 1898, at St. Louis, Mo.," Kurth Papers, Box 35.

72. J. B. White to Yellow Pine Manufacturers, Nov. 18, 1898, Kurth Papers, Box 12.

73. Unaddressed form letter from N. W. McLeod, Jan. 30, 1899, Kurth Papers, Box 18.

74. Unaddressed circular from J. J. White, President, and George K. Smith, Secretary, the Southern Lumber Manufacturers' Association, Nov. 9, 1896, Kurth Papers, Box 4. Box 7 of the Kurth Papers contains other scattered material on the clearinghouse.

75. Hickman, Mississippi Harvest, pp. 200-202.

76. J. Newton Nind to F. McCullam, undated but written in 1897, Kurth Papers, Box 7; McCullam to Angelina County Lumber Company, July 20, 1897, Kurth Papers, Box 7; McCullam to Angelina County Lumber Company, Sept. 24, 1902, Kurth Papers, Box 42; "Call for and invitation to 18th Annual Meeting of The Southern Lumber Manufacturers' Association," Kurth Papers, Box 47.

77. "Agreement Regarding Assessment for Advertising Fund, Extract from Minutes of Fifteenth Annual Meeting," Kurth Papers, Box 74; unaddressed letter from F. McCullam, Mar. 2, 1897, Kurth Papers, Box 7.

78. Circular from J. J. White and George K. Smith, Nov. 9, 1896, Kurth Papers, Box 4; Smith to Angelina County Lumber Company, Feb. 8, 1904, Kurth Papers, Box 67; "Call for and Invitation to 13th Annual Meeting of The Southern Lumber Manufacturers' Association," Kurth Papers, Box 47.

79. Circular from J. J. White and George K. Smith, Feb. 1, 1897, Kurth Papers, Box 7; "Call for and Invitation to 13th Annual Meeting of The Southern Lumber Manufacturers' Association," Kurth Papers, Box 47; M. R. Grant to Angelina County Lumber Company, June 28, 1897, Kurth Papers, Box 7; Circular from R. A. Long and George K. Smith, Jan. 11, 1906, Kurth Papers, Box 84.

80. Hickman, Mississippi Harvest, pp. 202.

81. George K. Smith to All Members, Dec. 20, 1905, Kurth Papers, Box 84.

82. George K. Smith to All Members, Jan. 27, 1906, Kurth Papers, Box 91; Hickman, Mississippi Harvest, p. 202.

83. U. S. Department of Commerce, Bureau of Corporations, Conditions in Production and Wholesale Distribution Including Wholesale Prices, Part IV of The Lumber Industry (Washington, D.C.: Government Printing Office, 1914), p. 159; Boyd, "Fifty Years," p. 65; Collier, First Fifty Years, pp. 36–37.

84. Boisfontaine, "Southern Pine Association in Retrospect," p. 109; Boyd, "Fifty Years," p. 65; Collier, First Fifty Years, pp. 36–37; Connolly, "Lumber Organization Activity," p. 107.

85. Oscar S. Tam to Louisiana and Texas Lumber Operators, Feb. 17, 1908, Kurth Papers, Box 127; "Constitution and By-Laws, Texas and Louisiana Saw Mill Association," Lumber Trade Journal (Feb. 15, 1908),

clipping in Records of the Bureau of Corporations, Drawer 1134, RG 122, National Archives, Washington, D.C.

86. Angelina County Lumber Company to Oscar S. Tam, June 8, 1908, Kurth Papers, Box 140.

87. Allen, East Texas Lumber Workers, p. 32; Boyd, "Fifty Years," p. 64; Hickman, Mississippi Harvest, p. 202.

88. The material on the origins and early period of the Operators' Association is taken from scattered materials in the Kurth Papers, Box 102. Several authors claim the Operators' Association was formed in 1907, but materials in the Kurth Papers show conclusively that it was organized in 1906.

89. The best published accounts of the early trouble in the southern lumber industry are in Charlotte Todes, Labor and Lumber (New York: International Publishers, 1931); Jensen, Lumber and Labor; F. Ray Marshall, Labor in the South (Cambridge, Mass.: Harvard University Press, 1967); Melvin Dubofsky, We Shall Be All: A History of the Industrial Workers of the World (Chicago: Quadrangle Press, 1969); George T. Morgan, Jr., "No Compromise--No Recognition: John Henry Kirby, the Southern Lumber Operators' Association, and Unionism in the Piney Woods, 1906-1916," Labor History, X (Spring, 1969), 193-204; and Philip S. Foner, "The IWW and the Black Worker," Journal of Negro History, LV (Jan., 1970), 45-64. There are also published treatments of the subject in Richard G. Lillard, The Great Forest (New York: Alfred A. Knopf, 1947), and James E. Fickle, "The Louisiana-East Texas Lumber War," Louisiana History, XVI (Winter, 1975), 59-85.

2

Development of the Industry
and the Southern Pine Association

The Yellow Pine Manufacturers' Association, the direct
predecessor of the Southern Pine Association, was formed
about the same time as the Southern Lumber Operators'
Association, and while the YPMA's main thrust was not the
same as that of the SLOA, the two organizations worked
closely together. On at least one occasion, the YPMA's
semi-annual meeting was simply turned over to the deliberations of the Operators' Association, with the president of that group actually taking the gavel until labor
matters were disposed of and then turning the meeting back
to the YPMA presiding officer.[1]

With the labor situation basically being handled by
the SLOA, the Yellow Pine Manufacturers' Association could
devote its energies to a variety of other matters. Its
main areas of interest were the old pillars of lumber
association work—grading standards and statistics. The
grading rules adopted by the YPMA represented a revision
and refinement of those developed by earlier associations,
the Southern Lumber Manufacturers' Association in
particular. The grading rules were published, and to
secure their adoption and proper application the association maintained a bureau of grades composed of a chief
inspector and several assistants who visited both the
mills and wholesale and retail lumber companies. By 1908,
the mills were inspected every thirty-five to forty days,
and the association soon estimated that approximately 95
percent of the total southern pine production was manufac-
turered according to its specifications.[2] Grading standards and the inspection service were the most positive
legacy of the YPMA to its sucessor, the Southern Pine
Association.

The New South and the "New Competition"

The biggest concerns of the Yellow Pine Manufacterers' Association and its staff were accounting and statistics at both the company and the industry level. During its first years of operation, the association sent out three men to gather more reliable information concerning production and stocks in the field and to establish offices in Houston, Shreveport, and Hatttesburg. Plans were made to add representatives in Alabama and Arkansas.[3] The work of these men proved so successful that their offices were closed in order to keep them in the field continuously.[4] During this period, the association was careful to prevent independent printing companies from controlling the issuance of price lists for the industry.[5]

The Yellow Pine Manufacturers' Association's efforts were not undertaken simply because of a fascination with accounting practices or statistics. The organization soon proved that a name change had not altered its basic purpose, and within a short time after assuming its new existence it was again attempting to stablize prices through production controls. The economic downturn that had spawned the labor troubles of 1906-7 propelled the YPMA into the shadowy area of influencing prices and production. A slight break in the market in May, 1907, developed into a full-scale depression, and late in the year many mills were idle in the face of what many hoped was merely a temporary recession. Of thirty-one mills in Mississippi listed by the YPMA early in 1908, only eight were running.[6]

A general manufacturers' conference at Memphis in November reported that the consensus from all sections of the South was "that similar conditions prevail in all localities . . . very little new business being placed . . . many old orders being cancelled, great difficulty in securing currency to meet payrolls and a growing necessity for great conservatism in the production of lumber during the next few months." The meeting's committee on resolutions recommended that the operators avoid complete shutdowns to provide their employees with the necessities of life, while endeavoring to curtail operations sufficiently to prevent a further drain on their own financial resources.[7]

While many millmen believed it better to shut down than to waste good timber at a time when the price of finished lumber often would not even defray manufacturing costs, the prevailing methods of financing in the industry kept many from halting operations:

Mill expansion, acquisition of timberlands, and provision of working capital were to a great extent financed through borrowing by the sale of bonds secured by what amounted to a lien on the standing timber. The millmen paid the taxes on the timber, insured it against the hazards of fire and tornado, and cut it only under conditions stipulated in the trust deed. Brooks-Scanlon, for example, issued $750,000 in 6 percent bonds on 47,474 acres of Louisiana timberland valued at $3,000,000 or about $1.50 on each thousand feet of lumber manufactured. The necessity of meeting such interest payments and of building up a sinking fund often compelled millmen to maintain operations when returns were little above, or in some instances, even below production costs. For this reason the available supply of lumber might exceed the demand even in a period of extremely low prices. Thus gentlemen's agreements to reduce the supply over an extended period had little chance of success.[8]

The YPMA's report of running time for sawmills in November showed that most mills had shut down entirely or curtailed production drastically in the hope that better conditions would return.[9]

Early in 1908, several large manufacturers made tentative plans to form a giant corporation to control the supply of lumber by consolidating the ownership of mills and timberlands and establishing a wholesale marketing agency. The firm would have included the major producers in the South with a combined output of about 20 percent of all yellow pine manufactured. The organizers included many prominent members of the YPMA, but the movement foundered when the attorney general of Missouri obtained an injunction to prevent the merger. His action prompted his counterparts in other states to take similar steps.[10]

Despite this setback, the Yellow Pine Manufacturers' Association kept trying for controls for the industry and urging its members to support legislation to make the Sherman Antitrust Act more lenient toward "reasonable" agreements to reduce the production of lumber. In June, it reported that members had achieved a steady decrease in stocks during the first five months of the year.[11]

Although the Panic of 1907 was short, the lumber industry remained in a general depression until late 1915. The YPMA and individual producers continued to try to

influence prices but in general were unsuccessful because
of the excessive productive capacity of the industry and
the inordinate production increases when small price
upturns did occur.[12] The association continued to plead
with its members to supply reliable statistics and
reports, often to no avail, and it continued to distribute
a variety of statistical information.[13] As the association came under the legal fire that eventually destroyed
it because of these activities, its secretary was reduced
to begging for support and issuing constant reassurances
to members that participation in the association's statistical programs would pose no legal problems.[14]

Despite the overriding significance of the YPMA's
statistical efforts, this was not all the association
did. Another major interest of the group and its officers
was the tariff, which had provided protection against
lumber imports, particularly from Canada, when the white
pine states of the Old Northwest had been the primary
lumber-producing centers of the nation. As these areas
were cut over, however, northern lumbermen began to
purchase Canadian timber that could be easily rafted to
mills in the United States. They favored free entry of
lumber into the United States because they knew that a
tariff on rough Canadian lumber would bring a retaliatory
Canadian export duty on logs. By 1888 there was a good
deal of sentiment among northern lumbermen for repealing
or lowering the tariff on rough Canadian lumber, and the
McKinley Act of 1890 brought a reduction from $2.00 to
$1.00 per thousand board feet on low-grade lumber. The
Canadians, as expected, repealed their duty on logs, but
they placed restrictions on holders of cutting rights on
government lands unless these men established mills in
Canada.[15]

As the South became a major producer, southern lumbermen complained that the duty on rough Canadian lumber was
too low, but their protests were in vain. The Wilson-
Gorman Tariff of 1894 completely repealed the tariff on
lumber and permitted Canadian rough lumber to enter the
United States duty-free. Competition from the low-grade
Canadian lumber seriously hurt southern producers, and in
1896 the Southern Lumber Manufacturers' Association led a
fight for restoration of the duties. Under the high-
tariff McKinley administration, Congress in 1897 passed
the Dingley bill, which placed a two-dollar duty on rough
lumber. Canada countered with an export duty on unmanu-
factured logs and passed an act requiring that logs cut

on Crown lands be manufactured into lumber before export,
thereby forcing American lumbermen who owned such stumpage
to construct mills in Canada.[16] Here the matter stood
until pressure for abolition of the duties began to come
from a number of quarters.

Conservationists believed that tariff revision would
allow imported lumber to come into the United States more
freely, thus reducing the drain on American timber, and
consumers felt that rising lumber prices were partially
a result of the high duties.   Added to this was the
pressure of Americans who owned Canadian mills and timber.
To combat   these forces, YPMA members were instructed
early in   1909 that each should "consider himself a committee of one to bring to the   attention of Congress the
deplorable effect   any change in lumber tariff will have
on the price of low grade lumber. . . ."[17] The Association's annual meeting passed a resolution on the proposed
tariff revision addressed to the House ways and means
committee.   It pointed out that lumber manufacturers had
just gone through a year of severe depression and that
removal of the tariff would seriously harm both the
lumber and the transportation interests of the South as
well as many related businesses and occupations.[18]

Southern   lumbermen were particularly afraid of the
competition of Canadian   lumber north of the Ohio River,
a consuming area that would be crucial to the fortunes
of yellow pine manufacturers for many years to come.   The
leader of the   fight against   reduction was peppery little
Edward Hines of Chicago, who owned mills and timber in
both Canada and the South.   Hines, one of the most colorful industry figures and a future   leader in the Southern
Pine   Association,   attacked   the   Canadian   lumbermen's
advantages in   cheap stumpage,   low taxes, and inexpensive
water   transportation.[19]   His   efforts   to get   a   higher
tariff led to his deep involvement in politics and charges
that he had   tried to   "buy" a U.S. Senate election in
Illinois in   cooperation with other lumbermen.[20] Mississippi lumbermen sent delegates to Washington to fight for
high duties, and a lobbying committee was formed to oppose
the free lumber provisions.   John E. Rhodes, who was to
be the   first   secretary-manager of   the   Southern   Pine
Association, led the lumbermen's fight as treasurer of the
committee.

The only member of the House ways and means committee
who favored retaining the duty on   low-grade lumber was
Joseph   Fordney   of Michigan, who also happened to be part

owner of the Gilchrist-Fordney Lumber Company at Laurel, Mississippi. Through some frantic horse trading, however, the southern lumbermen won a partial victory. The Payne-Aldrich Tariff carried a duty of $1.25 per thousand board feet on low-grade lumber.[21] In 1913, during the Wilson administration, however, the Underwood-Simmons Tariff was passed and lumber was placed on the free list. Although southern lumbermen were still strongly opposed to free Canadian lumber, they accepted the inevitable and did nothing to fight it.[22]

Southern concern about Canadian competition north of the Ohio River was reflected not only in the fight to retain the tariff, but also in the maintenance of the YPMA's traffic department. The department represented association members before the railroads and the Interstate Commerce Commission in determining rates for the shipment of southern pine lumber. The department conveyed semi-monthly rate information to yards east and west of the Mississippi River, and a separate freight claim department handled claims for overcharges. Freight and traffic matters were also among the major concerns of the YPMA's successor, and the different interests and rates of producers on opposite sides of the Mississippi River would play a central role in associational affairs.[23]

Another area of large-scale YPMA activity was advertising and trade promotion. To help its members enlarge their markets for southern pine products, the association maintained both advertising and trade promotion departments. The former was responsible for the preparation of literature advertising the virtues and uses of southern pine. In addition to the production and distribution of literature, the advertising department furnished a free consultation service for potential customers. Closely tied in with advertising were the association's trade promotion activities. In fact, the trade promotion department published a good deal of literature concerning the use of southern pine products which was quite similar to that of the advertising department. In order to combat heavy advertising campaigns by other lumber species, the YPMA maintained special funds supported by contributions to supplement the regular costs of association membership. It made special attempts to furnish architects, builders, and retailers with information about southern pine. Late in the association's existence, it was spending approximately $25,000 per year for advertising.[24]

Development of the Industry and the SPA

The association failed to take effective action in the fields of forestry and conservation, despite the support of Captain J. B. White, the existence of a standing committee on forest conservation, and the efforts of Secretary George K. Smith who tried to stimulate the interest and attention of his membership. Lumbermen in this early period had little use for the idea of conservation, and the first industry conservationists were subjected to considerable scorn and ridicule. Despite the unfavorable climate of opinion, Smith continued to distribute copies of the U.S. Forest Service reports, newspaper articles, and other related materials. Although the YPMA took no major steps to deal with conservation, it is quite possible that Smith's efforts stimulated industry figures who became pioneers in these areas.[25]

The last days of the Yellow Pine Manufacturers' Association and George K. Smith were tumultuous, stimulated by the heady vision of an age of "new competition" and finally shattered by a judicial decision which spelled the organization's demise. Smith was apparently a vigorous man whose interests reached out in several directions. During his tenure as head of the YPMA, he sent members information not only on freight rates, advertising, and forestry and conservation, but also on many other matters which he felt might affect the industry's welfare. In October, 1913, under the heading "The New Competition," Smith informed the members about the ideas of a Chicago lawyer, Arthur Jerome Eddy. Smith asked them to submit their thoughts on establishing a central office for the interchange of information and announced plans to meet Eddy in Chicago to discuss the yellow pine situation and secure his suggestions and advice.[26]

Eddy's thesis was presented in a book entitled The New Competition, published in 1912. This was only three years after the appearance of Herbert Croly's The Promise of American Life, which ushered in an age of business thought that wavered somewhat uncertainly from the American ideals of free competition and laissez faire. Eddy called for an end to secretive, cutthroat competition. His new millennium would feature an atmosphere in which competitors would freely exchange information and in which the Sherman Act would be abolished, allowing the free operation of trade associations with some friendly federal supervision. Ended would be the primitive days in which "competition is war . . . and war is hell."[27]

The New South and the "New Competition"

Eddy's "new-competition" approach inspired the "open-price," or "open-competition," associations spawned in the wake of the Supreme Court's decisions in the Standard Oil and American Tobacco cases in 1911. With these cases it became apparent that the Sherman Act applied to manufacturing and that federal antitrust policy had tremendous importance for trade associations. Eddy's plan and the variations adopted by numerous open-price associations required individual companies, or their representatives, to furnish complete information to their associations or related organizations concerning production, stocks on hand, unfilled orders, and prices. The association's staff then processed the raw data and channeled it back to the subscribers so that each producer had an intimate and comprehensive view of market conditions. Theoretically, the open-price system was designed to create order and stability in extremely individualistic industries like that already prevailing in those which were highly concentrated. Eddy hoped to bring about more equitable and freer competition by eliminating the unintelligent and vindictive actions of individual producers. Actually, the open-price system often provided simply another means of pursuing the old trade association objective of controlling production and prices.

According to its adherents, the overwhelming advantage of the open-price association was that it provided a completely legal means of achieving stability. The key was that members would not conspire to control future activities, but rather would provide complete information to one another about past transactions. If this was done with sufficient accuracy and speed, however, cooperators could obviously act in collusion to affect the future of the market. Eddy was so confident of his plan's legality that he maintained close contact with the U.S. Department of Justice and kept it informed about various open-price associations he helped form. For a while the department seemed to look favorably upon the new organization and for several years the government made no effort to obtain a test case and determine the legality of the plan.[28]

Smith's meeting with Eddy in Chicago and his enthusiastic interest led to a December, 1913, gathering of yellow pine manufacturers in St. Louis which featured an address by the Chicago lawyer. With Eddy's help, the lumbermen adopted a constitution and by-laws for the Yellow Pine Publicity Society. Smith reported that the St. Louis meeting indicated that about one hundred manufacturers with an annual producing capacity of nearly three billion feet favored the plan. Eddy's $2,500 speaking fee was prorated among the fifty firms represented in St. Louis.[29]

Unfortunately, however, time had run out for the YPMA because of its alleged production and price-fixing activities just when Smith was trying to move toward a new, effective, and legal means of achieving the same objectives. The members were reluctant to support a new venture in light of the YPMA's increasingly bleak legal situation. The ever-optimistic Smith informed the manufacturers that plans for the new group were being temporarily dropped while a reorganization of the YPMA itself was under consideration and that the publicity society might well be incorporated into the structure of the revised parent association.[30]

The Yellow Pine Manufacturers' Association's difficulties stemmed from alleged attempts to stabilize prices through production controls. The basic device for these activities had been the price list which YPMA members were urged to follow. Because of these activities, the Missouri attorney general brought a writ of quo warranto against forty-one lumber companies on July 30, 1908. The writ sought to oust the companies from their franchises in Missouri and to fine them for violating the state statutes outlawing pools, trusts, and conspiracies. All of the companies were licensed to do business in Missouri: thirty-five were incorporated under the laws of the state, and the other six merely operated there.[31] All forty-one respondents were members of the YPMA, but the association was not mentioned in the suit.[32] Charges against the defendants included issuing association price lists, curtailing output, agreeing to sell only to legitimate retailers, refusing to sell in carload lots to farmers' cooperatives, and dividing territory among retailers.[33]

The case became known as the Missouri Ouster Case and was heard before the Missouri State Supreme Court. The court appointed a commissioner to gather evidence, and in May, 1911, he began to hear testimony. The commissioner eventually collected 3,000 printed pages and 200 pounds of exhibits and filed this great mass of material, together with his findings of fact and conclusions of law, with the court.[34]

While the manufacturers were under indictment, George K. Smith and the YPMA tried to maintain an optimistic outlook and facade, and it appears that many lumbermen were not particularly alarmed by the charges. In June, 1912, the attorney for several YPMA members involved in the ouster proceedings addressed the association's semi-annual meeting. On the basis of his remarks, the secretary reported that every manufacturer could in good faith join the YPMA because "the manner in which the organization is now conducted precludes the possibility of any legal entanglements. . . ."[35]

Despite the real or feigned optimism of the lumber industry, on December 24, 1913, the Missouri Supreme Court found twenty-five companies incorporated in Missouri and six foreign corporations guilty of conspiring to limit the output of yellow pine and of fixing prices. The court entered judgments of forfeiture against each of the guilty respondents, dissolving those which had Missouri charters and repealing all of their licenses to do business in the state. It also fined the guilty defendants a total of $436,000, with the assessment for individual companies ranging from $500 to $50,000.[36]

The decision made the YPMA's demise inevitable. However, George K. Smith and the manufacturers waged a desperate struggle to bring their organization into harmony with the law by making basic changes in its stated purposes and structure. In January, 1914, Smith informed the members that the association's annual meeting in February would consider "some changes in the Constitution and By-Laws . . . to make them conform in all respects to the views of the Court in the recent decision. . . ."[37]

The YPMA's annual meeting heard a report by the committee on constitution and by-laws, and on March 24 Smith advised the members that a general meeting in St. Louis on April 7 would consider amendments to the constitution which would "provide for a change in the statement of the objects of our association . . . and eliminate the gathering and disseminating of information regarding sales and marketing."[38] At the same time, he submitted to the members a petition to the Missouri Supreme Court which was to be filed by the respondents' attorneys in the ouster suit. The document promised that the lumbermen would revise the constitution and by-laws of the YPMA to conform to the court's opinion and pledged to stop the collection and distribution of price lists. The petition further stated that the respondents would drop out of the association if it was not satisfactorily reformed and that they would no longer engage in the practices attributed to them.[39]

Development of the Industry and the SPA

A special YPMA meeting convened in St. Louis on
April 8, 1914, and two of the industry's most prestigious
leaders, Captain J. B. White, and R. A. Long of the
Long-Bell Company, who acted as chairman, led efforts to
reform the organization. Long was most concerned about
appearances and was an extremely moral man in his personal
life. He was dismayed by the lumber companies' troubles
with the Missouri Supreme Court.[40] The lumbermen amended
the YPMA's constitution to eliminate references to the
dissemination of information relating to sales and
marketing. At the suggestion of Captain White, a new
addition to the association's by-laws pledged: "Neither
this Association nor any officer, agent, or employee
thereof, shall hereafter publish or issue in the name of,
or for or on behalf of this Association, either directly
or indirectly, any market report, price current or price
list, or any other document or statement purporting to
quote or to recite market values of yellow pine lumber;
and it shall be the duty of the officers and board of
directors of this Association to see that this by-law is
rigidly enforced."[41]
The respondents' plea, which had been sent to the
yellow pine companies in March by George K. Smith, ended
with a request that the Missouri Supreme Court suspend the
ouster judgments and reduce the fines. Having evidently
been persuaded that the original decree was indeed too
harsh, on July 2, 1914, the court announced that it would
suspend its writ of ouster from corporate rights and
franchises if the respondent companies would comply with
certain conditions. Each defendant had to pay his fine
within sixty days and promise to treat all purchasers
equally. It had to refrain from blacklisting retailers or
selling in open competition with wholesalers. The defendants were also forbidden to issue any price lists unless
they represented actual and bona fide sales of their products and the prices paid for them. However, despite
these modifications, each defendant was required to file
evidence that it had withdrawn from the YPMA and similar
organizations.
The court's decision mentioned the Yellow Pine Manufacturers' Association directly only once, saying it was
powerless to act against, the YPMA since it was not a
respondent in the case. However, the court suggested
that its decision might act as "rules of ethics by which
it (the YPMA) may square its behavior, or as a chart by
which it may hereafter steer its course."[42] The irony of

43

this statement was that there was to be no future in which YPMA could attempt to "square its behavior" or "steer its course." The court's decree requiring the respondents to withdraw from YPMA membership made its demise inevitable. On November 10, 1914, the board of directors unanimously recommended the association's dissolution.[43]

The manufacturers continued to assert their innocence, and they declared that they had been persecuted by the state of Missouri. This position received some support from the Bureau of Corporations. In its 1914 report, which contained a survey of the lumber-producing areas of the United States, the bureau declared that the great diversity and wide geographical area of the yellow pine industry prevented the centralization of control over production and prices which was evident in some other species. The report also questioned the industry's adherence to the association's official prise lists, which had been one of the major charges against the lumbermen.[44]

After the dissolution of the YPMA, southern lumbermen immediately began to plan for the creation of its successor. On November 24, 1914, NLMA Secretary John E. Rhodes announced a New Orleans meeting of all yellow pine manufacturers in the name of the national association because of "its interest in the welfare of the yellow pine industry. . . ." The YPMA's board of directors had authorized such a call in their last meeting and recommended that any new organization should "carry on uniform grades and inspection only, with headquarters near the center of production. . . ."[45] So the new association would not share the reputation of the YPMA, only the old organization's transportation tariff files and technical materials were preserved. The remaining files were destroyed upon the advice of the counsel, so that the successor organization would have nothing to show that it was connected in any way with its defunct predecessor.[46]

The most tragic figure in the entire story of the YPMA's demise was Secretary George K. Smith, who had served long and valiantly to promote organization and progress in the southern pine industry. Smith's eternal optimism and frantic efforts went unrewarded, and after the YPMA's fall, he worked briefly for a firm of St. Louis lumber wholesalers. The former secretary was then involved in an abortive effort to take over the YPMA's inspection service. According to general opinion in the industry, Smith believed he had been ruined by the scandal and fall of the YPMA, and he finally ended his life by jumping out of a St. Louis hotel window.[47] It was thus in an atmosphere of personal tragedy, unsettled market conditions, labor turmoil, legal difficulties, and approaching warfare that the industry's greatest trade organization, the Southern Pine Association, was born.

While Captain J. B. White was the leading figure in early southern pine producers' association activities there is no doubt that he was succeeded as a dominant figure by Charles S. Keith, president of Central Coal and Coke Company, with headquarters in Kansas City. Keith seized the initiative at the time of the Missouri Ouster Suit and led the temporarily disorganized yellow pine producers into the new and stronger Southern Pine Association. At the time of the ouster suit Keith, a vigorous man who had just turned forty, was nearing the pinnacle of a bright career in the lumber industry. Keith was born into a prominent Kansas City mercantile family and spent his entire life in that old lumbering capital. His father was president of the Keith and Perry Company, later expanded into the Central Coke and Coke Company, with operations in eight states.

Keith was a quick, bright man who was particularly noted for his mastery of statistical information. He graduated at eighteen from Fordham University and joined his father's firm, where he started as an accounting clerk and moved up through the ranks becoming, successively, an engineer, traveling sales agent, and general sales agent. In 1902, at twenty-nine, Charles S. Keith became general manager of the company. Keith's father died in 1905, and his partner, W. C. Perry, became president, but Perry died two years later. Charles S. Keith thus found himself, in his thirties, directing one of the industry's largest businesses. The Central Coal and Coke Company by this time controlled nine subsidiary companies, operating mines, lumber camps, and manufacturing plants.[48]

Keith differed from most of his associates in many ways. He was not a self-made man in an age and industry which were still strongly influenced by their pioneering elements. There can be little doubt that his family background facilitated his rise to the top. He was a university graduate among generally uneducated contemporaries who prided themselves on being able to hire a college man if they needed one. He was a Roman Catholic running operations concentrated in heavily Protestant areas. Finally, Keith was extremely young. In a sense, he was a link between the pioneering generation and the era of managers which was to come. Perhaps because of his own distinctiveness and the fact that he was used to success and respect, Keith exhibited little of the hesitation of some of his colleagues. He seemed able to reach decisions in the industry's time of trial. Charles S. Keith, with his qualities of leadership, was the man needed to lead yellow pine producers in a new effort at organization.[49]

Keith was a member of the committee appointed during the YPMA's last days to devise a reorganization plan. Upon the advice of attorneys, that plan was never circulated or promulgated because of the Missouri ouster decision. However, the committee members consulted with attorneys, devised plans for the Southern Pine Association, and filed articles of incorporation with the Missouri Secretary of State.[50] On October 21, 1914, the association was chartered as a corporation for fifty years under the provisions of the Revised Statutes of Missouri of 1909. Capital stock was listed at $2,000, divided into 2,000 shares with a par value of one dollar each. Legal headquarters were initially established at St. Louis.[51]

Robert A. Long and Captain J. B. White were closely involved with Keith in organizing the Southern Pine Association. Judge John H. Lucas, a Kansas City businessman and lawyer, was the primary legal mind behind the organization. To win support for the SPOA and put it into operation, Keith, Long, and White scheduled a meeting for December 8, 1914, in New Orleans. Although the association had been chartered, it was not expected that a prospectus would be prepared in time for the New Orleans meeting. While Long, White and others worked on a prospectus, Keith began to elicit support for the new organization. One of his first steps was to ask the powerful Texas lumberman John Henry Kirby to attend the New Orleans meeting.[52] He knew that Kirby's affiliation with the SPA would almost insure success among the vitally important East Texas and western Louisiana producers.

The New Orleans meeting lasted three days and attracted over 80 percent of the southern lumber manufacturing interests. The lumbermen made plans to set the Southern Pine Association into operation and chose directors. Kirby attended the meeting and was favorably impressed. He hesitated about joining, however, until he had consulted his attorneys and learned "what others who had heretofore stood aloof intended to do." Kirby was happy that firms in his area that had previously abstained from associational activitites were favorable toward the new proposition and was particularly enthusiastic about the possibility of effective joint action in grading and inspection, statistics, advertising, and product research. Although selected as an SPA director, Kirby did not attend the directors' sessions which were held later in New Orleans.[53]

During late December, communications between Keith and the directors filled the mails. Plans were made for an early-January directors' meeting in St. Louis to work out details concerning SPA contracts, prices, and services. Preparations were to be made at this session for a mass meeting of lumbermen in New Orleans on January 19. Keith also planned to "make arrangements to secure the office furniture and other things belonging to the Yellow Pine Manufacturers' Association." The St. Louis directors' conference would fulfill the SPA's chartered obligation to have a directors' session in Missouri.[54]

In accordance with the board of directors' instructions, Keith negotiated with John E. Rhodes, secretary of the National Lumber Manufacturers' Association, to fill the same position with the SPA. On December 22, Keith received Rhodes's acceptance,[55] thus giving the Southern Pine Association the services of a well-trained and industrious trade association executive. As Kirby said, "Nearly everything depends upon the Secretary and this young man will bring a great deal of capacity and dignity into this new organization."[56]

Rhodes was originally a Minneapolis newspaperman. His initial connection with the lumber industry was as stenographer and secretary to Frederick Weyerhaeuser. Rhodes's first trade association work was as secretary of the Northern Pine Manufacturers' Association. From that position he was hired by the Weyerhaeusers and installed in their St. Paul office to analyze sales conditions. Together with Frederick E. Weyerhaeuser, Rhodes developed the idea of trade-marking and grade-marking lumber for species and quality.[57] Rhodes had thus been active in what would become one of the Southern Pine Association's most important endeavors long before he joined the SPA. Rhodes's ideas were not well received in the Weyerhaeuser firm, however, and in 1912, he became discouraged and left. He then served as secretary of the Mississippi Valley Lumbermen's Association and the National Lumber Manufacturers' Association.[58]

When Rhodes became secretary-manager of the SPA, he was widely known among the lumber fraternity and well versed in association work. He "was a small man, prematurely gray, wiry, very diplomatic and very impressive in what he said and did." Rhodes's diplomatic abilities were perhaps his outstanding asset and they were sorely needed during the association's early years. He was widely respected within the industry and could, therefore, deal with lumbermen on an equal basis. However, he was careful not to become an intimate of any particular individual or clique and thereby destroy his effectiveness. According to his closest associate within the association, "to harmonize all of these men in the first eight years of the Southern Pine Association was some job and he did it, and did it well." There is a tragic side to the story of John E. Rhodes and the Southern Pine Association, for when he came South he was incurably ill. A Christian Scientist, he told no one of his affliction, but toiled valiantly for the survival of the new organization and assiduously trained the man he had selected to be his successor.[59]

Before their December 8, 1914, New Orleans meeting, the lumbermen's common interests had been handled on a voluntary basis under the shadow of the dissolution of the Yellow Pine Manufactuers' Association. Efforts to organize a workable successor to the YPMA were made in informal meetings.[60] With the actual formulation of plans for the new association and the organizational meeting in New Orleans completed, Rhodes and leaders in the new endeavor turned to the most important matters at hand: convincing southern pine lumbermen that the SPA was organized in a way that would avoid legal difficulties and then winning their moral and financial support.

The basic difference between the structure of the Southern Pine Association and other trade organizations was that it was chartered as a non-profit corporation created to perform certain services for southern pine manufacturers who would subscribe and pay for them. Since the lumbermen were not members of the association, but merely subscribers for its services, they had no legal responsibility for the organization's actions.[61] This was the key legal distinction between the SPA and its predecessors. The objective was "to organize a company that could sell a service to the sawmills all over the South that would be perfectly legal."[62]

When a subscriber had any doubts concerning the legality of his relationship to the association, the board of directors provided a means by which he could withdraw. If the subscriber's attorneys considered an SPA action illegal, they could confer with the association's counsel. If the conference disagreed about the legality of the disputed matters, a third lawyer was to be selected as a referee. A majority opinion of these attorneys was to be final. The subscriber was permitted to cancel his contract after giving ten days' notice if the SPA's actions were ruled illegal and if it did not discontinue the disputed practices.[63]

Although southern pine manufacturers did not actually belong to the SPA, they controlled the organization and dictated the services it performed. The directors were "suggested" by the subscribing companies from among their own officers, and they held all the stock. Although under no legal obligation to do so, the board of directors at each annual meeting asked the subscribers to submit names to a nominating committee appointed by the president for possible election to the board by the stockholders. New directors received their predecessors' shares of stock. The directors chose the corporation's officers from among their own number. The president always served as chairman of the board.[64]

The president and vice-presidents of the Southern Pine Association acted largely in a general policy-making capacity. The secretary-manager was the actual administrative head of the organization. He was responsible for all record-keeping, correspondence, personnel, and the allocation of duties among departments and for representing the association in its relations with other organizations. The number and functions of departments varied from time to time, but there were usually about ten. Initially, they were concerned with trade extension, research, inspection, legal matters, accounting and statistics, traffic, forestry, filing and library, bookkeeping, and mailing.[65]

In addition to its headquarters organization, the SPA had several standing advisory committees. Their members and functions also changed periodically. The original committees dealt with grading, trade extension, advertising, accounting, transportation, forestry, standard weights, sales and distribution, and terms of sale. According to the by-laws, the board of directors was to appoint each committee. Every committee was to consist of representatives from one or more manufacturing establishments in each southern pine association state.[66] In practice, the board named only the chairmen, and they in turn selected their committee members without regard to the proper geographical distribution. As a matter of fact, in order to facilitate committee work members were usually chosen from a rather limited area.[67]

The association's secretary-manager called committee meetings on the request of the chairmen. Records of these meetings, together with all other information concerning committee activities, were filed with the secretary-manager so that they would be available to all subscribers. Each association committee was assisted by the appropriate departments. The departments investigated various subjects and made reports which were submitted to the committees through the secretary-manager. Copies of these reports also went to the board of directors and other interested committees.[68]

The Southern Pine Association obtained its funds from fees paid by subscribing companies. Each subscriber was required to pay a stipulated monthly sum for every thousand board feet of lumber it shipped. The decision to base the charge upon lumber shipments was made after considering other possible criteria, particularly the capacity or production of each manufacturing concern. This proposal was rejected because these factors did not necessarily reflect a company's financial position or ability to pay. In fact, the industry was plagued by over-production which brought on financial stringency and made it difficult for some mills to pay the subscription fees. A charge based upon lumber shipments, or sales, it was concluded, would provide the best and most dependable source of income.[69] To ensure that each subscriber paid his fair share, the association reserved the right to determine his production and shipments at any time and to cancel his contract for any violations.[70] The only lumber shipments exempted from the charge were those the subscriber intended to use in his own operations.

Since the subscribers actually controlled the Southern Pine Association, they established the amount of the fees. When the association was organized in late 1914, the subscription rate was set at five cents per thousand board feet of lumber sold, and it was thereafter periodically adjusted in accordance with fluctuations in the industry's economic health. From time to time, there were special assessments for concentrated efforts to meet problems of immediate importance in areas such as advertising and transportation.[71]

The Southern Pine Association's income was spent under the general supervision of the board of directors and its supervisory committee. The board had to authorize all substantial expenditures made by the advisory committees and departments, and the details of all such expenditures were available to the subscribers upon request.[72] At their insistence, the SPA supported and carried out only activities directly connected with the work which it contracted to perform for subscribers.[73] An auditor kept the association's accounts, under the supervision of an independent accounting firm.[74]

Since the Southern Pine Association's income depended upon both the amount of the subscription fee and the number of subscribers, Secretary-Manager Rhodes gave first priority to securing new members and attempting to bring old YPMA supporters into the fold. In January, 1915, Rhodes sent each SPA director a list of manufacturers in his state that showed whether they had been affiliated with the YPMA or had supported its statistical activities and whether they had signed SPA subscription contracts. He asked each director to call a manufacturers' meeting in his state to spur the membership drive.[75]

Organizational meetings were held throughout the southern pine region. In Texas John Henry Kirby summoned a gathering at the Lumberman's Club in Houston and representatives of fifteen prominent firms attended. Similar meetings were scheduled in Alabama, Arkansas, Louisiana, and Mississippi.[76]

Kirby was most responsible for swinging East Texas and western Louisiana into the Southern Pine Association. Despite his own fears about legal difficulties and his record of reticence in routine associational activities, Kirby actively recruited support for the new organization almost from the very beginning. The Texan's efforts were directed toward convincing other manufacturers of the nascent association's legality. In the pursuit of his goal, Kirby first had to overcome his own legal advisors' objections and then in turn to battle the counsels of other companies.[77] Lutcher and Moore of Orange, Texas, for example, stayed out of the association for a while simply because they received an adverse report on the SPA's legality from their attorney. Kirby's campaign— undertaken with the full approval of the firm's general manager—brought him into direct negotiation with the Lutcher and Moore counsel to try to convince him of the error of his decision.[78]

Lutcher and Moore eventually supported the Southern Pine Association, and there were still others who hesitated and finally joined. Even R. A. Long had to be shown after the decision in the Missouri Ouster Case. These men and firms could be counted on in the final analysis, but others consistently refused to join the organization for one reason or another and did not even follow the practice of those who drifted in and out. The Weston Lumber Company in Mississippi, for example, stayed out of the SPA because it produced mainly for export and saw no particular benefit in the services of the association.[79] Others, like J. A. Bentley of Alexandria, Louisiana, were individualists who had fought heated battles with competitors over timber purchases.

Organizations like the Bentley firm posed a tremendous problem for the fledgling SPA and in such cases, the big guns of the industry and the association were trained on the slacker. Secretary-Manager Rhodes tacitly acknowledged personal defeat in the Bentley matter in November, 1915, and called upon John Henry Kirby to intercede as "the only man who can possibly secure his subscription."[80] Kirby's action was quick, heavy-handed, and unsuccessful: "Why don't you join us? We need you and you need the Association. There must be a reason why you have not co-operated with us in the past and have not come in for your portion of these necessary expenses. Let me know what the reason is. I want you with us."[81] Bentley remained aloof from the Southern Pine Association.

The Bentley experience was not typical. Most organizational efforts were successfully directed toward firms considered of key importance in bringing entire regions into the SPA. In Texas, Kirby's confidants advised him that "with the Lutcher-Moore people, Alexander Gilmer, and the Sabine Tram coming in and becoming subscribers, the remaining Manufacturers in Texas would all fall right into line."[82] The emphasis in dealing with such concerns was on the benefits and legality of the association.

The decision to incorporate the SPA in Missouri was a deliberate one which, as one lumber journal said, "makes the Association a ward, so to speak, of a hostile Court and insures the plan of organization against the possibility of criticism by the courts of any state in which it may seek to do business."[83] The Missouri location, however, was opposed by many southern lumbermen who believed the old YPMA had not been sufficiently responsive to their desires. The president of the Carter-Kelley Lumber Company of Manning, Texas, expressed this point of view:

> . . . I am very much opposed to going into an organi-
> zation of this kind with its headquarters in Kansas
> City. . . . The largest part of the business done by
> the association would be in the department of inspec-
> tion of grades and arbitration. This I believe could
> be handled to very much advantage with its headquar-
> ters located in the south . . . and when trouble comes
> up such as we had during the I.W.W., the men on the
> ground behind the guns are the fellows who have to
> take care of the situation, and I feel in this we
> should have the association organized in some of the
> southern states where it can be close to the manufac-
> turing points, and where we can attend meetings
> conveniently.[84]

Kirby answered this objection by emphasizing that the
association's headquarters were to be in New Orleans. He
allayed another common fear by stating, "I have not found
any disposition among the Missouri lumbermen to run
things. They are willing that others shall have all the
honors and take all the responsibilities if they will but
recognize that some character of vigorous organization is
indispendable [sic] to the success of the industry."[85]

The association began operations in downtown New
Orleans and Rhodes started to assemble his staff and
grapple with the industry's problems. Staff work began in
March, 1915, in temporary headquarters in the Hibernia
Bank Building. Permanent offices were then established in
the old Interstate Bank Building at Canal and Camp
streets.[86] The physical beginnings were inauspicious.
Employees hammered up shelves and arranged the limited
equipment themselves. They were settled before the advent
of the long and humid New Orleans summer, which they faced
without the air conditioners and window screens later
generations would find indispensable. In fact, although
it later moved to better quarters the SPA never had elaborate equipment or offices and consciously cultivated a
frugal image. As long-time Secretary-Manager H. C.
Berckes said, "A lot of Associations that had our
influence had much better offices than we did. You know,
lumbermen are a difficult type of people. When you get a
fellow out there with a small sawmill and he comes in to
see you and you're puttin' on too much dog, he don't like
it."[87]

The image was especially important in the beginning,
for during its first year of existence the Southern Pine
Association's principal effort was directed toward

securing members.[88] This effort culminated successfully at the first SPA meeting of 1915, held in New Orleans's plush new Grunewald Hotel,[89] after President Charles S. Keith laid matters squarely on the line. He read a long list of companies which had already signed subscription contracts and then told his audience that unless a minimum production of four billion board feet could be enrolled in the association, "now is the time to stop." The response was overwhelming, and "as fast as two assistants to the secretary could accommodate them . . . contracts were signed."[90] During the SPA's first year, the total output of southern pine was 14,463,804,000 board feet. Of this figure, the association commanded a production of 4,053,000,000 board feet from 108 subscribers operating 127 mills.[91]

From its spartan headquarters the association began to struggle with industry problems, but these efforts were scarcely under way when the worsening diplomatic and military situation in Europe began to concern advocates of preparedness in the United States. In spite of wartime problems, however, the growth of the industry and of the SPA was steady throughout the remainder of the decade. By 1919 the association had 205 subscribers who operated 235 mills and produced approximately six and one-half billion board feet of lumber annually out of a total industry production of a little more than thirteen million board feet.[92] Association revenues more than doubled, from a little more than $200,000 in 1915 to over $475,000 by 1919.[93]

The run of uninterrupted progress soon ended for the industry, and for the association. During the 1920s southern pine producers and the SPA encountered a complex web of problems and challenges which do not lend themselves to easy compartmentalization. For example, the problem of cutover lands was a major factor in the Southern Pine Association's chronic financial difficulties of the 1920s as firms cut out in the South and left the association, in some cases migrating to the West Coast where they became competitors of the southern pine industry. The association faced many problems of adjustment as southern pine production increasingly came from small mills, SPA revenues declined, and the industry encountered growing competition from the West.

By the beginning of the 1920s the Southern Pine Association's professional leadership was well aware of the changing nature of the industry. In 1921 Secretary-

Manager John E. Rhodes noted that "while there has been a decline in the total lumber production, there has been an increase in the number of individual mills producing Southern Pine." He said that the new small mills were utilizing second-growth timber and optimistically described this as an indication that the industry would achieve permanence.[94]

The association favored the idea of permanence in the industry, but it did not view the arrival of the small or "peckerwood" mills with equanimity. In fact, during the 1920s small mills were viewed as at best irritants and at worst real threats to the survival of the large operators who dominated the Southern Pine Association. The most positive factor from the SPA's point of view was the fact that the arrival of the small mills meant that timber prices rose, and there was increasing emphasis upon complete utilization of the log as large operators strove to fend off the challenge of the small producers. The arrival of small producers also spurred the large operators to improve their manufacturing and grading standards. By the middle 1920s, the SPA's secretary-manager noted that "the activities of these small mills have made it necessary to revise our estimates of reserve scattered timber upwards. It is astonishing the amount of lumber these small mills can get out of a county that, theoretically, and to all appearances, has no timber." He concluded that "the competition of these small mills must be met, and this can best be done through better trade extension work on the part of the large mills and better manufacturing methods. A feature that will assist larger manufacturers in this will be grade-marking."[95]

To understand more fully the magnitude of the changes brought about by the advent of small mills, the Southern Pine Association in 1924 sponsored a comprehensive study to determine the amount of standing timber and the rate of production by both large and small mills. The SPA had conducted a similar investigation in 1919, and the results of the 1924 survey revealed two significant factors. First, large operators who had expected to cut out relatively soon in 1919 had acquired much of the available timber, thereby extending the life of their operations, and even in a few cases increasing their production facilities. Second was "the organization of the small mills by wholesalers and planning mill operators, and large increases in production by mills of this class, particularly of boards and framing." Secretary-Manager H. C.

Berckes reported to his subscribers that "as a consequence of the acquiring of additional holdings by operators, most of the timber that can be used by the larger mills is now in their ownership. This has prolonged the life of many mills now operating, which reported to us in 1919 that they would be cut out in two, three or four years."[96]

While the production of large mills since the 1919 survey had declined approximately 1,435,000,000 feet, the net decrease was probably only about 435 million feet for the industry, because of the influence of the small mills. The principal areas of small mill production were the Carolinas, Alabama, Florida, Georgia, and Mississippi, with the largest increase in Alabama. The area of most resistance to the small mill movement was Louisiana.[97] The report concluded that "today the production of the large mills of the South is inconsiderable. The small mills of the South represent 43 percent of the production of yellow pine."[98]

The report also commented on the changing nature of the small producers and hinted at the most effective ways of fighting their incursions. It emphasized that the small mills were "no longer a disorganized part of the industry." Rather, "every one of them has a wholesome arrangement. Those mills are financed from the purchase of the plant up to the financing of the pay roll." Furthermore, because of their small overhead and negligible amount of fixed capital, the small mills could produce lumber cheaply. The way out rested in the implementation of balanced or sustained-yield operations by the larger firms, who could buy up and control timber resources when prices increased as a result of increasing scarcity.[99]

The SPA survey was undertaken at a time when the organization's large producers regarded the small mills as at best "a pain in the neck." The realization that many large firms were going to cut out made planning and the position of the SPA professional staff difficult, and the report inadvertently contributed to the industry's difficulties in publicizing itself as an enduring source of lumber. Some of its findings, particularly a prediction that within ten years 80 percent of the southern pine mills would be cut out, were converted into chart form for display at the SPA's annual meeting. Unfortunately the trade papers photographed and publicized the chart, but blithley ignored other factors, notably the increasing production from small mills and the tendency toward sustained-yield operations. Ironically, the SPA's own report inadvertently contributed to a general concept that the association was doggedly trying to combat during the 1920s--the idea that the industry was cutting out and would not in the future be able to supply the lumber needs of even its own region.[100]

The Southern Pine Association was also increasingly concerned about damage to the reputation of southern pine caused by a growing flood of poorly manufactured and unseasoned lumber produced by the small mills. Despite this concern, and in the face of declining association revenues, there was no strong push to bring the smaller producers into the SPA until the late 1920s. Late in 1928 and early in 1929, however, the association undertook a survey to determine the amount of lumber produced by non-association and small mills in order to develop an accurate prediction of output from these sources during 1929.[101]

The association's survey covered Alabama, Arkansas, Florida, Louisiana, Mississippi, Oklahoma, and Texas. Georgia was covered in cooperation with the North Carolina Pine Association, which also surveyed North Carolina, South Carolina, and Virginia. The survey covered some 5,826 operations, of which 5,589 fell into the "small mill" category with individual outputs of under 6 million feet per year. The study found that in ten years the small mills had increased their share of the total southern pine production dramatically. In 1919, they had accounted for only 33 percent of the total production; according to the 1924 survey they produced 44 percent of the total production; and by 1928 that figure had increased to some 48 percent.[102]

Convinced by the end of the decade that small mills were a permanent fixture in the industry, the SPA and its subscribers began to consider ways to deal with their smaller competitors. One common suggestion was that the association determine the feasibility of organizing cooperative enterprises or corporations which would purchase or erect planing mills at strategically located concentration points and bring small mill products up to SPA standards through remanufacturing.[103] Nothing concrete came of this approach.

By the end of 1929, there were indications that the 1930s might bring efforts by the large SPA producers to attract smaller operators into the fold. In a free-wheeling discussion at the association's mid-summer meeting, a subscriber suggested that "the little mill is a source of future income for the Southern Pine Association."[104] One participant summed up the growing realization in the SPA that "the association had neglected the little mill and allowed them to be exploited by the wholesalers and various organizations."[105] He urged the SPA to "extend the activities and widen the scope of the association and get some of the smaller men into it," because "if you don't teach them anything but better merchandising you would be helping yourselves to better control the product."[106] By the end of the year, there were suggestions within the association for group meetings with the smaller producers to find a common ground for cooperation.[107] The expression of such sentiments was a portent of the later association of large and small producers during the days of the New Deal's National Recovery Administration.

The changing nature of the industry was reflected in changes in the SPA's personnel. In a sense, the World War I years constituted the last great fling of the giants and individualists who had developed the industry and organized the association, including John Henry Kirby, R. A. Long, Charles S. Keith, Edward Hines, W. H. Sullivan, and their chosen confidants and spokesmen, Judge John H. Lucas and John E. Rhodes. These men and their industry reached a production peak during the war years and achieved a symbolic recognition of their maturity and power when John Henry Kirby was apointed Lumber Administrator and the SPA designated as the agency through which the federal government would channel its lumber needs.

These men in a real sense were the southern pine industry during its pioneering period. Several remained active and influential during the 1920s; some passed from the scene with the migration of large producers to the West Coast; and others were removed from leadership positions by old age, infirmities, or death. In their place new leaders emerged. The new age that was dawning might be called the age of the managers. The lines were not perfectly defined, but during the 1920s men who were not themselves the principal owners of the properties they directed moved into positions of prominence.

The most important change in the Southern Pine Association's internal administrative leadership came in 1923 when John E. Rhodes died. During his eight-year tenure, Rhodes did more than anyone else to shape the organization and he never lost the good will or respect of the industry or SPA subscribers. He gave the Southern Pine Association efficient, constructive, and dedicated leadership which was continued by his personally selected successor, H. C. Berckes.[108]

Berckes's personal story was intertwined with the development of the Southern Pine Association from the very beginning of the organization until the 1950s. Rhodes apparently came South with the knowledge that he was suffering from a terminal case of cancer and began from the first to train Berckes as his successor. From Rhodes, Berckes learned that diplomacy was essential in trade association work and that in order to represent the industry effectively, the trade association manager could not become identified with any particular faction or group within the organization.[109]

Berckes became Rhodes's assistant about a year after the SPA's formation. At the time, Berckes had absolutely no background in the lumber industry and in fact preferred throughout the course of his SPA career not to become overly familiar with the technical aspects of lumbering and sawmilling. Berckes believed that in this way he could retain an open mind and serve as a conciliating force in the case of intra-industry disputes.[110] Despite his lack of technical expertise, by the time of Rhodes's death Berckes had been thoroughly trained in a practical school of trade association management. When he was immediately appointed acting secretary-manager by President John Henry Kirby, a leading trade journal hailed him as "a young man trained thoroughly in association work and a thorough student of the gentle art of diplomacy."[111]

As its executive and managerial personnel changed, the Southern Pine Association moved toward the expansion of its geographical coverage by absorbing subregional lumber trade associations. The first step came in 1920 as the SPA formed a committee to continue negotiations with the Georgia-Florida Sawmill Association that might lead to the absorption of that organization.[112] The Southern Pine Association was in a somewhat delicate situation because the Georgia-Florida Sawmill Association was still very much alive and there was disagreement within that organization about the desirability of joining forces with the SPA. Nevertheless, there was apparently some feeling in the region that the Georgia-Florida association was not adequately caring for the needs of its larger mills. Several of them applied for membership in the SPA, on the condition that the association place a branch office in Jacksonville. The SPA opened its branch office on July 1, 1921, under the direction of W. E. Gardner, who had been traffic manager of the Georgia-Florida Sawmill Association.

The Southern Pine Association actively solicited members and worked to absorb the Georgia-Florida Sawmill Association while at the same time trying to create the impression that it had no desire to eliminate the smaller organization. The officers and administrative staff of the Georgia-Florida association, supported by many of their members and the leading trade journal in the area, resisted the Southern Pine Association invasion vigorously.[113] By 1922 Gardner's job and the very existence of his office were under fire because of his failure to secure larger numbers of new SPA subscribers. Furthermore, other SPA states and sections were insisting that if Georgia and Florida were entitled to a separate Southern Pine Association office so was Arkansas, Texas, or any other SPA state. The following year, the Southern Pine Association closed its Jacksonville office.[114] Subscribers from Florida and Georgia who remained in the Southern Pine Association aparently did not strongly oppose the closing, but one subscriber in the area did assert that "the impression prevailing in this territory is that the Association has grown more into a Mississippi Valley local association and that other sections have suffered accordingly."[115]

In early 1926, the Southern Pine Association resumed its expansionist efforts. H. C. Berckes, cognizant of the declining production of his organization and the departure of many old leaders, was covetously eyeing the Georgia-Florida producers as a source of new strength and leadership. Berckes was convinced that the fear of the Georgia-Florida secretary, E. C. Harrell, that he would lose his job was one of the major impediments to the merger, and he was willing to promise the creation of a Jacksonville office, run by Harrell.[116] At the same time, negotiations were underway with the president and some members of the North Carolina Pine Association.[117]

By the middle of 1926, it appeared that the Georgia-Florida association was going to be liquidated. E. C. Harrell attended the SPA's mid-summer meeting in Memphis and returned home seemingly engaged in paving the way for the amalgamation of the two organizations.[118] When Southern Pine Association representatives met with a committee from the Georgia-Florida Sawmill Association at

Pensacola in August to make final plans for mergers, however, they were abruptly informed that plans had changed. Harrell announced "that they were going to endeavor to revive interest in the Georgia-Florida Association and bring it back to its old time standing."[119] The SPA secretary-manager attributed the change of heart to the influence of Harrell and J. Ben Wand, editor and publisher of the Southern Lumber Journal.[120]

The attempted revival of the Georgia-Florida Sawmill Association failed. The organization was taken over by the Southeastern Forest Products Association, which was in turn absorbed by the Florida Dense Long Leaf Pine Manufacturers' Association. On November 1, 1927, the long frustrating years of negotiation culminated in the absorption of the Florida Dense Long Leaf Pine Manufacturers' Association into the SPA. This expanded the Southern Pine Association's geographical coverage to the Atlantic Coast and gave it 90 percent of the total pine production in Florida. The Southern Pine Association again opened a branch office in Jacksonville, this time under the direction of J. S. Farish, former traffic manager of the Georgia-Florida Sawmill Association, who served as district manager.[121] The efforts of large firm leaders whose companies belonged to both organizations may have been decisive in enabling the SPA to absorb the Georgia-Florida, and southern Alabama producers.[122]

As the SPA was absorbing former members of the Georgia-Florida Sawmill Association, preliminary negotiations were also underway with representatives of the North Carolina Pine Association. The object was to disband the organization and absorb its entire membership into the Southern Pine Association. During December, 1929, the president and secretary-manager of the North Carolina Pine Association appeared before the Southern Pine Association's board of directors and reported that their subscribers were generally in favor of a merger. The SPA Board appointed a committee to confer with the North Carolina people and undertake a comprehensive survey of the entire situation.[123]

During the depression the shift toward small mill operations in the industry continued, but it was now also accompanied by a precipitous decline in total production. From a peak of more than 13 billion board feet in 1925, southern pine production collapsed to a low of around 3 billion in 1932, and then leveled off at between 7 and 8 billion during the latter half of the decade.[124] With

61

revenues declining as production plummeted, the Southern Pine Association attempted to survive through budget cutting, special assessments on its members, and, particularly, renewed efforts to bring small mills and subregional associations under the SPA banner.[125]

The association again attacked the small mill problem in 1930 as President F. W. Reimers advocated the extension of SPA services to the small operators.[126] The association offered standardization and education services, on a cost basis, to help the small mills improve their manufacturing and merchandising processes. During the year the SPA organized small mill meetings at various points to promote these objectives.[127] An association spokesman succinctly expressed the association's rationale for the program before an audience of small mill representatives: "This is a more or less selfish move on our part. . . . If we can raise the level of your product, and bring it up to a higher standard . . . you will sell it for more money, and, therefore, you will assist us in stabilizing our market. . . ."[128]

By the spring of 1931, the SPA had organized some sixty-five or sixty-six small mills in Mississippi, western Louisiana, western Florida, Georgia, Texas, and southwest Arkansas, representing about 20 percent of small mill production. The 1931 annual meeting devoted an entire day to subjects of particular interest to small mills, and the association decided to continue its activities among the small mills at the rate of five cents per thousand feet, as opposed to the regular fifteen cents, for the rest of the year.[129] In addition, the association hoped to extend its services to small mills in other sections of the South by absorbing other trade organizations.

The efforts of the Southern Pine Association to extend its influence into new areas were fraught with reminders of its 1920s expansion efforts. By the time of the 1931 annual meeting, the SPA was on the one hand considering closing its Jacksonville, Florida, office as an economy measure and on the other endeavoring to head off rumored efforts by southeastern lumbermen to recreate the old Georgia-Florida association.[130]

The effort to reestablish the old association was triggered by what appeared to be the imminent collapse of the North Carolina Pine Association, which had some subscribers in the Southeast, and by some dissatisfaction with the Southern Pine Association's services in the area. The SPA's Florida representative kept Berckes informed about the situation. While the south Florida mills were accusing one another of "being the offender in ruinous price cutting," he said, the longleaf mills were "displeased over grade marking and drying."[131]

The SPA entered prolonged negotiations with the North Carolina Pine Association. After several years of preliminary activities, in March, 1931, H. C. Berckes presented the SPA board with proposals for the absorption of mills in North and South Carolina, Virginia, and Georgia which were members of the NCPA. The board approved cooperation between April 1, 1931, and December 31, 1931, with absorption of the NCPA mills under regular subscription contracts to follow after January 1, 1932.[132]

The Southern Pine Association agreed to maintain an office in Norfolk, Virginia, as long as it received at least $1,500 in monthly revenues from the NCPA territory.[133] The movement into the Southern Pine Association was spearheaded by the Camp Lumber Company in Virginia, and the transition went rather smoothly.[134] The absorption of the North Carolina Pine Association was significant in bringing more small mills under the SPA's aegis with a corresponding uplifting of grading and manufacturing standards.[135] This was extremely significant, for by the middle 1930s over 90 percent of the more than ten thousand sawmills producing southern pine lumber were small, portable mills producing rough green lumber which had to be processed by planing mills and concentration plants to compete with the products of the large operators.

By the latter part of the decade the Southern Pine Association had approximately two hundred and seventy-five subscribers, who produced some 60 percent of the output for the entire industry. Southern pine remained the leading lumber specie utilized in building and construction work, accounting for more than 35 percent of the total, and it was also used extensively in export markets and for the manufacture of freight cars, railroad ties, boxes, and crates. Using an annual production rate of 6 million board feet as the dividing line between "large" and "small" mills or operators, by the mid-thirties only 4.2 percent of the manufacturers were "large" operators, but they produced 47 percent of southern pine production. The remaining 95.8 percent of the manufacturers, the "small" mill men, turned out the remaining 53 percent of total production. Despite its small-mill recruitment campaign, the SPA's board of directors and decision-making process were dominated by some forty firms drawn from the large-manufacturer sector of the industry, who manufactured approximately 50 percent of the southern pine lumber produced by all SPA subscribers.[136]

Southern pine production jumped to over 10 billion board feet annually during the early years of the 1940s, with a peak of nearly 12 billion in 1942, and then began to decline, reaching a low of about 7 1/2 billion board feet in 1945. The SPA blamed the decline on government price controls, as operators waited to cut their trees in anticipation of reaping rich monetary harvests following the explosion of consumer demand that was sure to follow World War II. During the first half of the decade southern pine represented between 26 and 33 percent of total United States annual lumber production.[137] The association fluctuated between approximately 200 and 270 subscribers during the period.[138]

The post-war era brought the expected burgeoning consumer demand for lumber and with it a tremendous number of new mills. By the end of the 1940s there were some 25,000 sawmills manufacturing southern pine lumber--the highest number in the industry's history. Most were small mills which did not belong to the SPA. There was a high mortality rate among these small producers; within a decade about 12,000, or nearly half, of the mills had gone out of business.[139] The southern pine industry was changing. Not only were many of the small manufacturers disappearing; many of the larger companies were being taken over by conglomerates. The Southern Pine Association, which had once represented manufacturers producing the bulk of the industry's production, had declined to the point where its subscribers manufactured only about 20 percent of total southern pine output.[140] The industry faced the end of its fourth decade grappling with internal change and under heavy attack from other wood products and various wood substitutes. The association was undergoing significant changes in personnel and leadership, and, like its industry, faced an uncertain future.

NOTES TO CHAPTER 2

1. S. J. Carpenter to John Henry Kirby, May 24, 1912, John Henry Kirby Papers, Box 221 (University of Houston

Development of the Industry and the SPA

Library, Houston, Tex.). Collection hereafter cited as Kirby Papers. H. C. Berckes says that the Operators' Association continued to exist on a small scale until the New Deal period. Interview with H. C. Berckes, Jan. 24, 1968.

2. George K. Smith to Angelina County Lumber Company, June 29, 1908, Kirby Papers, Box 135; "Adaptability of Southern Yellow Pine, the Wood of a Thousand Different Uses: Established Building Facts Worth Knowing," Southern Pine Association Records, Box 39a (Louisiana State University Archives, Baton Rouge, La.). Collection hereafter cited as SPA Records.

3. George K. Smith to Members and Manufacturers, Aug. 31, 1906, Kurth Papers, Box 93, (Forest History Collection, Stephen F. Austin State University Library, Nacogdoches, Tex.). Collection hereafter cited as Kurth Papers.

4. Smith to All Members and Manufacturers, Mar. 1, 1907, Kurth Papers, Box 108.

5. "An Open Letter to the Lumber Trade," Oct. 16, 1906, Kurth Papers, Box 101.

6. Nollie Hickman, Mississippi Harvest: Lumbering in the Longleaf Pine Belt, 1840-1915 (University: University of Mississippi Press, 1962), pp. 202-3. An investigator in the Bureau of Corporations charged in 1912 that the YPMA was definitely guilty of price-fixing and efforts to control production. Report of Special Agent Guy M. Cowgill, Oct., 1912, File 6584-16, Records of the Federal Trade Commission, Bureau of Corporations, RG 122, National Archives.

7. George K. Smith to Manufacturers of Yellow Pine, Nov. 15, 1907, Kurth Papers, Box 118.

8. Hickman, Mississippi Harvest, pp. 203-4.

9. "Yellow Pine Manufacturer's Association Present Running Time of Saw Mills," Kurth Papers, Box 118.

10. Hickman, Mississippi Harvest, pp. 203-4; Baltimore Sun, May 1, 1908; New York Lumber Trade Journal, May 15

and July 15, 1908; St. Louis Times-Democrat, Apr. 29, 1908; clippings in Records of Federal Trade Commission, Bureau of Corporations, RG 122, National Archives.

11. George K. Smith to All Members, Apr. 14, 1908, Kurth Papers, Box 135; Smith to Members and Manufacturers, June 4, 1908, Kurth Papers, Box 135.

12. Hickman, Mississippi Harvest, p. 205. There is extensive correspondence relating to the YPMA's production control efforts in File 6582-65, which contains materials collected by special Agent Walter B. Wooden, in the Records of the Federal Trade Commission, Bureau of Corporations, RG 122, National Archives.

13. George K. Smith to Angelina County Lumber Company, June 29, 1908, Kurth Papers, Box 135.

14. George K. Smith to Angelina County Lumber Company, Apr. 12, 1909, Kurth Papers, Box 150; Smith to Members and Manufacturers from Whom Information as to Weekly Running Time, Daily Cut, Shipments, Orders Booked, Etc. Is Requested, Apr. 30, 1909, Kurth Papers, Box 150; Smith to Members of Basic Price List Committee, June 29, 1909, Kurth Papers, Box 155; Smith to Members, May 28, 1912, Kurth Papers, Box 251; Smith to J. P. Dawson, June 8, 1908, and Dawson to Smith, June 10, 1908, both in File 6582-65, Records of the Federal Trade Commission, Bureau of Corporations, RG 122, National Archives.

15. Hickman, Mississippi Harvest, pp. 206-7.

16. Ibid., pp. 207-8.

17. Ibid., P. 208; George K. Smith to Angelina County Lumber Company, Jan. 22, 1909, Kurth Papers, Box 149.

18. "Resolution to Ways and Means Committee of the House of Representatives, January 20, 1909," Kurth Papers, Box 149.

19. Hickman, Mississippi Harvest, pp. 208-9.

20. File 4865-1, Records of the Federal Trade Commission, Bureau of Corporations, RG 122, National Archives.

21. Hickman, Mississippi Harvest, pp. 209-10.

22. Ibid., 210. There is nothing in the Southern Pine Association records or those of the Yellow Pine Manufacturers' Association seen by the author to indicate a concerted attempt was made to fight the Underwood-Simmons Tariff. While accepting the inevitability of a low tariff under a Democratic administration, many lumbermen remained restive and hoped for a higher tariff, although they sometimes found it difficult to reconcile this position with their southern, low-tariff, Democratic party backgrounds.

23. George K. Smith to Angelina County Lumber Company, June 29, 1908, Kurth Papers, Box 135. The matter of classification of lumber into rough or finished categories for rate-fixing purposes was of great importance to the producers because finished products were charged a higher tariff than rough lumber. For an example of the association's concern over this matter, see Smith to All Members, Apr. 14, 1914, SPA Records, Box 39a.

24. Smith to Members, June 8, 1912, Kurth Papers, Box 251; "Advertising Funds Collected and Disbursed, Oct.-Dec. Incl. 1913," Kurth Papers, Box 312; Smith to Angelina County Lumber Company, June 29, 1908, Kurth Papers, Box 135.

25. As in most other areas the extent of accessible information concerning the activities of the Yellow Pine Manufacturers' Association in forestry and conservation is extremely limited. There are scattered materials on these and other matters in the Kurth Papers, Boxes 118, 135, and 149, and in Files 4854-43 and 4854-44, Records of the Federal Trade Commission, Bureau of Corporations, RG 122, National Archives.

26. George K. Smith to Angelina County Lumber Company, Oct. 23, 1913, Kurth Papers, Box 312; Smith to Angelina County Lumber Company, Feb. 4, 1914, Kurth Papers, Box 320.

27. Eric F. Goldman, Rendezvous with Destiny: A History of Modern American Reform (rev. ed.; New York: Vintage Books, 1956), p. 160; Arthur Jerome Eddy, The New Competition (New York and London: D. Appleton, 1912), passim; Gabriel Kolko, The Triumph of Conservatism: A

The New South and the "New Competition"

Reinterpretation of American History, 1900-1916 (Chicago: Quadrangle Books, 1967. Orig. pub., 1963, Free Press of Glencoe), pp. 180-81.

28. Louis Galambos, Competition and Cooperation: The Emergence of a National Trade Association (Baltimore: Johns Hopkins University Press, 1966), pp. 78-81.

29. George K. Smith to Angelina County Lumber Company, Dec. 22, 1913, Kurth Papers, Box 312; Smith to Angelina County Lumber Company, Feb. 4, 1914, Kurth Papers, Box 320.

30. George K. Smith and George R. Hicks to Angelina County Lumber Company, Jan. 7, 1914, Kurth Papers, Box 320.

31. The State ex inf. Elliott W. Major, Attorney-General, v. Arkansas Lumber Company et al., 260 Mo. 212 (1914); Missouri, Revised Statutes (1909), c. 98, secs. 10298-301.

32. The State ex inf. Elliott W. Major, Attorney-General v. Arkansas Lumber Company et al., 260 Mo. 212 (1914).

33. Hickman, Mississippi Harvest, p. 205.

34. The State ex inf. Elliott W. Major, Attorney-General, v. Arkansas Lumber Company et al., 260 Mo. 212 (1914). There is extensive correspondence relating to the "Missouri Ouster Case" in File 6582-65, Records of the Federal Trade Commission, Bureau of Corporations, RG 122, National Archives.

35. "Official Proceedings of the Semi-annual Meeting of the Yellow Pine Manufacturers' Association, June 28-29, 1912," in File 4854-44, Records of the Federal Trade Commission, Bureau of Corporations, RG 122, National Archives; George K. Smith to Members and Manufacturers, July 17, 1912, Kurth Papers, Box 267.

36. The State ex inf. Elliott W. Major, Attorney-General, v. Arkansas Lumber Company et al., 260 Mo. 212 (1914).

37. George R. Hicks and George K. Smith to Angelina County Lumber Company, Jan. 7, 1914, Kurth Papers, Box 320.

38. George K. Smith to All Members, Mar. 24, 1914, Kurth Papers, Box 320.

39. "In The Supreme Court of Missouri En Banc, October Term 1913," Kurth Papers, Box 312.

40. Interview with H. C. Berckes, Feb. 10, 1968.

41. Constitution and By-Laws of Yellow Pine Manufacturers' Association as Amended April 8, 1914 (n.p., n.d.), Kurth Papers, Box 93; "Proceedings of Special Meeting of the Yellow Pine Manufacturers' Association, Held at Mercantile Club, St. Louis, Mo., April 8th, 1914," Kurth Papers, Box 320.

42. The State ex inf. Elliott W. Major, Attorney-General, v. Arkansas Lumber Company et al., 260 Mo. 212 (1914).

43. John E. Rhodes to Gentlemen, Nov. 24, 1914, Kurth Papers, Box 339.

44. U. S. Department of Commerce, Bureau of Corporations, Conditions in Production and Wholesale Distribution Including Wholesale Prices, Part IV of The Lumber Industry (Washington, D.C.: Government Printing Office, 1914), p. 74.

45. John E. Rhodes to Gentlemen, Nov. 24, 1914, Kurth Papers, Box 339.

46. Interview with H. C. Berckes, Jan. 24, 1968.

47. Ibid.; Charles S. Keith to Southern Pine Association Board of Directors, Dec. 22, 1914, Kirby Papers, Box 222.

48. Kansas City Times, Oct. 10, 1945.

49. Interview with H. C. Berckes, Jan. 24, 1968.

50. Charles S. Keith to John Henry Kirby, Nov. 27, 1914, Kirby Papers, Box 222.

51. "Prospectus: Incorporation, By-Laws, Departments," SPA Records, Collection Prospects, p. 8. In 1920 the legal headquarters were moved to Kansas City. "Minutes of a Meeting of the Southern Pine Association Board of Directors, July 9, 1920," SPA Records, Box 70b, p. 10.

52. Charles S. Keith to John Henry Kirby, Nov. 27, 1914, Kirby Papers, Box 222.

53. John Henry Kirby to F. H. Farwell, Dec. 17, 1914, Kirby Papers, Box 222.

54. Charles S. Keith to John Henry Kirby, Dec. 18, 1914, Kirby Papers, Box 222.

55. Charles S. Keith to the Southern Pine Association Board of Directors, Dec. 22, 1914, Kirby Papers, Box 222.

56. John Henry Kirby to G. A. Kelley, Dec. 28, 1914, Kirby Papers, Box 222.

57. Interview with H. C. Berckes, Jan. 24, 1968; Ralph W. Hidy, Frank Ernest Hill, and Allan Nevins, Timber and Men: The Weyerhaeuser Story (New York: Macmillan, 1963), pp. 316-17.

58. Interview with H. C. Berckes, Jan. 24, 1968.

59. Ibid.

60. Ibid.

61. "Proceedings of Fifth Annual Convention of Southern Pine Association, March 16, 17, 18, 1920," SPA Records, Box 73b, p. 240.

62. Interview with H. C. Berckes, Jan. 24, 1968.

63. "Prospectus: Incorporation, By-Laws, Departments," SPA Records, Collection Prospects, p. 2.

Development of the Industry and the SPA

64. "Proceedings of Fifth Annual Convention of Southern Pine Association, March 16, 17, 18, 1920," SPA Records, Box 73b, p. 240.

65. "Southern Pine Association: Outline of Organization and Work Proposed," SPA Records, Collection Prospects.

66. "Outline of Work under Supervision of the Committees of the Southern Pine Association," John E. Rhodes notebook, SPA Records, Box 39a.

67. "Pine and Patriotism: Official Report of the Third Annual Meeting of the Subscribers to the Southern Pine Association Held at Grunewald Hotel, New Orleans, Feb. 19, 20, 1918," SPA Records, Box 85b, p. 17.

68. "Outline of Work Under Supervision of the Committees of the Southern Pine Association," John E. Rhodes notebook, SPA Records, Box 39a.

69. "An Outline of Policies and Activities of the Southern Pine Association, 1915-1950," SPA Records, Collection Prospects, pp. 5, 6.

70. "Prospectus: Incorporation, By-Laws, Departments," SPA Records, Collection Prospects.

71. "Minutes of a Meeting of the Southern Pine Association Board of Directors, February 26, 1915," SPA Records, Box 70b, p. 2.

72. "Lumber Awakes! Official Report of the First Annual Meeting of the Subscribers to the Southern Pine Association Held at Grunewald Hotel, New Orleans, Feb. 23, 24, 1916," SPA Records, Box 85b, pp. 25, 28.

73. "Minutes of a Meeting of the Southern Pine Association Board of Directors, February 26, 1915," SPA Records, Box 70b, p. 2.

74. "Minutes of a Meeting of the Southern Pine Association Board of Directors, April 2, 1917," SPA Records, Box 70b, p. 38.

The New South and the "New Competition"

75. John E. Rhodes to Southern Pine Association Board of Directors, Jan. 28, 1915, Kirby Papers, Box 222.

76. Interdepartmental memorandum, B. F. Bonner to John Henry Kirby, Feb. 5, 1915, Kirby Papers, Box 222; John M. Collier, The First Fifty Years of the Southern Pine Association, 1915-1965 (New Orleans: Southern Pine Association, 1965), p. 52; "Minutes of a Meeting of the Southern Pine Association Board of Directors, February 26, 1915," SPA Records, Box 70b, p. 1.

77. In a five-page letter that was summed up in the warning "we regard it as unwise that the Kirby Lumber Company participate in the Southern Pine Association," Kirby's lawyers advised him to stay out of the SPA. Andrews, Streetman, Burns, and Logue to John Henry Kirby, Dec. 23, 1914, Kirby Papers, Box 222.

78. George E. Holland to Edwin B. Parker, Feb. 15, 1915, F. H. Farwell to John Henry Kirby, Feb. 17, 1915, Kirby to Parker, Feb. 22, 1915, and Kirby to J. Lewis Thompson, Feb. 22, 1915, all in Kirby Papers, Box 222.

79. Interview with H. C. Berckes, Feb. 10, 1968.

80. John E. Rhodes to John Henry Kirby, Nov. 9, 1915, Kirby Papers, Box 222.

81. John Henry Kirby to Joseph A. Bentley, Nov. 10, 1915, Kirby Papers, Box 222.

82. J. Lewis Thompson to John Henry Kirby, Feb. 17, 1915, Kirby Papers, Box 222.

83. Collier, First Fifty Years, p. 42.

84. G. A. Kelley to John Henry Kirby, Dec. 24, 1914, Kirby Papers, Box 222.

85. John Henry Kirby to G. A. Kelley, Dec. 28, 1914, Kirby Papers, Box 222.

86. Collier, First Fifty Years, p. 52.

87. Interview with H. C. Berckes, Jan. 24, 1968.

Development of the Industry and the SPA

88. John E. Rhodes to John Henry Kirby, Nov. 9, 1915, Kirby Papers, Box 222.

89. This hotel remained the traditional SPA meeting site under its old name and after it became The Roosevelt.

90. The first to do so was S. H. Bolinger & Company of Shreveport, Louisiana.

91. "Pine and Patriotism," SPA Records, Box 85b, p. 8.

92. "Growth of Association," Kurth Papers, Box 505; "Southern Pine Production and Stocks--Industry Totals," SPA Records, Box 12b.

93. "Revenue from Fees," SPA Records, Box 12B.

94. John E. Rhodes, "What the Southern Pine Association Has Done for the Industry and the Public," in "Lumber Liquidates: Official Report of the Sixth Annual Meeting of the Subscribers to the Southern Pine Association Held at Grunewald Hotel, New Orleans, April 5, 6, 1921," SPA Records, Box 85b, pp. 17-18.

95. H. C. Berckes, "Association Activities," in "A New Era: Official Report of the Ninth Annual Meeting of the Subscribers to the Southern Pine Association, Held at Roosevelt Hotel, New Orleans, March 11 and 12, 1924," SPA Records, Box 85b, pp. 25-26.

96. Ibid., p. 24.

97. F. V. Dunham, "How the Small Mills are Affecting the Southern Pine Industry," SPA Records, Box 68b.

98. Ibid.

99. Ibid.

100. Interview with H. C. Berckes, Feb. 10, 1968.

101. "Minutes of a Meeting of the Board of Directors of the Southern Pine Association, January 30, 1929," SPA Records, Box 70b.

102. "Address of Mr. C. W. Nelson," in "Proceedings of Fourteenth Annual Meeting of the Subscribers to the Southern Pine Association, New Orleans, Louisiana, March 26-27," SPA Records, Box 73b, pp. 105-7.

103. "Proceedings of Fourteenth Annual Meeting of the Subscribers to the Southern Pine Association, March 26-27," SPA Records, Box 73b, p. 97.

104. "Minutes of Joint Meeting of Trade Promotion Committee and Advertising Committee of the Southern Pine Association, June 26, 1929. And of Mid-summer Meeting of Subscribers, June 27, 1929," SPA Records, Box 68b, p. 61.

105. Ibid., p. 59.

106. Ibid., p. 60.

107. "Minutes of Meeting of Adv. and Trade Extn. Comms., 8-1-29," SPA Records, Box 70b.

108. Rhodes was memorialized at the Southern Pine Association's 1924 annual meeting, and the published annual report for that year contains fulsome praise for the departed secretary-manager from industry leaders such as R. A. Long, G. A. Kelley, E. A. Frost, and Charles S. Keith which indicates the industry's high regard for Rhodes. "A New Era," SPA Records, Box 85b, pp. 5-8. Perhaps the most interesting comments came not at the time but more than a quarter of a century later when a student writing a graduate thesis dealing with lumber trade associations was told by a longtime prominent industry figure that "J. E. Rhodes was one of the best association executives I have known in any field." R. S. Kellogg to R. C. Fraunberger, Mar. 24, 1951; quoted in R. C. Fraunberger, "Lumber Trade Associations: Their Economic and Social Significance" (M.A. thesis, Temple University, 1951), p. 31.

109. Interview with H. C. Berckes, Jan. 24, 1968.

110. Ibid.

111. Lumber Trade Journal (June 15, 1923), p. 15.

112. "Minutes of a Meeting of the Board of Directors of the Southern Pine Association, November 30, 1920," SPA Records, Box 70b.

113. W. C. Sherman to Charles S. Keith, July 19, 1921, Keith to Sherman, July 22, 1921, John E. Rhodes to John L. Kaul, July 30, 1921, Rhodes to W. E. Gardner, Sept. 3, 1921, and Gardner to Rhodes, Oct. 15, 1921, all in SPA Records, Box 27a.

114. Thomas Hamilton to A. G. T. Moore, Oct. 26, 1923, SPA Records, Box 27a.

115. Thomas Hamilton to H. C. Berckes, Oct. 24, 1924, SPA Records, Box 37a.

116. H. C. Berckes to Edward Hines, Jan. 25, 1926, SPA Records, Box 37b.

117. J. G. McGowin to H. C. Berckes, Feb. 20, 1926, J. W. LeMaistre to Berckes, Feb. 27, 1926, and LeMaistre to Berckes, Mar. 19, 1926, all in SPA Records, Box 37b.

118. J. S. Foley to H. C. Berckes, July 20, 1926, Berckes to Foley, July 24, 1926, and E. C. Harrell to Berckes, July 29, 1926, all in SPA Records, Box 37b.

119. H. C. Berckes to J. E. Cabler, Aug. 18, 1926, SPA Records, Box 37b.

120. H. C. Berckes to J. W. LeMaistre, Mar. 7, 1927, SPA Records, Box 37b. More than forty years later, Berckes would retain virtually the same beliefs and outlook on the episode. Interview with H. C. Berckes, Aug. 10, 1968.

121. "SPA News Release, 10-10-27," SPA Records, Box 27a; J. S. Farish, "Report of Year's Activities for Period Beginning April 1st, 1927 and Ending March 1st, 1928," SPA Records, Box 27a.

122. Interview with H. C. Berckes, Aug. 10, 1968.

123. "Minutes of a Meeting of the Board of Directors of the Southern Pine Association, December 11, 1929," SPA Records, Box 70b.

The New South and the "New Competition"

124. "Southern Pine Production and Stocks—Industry Totals," SPA Records, Box 12b.

125. H. C. Berckes to C. C. Sheppard, May 9, 1931, SPA Records, Box 39a.

126. Collier, First Fifty Years, p. 100.

127. "Minutes of a Meeting of the Board of Directors of the Southern Pine Association Held at the Roosevelt Hotel, New Orleans, La., Monday, March 24, 1930," SPA Records, Box 70b; "Annual Report of the Secretary-Manager," SPA Records, Box 9b.

128. "Proceedings of the Mid-Summer Meeting of the Southern Pine Association Held in Memphis, Tennessee at the Hotel Peabody, on July 16, 1930," SPA Records, Box 68a, p. 10.

129. "Small Mill Meeting, 3-23-31," SPA Records, Box 70b, pp. 1-2, 4, 105; "Proceedings of Cost Conservation Conference, July 8-9, 1931," SPA Records, Box 68a; A. S. Boisfontaine to V. M. Sondregger, Mar. 17, 1931, SPA Records, Box 9b.

130. H. C. Berckes to Edward A. Hauss, Apr. 11, 1930, SPA Records, Box 27a; J. S. Farish to Berckes, Apr. 21, 1930, SPA Records, Box 27a; "Minutes of a Meeting of the Board of Directors of the Southern Pine Association, March 24, 1930," SPA Records, Box 70b. The board decided to close the Jacksonville office on May 1, 1930.

131. J. S. Farish to H. C. Berckes, Apr. 21, 1930, SPA Records, Box 27a.

132. "Small Mill Meeting, 3-23-31," SPA Records, Box 70b; "Minutes of a Meeting of the Board of Directors of the Southern Pine Association Held at the Roosevelt Hotel, New Orleans, Louisiana, Monday, March 23, 1931," SPA Records, Box 70b.

133. "Minutes of a Meeting of the Board of Directors of the Southern Pine Association, November 11, 1931," SPA Records, Box 70b.

134. Interview with H. C. Berckes, Aug. 10, 1968.

Development of the Industry and the SPA

135. "Proceedings of Cost Conservation Conference, July 8-9, 1931," SPA Records, Box 68a.

136. "In the District Court of The United States for The Eastern District of Louisiana, New Orleans Division, Civil Action No. 275, United States of America, Plaintiff, versus Southern Pine Association, et al., Defendants," SPA Records, Box 70a.

137. "Southern Pine Production And Stocks—Industry Totals," SPA Records, Box 12b.

138. "Report of Meetings of SPA Board of Directors and Stockholders, February 19, 1943," SPA Records, Box 9a.

139. Collier, First Fifty Years, pp. 137, 143.

140. "The Time Is Now," pamphlet, SPA Records, Box 12b.

3

Mobilization for World War I

During World War I the southern pine industry and the SPA
compiled a mixed record of both great patriotism and
"business as usual." War in Europe seemed at first to
threaten the industry's well-being, but it became a shot
in the arm for lagging sales. Since the South was the
nation's most extensive wood-producing area, it bore the
brunt of providing material to construct cantonments,
ships, railroad cars, piers, wharves, and warehouses in
the United States and France.[1] The Southern Pine Association, representing over 50 percent of southern pine
production, was the logical agency to secure and coordinate the industry's cooperation with the government.[2]

When the war started in Europe in August, 1914, it
struck southern lumbermen, as it did most Americans, "like
lightning out of a clear sky." Like their agrarian
neighbors of the cotton-belt South, Dixie's lumber producers were intensely concerned about the disruption of
export markets.[3] The southern pine industry had not
enjoyed a good year since the depression of 1907. The
year 1913 had been "bad all the way through; 1914 was a
little better, getting a bad start, strengthening about
the middle of the year and then being smashed flat by the
sudden starting of the Great War. . . ."[4]

The first signs of the war were cables from Europe
cancelling all lumber shipments. The export market
appeared ruined. Lumber export contracts had cancellation
clauses in case of war, and export operations stopped
immediately. In the important East Texas-western
Louisiana area, the curtailment directly affected some
seventy sawmills representing about 4 to 5 percent of that

region's production. Many ships carrying southern pine
were at sea headed for Europe, but those still in port and
only partially filled were unloaded.[5] On August 3, the
major cotton exchanges failed to open, and that industry
plunged into a deep trough. This disruption of trade
helped trigger a decline in all kinds of normal lumber
orders by September. The downturn was also influenced by
the collapse of other facets of the U. S. export trade.[6]
In September, the Gulf Coast Lumberman reported that
lumber manufacturers were being forced to curtail their
output. The journal warned that scores of mills were
closed entirely and more were shutting down, and it predicted that hundreds of plants would be completely idle
within a month.[7]

Early in 1915, however, the trend began to reverse.
The United States as a neutral producer and carrier began
to profit from Europe's torment. The American economy
received a tremendous boost from several billion dollars
of purchasing power pumped into the country through money
borrowed in the United States by the Allies, who also
spent funds realized by the sale of their American securi-
ties between January, 1915, and April, 1917.[8]

The efforts of American producers and shippers to
supply the Allies during the flush period before the U. S.
declaration of war against Germany on April 6, 1917, were
not controlled or guided by any governmental machinery.
Allied purchasers had to pay whatever the traffic would
bear, and their confusion and frustration were matched
only by that of American businessmen who were forced to
fight for labor, raw materials, and facilities. Although
the United States made some preparations for hostilities
prior to 1917, not until the actual declaration of war was
it possible for the government to exercise the necessary
legal power to bring order, stability, and control to the
American mobilization effort.[9]

The United States had fought its earlier wars without
truly effective coordination between the military
establishment and the private economic sector. Within
the military there had been no systematic cooperation
between the services, or even within the various bureaus
of a single service in purchases and supply matters.
These traditions had to be overcome in the face of the
need for concerted advance preparations and planning for a
modern, mechanized war. To bring order and planning into
the joint efforts of the private sector and the government, a plethora of control agencies were created and

revised before a workable situation was achieved.[10] The confusion and turmoil of the planning and settling process undoubtedly contributed to some of the difficulties the SPA and its subscribers experienced during the war.

Coordination between the military services and the civilian economy was under congressional consideration as early as 1910, but was not implemented. In 1915, the idea of industrial coordination began to rise, and as a result of President Wilson's message to Congress on December 7, 1915, the United States began construction of "a navy second to none" and a large merchant marine. The Naval Consulting Board, headed by Thomas A. Edison, was created to coordinate the program's industrial requirements. In August, 1915, this board created a commission on industrial preparedness to deal with the requirements of the Army and Navy. The commission was supported by private contributions and was concerned primarily with the U.S. potential for munitions manufacturing. Its members became strong and influential advocates of industrial preparedness.[11]

The southern pine industry was immediately affected by the decision to construct large military and mercantile fleets. The government's shipbuilding programs began in 1916 and called for the construction of one thousand ships, each requiring at least a million board feet of lumber. Gulf Coast ports began to hum. The southern lumber industry strained to produce under government regulations controlling production, prices, and shipments. In Texas, Beaumont and Orange became major shipbuilding centers. In the two cities there were eleven vessels planned and under construction for the ocean trade by the end of 1916.[12] In November, the Gulf Coast Lumberman reported the launching of the schooner "City of Orange" which was the largest ship "ever built on the Gulf of Mexico or its tributaries. . . ." The vessel was built entirely of longleaf southern pine lumber and timbers.[13] Not surprisingly, the year was extremely prosperous for the southern pine industry.[14]

The Southern Pine Association had dealings with a number of agencies which mobilized and directed the economic aspects of the nation's military effort. One of the most important was the Council of National Defense, created by the Army Military Appropriations Act of August 29, 1916. This body was composed of a number of cabinet officers, but its work was done by an advisory commission of leaders from outside government. The council's legal authority was based on the Military Appropriations Act and the National Defense Act of June 3, 1916, which gave the President authority to place orders for war material directly with suppliers, to commandeer plants if necessary, and to set up an industrial mobilization board. Despite some congressional misgivings, the advisory commission started planning for the eventualities of war. Commissioner Bernard M. Baruch, who was particularly concerned about shortages in raw materials, began organizing industry committees so that resources in various areas could be surveyed and tapped for the preparedness effort.[15]

When America's declaration of war came, the nation still did not have a coordinated and centralized preparedness structure. The War Department, in despair, abandoned efforts to coordinate the various bureaus of the Army and finally asked Congress for a lump-sum appropriation. The advisory commission's efforts to coordinate munitions purchases between the military bureaus and civilian suppliers were similarly unsuccessful. Finally, on July 8, 1917, the Council of National Defense attempted to introduce centralization and systematization by creating the War Industries Board, which consisted of five civilians and one representative each from the Army and Navy. However, the board initially lacked executive authority and failed to coordinate government purchases; it simply provided a mechanism for contacts between industry and the government. The board's first two chairmen were frustrated and left because of its impotence.[16]

Within the Council of National Defense several committees to deal with particular problems eventually evolved into important full-fledged administrative organs. Through this process, the council's committee on transportation became by act of Congress the Railroad Administration, and the Food and Fuel administrations developed from other committees, as did the War Trade Board and the U. S. Shipping Board.[17] The War Industries Board remained a subordinate body to the Council of National Defense, which had only advisory powers.[18]

The War Industries Board had several subordinate sections and committees, including supervisors or commissioners of raw materials, finished products, priorities, and labor. The committees were supposed to represent the views of individual industries to the board and included experienced people from those industries. The committees grew in importance and became the main vehicles for conveying information from the industry level to the divisions and agencies of government that made general policies. At first, however, the committees had difficulty reaching or representing all members of a particular industry and thus began to depend upon groups who could "represent before the commodity sections and the functional divisions or the Board the interests of all members of the respective trades to be affected by a war regulation."[19] Of course the SPA was such a group, and it became the main channel of information from the southern pine industry to the government.

By the summer of 1917, the War Industries Board had defined the main outlines of its problems. It felt there would be a shortage of certain commodities and to supply the nation's military needs for these goods the government would have to outbid other purchasers in the open market or attempt to control production and prices. According to Bernard M. Baruch, "the most significant, and for us the most novel, functions of the Board were the solutions which it developed for these problems in the form of the priority system and the price-fixing plan."[20] During the summer and fall of 1917, priority rules were put into effect, prices were fixed, and projects to increase production were inaugurated through voluntary agreements with the industries. These efforts were conducted with the support of the President and the Secretaries of War and the Navy, as well as other legally constituted agencies. The board had no legal responsibility, however, and it was sometimes difficult to impose its decisions on other governmental agencies.[21]

Among the major problems facing the United States at the outset of war were its distance from Europe and the fact that German submarines had decimated Allied shipping. Long before the United States entered the conflict, there was tremendous agitation from the business community for building up the American merchant marine for both commercial and military reasons. Although specific government action did not come until late in the year, American shipyards boomed, turning out a greatly increased tonnage in response to orders from both American and foreign governments.[22]

Finally in September, 1916, Congress passed and the President signed a bill creating the U. S. Shipping Board to control shipping for the government and appropriating $50 million for a subsidiary corporation to build new ships. Ten days after the U. S. declaration of war, the

subsidiary, the American Emergency Fleet Corporation, was
chartered in Washington, D. C. Following early quarrels
between officials of the Shipping Board and the Fleet
Corporation, the original leaders were replaced. In July,
1917, Edward N. Hurley, a Democratic politician from
Chicago, became chairman of the Shipping Board, where he
remained until the end of the war. Direction of the
Emergency Fleet Corporation was finally taken over by
steel executive Charles N. Schwab on April 16, 1918.[23]
These men were in direct contact with the Southern Pine
Association, as were R. H. Downman, who became head of
lumber under the raw materials division of the Council of
National Defense on April 7, 1917, and his successor,
Charles Edgar, who took over on January 1, 1918.[24]

The U. S. declaration of war created an immediate need
for over one billion feet of lumber for cantonments. The
lumber committee of the raw materials division of the
Council of National Defense was immediately organized to
develop a plan for the government to purchase lumber
directly from sawmills at reasonable prices. Since it
produced the nation's leading construction timber, and
because it was located near the sites of the proposed
cantonments, the southern pine industry was the logical
supplier.[25] The use of southern pine for army cantonments
and wooden ships created such a demand for lumber that by
mid-April, 1917, over 70 percent of the southern pine
mills west of the Mississippi were producing exclusively
for government orders, and by August the government had
already purchased more than 700 million board feet of
southern pine.[26]

However, these early achievements did not come without
difficulty and conflict. The Southern Pine Association
had anticipated both the U. S. entry into the war and the
difficulties the industry would face in meeting government
needs. Before the declaration of war, the SPA on February
7, 1917, sent a resolution to President Wilson advising
him that southern pine manufacturers were offering their
facilities to the government "in any manner that may best
serve to maintain the dignity and honor of the Nation."[27]

The SPA's first official contact with the war effort
came in March, 1917, when the U. S. Shipping Board
inquired about the industry's ability to support a wooden-
ship-building program. The SPA responded enthusiastically
that both the raw materials and the construction facilities would be readily available. Then, on April 12,
Frederick W. Allen, a member of a subcommittee of the

84

Council of National Defense who was representing Chairman Bernard M. Baruch of the commission on raw materials, suggested to President Charles S. Keith that he organize the association's subscribers to facilitate the immediate negotiation of agreements for the delivery of lumber supplies to the government, especially for the ship-building program."[28] Allen also asked Keith to appoint a committee with authority to represent southern pine manufacturers in establishing prices for their products and binding the industry to furnish and deliver lumber for war efforts.[29] Two days later, F. A. Eustis, subagent of the U. S. Shipping Board, wired Secretary-Manager John E. Rhodes about the possibility of forming an industry committee to fix prices and distribute orders for southern pine needed by the Emergency Fleet Corporation.[30] Keith and Rhodes gave their assurance that southern pine manufacturers would furnish every assistance to the war effort.[31]

Rhodes telegraphed SPA subscribers to ask for authorization for the board of directors to appoint a committee to represent them in negotiations with the Council of National Defense and to bind their companies to furnish lumber for the war programs. Within three days, over 90 percent of the subscribers had agreed to the creation of the committee and promised to place their stocks and production facilities at its disposal and to abide by any commitments concerning quantities, specifications, and prices which the committees might make with the Council of National Defense or other government agencies.[32]

Even before the establishment of its mobilization structure, the SPA was involved in the defense effort. During the first week of the war, the association received a government request to supply 6 million feet of lumber for the immediate construction of cantonments at Camp Pike, Arkansas. The request came on a Saturday, when the SPA office was closed, but three employees worked through Saturday night and Sunday contacting both mills in Arkansas and north Louisiana and railroad shipping agents to fill the government's order. On Monday, lumber began rolling into Camp Pike in such quantities that a temporary halt in shipments was ordered because of a shortage of storage space and railroad cars.[33] Such intensive efforts were not limited to this occasion: later, during a similar emergency, 25 billion feet of lumber were loaded and shipped within three days.[34]

The New South and the "New Competition"

On April 24, 1917, the SPA board of directors met in Memphis and appointed an emergency committee, composed of one representative from each state with association subscribers. The responsibility of the committee was to secure information about government lumber requirements and to report to SPA subscribers. It was also empowered to bind subscribers for the amount of lumber they would furnish, depending upon their facilities, to recommend specifications and inspections, and to fix minimum prices and divide orders for all government southern pine purchases.[35]

The emergency committee promptly traveled to Washington, where by April 30 it was conferring with the U. S. Shipping Board, the Emergency Fleet Corporation, and the lumber committee of the Council of National Defense and establishing specifications and prices for ship and cantonment lumber. The committee established a Washington office and appointed an industry representative who served as a liaison officer with the several government purchasing agencies.[36] On May 23, several hundred SPA subscribers and nonsubscribing southern pine manufacturers met in Memphis to hear the emergency committee report on its Washington activities. The subscribers approved the price schedule and authorized the committee to distribute orders and arrange for the delivery of lumber to the government, directing it in so doing to treat non-SPA producers equitably.

At the same meeting, the emergency committee became a permanent organization called the Southern Pine Emergency Bureau, and its membership was enlarged by the addition of representatives from non-SPA producers. The SPA promised to furnish the bureau information on mill locations, production capacities, stocks on hand, shipping facilities, and freight rates. The association also contributed $2,000 toward the bureau's organizational expenses. Operating income was to be derived from assessments on producers' sales to the government, whether made through the bureau or not. The original assessment rate was five cents per thousand board feet. This was subsequently raised to ten, and later fifteen, cents.[37]

At first, the Southern Pine Emergency Bureau represented no clearly defined area. However, as its activities developed, Charles Edgar, acting lumber director of the War Industries Board, outlined its territory as the southern pine-producing region west of the main line of the Louisville and Nashville Railroad in Alabama and south of a line drawn west from Montgomery, Alabama, to Meridian, Mississippi, all of the state of Mississippi south of the Alabama and Vicksburg Railroad, and the entire states of Louisiana, Arkansas, Oklahoma, and Texas. The bureau did not represent southern pine areas along the South Atlantic Seaboard and in the extreme southeastern part of the country.

While maintaining the office established by the Emergency Committee in Washington, the Southern Pine Emergency Bureau established its main office in New Orleans. The work of that office was divided into five categories: (1) ship schedules for the Emergency Fleet Corporation; (2) cantonment lumber and the requirements of the Allied countries; (3) car material for the U. S. Railroad Administration; (4) auditing; and (5) production.[38]

The Southern Pine Emergency Bureau's principal function was to allocate lumber orders from the Emergency Administration and Allied purchasing agents to the manufacturers. The Washington office maintained close contact with all government agencies concerned with procuring southern pine lumber. The bureau's capital personnel worked especially closely with the lumber committee of the Council of National Defense, which later became the lumber section of the War Industries Board. In fact, upon formation of the War Industries Board, the Southern Pine Emergency Bureau, like bureaus representing other groups of lumber manufacturers, was recognized as a semi-governmental organization working under the supervision of the director of the lumber section.[39] The Southern Pine Emergency Bureau handled only orders of government and Allied purchasing agencies which were duly authorized and recommended by the lumber section.

The Washington office also helped government engineers determine specifications for lumber to be used in buildings, ships, and other projects. It kept the proper departments and agencies fully advised of orders placed with particular manufacturers, each day's shipments, and other useful information. The office also handled problems, for instance, producers' delinquencies in filling orders and controversies over terms of settlement.[40]

Periodically during the war southern pine producers were accused of profiteering and of failing to supply the government's needs. It was charged that they preferred to save their timber supply for more profitable private markets. The first clash came in June, 1917, when the lumber committee of the raw materials division, Council of National Defense, called representative southern pine producers to Washington to discuss cantonment requirements. At a meeting on June 13, R. H. Downman and the producers agreed upon basic southern prices, but only after a figure higher than the going market price was temporarily adopted. The lumbermen said their attempt to make the government pay more than the public was justified because of the emergency nature of the order. This explanation was rejected.[41] This was the first, but not the last, time that the facts contradicted later industry statements that the lumbermen acted with "little thought of cost and profit"[42] or that the government was "well pleased with prices. . . ."[43] In fact, at the beginning of August Chairman Hurley called a conference with southern pine producers to discuss prices and try to get them to live up to their commitments to produce lumber for the shipbuilding program.[44]

Prices continued to be a matter of controversy. Prices for all government agencies, except the Emergency Fleet Corporation, were initially established by agreement beween the Lumber Committee and representatives of the agency.[45] Later, these prices were periodically adjusted by agreements between the Southern Pine Emergency Bureau and representatives of the lumber section of the War Industries Board and the Emergency Fleet Corporation. In the fall of 1917, and again a short time later, the Federal Trade Commission investigated the costs of lumber production. On the basis of these inquiries, officials of the appropriate government agencies insisted upon price reductions, which were then made.[46]

However, lumbermen regarded prices in the industry as too low. During late 1917 and early 1918, Edward Hines of Chicago's Hines Lumber Company, with other leading southern pine lumbermen and SPA officials, attempted to gain a price increase.[47] The manufacturers could get higher prices for their lumber in the civilian market than from the government, and their "often heroic" efforts in supplying the government's needs were "not untinged with the color of human weakness and errancy."[48] Their attitude was typified by the statement of the Kirby Lumber Company's sales manager that "these Government prices are so much lower than the regular commercial market, that we of course do not want to take any more than our share of the orders. . . ."[49]

During early 1918, lumber prices in the commercial trade rose to $5 to $7 per thousand board feet above those paid by the government. For a number of reasons, the government believed that production for civilian purposes should not be stimulated by high prices.[50] Conservation of the softwood supply was a factor, but the primary consideration was the conservation of other materials and transportation needed for the war. Reducing nonmilitary production would conserve men, machinery, materials, and transportation facilities. Civilian lumber needs were considered deferrable.[51]

The industry's size and fragmented nature made general commandeering impossible, and so the War Industries Board attacked the problem by manipulating priorities and by price fixing. The non-war construction section of the War Industries Board's priorities section discouraged production beyond minimum civilian requirements by requiring lumber manufacturers and distributors to sign pledges to deliver lumber only for essential purposes or on express, written permits. Southern pine was not placed on the board's preferred list of essential war industries and it was thus deprived of any general priority classification. However, for government production the lumbermen were given top priority privileges.[52]

Early in 1918, the War Industries Board concluded that it was necessary to fix maximum prices for southern pine lumber. In March, the producers were granted a hearing before the War Industries Board's price-fixing committee. No changes were made, however, until after further hearings on June 12, 13, and 14, 1918, and then an agreement was reached to fix prices on the basis of cost figures provided by the Federal Trade Commission's production cost studies. The manufacturers also agreed that commercial sales would be subject at any time before delivery to an option in favor of the government. They further agreed to comply with War Industries Board directions with reference to filling commercial requirements in the order of their importance. In general, prices were fixed at levels low enough to discourage production, and in many instances they actually caused a curtailment.[53] Southern pine prices were controlled from June 14 through December 23, 1918.[54]

Prices were only one of the problems facing the southern pine industry. Despite efforts to reduce production for domestic use, the industry faced the tremendous task of supplying the government's needs. Most pressing

was the shipbuilding program inaugurated in late 1916.
This called for the construction of one thousand ships,
each requiring at least one million feet of lumber.[55] The
peak demand for southern pine came in October, 1917, when
Gulf Coast mills were instructed to hold all longleaf timbers measuring twelve inches by twelve inches by twenty-
four inches and larger for the shipbuilding program. The
mills were not to accept any new orders for such materials
and not to fill old orders.[56] On November 2, the government's demand was extended to cover all southern pine
timber thicker than two inches, wider than ten inches, and
longer than twenty feet. Government agents moved into the
South to watch the sawmills and be sure that timbers
suitable for war use were not diverted into the domestic
trade.[57]

The tremendous government demands required drastic
efforts in the southern pine industry. To procure the
extra-large sizes needed for ship timbers, southern lumbermen went far beyond their normal logging operations to
secure specially selected trees.[58] The manufacturers
instituted a speedup program to increase the output of
ship timbers from 850,000 to 2 million linear feet daily.
They overhauled and reorganized machinery and installed
new equipment as many mills worked night and day to meet
the government's demands.[59]

During the first ten months of America's involvement
in World War I, the southern pine industry furnished
37,803 carloads, or 750 million feet, of lumber to the
military and supplied ship timbers at the rate of 75
carloads, or 1,500,000 feet, per day. In addition,
southern pine supplied huge quantities of lumber for war
industries, foreign governments, war housing, and other
purposes.[60] However, the producers encountered some difficulty in meeting the government's demands. During late
1917 and early 1918, the industry came under both public
and internal criticism because of its failure to fill
government orders satisfactorily in terms of both quantity
and price.[61]

Newspapers publicized the fact that late in 1917 the
Shipping Board had to obtain large ship timbers, ordered
originally from southern pine producers, from West Coast
manufacturers. In the spring of 1918, the U. S. committee
on commerce investigated this matter. At the hearing, the
industry's spokesman denied that the Shipping Board had
been forced to secure West Coast lumber because of

southern pine producers' failure to fulfill their commitments. Rather, he declared, the Shipping Board had acted on the suggestion of the southern pine manufacturers in securing fir timbers for certain larger sizes, and the producers ought therefore to be commended for their "prevision."[62]

Southern pine manufacturers were having difficulty delivering large timbers used for keels, keelsons, ribs, frames, and side timbers in the wooden-ship construction program. In February, 1918, J. O. Heyworth, director of the wooden ship division of the Emergency Fleet Corporation, stated that 100 million board feet of such timbers were required for ships then on order, but that only 38 million feet had been shipped. It had thus been necessary for the Emergency Fleet Corporation, at the request of the southern pine producers, as noted above, to order more than half the total requirement from West Coast manufacturers. Nevertheless, the need for yellow pine timbers remained great, and Heyworth exhorted the industry to maximize its efforts.[63] President Keith urged all southern pine manufacturers to exert themselves to satisfy the needs of the ship construction program. "Any manufacturer," he wrote, "who does not do his part by going in advance of his logging for the necessary timber, and who will not refuse to take orders for material which interferes with Government orders is a slacker and a traitor, and is encouraging and assisting our enemies."[64]

Heyworth's concern was shared by other government officials and by prominent figures in and out of the southern pine industry. Edward N. Hurley, chairman of the U. S. Shipping Board, wrote the Southern Pine Emergency Bureau that "there is a strong feeling in the country that there is only enough lumber to complete three hundred and sixty ships each year. . . . The sooner you present some facts to counteract this information, the better it will be for the lumber industry." Stating that "we have not received enough lumber to keep our program going . . .," Hurley said, "It is up to the lumbermen . . . so far the southern pine people have not produced sufficient timbers of large sizes to carry out our program."[65]

Having the same concern, the editor and general manager of the Manufacturers' Record in Baltimore wrote John Henry Kirby to get the Texan's reaction to charges against his industry. According to the editor:

The New South and the "New Competition"

There is a feeling in Washington that the Southern
pine lumber people have very badly fallen down in the
promised deliveries of timber for wooden ships, and in
the minds of those who have been studying the matter,
there is a question as to whether this is due to the
inability to get the timber specified, or whether the
lumber people have been taking care of their private
trade at the expense of delaying the fulfillment of
their contracts to provide timbers for ships.

As you know a large amount of timber is being
brought across the Continent from the Pacific Coast to
Southern shipyards. If this is to be continued, it
will mean that the wooden ship program when existing
contracts have been finished, will naturally probably
be switched to the Pacific Coast. . . .

To what do you attribute the delay in the delivery
of pine to Southern shipyards which has brought about
a delay of four to six months in the completion of
ships under contract as compared to specifications
when they were begun? Have the lumber operators done
their best to hunt out in their timber properties for
trees big enough to provide the necessary lumber, or is
there an actual shortage of such trees?[66]

The last part of the question was answered in a manner
favorable to Kirby's own operations by an Emergency Fleet
Corporation official. He reported that he had been to
most of the Kirby mills and found "their managers have
instructions . . . to cut every piece of timber possible
that will go into ships and to spare no expenses whatever
in getting these pieces." The official further stated:
"I also found that in their logging operations they have
had a man in the woods to go four miles ahead of the
operations and mark trees suitable and the men in the
woods hauling them to their tram. All of these trees that
I have seen are very fine, and it seems that the Kirby
Lumber Company as a whole, are doing everything possible
to increase the production over what they had been doing
and I already had evidence that they were doing that."[67]
The situation was somewhat confused in the spring of
1918. When J. O. Heyworth addressed the SPA in February,
the reaction was mixed. The producers made no effort to
present to him their feeling that part of the production
difficulties were due to the fact that southern pine manufacturers were being called on to produce timbers for
shipbuilding which would better have been obtained on the

92

Pacific Coast.[68] In fact, Heyworth was introduced with an admission that "we have not done our duty. . . . It is perhaps not possible to get out everything demanded by the Fleet Corporation, but in some respects we could have done better than we have done."[69] Heyworth, however, replied, "No man here . . . need be ashamed of the product or the production of the last six or seven months."[70]

Actually, at that time the federal government was investigating the industry's performance in the war effort, and the manufacturers were restive about what they regarded as unwise and unfair governmental policies. In the spring of 1918, the government turned to John Henry Kirby for assistance, but Kirby's efforts only caused more trouble.

Kirby became active in the war effort shortly after America's entry. On April 27, 1917, Kirby received a telegram from Bernard Baruch asking him to serve as a member of the raw materials committee of the Council of National Defense. Kirby accepted and moved to Washington. In May, Kirby became president of the National Lumber Manufacturers' Association, while continuing to work for the government. In March, 1918, Chairman Edward N. Hurley of the U. S. Shipping Board asked Kirby to become Lumber Administrator for the South and to secure the timbers and other materials needed so badly for the Emergency Fleet Corporation's wooden-ship program. It was hoped that Kirby could bring order to and increase production out of the chaotic southern industry.[71]

Kirby accepted the position with the blessing of J. O. Heyworth, who said that he was "sure a direct personal attention by a man like you will straighten matters out and will give to Southern Pine Producers a much better chance to deliver."[72] Kirby immediately moved to New Orleans, and on March 20, 1918, took charge of the timber section of the Emergency Fleet Corporation as Lumber Administrator for the South. He was assisted by fifteen industry leaders from all parts of the region who served without pay.[73] They included not only SPA subscribers but members of other organizations and independents.[74]

Kirby's appointment coincided with a governmental decision that seemed to foreshadow better days for the industry in meeting the government's timber needs. As we have seen, southern lumbermen from the first recommended that some large timbers that were scarce in their timber stands should be obtained in the West where they were more

The New South and the "New Competition"

plentiful. The chairman of the Southern Pine Emergency
Bureau had expressed this attitude in January, 1918, to
Edward N. Hurley.

Early in 1918, because of charges in the press that
southern pine lumbermen were failing to meet their
responsibilities to the shipbuilding program, the industry
requested a hearing before the committee on commerce of
the U. S. Senate, which was investigating the ship-
construction effort. On March 10, 11, and 12, 1918, a
group of lumbermen representing approximately 20 percent
of southern pine production met in Washington with the
U. S. Shipping Board. At this conference, the recommendations which had been consistently made by southern pine
producers were finally adopted by the Shipping Board. As
early as December 1, 1917, the board had started obtaining
large sizes in the western fir forests, and at the March
conference it agreed that this practice would be continued
and also that the government would start to permit the use
of laminated, or built-up, materials, thus making it
easier for the southern pine industry to meet the government's requirements.[75] Because of the Shipping Board's
decision, the industry decided merely to file a statement
of record rather than taking up the commerce committee's
time with long hearings. In this statement it predicted
that the appointment of Kirby as lumber administrator
would straighten out conditions in the industry and its
relations with the government.[76]

Official notice of the Kirby appointment came on
March 15, in a letter from the general purchasing officer
of the Emergency Fleet Corporation. It outlined the
Texan's duties as being in "charge of supplying lumber for
ships built on the Atlantic and Gulf Coasts and such other
lumber for shipyards and other purposes as may be needed
by the Emergency Fleet Corporation from time to time."
Kirby was "expected to use whatever new methods that may
occur to you in order that lumber may be obtained at a
sufficient rate that the construction of wooden ships will
not be delayed."[77] W. J. Haynen, the assistant purchasing officer, acted as Kirby's direct assistant. The lumbermen perhaps unknowingly faced immediate hostility from
the general purchasing officer, who believed Kirby would
be usurping his authority.[78]

Late in April, 1918, came the first rumblings of matters that would eventually involve Kirby and the southern
pine industry in difficulties with the government. SPA
Secretary-Manager John E. Rhodes advised his board of

94

directors that, because of the demands of retail dealers
that they receive lumber at the same price as the government, and because many mills preferred to take higher-
priced commercial orders and not accept those for government material from the Emergency Bureau, Chairman Baruch
and Acting Director of Lumber Edgar hoped the lumber
industry would agree with the government on southern pine
prices for the government and public alike.   Rhodes
reported, however, that R. H. Downman had left New Orleans
for Washington, where he would "vigorously protest against
the plan of the government to fix a price for retail
trade."[79]

Nevertheless, on June 14, after three days of conferences with the southern pine manufacturers' representatives, including Kirby, Dr. F. W. Taussig, the acting
chairman of the War Industries Board's price-fixing
committee, drew up a list of maximum prices for all lumber
sales, civilian or private, "by agreement with the said
representatives of the manufacturers of Southern or Yellow
Pine lumber. . . ."[80]

Kirby was soon called to task by his superiors, on
grounds of conflict of interest, for serving as chairman
of the southern pine industry's committee to negotiate
prices with the government while acting at the same
time as lumber administrator for the Emergency Fleet
Corporation.   Kirby explained that he saw no conflict
of interest because the prices of ship timbers, which he
was procuring in his government job, were not discussed.
Furthermore, his government position had nothing to do
with setting prices:

> As lumber administrator I have nothing to do with the
> matter of the price which the government pays for
> the timbers it acquires.   That is a matter of
> agreement between the producers and the purchasing
> officer of the Shipping Board or with the Lumber
> Director of the War Industries Board. The Purchasing
> Officer or the Lumber Director or both will fix the
> price by agreement with the producers and when that
> factor has been determined the Purchasing Officer
> passes to me an order to distribute among the con-
> senting mills, in accordance with their capacity to
> produce logs for the timbers required.[81]

Kirby continued, ". . . the lumber manufacturers were
opposed to the government's price fixing program both on
price and as a matter of current governmental policy."
However, said Kirby, "the manufacturers waived their own

opinions and convictions on the subject and entered in good faith upon the discussion looking to an agreement with the government fixing a maximum price, both to the trade and the government. . . ." Kirby concluded that he had "not understood that it was any part of my duty or prerogative to have any views in the matter of fixing or agreeing upon a price. . . ."[82] A few days later, in his capacity as president of the National Lumber Manufacturers' Association, Kirby called upon all lumber manufacturers to support the war effort through the various lumber associations. He announced that "manufacturers of lumber in spirit of patriotism have yielded their convictions on subject of price fixing." They, he wrote, "are attempting in good faith and in proper spirit to put into efficient action rules which government at Washington has prescribed for them."[83] Kirby's statement in regard to price-fixing would prove interesting in the light of his later activities and words.

Just three days later, on June 28, Kirby, along with R. A. Long and Charles S. Keith as members of a committee representing southern pine interests, sent a telegram to Dr. F. W. Taussig of the price-fixing committee stating:

> . . . we have just learned that the order of June fourteenth . . . fixing the maximum for southern pine lumber items as approved by the President, contains the language that the price fixed was reached by agreement. This is an error. Aside from the question as to whether Southern Pine interests will accept the prices as fixed, we do want it understood at the outset that we have not agreed to the price . . . nor did we consent to administrative features covered by the order. We respectfully request that these errors be called to the President's attention and the order corrected to conform with the facts.[84]

Kirby soon received a telegram from Bernard M. Baruch asking if Kirby had indeed signed the Taussig telegram, saying that because of "the understanding I had when you left" the telegram had "caused me surprise and astonishment. . . ." Baruch continued that he "would be surprised and regret exceedingly to have a confirmation of such telegram especially in view of your personal attitude when I last saw you."[85] Kirby wired Charles S. Keith for instructions and was advised to "wire Mr. Baruch that you signed telegram" and to tell him that Kirby, Long, and F. W. Stevens were on the way to Washington and that Kirby would confer with Baruch on his arrival. Kirby carried

out Keith's instructions and also informed Baruch that a
large meeting of southern pine manufacturers in Memphis
had passed a resolution requesting an additional conference with the War Industries Board. They appointed Long,
Kirby, and Stevens to represent the industry.[86] These communications marked the beginning of a fiery clash between
Baruch and Kirby.

The meeting in Memphis had been a heated one in which
both the government's price for lumber and its administrative figures had come under heavy fire. Kirby, Long, and
Keith portrayed the June 14 price-fixing session with the
War Industries Board as stormy, and all three centered
their criticism on Charles Edgar, acting director of lumber on the War Industries Board. At one point, the
Memphis meeting adopted a resolution saying that the
industry had no faith in Edgar's ability to treat pine
manufacturers fairly. The resolution was reconsidered and
rejected on the advice of industry leaders because it
would have embarrassed those trying to negotiate new prices with the government. SPA President Charles S. Keith
pledged that the industry would continue to meet its commitments to the government and expressed confidence that
it would eventually receive fair treatment, but, he concluded, "I don't accept Mr. Baruch and Mr. Edgar as my
government and I strongly favor appealing from their decision in fixing prices for our product."[87]

On July 1, Kirby left New Orleans for Washington after
writing Keith to ask if he approved of Kirby's telegram to
Baruch. Kirby voiced his concern over wire service
reports which quoted the Federal Trade Commission as the
authority for statements that lumber manufacturers were
"among the present selfish interests which are profiteering in a reprehensible way." Kirby said that he did "not
know how far that thought has currency in Washington, but
I trust it will not be serious or embarrassing to our
committee."[88]

On July 3, the southern pine committee arrived in
Washington, went into conference, and drew up a letter
setting forth their reasons for opposing the June 14
price-fixing agreement. Among these was the fact that
the agreement set prices FOB mills to the public on the
same basis as those for the government. The lumbermen
said this would disrupt normal and established channels of
trade, since many mills sold through commission men,
brokers, and wholesalers. There were many other distribution variations which made it difficult to set prices

effectively and clearly. The committee also charged that prices for the public should be higher than government prices, since the costs of producing for the public were higher. Price-fixing, it added, was not necessary to assure adequate government supplies. Furthermore, the prices set were too low and did not adequately consider widely varying conditions in the industry. The efficiency and structure of some firms might enable them to survive under the government's prices, while others could not. The lumbermen said that labor and material costs were changing so rapidly under war conditions that cost figures used by the government to determine prices were too low and did not adequately protect the industry. Thus the committee members recommended that the fixed prices be adjusted every thirty days. Finally they asked the government to stop placing extremely large orders at the current prices on the eve of new price adjustments.[89]

Armed with a copy of this letter, Kirby called on Bernard M. Baruch. According to Kirby, he was kept waiting for two hours, and when he finally got to see Baruch, the first thing the chairman said "was that as a condition precedent to any discussion, we must withdraw the telegram to Dr. Taussig and accept the order of June 14 as having been put in by agreement, because he had represented to the President that it was by agreement, and the committee must not put him in the attitude of having made a misrepresentation."[90] Kirby contested the statement that lumbermen had agreed to the June 14 order, but Baruch "said if this new committee would accept that order as by agreement, he and the War Industries Board would then go into all our grievances with us and do everything they thought possible to conform to our ideas and give us the relief sought."[91]

Kirby then filed his letter with Baruch, who sent copies to members of the War Industries Board. The men arranged for the committee to meet with Baruch on Monday, July 8, to try to settle things. Kirby expressed his hope that the matter could be handled without a hearing before the full board and said the lumbermen "were perfectly willing to leave . . . matters to his [Baruch's] sole adjudication."[92] On Monday, Kirby called for an interview with Baruch, but was told the chairman was too busy and that the lumbermen could present their case before the entire board on Tuesday, July 9, "provided we would file at once an agreement." Kirby later complained that "we were combatting this thought all the time. To our minds it was a species of coersion [sic] that was wholly indefensible. . . . We were told positively, definitely, unequivocally, and I might say irritably, that the War Industries Board would not give us a hearing, nor would any other tribunal give us a hearing until we had formally agreed in writing that the order of June 14 was predicated upon an agreement between the Price Fixing Committee and the lumber industry."[93]

On July 9, under War Industries Board pressure, the lumbermen's committee finally adopted a reluctant statement that the price-fixing order "may be considered as now agreed to as of June 14th."[94] However, they strongly qualified their statement with a reminder that "the committee that was in charge of this matter for the Southern Pine industry left Washington June 22nd, with the distinct impression that no agreement had been entered into." They said further, "The committee now acting for the industry came to Washington on this occasion in the firm belief that no agreement had been reached. However . . . as we are not permitted to discuss our problems except this element is eliminated, we have, as stated, agreed to waive all objections to the recital in the order that it had been assented to."[95]

Having fulfilled this condition, the committee was granted a hearing before the board in Baruch's office. The session began with Baruch calling for the filing of the committee's assent to the June 14 order, and Kirby presented the committee's July 9 written statement. Kirby then read a list of southern pine industry grievances, which were basically the same as those cited in the committee's July 3 letter to the board. The committee also suggested that the board accept it or a similar body to "be recognized by the Government as a standing committee representing the Southern Pine industry, and that as important questions arise affecting the economic or commercial status of the industry, this committee be called into conference for suggestion and counsel." They also urged that "all lumber sold the Government shall be billed at the price in effect at the time of shipment, rather than at the price in effect when the order was placed." Finally, the committee asked that railroad orders be placed through the emergency bureaus, and that the industry be permitted to continue its traditional practice of allowing discounts for prompt payment.[96]

The board claimed no jurisdiction over the price-fixing committee, whose power they said rested with the

President, but they did agree to set up a subcommittee to consider complaints dealing with administrative features of the price-fixing agreement.[97] The subcommittee eventually suggested that producers in the Southern Pine Emergency Bureau territory choose a permanent representative committee of all manufacturers to represent them before the War Industries Board, that railroad orders be placed through the Emergency Bureau, and that "on all Government orders on which the price is fixed by the Government the price in effect on the date of delivery rather than the price in effect on the date the order is placed shall control. . . ." Matters concerning price adjustments and terms of sales were referred to the price-fixing committee,[98] which adopted the suggestion that prices in effect on the date of shipment, rather than those in effect at the time an order was placed, would apply to government orders.[99]

At this point, the situation deteriorated and acrimonious words and actions flew among the lumbermen themselves and between industry and government leaders. Kirby was relieved of his duties with the government: some said in dishonor, but others claimed because he had the temerity to tangle with Baruch, Charles Edgar, and other government officials. For whatever reason, on July 16 J. L. Ackerson, assistant to the director general, acting for the vice-president of the Emergency Fleet Corporation, advised Kirby that, because of administrative consolidations within the Fleet Corporation, the positions of lumber administrator and assistant lumber administrator were being abolished. Ackerson very formally expressed "the Emergency Fleet Corporation's appreciation of the service you have rendered," and expressed the "hope that your connection with the Fleet Corporation has been as satisfactory to yourself as it has been to us." The letter did not announce a _fait accompli_; rather it anticipated actions "if this consolidation is as successful as we hope. . . ."[100]

Later in July the Southern Pine Association Board of Directors met in Chicago to hear a report by the special committee composed of Kirby, R. A. Long, and F. W. Stevens. Kirby reported that the board's subcommittee that had met with him, Long, and Stevens in Washington had recommended that the manufacturers in the Southern Pine Emergency Bureau territory select a trade committee to permanently represent them in dealing with the War Industries Board, thus getting away from undue influence by any particular association, group of mills, or faction of the industry.[101]

The SPA board then dissolved the Southern Pine Emergency Bureau and authorized the SPA president to appoint a permanent, five-man, war service committee of the Southern Pine Industry. The committee was authorized to represent the association, its subscribers, and cooperating manufacturers in all matters involving the production and sale of their lumber under conditions set by the War Industries Board.[102] The committee members appointed by President Keith included R. A. Long, F. W. Stevens, John H. Kirby, A. L. Clark, and Charles Green.[103]

The action of the SPA board was not acceptable to the government's representatives, who had reached the end of their rope with the southern lumbermen. A contemporary involved in the mobilization of industry during World War I later recalled that "the greatest friction between the lumbermen and the Board was with three members of the Southern Pine Association."[104]

The men referred to were, of course, Long, Kirby, and Keith, and Baruch's decision to have nothing more to do with them was expressed in a telegram to R. A. Long on July 30. Baruch said the SPA board's Chicago action abolishing the Emergency Bureau and setting up the new War Service Committee was not in accord with the wishes of the War Industries Board's subcommittee, because the "Chicago committee was not selected by the lumber manufacturers but by [the] Board of Directors of [the] Southern Pine Association which association does not include a large number of independent and small mills in that territory." Furthermore, Baruch said he had read Kirby's letters to Keith of July 10 and 13 which had been published in the lumber journals, and he thundered, "I am astonished at the representations contained therein and advise you that [the] War Industries Board will deal with no committee of which those responsible for these representations or their circulation are members."[105]

Charles Edgar, acting director of lumber for the War Industries Board, immediately attempted to explain Baruch's and the Board's position to prominent members of the southern pine industry. On July 31, he wrote W. H. Sullivan of Bogalusa, Louisiana, a sometime Kirby foe, that the War Industries Board would consider the Southern Pine Emergency Bureau, of which Sullivan was chairman, a functioning organization until the southern pine industry could hold a general meeting and form a truly representative committee. Edgar attempted to refute Kirby's statement about the price-fixing episode and stated that Kirby "definitely understood the ruling was to be written by agreement."[106] Edgar also submitted statements by two of his assistants that they had heard M. J. Scanlon, a member of the original southern pine group that had met with the price-fixing committee, state that it was his understanding that prices had been fixed by agreement and that he could not understand why Kirby, Keith, and Long said otherwise.[107]

Kirby's public statements, circulated throughout the industry, seem to have been the final straw in his break with Baruch. Ironically, Kirby had received a promotion of sorts in July, moving from Lumber Administrator for the South to national Lumber Administrator. The promotion came about the same time as his letter of July 10 to Charles S. Keith reporting on the industry committee's activities in Washington and accusing Baruch and his cohorts of coercion, but apparently before his letter was published and circulated. The letter infuriated Baruch, and members of the industry saw a relationship between the letter incident and Kirby's later difficulties.[108]

On July 31, shortly after the publication of Kirby's letter, newspapers throughout the country reported that Kirby was no longer lumber administrator of the Emergency Fleet Corporation. Emergency Fleet Corporation officials were quoted as saying that the wooden-ship building program was being "seriously hampered . . . because southern yellow pine interests have not met more fully and promptly the demand for heavy timbers required in ship construction." Bernard Baruch was said to be considering commandeering the yellow pine industry "unless the government's needs are fully supplied." Kirby was identified as a prominent member of the Southern Pine Association "virtually controlling it is said, with two other yellow pine operators, the yellow pine industry." Since the time yellow pine lumber prices were approved by President Wilson, it was reported, "difficulties have constantly arisen as to interpretation, discounts, and territory to be covered by the Southern Pine Association." The story said that the decision to dispense with Kirby's services was made by Director-General Charles M. Schwab and Vice-President Charles Piez of the Shipping Board, and that the Texan's resignation had been announced the previous evening in New Orleans. Kirby denied the charges against him and the industry and demanded that Chairman Hurley of the United States Shipping Board correct them.[109]

Despite later pious words and expressions of gratitude from both the lumber industry and the government, the southern pine industry's problems and the charges against it continued through the end of the war. As late as November 1, 1918, the war service committee was facing charges from Washington that the industry was dragging its feet on orders intended for railroads and railroad cars because the orders had been placed early and thus carried lower prices than more recent ones. Although it denied the charge, the committee urged industry members to fill these orders to clear the industry of any suspicion of delay.[110]

It was evident that the war experiences left a bad taste in the mouths of many industry figures. During the last days of the war, the advisory board which Kirby had selected to help with his duties as lumber administrator submitted a lengthy report on the achievements of his administration. The report was extremely critical of the conditions Kirby inherited from W. J. Haynen and concluded with the charge that Haynen had utilized an informer on Kirby's staff to spy on the Texan during his tenure as lumber administrator. The general tenor of the committee's comments was to the effect that Haynen had done everything within his power to discredit Kirby and the advisory committee.[111]

The effort to discredit Kirby, if indeed it can be called that, was certainly not successful within the industry. When southern pine lumbermen assembled in New Orleans in August, 1918, to choose a permanent war committee, Kirby's services were lauded and he was introduced to "storms of applause." According to accounts of the meeting, "so rousing was Mr. Kirby's reception when he arose to speak that for some moments he was unable to proceed. He seemed noticeably affected by the voluntary expressions of confidence displayed by the audience."[112] It was evident that the industry regarded Kirby as a victim and a symbol of the charges leveled against the entire industry. In the latter part of 1918, the SPA began placing large advertisements playing up the industry's role in war mobilization in metropolitan newspapers. These campaigns were designed not only to repair the industry's image, but also to demonstrate the broad adaptability of southern pine as a construction material.[113]

The New South and the "New Competition"

On November 11 the armistice was signed, and the following day the government began cancelling contracts as an unplanned, headlong plunge toward demobilization began. Two days after the armistice, the War Industries Board began to remove price controls, and within approximately a month no more priority orders were issued. The "dollar-a-year" men almost ran one another down in their haste to close down the war-created bureaucratic machinery and get back to civilian life.[114] On November 23, Acting Lumber Director Charles Edgar officially notified the Southern Pine Emergency Bureau that the War Industries Board would be making no further recommendations concerning the placing of lumber orders with the various bureaus. The SPEB immediately stopped taking orders, and its Washington office was closed by December 1. The New Orleans office continued to function in a restricted fashion until February 15, 1919, when the last of the government orders was filled, and then the Southern Pine Emergency Bureau went out of existence.[115]

By the end of the war, or more precisely by November 23, 1918, when the Southern Pine Emergency Bureau ceased to allocate government purchases, the industry had delivered a total of 1,904,308,523 board feet of lumber for the United States and Allied governments. Of this vast quantity of lumber products, 295,178,221 feet went to the Emergency Fleet Corporation for the construction of ships, and 1,345,648,542 feet to the War Department for the building of cantonments and other structures for the use of the army and related service organizations, like the YMCA and the Knights of Columbus. The Railroad Administration received 224,722,713 feet for use in the construction of railroad cars, and 38,759,047 feet were shipped to the Allies.[116] This was unquestionably a major accomplishment despite the war's controversies.

In the afterglow of victory, the government and the southern pine industry momentarily forgot the strife, conflict, and difficulties of the war years and basked in the glory of their accomplishments. The Southern Pine Emergency Bureau, the Southern Pine Association, and the southern pine industry received wide praise from high-ranking government officials for their services in behalf of the U. S. war effort. Among the more prized expressions of gratitude were those of former nemesis Bernard M. Baruch and of the acting director of the War Industries Board's lumber section, Charles Edgar. On December 5, 1918, Baruch wrote:

Mobilization for World War I

I offer in behalf of my associates and myself a tribute of thanks to the patriotism and service shown by the entire commercial body of America. Its members have made service and not profit their rule. They have shown a desire to subordinate self and exalt public interest, and to this readiness to make sacrifice in the common cause has largely been due whatever success we may have been able to attain. I would be doing the industry of America an injustice if I did not make this acknowledgment. May I express the hope that this same spirit may continue in times of peace, so that the problems affecting all may be handled in the same spirit of helpful co-operation that had prevailed during the War. May I send this message of gratitude to the loyal co-workers in the great lumber industry which you have so ably represented.[117]

Following the end of the war, the southern pine industry, like the rest of the economy, faced the problems referred to by Baruch, and it looked to the Southern Pine Association to help lead it through the maze of matters postponed, created, or intensified by the wartime experiences and disruptions. The southern pine industry faced the problems of reconstruction, the return to "normalcy," and "profitless prosperity" of the post-war decade with the assistance of a well-organized trade association which had been tempered in the fires of war.

Although controversial, the SPA's service in the mobilization effort, like that of other associations, built a reservoir of good will with the government which helped shape a more favorable or lenient attitude toward trade association activities during the 1920s. Business practices which were not tolerated during peacetime—price-fixing and production controls—were essential for the defense effort and would thus seem less objectionable in the post-war period.[118] The experience of business-government cooperation also provided valuable knowledge and experience that would prove significant for future mobilization for total war, as well as for peacetime government-business economic planning and coordination. The southern pine experience provides a good insight into the World War I mobilization effort.[119]

NOTES TO CHAPTER 3

1. "War Activities of The Southern Pine Association: An Outline of the Co-operation of the Southern Pine Lumber Industry with Various Departments of the United States Government during the War," Southern Pine Association Records, Box 84b (Louisiana State University Archives, Baton Rouge, La.). Collection hereafter cited as SPA Records.

2. Ibid.

3. George Brown Tindall, The Emergence of the New South, 1913-1945 (Baton Rouge: Louisiana State University Press, 1967), p. 33.

4. "Yellow Pine Industry of 1916," Gulf Coast Lumberman, IV (Jan. 1, 1917), 4.

5. "European War and the Lumber Situation," Gulf Coast Lumberman, II (Aug. 15, 1914), 4.

6. Hamilton Pratt Easton, "The History of the Texas Lumbering Industry" (Ph.D. dissertation, University of Texas, 1947), p. 202; Harold Underwood Faulkner, The Decline of Laissez Faire, 1897-1917 (New York: Holt, Rinehart and Winston, 1951), pp. 32-33; Tindall, Emergence of the New South, pp. 33-34.

7. "European War and Its Results," Gulf Coast Lumberman, II (Sept. 1, 1914), 7.

8. Faulkner, Decline of Laissez Faire, p. 35; George Soule, Prosperity Decade: From War to Depression: 1917-1929 (New York: Holt, Rinehart and Winston, 1947), p. 71.

9. Soule, Prosperity Decade, pp. 7-8. There is a detailed examination of the origins and development of American war mobilization in Daniel R. Beaver, Newton D. Baker and the American War Effort, 1917-1919 (Lincoln: University of Nebraska Press, 1966).

10. Soule, Prosperity Decade, p. 9. American war mobilization is treated at length in Robert Sobel, The Age of Giant Corporations: A Microeconomic History of American

Business, 1914-1970 (Westport, Conn.: Greenwood Press, 1972), pp. 3-24.

11. Paul A. C. Koistinen, "The 'Industrial-Military Complex' in Historical Perspective: World War I," Business History Review, XLI (Winter, 1967), 378-82; Soule, Prosperity Decade, p. 9.

12. Easton, "History of Texas Lumbering," pp. 287-89.

13. "Orange Will Celebrate," Gulf Coast Lumberman, IV (Nov. 1, 1916), 30.

14. Easton, "History of Texas Lumbering," p. 201.

15. Bernard M. Baruch, American Industry in the War: A Report of the War Industries Board (Washington, D. C.: Government Printing Office, 1921), pp. 19-20; Soule, Prosperity Decade, pp. 10-12; Koistinen, "World War I," pp. 382-87. The development of the war mobilization structure is outlined in Paul A. C. Koistinen, "The 'Industrial-Military Complex' in Historical Perspective: The Interwar Years," Journal of American History, LVI (Mar., 1970), 819-23.

16. Soule, Prosperity Decade, p. 12; Koistinen, "World War I," pp. 387-95. There is an exhaustive account of the origins and operations of the War Industries Board in Robert D. Cuff, The War Industries Board: Business-Government Relations during World War I (Baltimore: Johns Hopkins University Press, 1973).

17. Baruch, American Industry in the War, pp. 29-21.

18. Ibid., p. 24.

19. Ibid., p. 23. For a description of the further development and wartime problems of the War Industries Board see Koistinen, "World War I," 395-403.

20. Baruch, American Industry in the War, p. 21.

21. Ibid., p. 24.

22. Soule, Prosperity Decade, p. 29.

23. Ibid. pp. 29-31.

24. Baruch, American Industry in the War, p. 219; Grosvenor B. Clarkson, Industrial America in the World War: The Strategy behind the Lines, 1917-1918 (Boston: Houghton Mifflin, 1923), pp. 426-27.

25. Baruch, American Industry in the War, p. 211.

26. Tindall, Emergence of the New South, pp. 55-56.

27. James Boyd, "It Is War!" SPA Records, Box 77a, p. 1.

28. U.S. Shipping Board to Central Coal and Coke Company, Mar. 24, 1917, and Southern Pine Association to U.S. Shipping Board, Mar. 24, 1917, both in Records of the U.S. Shipping Board, Construction Division, General File, RG 32, National Archives; Senate Committee on Commerce, Hearings on S. 170, Building of Merchant Vessels under the Direction of the United States Shipping Board Emergency Fleet Corporation, 65th Cong., 2d Sess., 1918, p. 10.

29. "Report of Southern Pine Emergency Bureau," SPA Records, Box 84b.

30. Hearings on S. 170, p. 11.

31. Ibid., pp. 10-11. However, Keith strongly noted that the SPA had never dealt with prices in any way previously. Charles S. Keith to F. R. Eustis, Apr. 18, 1917, Records of the U.S. Shipping Board, Construction Division, General File, RG 32, National Archives.

32. Boyd, "It Is War!" SPA Records, Box 77a, pp. 2-3; "Report of Southern Pine Emergency Bureau," SPA Records, Box 84b; "War Activities of the Southern Pine Association," SPA Records, Box 846. In response to an inquiry from Eustis, Secretary-Manager Rhodes reported that lumber prices were rising but that there would be no attempt by producers to extort the government. John E. Rhodes to F. A. Eustis, Apr. 17, 1917, Records of the U.S. Shipping Board, Construction Division, General File, RG 32, National Archives.

33. Herbert C. Berckes, "The Pitch in Pine: A Story of the Traditions, Policies, and Activities of the Southern Pine Industry and the Men Responsible for Them" (unpublished manuscript in possession of the author), p. 68. Car shortages would be a continuing problem during the war. Charles S. Keith to Edward N. Hurley, Dec. 24, 1917, and James O. Heyworth to Keith, Jan. 3, 1918, both in Records of the U.S. Shipping Board, Construction Division, General File, RG 32, National Archives.

34. Clarkson, Industrial America in the World War, p. 421.

35. "Minutes of a Meeting of the Board of Directors of the Southern Pine Association Held at the Gayoso Hotel, Memphis, Tenn., Tuesday, April 24, 1917," SPA Records, Box 70b, 2-3. For a description of the mobilization structure established for the entire lumber industry see Cuff, War Industries Board, pp. 75-81.

36. "Report of Southern Pine Emergency Bureau," SPA Records, Box 84b.

37. Ibid.

38. Ibid.

39. Ibid.

40. "Pine and Patriotism: Official Report of the Third Annual Meeting of the Subscribers to the Southern Pine Association Held at Grunewald Hotel, New Orleans, Feb. 19, 20, 1918," SPA Records, Box 85b, p. 95.

41. Ibid.

42. Berckes, "Pitch in Pine," p. 68.

43. John M. Collier, The First Fifty Years of the Southern Pine Association, 1915-1965 (New Orleans: Southern Pine Association, 1965), p. 63. For materials relating to alleged SPA price-fixing and profiteering before, during, and after the war see File 60-160-21, Records of the Justice Department, RG 60, National Archives.

44. "Conference with Lumbermen Relative to Expediting Production of Lumber for Ships, Wednesday, August 1, 1917," typescript in Records of U.S. Shipping Board, Construction Division, General File, RG 32, National Archives.

45. "Report of Southern Pine Emergency Bureau," SPA Records, Box 84b.

46. "Before the Federal Trade Commission: Conference with Representatives of the Yellow Pine Lumber Industry, Federal Trade Commission Building, Washington, D. C., Oct. 30, 1917," SPA Records, Box 67a.

47. Report of the Federal Trade Commission on Lumber Manufacturers' Trade Associations, Incorporating Reports of January 10, 1921, June 9, 1921, February 15, 1922 (Washington, D. C.: Government Printing Office, 1922), pp. 15-19.

48. Clarkson, Industrial America in the World War, p. 423.

49. Report of the Federal Trade Commission on Lumber Manufacturers' Trade Associations, p. 20.

50. Baruch, American Industry in the War, p. 212.

51. Clarkson, Industrial American in the World War, pp. 423, 426.

52. Ibid., pp. 423, 425-26.

53. Baruch, American Industry in the War pp. 212-13; Report of the Federal Trade Commission on Lumber Manufacturers' Trade Associations, pp. 19-21.

54. "Report of Southern Pine Emergency Bureau," SPA Records, Box 84b.

55. Easton, "History of Texas Lumbering," p. 287; Soule, Prosperity Decade, p. 31.

56. "Government Takes All Long Leaf Timbers," Gulf Coast Lumberman, V (Oct. 15, 1917), p. 30.

57. "Government Conscripts All Lumber over 2 Inches Thick," Gulf Coast Lumbermen, V (Nov. 15, 1917), p. 22; W. H. Sullivan to Admiral W. L. Capps, Oct. 31, 1917, records of the U.S. Shipping Board, Construction Division, General File, RG 32, National Archives.

58. Berckes, "Pitch in Pine, " pp. 69-70.

59. "Forcing Ship Timber Production," Gulf Coast Lumberman, V (Nov. 15, 1917), 22.

60. Berckes, "Pitch in Pine," pp. 69-70.

61. Directors, Southern Pine Association, to Long Leaf Southern Pine Manufacturers, Members of Southern Pine Association, and Those Who Are Not Members, Nov. 3, 1917, Frank A. Browne, Memorandum for Admiral Capps, Nov. 3, 1917, Charles Piez, Memorandum for Mr. Hurley, Edward N. Hurley to W. H. Sullivan, Dec. 1, 1917, all in records of the U.S. Shipping Board, Construction Division, General File, RG 32, National Archives.

62. Hearings on S. 170, pp. 24-25.

63. "Pine and Patriotism," SPA Records, Box 85b, pp. 111-12. On Feb. 1 the SPEB promised to deliver sizable quantities of timber if the Western fir producers would supply some of the longer sizes. Southern Pine Emergency Bureau to James O. Hayworth, Feb. 1, 1918, records of the U.S. Shipping Board, Wood Ship Division, RG 32, National Archives.

64. Charles S. Keith to Long Leaf Yellow Pine Manufacturers, Nov. 3, 1917, records of the U.S. Shipping Board, Construction Division, General File, RG 32, National Archives.

65. Berckes, "Pitch in Pine," p. 70.

66. Richard H. Edmonds to John Henry Kirby, Feb. 25, 1918, John Henry Kirby Papers, Box 144 (University of Houston Library, Houston, Tex.). Collection hereafter cited as Kirby Papers.

67. Frank Comstock to Wood Beal, Mar. 9, 1918, Kirby Papers, Box 192. However, another official found

widespread violations of the embargo on large-size timbers and many other problems among other firms. C. F. Holek to Mr. Haynen, Jan. 3, 1918, Records of the U.S. Shipping Board, Construction Division, RG 32, National Archives.

68. "Southern Pine Association Third Annual Mass Meeting Held at New Orleans, La., February 19 and 20, 1918," Lumber World Review (Feb. 25, 1918) (reprint in SPA Records, Box 9a).

69. "Pine and Patriotism," SPA Records, Box 85b, p. 108.

70. Ibid., p. 111. In March, Emergency Fleet Corporation Logging Officer Wood Beal reported very favorably on the Southern lumbermen's war efforts. Wood Beal to James O. Heyworth, Mar. 8, 1918, Records of the U.S. Shipping Board, Wood Ship Division, RG 32, National Archives.

71. Mary Lasswell, John Henry Kirby, Prince of the Pines (Austin, Tex.: Encino Press, 1967), pp. 160–61. For a study of a more prominent "dollar-a-year man" see Robert D. Cuff, "A 'Dollar-a-Year Man' in Government: George N. Peek and the War Industries Board," Business History Review, XLI (Winter, 1967), 404–20. Cuff also has valuable discussions of the entire concept of "voluntarism" during the war in "Bernard Baruch: Symbol and Myth in Industrial Mobilization," Business History Review, XLIII (Summer, 1969), 115–33, and "Herbert Hoover, The Ideology of Voluntarism and War Organization during the Great War," Journal of American History, LXIV (Sept., 1977), 358–72.

72. James O. Heyworth to John Henry Kirby, Mar. 11, 1918, Records of the U.S. Shipping Board, Wood Ship Division, RG 32, National Archives.

73. Lasswell, John Henry Kirby, p. 161. John Henry Kirby to Charles Piez, Mar. 25, 1918, Records of the U.S. Shipping Board, Construction Division, General File, RG 32, National Archives.

74. John Henry Kirby to James O. Heyworth, Mar. 13, 1919, Kirby Papers, Box 144.

75. F. L. Sanford to Duncan U. Fletcher, Mar. 12, 1918, Kirby Papers, Box 144; L. C. Boyle, "The Southern Pine Lumbermen's Co-operation in the National Wood Ship

Program, Statement on Behalf of the Southern Pine Association and Southern Pine Emergency Bureau, before the Committee on Commerce, United States Senate, Sixty-Fifth Congress, Second Session on S. Res. 170," SPA Records, Box 143b.

76. Boyle, "Southern Pine Lumbermen's Co-operation," SPA Records, Box 143b, p. 29.

77. Frank A. Brown to John H. Kirby, Mar. 15, 1918, Kirby Papers, Box 144.

78. Frank A. Brown memorandum to Charles Piez, Mar. 14, 1918, Records of U.S. Shipping Board, Construction Division, RG 32, National Archives.

79. J. E. Rhodes to Board of Directors, April 29, 1918, ibid.

80. "June 14, 1918. Maximum Prices for and Procedure for Distribution of Southern or Yellow Pine Lumber," ibid.

81. John H. Kirby to Charles Piez, June 15, 1918, ibid.

82. Ibid.

83. "Bulletin No. 38, June 25, 1918," Kirby Papers, Box 144.

84. Telegram (undated copy), Kirby Papers, Box 144.

85. B. M. Baruch to John Henry Kirby, June 28, 1918, Kirby Papers, Box 144.

86. John Henry Kirby to Charles S. Keith, June 29, 1918, Keith to Kirby, June 29, 1918, and Kirby to B. M. Baruch, June 30, 1918, all in Kirby Papers, Box 144.

87. Commercial Appeal (Memphis), June 29, 1918.

88. John Henry Kirby to Charles S. Keith, July 1, 1918, Kirby Papers, Box 144. The report that bothered Kirby quoted the Federal Trade Commission's report on profiteering, which charged southern pine producers with making unnecessary and unusually large profits "running as high as 121 per cent on the net investment." It claimed

that forty-eight southern pine companies had made an average profit on net investment of 17 percent during 1917 as opposed to only about 5 percent in 1916. During 1917, according to the report, 47 percent of the footage of the covered companies brought a profit of over 121 percent net on investment. Houston Post, June 3, 1918.

89. John Henry Kirby, R. A. Long, and F. W. Stevens to Members of the War Industries Board, July 3, 1918, Kirby Papers, Box 144.

90. John Henry Kirby to Charles S. Keith, July 10, 1918, Kirby Papers, Box 144.

91. Ibid.

92. Ibid.

93. Ibid.

94. John Henry Kirby, R. A. Long, and F. W. Stevens to the War Industries Board, July 9, 1918, Kirby Papers, Box 144.

95. Ibid.

96. "Exhibit 'C' Statement Filed by the Southern Pine Lumbermen before the War Industries Board," Kirby Papers, Box 144.

97. John H. Kirby to Charles S. Keith, July 10, 1918, Kirby Papers, Box 144.

98. "Exhibit 'D' Memorandum of Report by a Committee of the War Industries board Appointed to Hear the Protest Filed by the Southern Pine Lumbermen," Kirby Papers, Box 144.

99. John E. Rhodes to Manufacturers of Southern Pine, July 16, 1918, Kirby Papers, Box 144.

100. J. L. Ackerson to John Henry Kirby, July 16, 1918, Records of the U.S. Shipping Board, Construction Division, General File, RG 32, National Archives.

101. "Minutes of a Meeting of the Board of Directors of the Southern Pine Association Held at the Blackstone

Hotel, Chicago, Illinois, July 20, 1918," SPA Records, Box 70b, pp. 6-7.

102. Ibid., p. 7.

103. Ibid., p. 8.

104. This writer notes that the three SPA subscribers fought many battles with Charles Edgar of the War Industries Board. According to his account, Edgar "was a veteran in the industry and knew it from the woods to the dry-kiln. His old associates affected to think that he was a sort of trade traitor because he was adamant for fair prices. They made extraordinary efforts to get rid of him. Even Baruch thought at first that Edgar lacked diplomacy. But these men were not subjects for diplomacy. They drove to their ends with the brutal energy of a donkey engine jerking a lurching log through the forest. Baruch found that out later when they sought to batter him down. Then, like Edgar, he tossed diplomacy out of the window, and figuratively speaking, threw the three obstructionists after it. He refused to have anything to do with any bureau or committee which included them. Whereupon the axemen were retired to obscurity for the rest of the war. Thereupon the lumber sailing of the War Industries Board was smooth." Clarkson, Industrial America in the World War, pp. 423-24.

105. Bernard M. Baruch to R. A. Long, July 30, 1918, Kirby Papers, Box 144.

106. Charles Edgar to W. H. Sullivan, July 31, 1918, Kirby Papers, Box 144.

107. Both statements are attached to a letter from Charles Edgar to W. H. Sullivan, July 31, 1919, Kirby Papers, Box 144.

108. "Mr. Kirby and the Southern Pine Industry," Gulf Coast Lumberman, VI (Aug. 15, 1918), 9.

109. Globe and Commercial Advertiser (New York), July 31, 1918; John Henry Kirby to E. N. Hurley, Aug. 1, 1918, Records of the U. S. Shipping Board, Construction Division, General File, RG 32, National Archives. Kirby's formal notification of his dismissal came on Aug. 9. J. L.

Ackerson to John Henry Kirby, Aug. 9, 1918, Records of the U. S. Shipping Board, Construction Division, General File, RG 32, National Archives.

110. George R. Hicks to Southern Pine Mills, Nov. 1, 1919, Kurth Papers, Box 489 (Forest History Collections, Stephen F. Austin State University Library, Nacogdoches, Tex.).

111. "Report of Advisory Board to the Lumber Administrator of the U. S. Shipping Board, E.F.C.," Kirby Papers, Box 144.

112. Collier, First Fifty Years, p. 67. For an account of the difficulties of another "dollar-a-year man" in separating private from public affairs see Cuff, "George N. Peek," pp. 411-15.

113. Collier, First Fifty Years, p. 67-68.

114. Soule, Prosperity Decade, p. 81.

115. "Report of Southern Pine Emergency Bureau," SPA Records, Box 84b.

116. Ibid. The total southern pine production for 1917-18 was 24,384,464,000 board feet. "Southern Pine Production and Stocks Industry Totals," SPA Records, Box 12b.

117. James Boyd, "Gross Darkness Then Comes Dawn," SPA Records, Box 77a, p. 22.

118. Robert F. Himmelberg, "Business, Antitrust Policy, and the Industrial Board of the Department of Commerce, 1919," Business History Review, 42 (Spring, 1968), 1-23.

119. The relationship between World War I mobilization and the NRA is examined in Gerald Nash, "Experiments in Industrial Mobilization: WIB and NRA," Mid-America, XLV (July, 1963), 157-74.

4

The SPA and the NRA

The 1920s were years of mixed economic fortunes for the lumber industry. Profits lagged behind those in other industries, and processing facilities frequently stood inactive because the industry's persistent economic problem was overproduction. These problems were not confined to the South. The president of the West Coast Lumbermen's Association later recalled the depression in lumbering as stemming from overproduction, competition from other consumer products, and a "tremendous increase" in substitute materials.[1] There was also a tendency to cut timber without regard to market demand because of property tax burdens on timbered lands.[2]

The southern pine industry felt the impact of the Great Depression before it seriously affected many other sectors of the economy. Evidence of the nation's economic collapse appeared in industry statistics for 1930, which showed that lumber production had fallen below the figures for any year during the previous decade and SPA revenues declined drastically.[3] By 1931 the association had about 140 subscribers, who produced about one third of all southern pine.[4] There was a continuing problem with subscribers such as the Southern Pine, Temple, and Texas Long Leaf lumber companies of Texas and various concerns in other states who tried to leave the association because of financial difficulties.[5]

With revenues already on shaky ground before the depression, the association had to take some firm action to survive. The policies adopted were threefold: an attempt to get out of debt through special assessments and budget-cutting, an effort to bring small mills under the SPA banner, and expansion through amalgamation with the last remaining subregional association.[6]

In 1930 the SPA employed about sixty people and its 1929 net budget was over $600,000. By 1931 it was down to forty-five employees and revenues were declining drastically.[7] Within a year the association had cut all salaries 40 percent, dismissed additional staff members, and seriously curtailed its services.[8] By February, 1933, plans were underway to reduce the annual budget to $80,000, along with a fifth reduction in salaries until they were at only 50 percent of the January, 1930, level.[9] These and the efforts in other areas still seemed inadequate.

The Hoover administration proved no more effective than the southern pine manufacturers in dealing with the industry's problems. Characteristic of the government's approach was a note from the chief of the Commerce Department's Lumber Division, who requested the SPA president's assistance in carrying out the department's war against gloom and depression: "We are endeavoring to learn of hopeful and optimistic events happening in the industry, and it is our intention--where possible--to give such events publicity, thereby working toward a helpful change in the psychology of the public as a whole. We feel that now is the time to give publicity to all optimistic happenings. If you can send us such items as may come to your attention kindly drop me a line and let me know."[10]

The only significant action of the Hoover administration was the formation in 1930 of the U. S. Timber Conservation Board, which was to determine methods of dealing with overproduction in the lumber industry. The board issued statements recommending drastic reductions in inventories, assembled and published statistical data, and attempted to publicize new and neglected opportunities for the lumber industry. Even this scheme originated not with the administration, but with the National Lumber Manufacturers' Association.[11] The U. S. Timber Conservation Board ultimately recommended "regulation of timber cutting, mergers, state agreements and interstate compacts for control of production, and modification of the antitrust laws," plus sustained yield management of both public and privately owned lands.[12] The Southern Pine Association was represented on the board by John Henry Kirby of Houston and was also represented on the board's advisory committee.

Despite misgivings among its members, some of whom believed the U. S. Timber Conservation Board was a first step toward government control of the lumber industry, the Southern Pine Association attempted to comply with and garner support for the board's number one recommendation-- the reduction of excessive lumber stocks to restore a balance between supply and demand. Because of the vast number of small mills in the southern pine region and the necessity of getting the Timber Conservation Board's message to all of them, the SPA divided the entire southern pine territory into eleven districts with three-man committees of manufacturers supervising activities in each district. Frequently throughout the year, group meetings were held in the various districts to review business conditions and evaluate the performance of the mills. Although no effort was made to force agreements to curtail production, during 1932 southern pine manufacturers partially carried out the Timber Conservation Board's recommendations, cutting down their stocks on hand by some 25 percent.[13] However, voluntary action and recommendations were obviously not sufficient to deal with the problems ushered in or aggravated by the Great Depression. While production dropped, demand was lower than it had been in years.[14]

The industry was in serious difficulty, and in the absence of effective government action the SPA was working with its subscribers to develop depression-fighting weapons. Throughout the entire lumber industry there were plans and rumors of plans for the formation of joint selling agencies and mergers, all aimed at bringing production and consumption into balance. There was also strong agitation for a relaxation of the antitrust statutes to permit the industry to regulate itself and control production. The most important result of this movement was the introduction by Senator Gerald P. Nye of North Dakota of legislation calling for an investigation and possible revision of the antitrust laws. However, it was never passed. The industry's attempts to police itself were also largely ineffective, with the exception of the cooperative efforts with the U. S. Timber Conservation Board, which remained in effect until the beginning of the agitation which eventually led to the National Recovery Administration.[15]

During this period the association's long-time secretary-manager, H. C. Berckes, saw his subscribers undergoing what he regarded as a dangerous transformation.

119

The New South and the "New Competition"

At the beginning of 1932, Berckes had been vehemently opposed to the "infectious germ of government cooperation," which he feared was getting into even the bones of his subscribers, whom he described as "mostly good Democrats and believers in states rights . . . great individualists." He warned against the "encroachment of federal bureaus upon the operations of legitimate business" and lamented that if this viewpoint was lost, he did "not see much hope for businessmen to handle their own problems."[16] Berckes later recalled that "the industry . . . was seeing attitudes of free enterprise giving way to the necessity of firmer controls. Everyone was being conditioned by circumstances to the acceptance of regulation of prices and production. . . . All emphasis was on how to get controls—by government itself or by industry self-regulation."[17]

By the spring of 1933 and Franklin Delano Roosevelt's inauguration the vague outlines of a major effort to fight the depression began to appear, and it was becoming clear that trade associations would play an important role.[18] The Southern Pine Association's leaders were maintaining a close watch on developments in Washington, and they realized that for the SPA to be effective in industry affairs, and for it to be accepted by the federal government as truly and adequately representing all southern pine manufacturers, it would have to broaden its membership base. Thus in an effort to regain lost members and secure new ones, especially among smaller producers, the Southern Pine Association reduced its membership fees in February, 1933. This seemed to produce some immediate favorable results.[19]

During March, April, and May, 1933, the Southern Pine Association's officers, committees, and directors carefully observed developments in Washington. Anticipating the general outlines of what would become the National Industrial Recovery Act, the SPA kept the entire southern pine industry informed of the government's actions and of its own expectations through industry meetings, the trade papers, and the general press.[20]

The Southern Pine Association, like trade associations generally, had for many years favored the relaxation of the federal antitrust statutes in order to allow intelligent business planning or, in the case of the lumber industry, to enable manufacturers to bring production into balance with consumption and thereby stabilize prices.

120

Some associations, such as the Cotton Textile Institute, had conferred with the Hoover administration in the hope of working toward antitrust relaxation. The U. S. Chamber of Commerce had endorsed relaxation of the laws to permit business cooperation, with trade associations playing an important role, and President Gerard Swope of the General Electric Company had published a plea for production control through trade associations. The Swope plan and the Chamber of Commerce proposals advocated the concepts of work sharing and the adjustment of wages to bring purchasing power into balance with productivity, thus anticipating somewhat the provisions of the National Industrial Recovery Act.[21] The Window Glass Manufacturers' Association, the Cotton Textile Institute, and the National Lumber Manufacturers' Association were also deeply involved in an effort to induce the Supreme Court to change its interpretation of the antitrust statutes by filing a brief as amici curiae in the Appalachian Coals case in December, 1932. The court's decision, in March, 1933, seemed to permit trade association efforts to improve marketing conditions in the abnormal depression situation.[22]

Even before the Appalachian Coals case was decided, some trade association interests and individuals sought to persuade President-elect Roosevelt and his advisers to accept a general concept of industrial self-regulation through trade associations with a moderate amount of government supervision.[23] However, despite the economic crisis some prominent trade association figures involved in the negotiations were hesitant, because they feared they might not be able to withdraw after becoming involved in a full alliance with the government.[24] Although not directly involved, the Southern Pine Association apparently fell into this category. Secretary-Manager Berckes was pleased with the decision in the Appalachian Coals case and enthusiastically in favor of "cooperative action through our trade association, and of these various associations with each other," but he saw major threats to the nation's "greatly weakened business structure" coming from "the germs of communism" and "a rush to strong centralized government which in itself is fast placing the yoke of socialism upon business."[25]

By mid-April, 1933, President Roosevelt had apparently accepted the concept of production controls and cooperative efforts to eliminate wasteful competition. The National Industrial Recovery bill embodying this concept was drafted at the President's direction and was introduced in Congress on May 17, 1933.[26] The National Lumber Manufacturers' Association sponsored the formulation of a code of fair competition for the lumber and timber products industries and called a conference for the industry's various association officers and directors in Chicago on May 24 and 25 to make plans so they could act promptly when the new law went into effect. The secretaries and managers of the regional lumber associations met in Chicago on May 19. These meetings resulted in endorsement of a tentative code of fair competition. The National Industrial Recovery Act was passed and signed by the President on June 16.[27]

On June 7, 1933, nine days before the enactment of the National Industrial Recovery Act, the Southern Pine Association called an industry-wide meeting of southern pine manufacturers in New Orleans at which more than three hundred lumbermen learned about the provisions and ramifications of the pending legislation. SPA President C. C. Sheppard singled out as the "underlying principle" of the measure the "spreading and increasing employment of labor."[28] The association's legal counsel, R. C. Fulbright of Fulbright, Crooker, and Freemon in Houston, Texas, praised the expected appointment of General Hugh S. Johnson as administrator of the new law, describing him as a "hardboiled and unromantic" man who would be "fearless and fair and not truckle to any interests."[29] The lumbermen selected four prominent Southern Pine Association subscribers and empowered them to "commit the industry and to work with the government and other branches of the lumber industry" in hammering out the new economic relationships.[30] The meeting also approved the selection of the SPA to act as the industry's administrative agency and enlarged its board of directors to make it more representative of all geographical sections and classes of mills.[31]

Almost immediately after the National Industrial Recovery Act became law, the Southern Pine Association became involved in formal negotiations leading to the adoption of a code for the lumber industry. From June 27 through July 6, southern pine representatives met in Chicago with men from the other producing sections and the National Lumber Manufacturers' Association to formulate a code. The main accomplishment of the Chicago meeting was the formation of a twenty-man emergency national committee which was to consider a tentative lumber code and go to

Washington to represent the industry before the federal government.[32]

The emergency national committee completed work on a draft of a lumber code on July 9 and the following day presented it to National Recovery Administrator Hugh S. Johnson. The code regulated production, prices, wages and hours, and conservation policies. It was the product of representatives of a broadly dispersed industry with many producers, a great variety of lumber products, and widely divergent practices and conditions. As such it was a monument to the art of compromise. Hearings on the proposed code for all interested parties—industry, government, labor, and others—were scheduled for July 20.[33]

In the meantime, the Southern Pine Association prepared for the code's implementation. On July 13 the SPA board of directors held preliminary discussions about administering the code, noting particularly the necessity of enlarging the association's staff.[34] On August 4 the SPA mailed all southern pine manufacturers a form requesting a report of their production from 1925 through 1933, and on August 11 the association attempted to obtain a complete listing of all producers. The original effort netted nearly five thousand additional names. Anticipating final approval of the code, SPA President L. O. Crosby, the southern pine control committee, and industry officials divided the southern pine territory into twenty-eight districts and appointed local committees to handle code problems in each one.[35]

NRA Administrator Johnson approved the Lumber Code after it was revised, and the President signed it on August 19.[36] That night the SPA informed all southern pine manufacturers of the code's adoption and of the minimum wages of twenty-four cents an hour and maximum forty-hour work week that would become operative on August 22. The association also notified all manufacturers and SPA committees that there would be a meeting in New Orleans on August 25 and 26 to discuss the code and authorize steps for its proper administration.[37]

In late August, the Southern Pine Association received official notification from C. W. Bahr, the secretary and treasurer of the Lumber Code Authority, that the SPA had been "designated by the Lumber Code Authority as the agency for the administration of the Code in the Southern Pine Division."[38] The SPA board of directors immediately authorized the association's president and the

123

secretary-manager to appoint the necessary committees and establish the required facilities to administer the code. It accepted the finance committee's recommendations that, effective August 21, 1933, the SPA should collect a monthly code fee of fifteen cents per thousand feet on shipments. The secretary-manager reported to the board that the SPA was compiling the necessary statistics and information to determine production costs and permit the establishment of minimum prices for various items of southern pine lumber.[39]

The SPA-sponsored meeting in New Orleans on August 25 and 26 attracted over five hundred manufacturers from sixteen southern states. It was the largest meeting of lumbermen ever held in the South. Those present were enthusiastic about the new experiment and pledged their "active and sincere support to the provisions of the Code." Those provisions were completely explained to them by members of the committee who had been involved in the code's preparation in Washington. To further disseminate information about the new code, the SPA ordered 15,000 copies of it for distribution and circulated a press release describing developments at the meeting to the major wire services, trade journals, and newspapers throughout the southern pine area. It also arranged for meetings throughout the South for manufacturers who could not conveniently get to New Orleans.[40] Thirteen district and local meetings were held, with an SPA department head in attendance at each, between September 5 and 22. The meeting at Houston on September 12 attracted sixty Texas lumbermen.[41]

To administer the code in the southern pine region, the SPA set up an elaborate structure headed by the association through its board of directors and headquarters and field personnel. To make decisions and rulings on code matters, there was an eleven-man control committee. It included the chairmen of the four administrative committees and acted as the executive agency of the board of directors. The administrative committees were those on labor, production, cost protection, and trade practices and conservation. They handled the matters falling within their jurisdiction and made recommendations to the board of directors and control committee. Finally, there were three-to-ten-member district advisory committees for each district, with representatives of both large and small mills included on each. The district committees were to furnish information on conditions in their localities and make recommendations concerning individual mill problems, especially requests for exceptions from the administration's rulings. The SPA also assigned an inspector to each district and a supervisor for each state generally to check on conditions and enforcement and act as the association or code agency's official field representative.[42] At first, the cost of administering the code in the southern pine area was approximately $47,000 monthly.[43]

As the code was put into operation, SPA Secretary-Manager H. C. Berckes's attitude shifted from hostility to support. Shortly after the code's inception, he declared in an address before the American Trade Association Executives in Chicago that "for the first time the lumber industry feels that its conditions can be rectified, and that the Code provides the way out of chaos and misunderstanding. The lumber industry has faith in its program. . . ."[44]

The Southern Pine Association found new life with the advent of code administration. SPA publications praised the new effort at industry-government cooperation. The magnitude of the administrative task was enormous. Starting with some five thousand registered southern pine mills, by the end of the NRA experiment the SPA was supervising the activities of approximately twenty-two thousand different mill operations. The association's staff had been enlarged by about two hundred, and the amount of paperwork handled by the New Orleans office was staggering.[45]

Despite the bustle and reassurances of the association, however, from the very beginning administration of the Lumber Code was plagued with such difficulties as arriving at accurate production cost figures, disputes over production allotments, evasions of the labor provisions, and charges of discrimination against small mills. Basic to all these were the problems of devising administrative policies that would be equitable for the thousands of diverse units covered by the code in the southern pine region and of eliminating violations, particularly of the labor, production, and price requirements.[46] The Southern Lumberman, the leading southern trade journal, warned that compliance would be the key to the Lumber Code's success or failure. There was also open skepticism, such as that of the Alabama lumberman who warned that "this is not going to work, but its not going to be the fault of the W. T. Smith Lumber Company."[47]

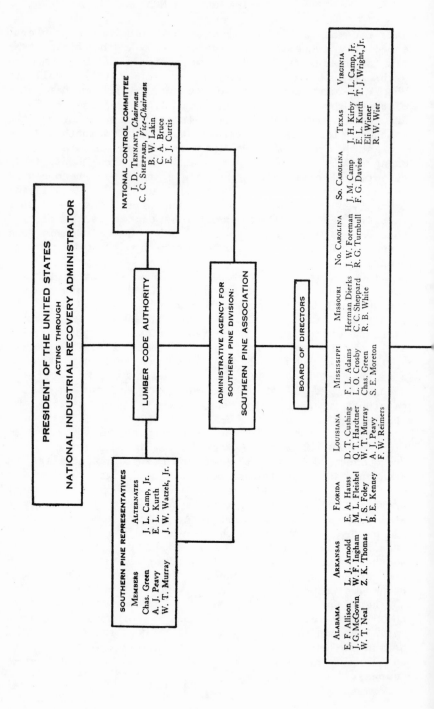

PRESIDENT OF THE UNITED STATES
ACTING THROUGH
NATIONAL INDUSTRIAL RECOVERY ADMINISTRATOR

NATIONAL CONTROL COMMITTEE
J. D. Tennant, *Chairman*
C. C. Sheppard, *Vice-Chairman*
B. W. Lakin
C. A. Bruce
E. J. Curtis

LUMBER CODE AUTHORITY

ADMINISTRATIVE AGENCY FOR
SOUTHERN PINE DIVISION:
SOUTHERN PINE ASSOCIATION

SOUTHERN PINE REPRESENTATIVES
MEMBERS   ALTERNATES
Chas. Green   J. L. Camp, Jr.
A. J. Peavy   E. L. Kurth
W. T. Murray   J. W. Wazek, Jr.

BOARD OF DIRECTORS

ALABAMA   ARKANSAS   FLORIDA   LOUISIANA   MISSISSIPPI   MISSOURI   No. CAROLINA   So. CAROLINA   TEXAS   VIRGINIA
E. F. Allison   L. J. Arnold   E. A. Hauss   D. T. Cushing   F. L. Adams   Herman Dierks   J. W. Foreman   J. M. Camp   J. H. Kirby   J. L. Camp, Jr.
J. G. McGowin   W. F. Ingham   M. L. Fleishel Q. T. Hardtner L. O. Crosby   C. C. Sheppard R. G. Turnbull F. G. Davies   E. L. Kurth   T. J. Wright, Jr.
W. T. Neal   Z. K. Thomas   J. S. Foley   W. T. Murray   Chas. Green   R. B. White   Eli Wiener
                                B. E. Kenney   A. J. Peavy   S. E. Moreton   R. W. Wier
                                                F. W. Reimers

126

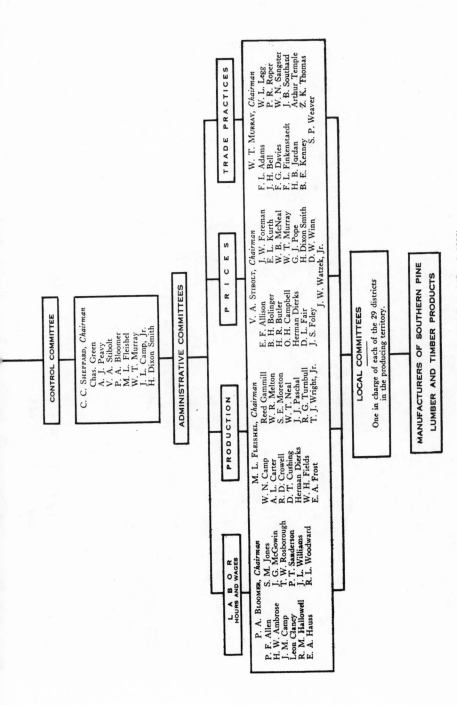

Source: *Southern Pine Division Code Bulletin,* I (Oct. 5, 1933).

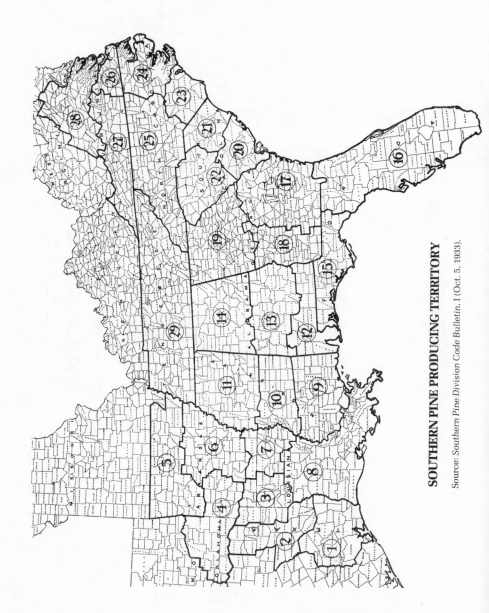

SOUTHERN PINE PRODUCING TERRITORY

Source: *Southern Pine Division Code Bulletin*, I (Oct. 5, 1933).

The lumber code provided for the establishment of minimum prices which were originally below the average cost of production, an extremely difficult thing to ascertain considering the thousands of different items, grades, and sizes made under the same operations. In addition, vast differences in efficiency and procedures among mills and the lack of complete statistics covering the entire industry, particularly the small producers, hampered efforts to fix equitable minimum price levels. Eventually, these prices were established at levels that would cover costs of production and the support of code administration, with differentials allowed for poorly equipped mills. Efforts to classify the mills in order to work out the differentials were a constant headache for the association and a frequent cause for complaints against the code administration, particularly from small mills.[48] To enforce the price provisions, the Southern Pine Association required weekly reports covering all orders booked from all mills under its jurisdiction. The accuracy of these reports was checked by field men who periodically inspected the mills' order files.[49]

The distribution of production allotments was an even touchier area. In line with the NRA's effort to bring production into line with consumption, the Lumber Code Authority attempted to determine for three-month periods the probable consumption of lumber and, based upon its findings, assigned production quotas to each of the divisions within the industry. There was naturally a good deal of competition between the producing regions for large quota allotments. The problem was particularly acute within the southern pine division because of the enormous number of small mills which began production after the creation of the National Recovery Administration. Eventually, there were some sixteen thousand small operations in the South applying to the Southern Pine Association for quotas, which they were given despite some strong industry sentiment for the development of a method to ensure they were not simply small fly-by-night operations organized to take advantage of the code. "Birth control" provisions of this sort were not adopted, and 4,200 new sawmills began operating within a few months after the code's adoption. The small mills were given their allotments, but nevertheless they did a good deal of grumbling about alleged discrimination in code administration in favor of the large producers.[50]

The New South and the "New Competition"

The Southern Pine Association had, of course,
purposely opened its meetings to all southern pine
manufacturers in an effort to qualify before the government as an effective and impartial code administration
agency and in order to defuse any possible charges of
discrimination which might have been lodged by non-SPA
mills functioning under the Lumber Code. Clearly, it
was anticipated that much of this opposition or activity
might come from the traditionally unorganized ranks of the
small operators. This opposition materialized in some
quarters almost from the very beginning of the code
administration, with charges of discrimination against
small mills in the administration of the NRA code, particularly with regard to production quotas. By
September, 1933, only a month after the SPA's official
designation as code agency for the Southern Pine Division,
efforts were underway in some areas of the South to organize yellow pine operators who were not members of any
other association into an organization to present the
views and needs of independent operators. One such effort
was extremely pointed in its organizational announcement,
noting that "through our legal department we intend to
present within the very near future to the Lumber Code
Authority in WASHINGTON (not the SPA) such suggestions as
are necessary for the continued operation of the independent saw mills, large and small, WITH THE LEAST
INTERFERENCE."[51]
The Southern Pine Association and the Lumber Code
Authority generally were fully aware of the small operators' criticisms and did their best to refute them, often
overstating their case in the process. By November,
1933, SPA Secretary-Manager H. C. Berckes was warning his
department heads that "prodded by southern Senators and
Representatives whose constituents are complaining," the
National Recovery Administration was undertaking an
investigation of the "beneficial and harmful effects of
the Lumber Code, particularly upon the smaller operators
in the South."[52] Since the investigation was carried out
by the code agencies themselves, its impartiality could be
open to serious question. However, by the end of the year
the information service of the National Lumber Manufacturer's Association had put out a release which noted that
the "correspondence of the Lumber Code Authority reveals
complaints and possibly somewhat of a widespread feeling
that the small lumber mill operators are being discriminated against through the administration of the Lumber

Code," but the release stated that "as viewed by the Code administrators . . . the Code is inherently and unavoidably favorable to the small operator and more burdensome to the large sawmills." The feelings of the small operators were attributed to their lack of knowledge of true conditions in the industry, which was played upon by "interested agencies of one kind or another," and "gossips and rumor mongers." Small mills were urged to make their grievances known to the proper Lumber Code agency, since "if there is one thing that the Lumber Code Authority desires above any other it is that the small operators shall be in fact a cooperative or constructive part of the lumber industry."[53] The assistant deputy administrator of the code argued that the SPA would give small mills a "square deal" and that it was "meeting small mill men more than half way."[54]

Small mill operators were not the only ones who found fault with the administration of the Lumber Code. From the very beginning, there was great concern from firms that were trying to live up to the code provisions about violations of the NRA requirements, particularly in the area of wages and hours of labor. The code had raised the minimum wage of southern pine workers by more than 100 percent from nearly twelve cents to twenty-four cents an hour, and compliance was a major problem that worsened as the code's life continued.[55] During the first stages of code administration, part of the problem was a shortage of field men. Early in the course of code administration, the SPA received a warning, which was to become familiar, that "unless we can coerce the unruly fellows into complying as to wages and hours, the fellows that are trying to live up to the law will become discouraged and also become violators."[56] The SPA's district manager in the North Carolina pine area reported about the same time that both small and large operators were concerned about enforcement, and he noted that "they are not of the opinion that the Southern Pine Association will be negligent, but they are fearful of the support that the Southern Pine Association will receive in their efforts to administer this law from the NRA administrators."[57]

The Southern Pine Division and the National Recovery Administration purposely were tolerant in enforcement during the early days of the lumber code, concentrating their efforts upon education and explanation. Under the NRA, there was originally a procedure for handling violations which culminated in the U. S. Department of

Justice's instructing the federal district attorney in the district concerned to institute court proceedings in cases of code violations. However, there was a good deal of caution and deliberation in code enforcement at both the regional and national levels. It was only after the general period of codemaking and education was ended, and after there was increasing concern about violations and noncompliance, that the National Recovery Administration permitted the lumber industry to set up its own enforcement agencies. Under this authority, the Southern Pine Trade Practice Complaints Committee began to function on June 15, 1934. The SPA and NRA officials believed, probably correctly, that many of the complaints about alleged violations were filed by people who were simply antagonistic toward the NRA. Many were extremely vague and indefinite. Most were groundless.[58]

As the Lumber Code Authority moved into its second year of operation, its efforts were increasingly directed toward defense of its policies and attempts to shore up enforcement. The old conflict over labor provisions and price controls became acute. In the Southern Pine Division the code administrators were never able to settle into a comfortable groove of routine operation. Much of the controversy in the southern lumber industry continued to be between large and small mills, with various small mill spokesmen claiming at various times that the Southern Pine Association as the NRA's code division discriminated against them.

The Southern Pine Association began the year with an effort to increase small mill representation on its board of directors and the administrative committees of the Lumber Code Authority's Southern Pine Division.[59] Nevertheless, the SPA continued to feel the wrath of many small producers. One small mill operator described the SPA and the Code Authority as "an organization built up by the large mills with a view to eliminating the small mills."[60] Another charged through his attorney that "the small saw mill men who make about seventy five percent of the lumber manufactured are not represented at all so far as the Code Authority is concerned" and that "the small saw mill man has already been entirely ignored from the beginning so far as the Code is concerned." This complainant leveled the recurring charge that "price fixing, higher wages, and various restrictions have already so hampered the little fellow, that he is

The SPA and the NRA

practically choked out of business."[61] Another small
operator complained that "my business is too insignificant
for the work required from N.R.A. lumber code. . . .
There is no market, & I get less than I did before all
this protection began. . . . I am just about ready to
quit everything, its all in favor of the capitolis [sic].
This irate correspondent returned a hotel reservation card
for the SPA's annual meeting with the scrawled question,
"Do they have any Transent homes for the average small
mill man?"[62]

While the Southern Pine Division and the SPA could
muster convincing evidence and testimony against the small
mill charges, there was sufficient interest in the matter
to provoke the NRA leadership into an investigation of
southern small mill conditions under the Lumber Code.
Public hearings were held by the National Recovery
Administration from January 9 to 13 in Washington to hear
complaints, which included charges by Georgia Congressman
M. C. Tarber that small mill operators in his district
were forced to shut down because of inability to pay code
wages, and by Congressman H. P. Fullmer from South
Carolina that it was impossible for small mill operators
in his district to operate under code wages. Tarber
asked for an investigation of small mill conditions in the
South. While the Southern Pine Division reported that
none of the complaints "were of a serious nature," the
National Recovery Administration considered them serious
enough to authorize an investigation.[63]

The investigation was requested by NRA Assistant
Administrator Alvin Brown on January 18, 1934. It was
undertaken by the Federal Trade Commission, which submitted its report to NRA Administrator General Hugh S.
Johnson on May 7, 1934. The investigation was to determine how the operation of the lumber code had affected
southern sawmills: had it made it impossible for them to
operate or had it made it possible for many of them to
resume operations; was it possible for the small mills to
obey code labor standards and still break even or earn a
profit; and were the prices received by the small operators held down by either the operation of the code or any
improper influence from the larger operators?

The study covered about two hundred and fifty individuals from Virginia, Tennessee, Arkansas, Missouri,
Louisiana, Florida, Georgia, South Carolina, and North
Carolina. The majority were small mill operators,
although large mill owners, wholesalers, retailers, and

owners of concentration yards were also visited. The FTC's investigation disclosed that the code had not made it impossible for sawmills to operate, and that it had made possible the opening of new mills, the reopening of old mills, and an increase in production. The commission also concluded that it was possible for small mill operators to pay code wage rates and still break even at the minimum code prices. It found no attempt by large operators to hold down the prices received by the small mill men. In fact, the Federal Trade Commission found that the Lumber Code had substantially increased prices. The report to the National Recovery Administration concluded by highly praising the officers and agents of the principal code agencies covered, including the Southern Pine Division, and noted an amazing lack of criticism from the small mill sectors concerning production allotments as evidence of the impartiality of code administration in the South.[64]

The Federal Trade Commission's rosy report could not, however, completely mask the continuing debates between small and large producers. At the Southern Pine Association's annual meeting in April there was a prolonged debate between representatives of the two groups over code price differentials which were adopted to protect small producers. The large mills by this time were charging that the lower prices charged by their smaller competitors under the lumber code were causing a shift in business away from the large mills. As a result of hearings on the matter in New Orleans from March 13 through 15, a special committee of three large and three small manufacturers drew up a plan for redefining the large and small categories and reducing the differentials to correct the situation. This plan was submitted to the SPA's board of directors at the annual meeting and adopted. Despite small mill representation on the committee that had drawn up the plan, there was strong opposition from the small mill sector and charges that changing the differentials would seriously hurt already wounded producers.[65]

On the other hand, in the wake of the SPA's annual meeting large mills continued to press their charges that the price differentials accorded small mills were so generous that the big operations were losing business. As a result of these protests, a Lumber Code Authority review board conducted hearings in Atlanta, Shreveport, and Jackson, Mississippi, to investigate the situation. Out

134

of these hearings the authority hoped to obtain the facts and figures necessary for an equitable adjustment.[66] The result of the hearings was basically the maintenance of rates worked out at the time of the Southern Pine Association's annual meeting, but some additional price advantages were given to the small mills.[67] Nevertheless, the Southern Pine Division continued to hear complaints from small mills on this and other matters.

Much of the criticism leveled against the Code Administration centered around lack of enforcement in all areas of the Lumber Code's concern, for instance prices, production quotas, and wages and hours. By the spring of 1934 the Southern Lumberman noted the lack of enforcement and praised plans underway to step up compliance efforts. The American Lumberman was running a series of stories under the headline "Compliance Becoming Chief Concern in Administering Lumber Codes."[68] Early in the year, the SPA board of directors requested that the Southern Pine Division's representatives on the Lumber Code Authority push for more rigid enforcement by the National Recovery Administration. By the time of the association's annual meeting in April, however, the compliance situation remained so bad that a leading figure in negotiating the code, C. C. Sheppard of Clarks, Louisiana, acknowledged that many of the lumbermen were "without hope with respect to the matter of compliance" and admitted that he could not "help but share your own [the lumbermen's] feeling of depression and disappointment that the [Roosevelt] Administration has moved so slowly and ineffectively and apparently without regard to the seriousness of the situation affecting this great industry." Sheppard noted, however, that, based on his contact with the administration, he knew that "they are making now an earnest effort and a more vigorous effort to reorganize their compliance set up," and he stated his "firm conviction that the Administration is determined to bring about compliance with our Code."[69] Not all industry figures were so confident. In an SPA labor committee session during the annual meeting, a prominent industry leader noted the widespread lack of enforcement and asked how one could expect the large majority who were complying "to continue this indefinitely when the Government apparently does not care to give the necessary enforcement assistance and, to add to our chagrin, it is reported that certain members of Congress give their approval to the acts of these non-conformists."[70] In June Deputy Code Administrator A. C. Dixon also pointed out the lack of enforcement.[71]

The New South and the "New Competition"

There was, in fact, increasing skepticism about the government's desire to institute vigorous enforcement of the code provisions, which the Southern Pine Division attributed to a "'Whisper' campaign to discredit the Lumber Code generally and to bring about a breakdown or elimination of minimum cost protection prices, being instigated in the main by a very small minority of manufacturers who are opposed to the Code and by certain individuals or groups who have a selfish motive in trying to break down Code prices." The division labeled as "unfounded gossip and rumors" reports that cost-protection prices and the lumber code generally were to be abandoned in the near future. It charged that "a very great percentage of the reports circulated concerning violations of the code and of selling below the established minimum prices, upon investigation have been proven to be entirely unfounded and the result of loose talk and willful misrepresentation on the part of persons having selfish motives."[72] Nevertheless, the SPA's district manager in the North Carolina pine area reported that large manufacturers were "rather skeptical regarding the possibility of the enforcement of the Code."[73]

By late June, 1934, when the Lumber Code Authority met, the compliance or enforcement problem was so serious that the authority appointed a committee to meet with General Hugh S. Johnson and urge a vigorous enforcement program. Johnson reassured the lumbermen, reaffirmed the administration's support of minimum prices for their products, and promised that the government would support Lumber Code enforcement efforts. By mid-August, one-third of the NRA's Compliance Division was working exclusively on Lumber Code violations. At the same time, the Southern Pine Division promised strict enforcement through its general and state trade complaints committees and an end to the "attitude of toleration of 'chiselers.'"[74] This pledge came none too soon for producers who were questioning the SPA's efforts.[75] From this time through the middle of September, the Southern Pine Association or Division was in full agreement with the view of Assistant Secretary-Manager Albert S. Boisfontaine that "there is no question but that vigorous steps must be taken with respect to enforcement," and according to him the Southern Pine Division's personnel were "really now concentrating all of our efforts in this direction."[76] These efforts were somewhat successful. During this period the Southern Pine Association pumped out an incessant stream of press releases reporting action against violators of the code's price-control and labor provisions.[77]

Despite the push for enforcement in the Southern Pine Division and from the national Lumber Code Authority, by the time the authority met in Chicago in early October, 1934, there were again strong rumblings from many quarters, particularly the West Coast producers, that the cost-protection program of the Lumber Code should be abandoned.[78] At an open Code Authority meeting on October 3, Executive Officer David T. Mason suggested four possible alternatives which were open to the industry: abandonment of the code, enforcement of the code as it then existed, maintenance of the code with the exception of wholesalers' discounts, or the elimination of cost-protection prices but maintenance of the remainder of the code. The Southern Pine Association's board of directors and the Southern Pine Division's code control committee met jointly the same day and voted that the Lumber Code be maintained with cost-protection prices, but strongly urged vigorous enforcement by the federal government. The Lumber Code Authority and the code survived the Chicago meetings intact, but the walls were beginning to crumble even as the industry's representatives met.[79]

On October 6, 1934, Federal Judge Harry B. Anderson of Memphis, Tennessee, granted an injunction restraining the U. S. District Attorney from proceeding with criminal prosecutions against hardwood lumbermen who were violating the minimum price provisions of the Lumber Code. His action was followed almost immediately by similar steps by federal judges in Mississippi and Texas. There was also continuing turmoil within the various producing regions over the question of maintaining cost-protection prices.[80] Both the Lumber Code Authority and the Southern Pine Association continued to calm the members and the industry and to reassure themselves. The SPA hailed the Chicago decisions to maintain the code and cost-protection prices and pledged even stricter enforcement. The Lumber Code Authority dismissed the importance of Judge Anderson's decision, noting that it applied only to that specific case, that it would be appealed, and that the temporary injunction did not relieve anyone of his responsibilities or obligations under the code.[81] Nevertheless, there was continuing agitation against cost-protection prices in all lumber-producing sections. By December the Southern Pine Association's board of directors and controls committee were reconsidering the

137

question and finally decided, because of the many difficulties in enforcement and the recent federal court decisions, to work toward the abandonment of Lumber Code Authority price controls. Very few in the industry were therefore surprised or disappointed when the National Industrial Recovery Board on December 22 announced the suspension of the cost-protection price program of the Lumber Code Authority. What remained, essentially, were production and wage and hour controls. The Southern Lumberman summarized the situation in a pessimistic editorial: "The whole problem boils down to one thing-- enforcement. If the Lumber Code had been vigorously enforced from the beginning it might have been a different story. If an actual effort at enforcement is made next year it may still be possible to salvage something from the wreck. One more year of slipshod enforcement like the one from which we have just emerged, and there won't be any Lumber Code."[82]

By 1935 almost complete disillusionment with the Lumber Code was evident in the Southern Pine Division. SPA Secretary-Manager H. C. Berckes, although calling for adherence to the provisions of the code, had reverted to his concern about the threat of government domination of business. Berckes urged the industry to regulate itself by upholding the code as an alternative to complete government regulation. In a statement before the SPA board of directors on January 28, the secretary-manager ominously noted that "when this cooperation between Government and Business was begun it was called 'a Partnership,' then later, 'industry self-regulation under Public Sanctions,' then 'with Government approval,' then 'under Government supervision,' next 'under Government regulation,' and now 'under Government control,' and the next remaining step is 'Government ownership.'"[83] During the board meeting, the SPA directors heard reports, considered many aspects of code administration, and reduced Southern Pine Division code fees from twenty cents to fifteen cents per thousand feet on shipments.[84] The SPA's annual meeting in March was similarly characterized by general disillusionment with the code experiment, and the 450 operators in attendance unanimously adopted a resolution calling for abandonment of the lumber code if it was not going to be vigorously enforced.[85]

By the end of the month, it was obvious that the code was not going to be enforced. In fact, the National Recovery Administration itself was in danger of collapse.

The situation was apparent when the Department of Justice announced that it was dropping a long-standing case involving violation of the Lumber Code. The code's administrative provisions extending discretionary powers to non-governmental agencies were under attack, and the department wished to wait for a review of this feature and new legislation before proceeding. The Lumber Code Authority commented on the Deparment of Justice's action, saying that, on the basis of confirmation from high administration quarters, enforcement of the code would be stopped, although technically it was still in effect.[86]

On March 26 the Lumber Code Authority decided that "for reasons of equity" the code should be suspended and it asked the various divisions to submit their views on the matter. The Southern Pine Association passed this information along to manufacturers in its area, and although thoroughly dissatisfied with the situation, promised to do everything possible to minimize the destructive effects of the government action and to maintain the industry's organization until matters cleared up. Everything now seemed to be pointing toward June 16, when the National Industrial Recovery Act was due to expire and would possibly be rewritten with the objectionable features eliminated.[87] On April 9, after a week of conferences, compliance with the provisions of the code was placed on a purely voluntary basis by the national control committee of the Lumber Code Authority, with the approval of the National Industrial Recovery Board.[88] When in May, 1935, the United States Supreme Court ended the procrastination and delay by unanimously ruling in the Schecter case that the NRA was unconstitutional, "few lumbermen mourned its passing."[89] H. C. Berckes said his industry viewed the decision "with satisfaction," and looked forward to "an era of relief from the uncertainty which has surrounded and retarded us for some time."[90]

In the southern pine industry the basic weakness of the code had obviously been a lack of enforcement, which was largely out of the control of the Southern Pine Association. The SPA itself, although subjected to periodic attacks especially from small producers, seems to have performed creditably in a difficult situation. In fact, even with regard to small producers the SPA's designation as code agency gave the association an interest in and entree into an increasingly important segment of the industry which might otherwise have lined up overwhelmingly in opposition to the industry's older leaders. Concerning the

The New South and the "New Competition"

provisions of the code, there were mixed feelings--those on conservation were essentially preserved and advocated voluntarily by the SPA and its industry, while attempts to reenact the wages and hours provisions by new legislation were bitterly resisted.[91]

The southern pine experiences differed somewhat from those in other industries. In the automobile industry the code was basically a labor code and it did not include any trade practice regulations. Thus, it had its major impact in forcing management to recognize employee grievances and formulate new labor relations policies with far-reaching implications for the future. However, during the code's life business had a much greater voice in the NRA "partnership" of government, industry, and labor than did organized labor.[92] If anything, the Lumber Code's positive influence on southern pine laborers was even less noticeable in its long-range impact.

In the cotton textile industry conditions also differed markedly from those of southern pine. The Cotton Textile Institute originally had greater influence over its industry than did the Southern Pine Association, and the Code Authority seemed not to have any major enforcement problems in the areas of production control, prices, or labor matters. As in the automobile industry cotton manufacturers had a much greater voice in code operations than either government or labor. There were differences, however, between the automobile industry, where there had been little or no trade association activity prior to 1933, the cotton textile industry, where there was a trade association, the Cotton Textile Institute, which sometimes acted somewhat independently of manufacturers in its own industry, and the southern pine industry, where the Southern Pine Association served as a service organization and seldom opposed the ideas of the large firms in the industry. The Cotton Textile Institute as the heart of the Code Authority had become, in effect, a policy-making body for its industry. In the wake of the code's demise it fell back into the role of being primarily a service agency for its members. The Southern Pine Association never really went beyond this function, even during its Code Authority period, and thus its institutional image and functions did not change so drastically with the end of the NRA.[93]

One student of the New Deal's attitudes and policies toward monopoly argues that in highly competitive industries the absence of governmental enforcement led to

140

the breakdown of the NRA codes and says that the problem was particularly acute in industries that had many units producing unstandardized products and in which there was easy access. Problems between industry factions and with competing substitute materials or products complicated such situations. This student cites the lumber industry as an excellent example of this situation. The experience of southern pine producers under the NRA strongly supports his arguments.[94]

There were in all 557 basic codes approved during the NRA era, and the lumber code was not necessarily representative. However, it does demonstrate one example of the NRA experience and when compared with the activities of other industries the southern pine story will provide students with a means of assessing the agency's overall performance. In any case, neither the actions of the southern pine industry and SPA leaders themselves nor the policies and programs of either the Hoover or Roosevelt administrations resolved the lumbermen's economic problems. For most, the solution would not come until the advent of defense production mobilization for World War II.

NOTES TO CHAPTER 4

1. Ellis Lucia, Head Rig: Story of the West Coast Lumber Industry (Portland, Ore.: Overland West Press, 1965), p. 169. For a brief general description of industry conditions see Ralph W. Hidy, Frank Ernest Hill, and Allan Nevins, Timber and Men: The Weyerhaeuser Story (New York: Macmillan, 1963), pp. 434-35.

2. A. C. Dixon et al., "History of the Code of Fair Competition for the Lumber and Timber Products Industries, Code No. 9, Approved August 19, 1933," Box 7573, pp. 322-23, Division of Review, National Recovery Administration Records, RG 9, National Archives. Hereafter cited as Dixon, "History of Lumber Code." Peter A. Stone et al., "NRA Work Materials 79: Economic Problems of the Lumber and Timber Products Industry" p. 48, Consolidated Reference Materials, Work Materials Prepared by the Division of Review, National Recovery Administration Records, RG 9, National Archives.

3. "Southern Pine Association and Stocks--Industry Totals," mimeographed report, Southern Pine Association Records, Box 72a (Louisiana State University Archives, Baton Rouge, La.). Collection hereafter cited as SPA Records. "Revenue from Fees," mimeographed report, SPA Records, Box 12b. This report shows that SPA revenues fell from $565,131.13 in 1928 to $369,292.11 in 1930.

4. "Economic Conditions in Southern Pine Industry" (Pamphlet presented by the Southern Pine Association to U. S. Conservation Board, July 1, 1931), SPA Records, Box 35a, pp. 32-33, 112. In 1929 the SPA had estimated there were about 7,090 southern pine mills in operation, and of those 239 were large mills producing at least six million feet annually. These large mills produced 47 percent of the industry's aggregate production, and it was operations of this sort that were generally subscribers of the SPA. Ibid., pp. 32-33.

5. "Minutes of a Meeting of the Board of Directors of the Southern Pine Association . . . March 21, 1932," SPA Records, Box 70b. Later in the year Ben S. Woodhead, president of the Beaumont Lumber Company, which had dropped out of the SPA, wrote to H. C. Berckes that his company was still using the association's emblem on its stationery because "we cannot afford to throw these letter-heads away, having bought 50,000 some years ago, when one of our officers thought he was at a convention and drunk; we are members in spirit, anyway." Woodhead to Berckes, Nov. 15, 1932, SPA Records, Box 39a.

6. H. C. Berckes to C. C. Sheppard, May 9, 1931, SPA Records, Box 39a.

7. Ibid.

8. "Minutes of a Meeting of the Board of Directors of the Southern Pine Association . . . March 21, 1932," SPA Records, Box 70b; H. C. Berckes to E. Mark Ferree, Apr. 20, 1932, SPA Records, Box 39b.

9. "Minutes of a Meeting of the Board of Directors of the Southern Pine Association . . . February 15, 1933," SPA Records, Box 70b.

The SPA and the NRA

10. Leighton H. Peebles to C. C. Sheppard, July 13, 1931, SPA Records, Box 11b.

11. Stone, "NRA Work Materials 79," pp. 247-49.

12. Hidy, Hill, and Nevins, Timber and Men, 435.

13. C. C. Sheppard, "Looking Forward with Lumber," SPA Records, Box 39a. At the end of 1931 a leading trade journal reported that because of "adherence to the policy of curtailed production . . . surplus stocks are being steadily reduced." Southern Lumberman, vol. 144, no. 1817 (Dec. 15, 1931), 50a.

14. Southern Lumberman, vol. 145, no. 1818 (Jan. 1, 1932), 61.

15. Stone, "NRA Work Materials 79," pp. 237-47, 250-52, 255-60; Hidy, Hill, and Nevins, Timber and Men, pp. 434-35; H. C. Berckes to Chairmen and Members of District Committees, July 25, 1932, SPA Records, Box 28a; Southern Pine Association to U. S. Timber Conservation Board, Sept. 19, 1932, SPA Records, Box 35a; Wayne S. Cole, Senator Gerald P. Nye and American Foreign Relations (Minneapolis: University of Minnesota Press, 1962), p. 55. Also see miscellaneous correspondence between H. C. Berckes and numerous southern pine industry figures in SPA Records, Box 39a. For a concise summary of the SPA's point of view on the difficulties of the antitrust situation see H. C. Berckes to W. DuB. Brookings, Aug. 22, 1932, SPA Records, Box 39a. There is a detailed account of the movement for antitrust revision during the early 1930s in Robert F. Himmelberg, The Origins of the National Recovery Administration: Business, Government, and the Trade Association Issue, 1921-1933 (New York: Fordham University Press, 1976), pp. 110-65.

16. H. C. Berckes to Merle Thorpe, Feb. 6, 1932, SPA Records, Box 39a.

17. H. C. Berckes, "The Pitch in Pine: A Story of the Traditions, Policies and Activities of the Southern Pine Industry and the Men Responsible for Them" (unpublished manuscript in possession of the author), p. 154.

18. For the relationship between the NRA and trade associations see President's Committee of Industrial Analysis, "A Report on the Operation of the National Recovery Administration, Which Has Been Prepared by Those Members of the Committee of Industrial Analysis Who Have No Official Relationship to the Government," pp. 78–104, mimeographed report in records of the Division of Industrial Economics, NRA Records, RG 9, National Archives. Report hereafter cited as CIA, "National Recovery Administration." This report appeared as House Document 158, 75th Congress, 1st Session, 1937. The Southern Lumberman suggested in June that prudent lumbermen would join the associations which had been "wondering whether they could much longer survive." Southern Lumberman, vol. 146, no. 1852 (June 1, 1933), 8.

19. "Minutes of a Meeting of the Board of Directors of the Southern Pine Association . . . February 15, 1933," SPA Records, Box 70b; Southern Lumberman, vol. 146, no. 1848 (Apr. 1, 1933), 13.

20. "Administration of the Lumber Code in the Southern Pine Division," Southern Pine Division Code Bulletin, I (June 16, 1934), 3 (copy in SPA Records, Box 103b).

21. Louis Galambos, Competition and Cooperation: The Emergence of a National Trade Association (Baltimore: Johns Hopkins University Press, 1966), pp. 176–84; Broadus Mitchell, Depression Decade: From New Era through New Deal, 1929–1941 (New York: Holt, Rinehart and Winston, 1947), p. 231; Himmelberg, Origins of the National Recovery Administration, pp. 125–35, 143–50; Robert Sobel, The Age of Giant Corporations: A Microeconomic History of American Business, 1914–1970 (Westport, Conn.: Greenwood Press, 1972), pp. 89–91.

22. Galambos, Competition and Cooperation, pp. 185–86, 191–92; Southern Lumberman, vol. 146, no. 1843 (Jan. 15, 1933), 13; and vol. 146, no. 1848 (Apr. 1, 1933), 10–11; Himmelberg, Origins of the National Recovery Administration, pp. 151–53.

23. Galambos, Competition and Cooperation, pp. 186–91, 192–95.

24. Ibid., pp. 190-91.

25. "Statement of Secretary-Manager to the Board of Directors of the Southern Pine Association, February 15, 1933" in "Minutes of a Meeting of the Board of Directors of the Southern Pine Association . . . February 15, 1933," SPA Records, Box 70b.

26. Mitchell, Depression Decade, p. 238. For an excellent analysis of the rise and decline of the NRA see Ellis W. Hawley, The New Deal and the Problem of Monopoly: A Study in Economic Ambivalence (Princeton, N.J.: Princeton University Press, 1966), pp. 19-146. A somewhat different interpretation of the NRA's origins is presented by Himmelberg, Origins of the National Recovery Administration, pp. 181-218. A work which concentrates on the labor experience under the NRA is Bernard Bellush, The Failure of the NRA (New York: W. W. Norton, 1975).

27. Dixon, "History of Lumber Code," pp. 42-45; Southern Lumberman, vol. 146, no. 1852 (June 1, 1933), 9. There is a brief account of the NRA story in Sobel, Age of Giant Corporations, pp. 103-8.

28. Berckes, "Pitch in Pine," p. 158; "Statement of Mr. Sheppard," SPA Records, Box 9b; Southern Lumberman, vol. 146, no. 1852 (June 1, 1933), 9, and vol. 146, no. 1853 (June 15, 1933), 9.

29. "Remarks of Mr. Fulbright," SPA Records, Box 9b. The guarded optimism of the speakers was reflected in the remarks of the assembled lumbermen at the mass meeting. A. J. Peavy of Shreveport, Louisiana, a long-time prominent SPA subscriber, vowed that there was no doubt that the lumbermen had "made a failure" in managing their own businesses, and he lamented that he didn't think the conditions they were presently in could be any worse. Charles Green of Laurel, Mississippi, noted that "our President is certainly making an effort to bring us back on our feet" and urged the lumbermen to "meet him halfway . . . the only way we can do it is to cooperate in this plan to the fullest extent, be broad-minded and overlook these difficulties and meet them as well as we possibly can." "Proceedings of Meeting of Subscribers to the Southern Pine Association and Other Representatives of the Southern Pine Industry Held at New Orleans, Louisiana, June 7, 1933," SPA Records, Box 68a.

30. Berckes, "Pitch in Pine," p. 158. There had been a similar mass meeting on May 9 that had chosen the original three-man steering committee, which was simply enlarged and continued on June 6. H. C. Berckes to Manufacturers of Southern Pine, June 8, 1933, SPA Records, Box 68a.

31. Berckes, "Pitch in Pine," p. 158. In preparing the industry for the mass meeting, SPA Secretary-Manager H. C. Berckes had written a pamphlet explaining the opportunities in the forthcoming National Industrial Recovery Act, but noting that it would also provide opportunities for "government officials and . . . an ever widening circle of economists, who see in the act an opportunity for exploiting long repressed theories and shades of philosophic thought that have flowered as the depression grew more serious." Berckes warned that many who were "enthusiastic about this New Deal for business . . . would have us cut loose permanently from the old order and embrace the new." "They hold that it is impossible for business to remain to any extent rooted in the old order while it gradually learns the new way," wrote Berckes. "The dangers before industry lie in this type of thinking; acute suffering has led many businessmen to adopt this view." The SPA secretary-manager also pointed out that it would be necessary to have compulsion to enforce the terms of the various codes, and that while "it is contemplated that this compulsion may come from within industry itself . . . lacking that will for self-government, even with the force of Law behind it, industry may expect direct government regulation to protect the willing cooperators from the recalcitrants. . . ." H. C. Berckes, "Southern Pine and the Industrial Recovery Act," SPA Records, Box 7.

32. "Administration of the Lumber Code in the Southern Pine Division," SPA Records, Box 103b, p. 3; Berckes, "Pitch in Pine," pp. 159-61; William B. Greeley, Forests and Men (Garden City, N.Y.: Doubleday, 1951), p. 134; Hidy, Hill, and Nevins, Timber and Men, p. 437; Lucia, Head Rig, p. 170; Dixon, "History of Lumber Code," pp. 45-47; Southern Lumberman, vol. 147, no. 1855 (July 15, 1933), 9-10.

33. "Administration of the Lumber Code in the Southern Pine Division," SPA Records, Box 103b, p. 3; Berckes, "Pitch in Pine," p. 163; Hidy, Hill, and Nevins, Timber

and Men, p. 437; Dixon, "History of Lumber Code," p. 47-48; Southern Lumberman, vol. 147, no. 1855 (July 15, 1933), 12-13.

34. "Administration of the Lumber Code in the Southern Pine Division," SPA Records, Box 103b, p. 3. The board also authorized the SPA secretary-manager to levy a five-cents-per-thousand-feet fee upon all mills, both subscribers and nonsubscribers, to pay for the costs of the Emergency National Committee and code preparation, with those paying the assessment being given credit "at such time as the Southern Pine Association will have the authority under the code to provide for a legal assessment." "Minutes of a Meeting of the Board of Directors of the Southern Pine Association Held at the Roosevelt Hotel, Thursday, July 13, 1933," SPA Records, Box 70b.

35. "Administration of the Lumber Code in the Southern Pine Division," SPA Records, Box 103b, p. 3; ASB (Albert S. Boisfontaine) to H. C. Berckes, Aug. 15, 1933, SPA Records, Box 40a. A form letter explaining the division of the southern pine area is attached to the Boisfontaine-Berckes letter.

36. Hidy, Hill, and Nevins, Timber and Men, p. 438; Hugh Johnson, The Blue Eagle from Egg to Earth (Garden City, N.Y.: Doubleday, Doran, 1935), p. 235; Dixon, "History of Lumber Code," p. 58. The major delay in Johnson's acceptance of the code was due to the wages and hours provisions. Southern Lumberman, vol. 147, no. 1856 (Aug. 1, 1933), 10-12, and vol. 147, no. 1857 (Aug. 15, 1933), 13.

37. "Administration of the Lumber Code in the Southern Pine Division," SPA Records, Box 103b, p. 3. The southern lumber industry was allowed a lower wage scale than other sections of the country in order to preserve existing and traditional competitive relationships.

38. C. W. Bahr to H. C. Berckes, Aug. 23, 1933, SPA Records, Box 70b.

39. "Minutes of a Meeting of the Board of Directors of the Southern Pine Association . . . August 25, 1933," SPA Records, Box 70b.

40. Ibid.; Southern Lumberman, vol. 147, no. 1858 (Sept. 1, 1933), 11-12.

41. "Minutes of a Meeting of the Board of Directors of the Southern Pine Association . . . August 25, 1933," SPA Records, Box 70b; Southern Pine Division Code Bulletin, I, no. 5 (Oct. 5, 1933)(copy in SPA Records, Box 103b); Southern Lumberman, vol. 147, no. 1859 (Sept. 15, 1933), 11.

42. "Minutes of a Meeting of the Board of Directors of the Southern Pine Association . . . August 25, 1933," SPA Records, Box 70b; Dixon, "History of Lumber Code," pp. 106-7.

43. "Minutes of a Meeting of the Board of Directors of the Southern Pine Association . . . August 25, 1933," SPA Records, Box 70b; "Monthly Budget Code Administration Southern Pine Association," SPA Records, Box 70b.

44. H. C. Berckes, "The Lumber Code and its Administration in the Southern Pine Industry: Address before the American Trade Association Executives, Chicago, Illinois, September 21, 1933," pamphlet published by the Southern Pine Association (copy in SPA Records, Box 7).

45. "Administration of the Lumber Code in the Southern Pine Division," SPA Records, Box 103b, p. 3.

46. For a discussion of the origins and development of NRA compliance efforts and an evaluation of their effectiveness see CIA, "National Recovery Administration," pp. 59-77.

47. Southern Lumberman, vol. 147, no. 1862 (Nov. 1, 1933), 10; Elwood R. Maunder, comp., James Greeley McGowin—South Alabama Lumberman: The Recollections of His Family (Santa Cruz, Calif.: Forest History Society, 1977), p. 52.

48. "Administration of the Lumber Code in the Southern Pine Division," SPA Records, Box 103b, pp. 9-12; Berckes, "Pitch in Pine," pp. 169-70; Dixon, "History of Lumber Code," pp. 324-25, 354-55.

49. "Administration of the Lumber Code in the Southern Pine Division," SPA Records, Box 103b, p. 13.

50. Ibid., p. 14; Dixon, "History of Lumber Code," pp. 77-78; interview with H. C. Berckes, Jan. 24, 1968.

51. "Independent Southern Pine Operators," Southern Pine Association circular, Sept., 1933 (copy in SPA Records, Box 40a). The Southern Lumberman warned from the beginning that the small mills would be a problem and should be treated fairly. Southern Lumberman, vol. 147, no. 1858 (Sept. 1, 1933), 10, and vol. 147, no. 1864 (Dec. 1, 1933), 10.

52. H. C. Berckes to All Departments, Nov. 25, 1933, SPA Records, Box 40a.

53. "Lumber Code Is Held Especially Helpful to Small Sawmill Operators," National Lumber Manufactuers' Association press release, Dec. 6, 1933 (copy in SPA Records, Box 36a).

54. Frederick F. Robinson to Luther Creason, Jan. 24, 1934, Box 3446, Consolidated Files on Industries Governed by Approved Codes, NRA Records, RG 9, National Archives.

55. Dixon, "History Of Lumber Code," pp. 293-95.

56. H. Dixon Smith to Albert S. Boisfontaine, Sept. 28, 1933, SPA Records, Box 40b.

57. G. L. Hume to H. C. Berckes, Sept. 25, 1933, SPA Records, Box 70b.

58. "Administration of the Lumber Code in the Southern Pine Division," SPA Records, Box 103b, pp. 25-27. It should also be noted that many industry sources and trade journals praised the SPA's performance. For example, a Southern Lumberman editorial lauded the association's performance as the NRA code agency. Southern Lumberman, vol. 147, no. 1860 (Oct. 1, 1933), 8.

59. "Minutes of a Meeting of the Board of Directors of the Southern Pine Association . . . January 5, 1934," SPA Records, Box 70a; Southern Lumberman, vol. 148, no. 1867 (Jan. 15, 1934), 9-10, 12.

60. A. P. Williams to Hon. John McDuffie, Mar. 4, 1934, Box 3446, Consolidated File of Industries Governed by Approved Codes, NRA Records, RG 9, National Archives.

The New South and the "New Competition"

61. A. D. Watson to H. C. Berckes, Mar. 6, 1934, SPA Records, Box 70a. Watson made the same charges in a Feb. 21, 1934, letter to Hugh S. Johnson, Box 3446, Consolidated Files of Industries Governed by Approved Codes, NRA Records, RG 9, National Archives.

62. J. H. Wells to Southern Pine Association, Mar. 29, 1934, SPA Records, Box 70a.

63. "Hearing before National Recovery Administrator," Southern Pine Division Code Bulletin, I (Jan. 27, 1934), 3 (copy in SPA Records, Box 103b). At least one small operator charged that a legitimate investigation of southern conditions undertaken by someone other than the Lumber Code Authority or the SPA would produce far more reliable information than the hearings. C. H. Armbrecht to Hugh Johnson, Jan. 16, 1934, Box 3446, Consolidated Files of Industries Governed by Approved Codes, NRA Records, RG 9, National Archives; Southern Lumberman, vol. 148, no. 1867 (Jan. 15, 1934), 11, 18A–18D.

64. Garland S. Ferguson, Jr., to General Hugh S. Johnson, May 7, 1934, and "Federal Trade Commission Memorandum on Effect of Lumber Code on Small Saw Mill Operators in the South," Box 3446, Consolidated Files of Industries Governed by Approved Codes, NRA Records, RG 9, National Archives. The FTC report is summarized and extracted in Southern Pine Division Code Bulletin, I (July 13, 1934), 10–13 (copy in SPA Records, Box 103b); Southern Lumberman, vol. 149, no. 1881 (Aug. 15, 1934), 24.

65. "General Session, Thursday Afternoon, April 5, 1934," typescript in SPA Records, Box 73b; "Memorandum for the Chief Examiner Re: Code Conferences and Annual Meeting of the Southern Pine Association in New Orleans on April 4–5, 1934," Box 8480, pp. 14–16, Central Records Miscellaneous Reports and Documents, NRA Records, RG 9, National Archives.

66. "Big Lumber Mills Complain of Small Mill Competition," National Lumber Manufacturers' Association press release, Apr. 17, 1934, SPA Records, Box 36a.

67. "Lumber Code Authority Grants Additional Differentials to Small Mills," National Lumber Manufacturers' Association press release, Apr. 29, 1934,

SPA Records, Box 36a; Dixon, "History of Lumber Code," pp. 330-31; Southern Lumberman, vol. 148, no. 1874 (May 1, 1934), 17.

68. Southern Lumberman, vol. 148, no. 1871 (Mar. 15, 1934), 12; American Lumberman, no. 3022 (May 26, 1934), 20-21.

69. "Minutes of a Meeting of the Control Committee, Southern Pine Association . . . February 26-27, 1934," SPA Records, Box 70a; "Proceedings of 19th Annual Meeting, Southern Pine Association . . . April 4 and 5, 1934," SPA Records, Box 73b.

70. "Minutes of a Meeting of the Southern Pine Association Labor Committee . . . April 4, 1934," SPA Records, Box 70a.

71. Dixon, "History of Lumber Code," p. 81.

72. "Minutes of a Meeting of the Control Committee, Southern Pine Association . . . May 23-24, 1934," SPA Records, Box 103b; Southern Pine Division Code Bulletin, I (May 31, 1934) (copy in SPA Records, Box 103b). The Southern Lumberman was still bemoaning the lack of enforcement. Southern Lumberman, vol. 148, no. 1873, (Apr. 15, 1934), 14.

73. G. L. Hume to H. C. Berckes, July 6, 1934, SPA Records, Box 40a.

74. "Prompt, Stern Enforcement Initiated In Southern Pine," Southern Pine Division Code Bulletin, I (Aug. 18, 1934), 1-2, 4 (copy in SPA Records, Box 103b); Southern Lumberman, vol. 149, no. 1878 (July 1, 1934), 14.

75. Resolution, Small Mill Pine Association, Aug. 7, 1934, Box 3247, Consolidated Files of Industries Governed by Approved Codes, NRA Records, RG 9, National Archives; Middleton L. Wooten to H. C. Berckes, Sept. 1, 1934, Box 3316, Consolidated Files of Industries Governed by Approved Codes, NRA Records, RG 9, National Archives.

76. Albert S. Boisfontaine to G. L. Hume, Aug. 29, 1934, SPA Records, Box 40a.

The New South and the "New Competition"

77. See several SPA press releases written during Aug. and Sept., 1934, in SPA Records, Box 103a. <u>Southern</u> <u>Lumberman</u>, vol. 149, no. 1883 (Sept. 15, 1934), 18, 23.

78. Hidy, Hill, and Nevins, <u>Timber and Men</u>, pp. 438-39; Lucia, <u>Head Rig</u>, pp. 172-73; Dixon, "History of Lumber Code," p. 338. There were also doubts about the Roosevelt administration's commitment to price regulation and continuing concern about enforcement. <u>Southern</u> <u>Lumberman</u>, vol. 149, no. 1883 (Sept. 15, 1934), 16, and vol. 149, no. 1884 (Oct. 1, 1934), 14.

79. "Minutes of the Board of Directors of the Southern Pine Association . . . October 3, 1934," SPA Records, Box 70a; <u>Southern Lumberman</u>, vol. 149, no. 1885 (Oct. 14, 1934), 17-18; <u>American Lumberman</u>, no. 3032 (Oct. 13, 1934), 18-29.

80. H. C. Berckes to Southern Pine Association Board of Directors, Nov. 30, 1934, SPA Records, Box 70a; "Anderson Decision In Tennessee No Barrier to Continued Price Compliance Program," <u>Southern Pine Division Code Bulletin</u>, I (Oct. 9, 1934) (copy in SPA Records, Box 103b); <u>Southern Lumberman</u>, vol. 149, no. 1885 (Oct. 15, 1934), 15, 16, 18; <u>American Lumberman</u>, no. 3032 (Oct. 13, 1934), 44.

81. "Price Compliance Campaign in Full Swing," <u>Southern Pine Division Code Bulletin</u>, I (Oct. 9, 1934) (copy in SPA Records, Box 103b); <u>Southern Lumberman</u>, vol. 149, no 1885 (Oct. 15, 1934), 19. By this time, however, the legal situation was so confused that the <u>Southern Lumberman</u> described the Lumber Code enforcement program as simply "marking time" until the Supreme Court could make a definitive ruling. <u>Southern Lumberman</u>, vol. 149, no. 1887 (Nov. 15, 1934), 15, 16, 17.

82. "Minutes of a Meeting of the Control Committee of the Southern Pine Association . . . December 9, 1934," SPA Records, Box 70a; "N.R.A. Suspends Cost Protection Prices; Reporting Of Sales Still Essential," <u>Southern Pine Division Code Bulletin</u>, I (Dec. 24, 1934) (copy in SPA Records, Box 103b); Dixon, "History of Lumber Code," pp. 82, 338; <u>Southern Lumberman</u>, vol. 150, no. 1884 (Jan. 1,

1935), 15-17; American Lumberman, no. 3038 (Jan. 5, 1935), 29-30.

83. "Statement to Board of Directors of the Southern Pine Association by H. C. Berckes, Secretary-Manager, New Orleans, January 28, 1935," SPA Records, Box 84b. Berckes's remarks were highly praised by the Southern Lumberman. Southern Lumberman, vol. 150, no. 1886 (Feb. 1, 1935), 16.

84. "Directors Set Annual Meeting of Southern Pine Association and Code Conferences for March 13 and 14; Code Fees Are Reduced 25 Per Cent," Southern Pine Division Code Bulletin, I (Feb. 6, 1935) (copy in SPA Records, Box 103b).

85. "Highlights of Code Conference and 20th Annual Meeting of Southern Pine Association Held in New Orleans, March 12 to 14, 1935," Southern Pine Division Code Bulletin, I (Mar. 20, 1935) (copy in SPA Records, Box 103b); Southern Lumberman, vol. 150, no. 1889 (Mar. 15, 1935), 19.

86. Southern Lumberman, vol. 150, no. 1890 (Apr. 1, 1935), 18-20.

87. "Present Situation of Lumber Code Resulting from Justice Department's Dismissal of Belcher Case Appeal before Supreme Court," Southern Pine Division Code Bulletin, I (Mar. 28, 1935) (copy in SPA Records, Box 103b).

88. Southern Pine Division Code Bulletin, I (Apr. 10, 1935); "Lumber Code Placed on Voluntary Compliance Basis by National Industrial Recovery Board," Southern Pine Division Code Bulletin, I (Apr. 13, 1935) (copies of both in SPA Records, Box 103b). The Southern Lumberman noted that "the Lumber Code has been made a political football" and that "to all intents and purposes the Lumber Code, as established in 1933, is dead." Southern Lumberman, vol. 150, no. 1897 (Apr. 15, 1935), 20.

89. Hidy, Hill, and Nevins, Timber and Men, 439.

90. Southern Lumberman, vol. 150, no. 1900 (June 1, 1935), 19.

The New South and the "New Competition"

91. Deputy Administrator A. C. Dixon listed inability to secure compliance as one of the major problems of the Code Authority, concluding that ironically "those who complied with the code made the least progress toward recovery." Dixon, "History Of Lumber Code," p. 92. Assistant Deputy Administrator C. Stowell Smith also considered compliance the major problem. Ibid., p. 117. For a manufacturer's view, see Maunder, James Greeley McGowin, pp. 52-54.

92. Sidney Fine, The Automobile under the Blue Eagle: Labor, Management, and the Automobile Manufacturing Code (Ann Arbor: University of Michigan Press, 1963), pp. vii, 427-30.

94. Hawley, New Deal and Monopoly, pp. 114-15. For information on the specifics of the lumber situation see Stone, "NRA Work Materials 79," pp. 103-10; Saul Nelson, "NRA Work Materials 56: Minimum Price Regulation under Codes of Fair Competition," pp. 49-54, 56; Consolidated Reference Materials, Work Materials Prepared by the Division of Review, National Recovery Administration Records, RG 9, National Archives; Herbert F. Taggert, Minimum Prices under the NRA (Ann Arbor: University of Michigan Press, 1936), pp. 52-54; A. C. Dixon et al., "NRA Code History 9" (Lumber), pp. 229-31, 260, Code History Files, NRA Records, RG 9, National Archives; C. A. Pearce, NRA Trade Practice Programs (New York: Columbia University Press, 1939), pp. 96-98; Business Week (Dec. 29, 1934), p. 12; and U. S. Senate, Committee on Finance, Investigation of the NRA, 75th Cong., 1st Sess., 1935, pp. 892-93. CIA, "National Recovery Administration," pp. 70-77, also presents a rather unfavorable assessment of NRA compliance efforts.

5

Statistics – the Heart
of a Trade Association

Gathering and disseminating statistical information among members have traditionally been at the heart of trade association activities. It has also been their most controversial function. From the members' viewpoint, the exchange of statistical information on production, prices, and stocks is seen as both sensible and socially beneficial, for it avoids waste and allows businessmen to plan more intelligently, thus benefiting them, the consumer, and society generally. From the critics' viewpoint, however, the exchange of such information within a closed membership is seen as promoting price-fixing and production controls and leading to oligopolistic or even monopolistic conditions in an industry.

From its inception the Southern Pine Association was deeply involved in statistical activities, and its fortunes rose and fell according to the changing public attitudes toward these functions and varying interpretations and enforcement attitudes with regard to the antitrust laws. Like many trade associations, the SPA walked a narrow line with respect to these laws.

Perhaps one of the reasons for the SPA's strong early interest in accounting and statistics was that President Charles S. Keith was an industry leader in statistical activities and knowledge. In addition, there was also the long tradition of other southern lumber trade associations, particularly the Yellow Pine Manufacturers' Association, which had emphasized statistical activities.

When it was established, the SPA organized a committee on accounting and statistics which was to supervise the gathering and dissemination of information about the accounting systems of association subscribers and to make studies of southern pine lumber production costs. The committee was also to direct the compilation of statistics on southern pine production, shipments, and stocks on hand. To assist the committee in the performance of these functions, the SPA established a statistical department.[1]

While actual SPA operations in accounting and statistics varied, they were typified by and centered around activities such as the preparation of a publication called The Weekly Trade Barometer, which was distributed to all subscribers and other interested parties. The Barometer was a prototype which was later picked up and copied by other associations and trade journals. It showed the production, orders, and shipments of SPA subscribers during the week and, in the eyes of the Federal Trade Commission, served as "a device . . . by which, through concerted action, the association instructs its membership how to restrict production and thereby to increase the price of lumber, by an artificial control of supply as balanced against current demand."[2]

The Barometer in its original form had contained devices to tell producers whether the market was advancing or declining and whether they should increase or decrease production. The memory of the YPMA's experience was still fresh in the minds of many subscribers, however, and direct words of advice were taken off the barometers. However, the lessons remained graphically clear so that, as Keith said, "while we are not advising our people what to do, the barometer itself will tell the story."[3] On the other hand, the accounting and statistics committee, which had been planning in 1916 to prepare a compilation of prices at which lumber had sold by SPA subscribers, received very little cooperation, primarily because of the subscribers' fear of running afoul of state and federal antitrust laws.[4]

The following year the association established statistical exchanges at Kansas City, Missouri; Hattiesburg, Mississippi; Alexandria, Louisiana; and Little Rock, Arkansas, to receive, compile, and disseminate information on prices charged for lumber products by cooperating mills. These exchanges reported their price summaries to the SPA, which consolidated them for distribution among its subscribers.[5] The Federal Trade Commission questioned the legality of this price reporting system, but it was defended by the SPA and nothing was done immediately to alter or eliminate its operations.[6]

Nevertheless, the FTC was convinced that the Southern Pine Association and its leaders, often acting in conjunction with lumber trade journals, were "busily engaged in a movement not only to curtail production but to advance prices."[7] These activities, getting under way in the formative years of the SPA, erupted into major controversies during and after World War I as the association and its leaders were lashed with stinging charges of failing wholeheartedly to support the defense effort and of war profiteering.

During the war the federal government relied heavily on trade associations to mobilize their industries for defense production. It seemed that the associations had every reason to look forward to a continued friendly relationship with the government which had utilized their cooperative efforts and statistical services during the period of crisis.[8] In the post-war period the trade associations began to expand their activities, and in the lumber industry some organizations were emphasizing statistical activities built around the open-competition ideas of Arthur Jerome Eddy. The Federal Trade Commission had not issued a clear statement concerning the plan's legality, but statements by government officials and the experience of the war seemed to give every indication that such activities would be approved and possibly even encouraged.[9]

Southern pine manufacturers were still chastened by their experience in the Missouri Ouster Suit and did not openly take the position of a Hardwood Manufacturers' Association spokesman who volunteered to the Federal Trade Commission that price stabilization was one of the objectives of his organization and that "this can be attained by hardwood manufacturers keeping thoroughly informed about prices at actual sales, stocks on hand, and other data."[10] Nevertheless, in addition to its Weekly Barometer, the SPA in 1918 added a Monthly Barometer, which indicated stocks on hand; a Monthly Statistical Statement, which supplied data on production, shipments, stocks, and unfilled orders; a Monthly Statement of Costs; and, perhaps most significantly, a Sales Report, which gave prices at which lumber had been recently sold and thus represented an up-to-date reflection of market conditions. These publications were distributed to association subscribers, trade papers, and other interested news media and provided the statistical information required by the open-competition system.[11]

The New South and the "New Competition"

By 1919, however, the federal government was taking a closer look at those trade associations openly practicing the "open-competition" or "open-price" plan. The Wilson administration was concerned about the rising cost of living, and the President reported to Congress that "there is reason to believe that the prices of leather, of coal, of lumber, and of textiles have been materially affected by forms of concern and co-operation among the producers and marketers."[12] Some segments of the lumber industry were troubled. A major lumber journal pointed out that "the unbiased, unembellished fact must be taken into consideration, that the lumber industry must deal with the public--and the public cannot be damned."[13]

In September, 1919, the U. S. Attorney General requested the Federal Trade Commission to continue and bring up-to-date the investigation of the lumber industry begun prior to World War I under the Department of Commerce's Bureau of Corporations. The FTC resolved to conduct the investigation, and on November 26 the commission's examiner requested access to the files and records of the Southern Pine Association. Secretary-Manager John E. Rhodes submitted the minutes of board of directors' meetings and the printed reports of the annual meetings since the organization's incorporation to the FTC's examiners. He stated that he wanted to submit the matter to his board of directors before producing additional records. Southern Pine Association Chief Counsel John H. Lucas recommended that the examiners be allowed access to all SPA records, and the board endorsed Rhodes's conduct of the matter and Lucas's recommendations. Former Missouri Attorney General Louis C. Boyle was the national lumber industry's attorney, and he endorsed the SPA's position, stating that he believed the Federal Trade Commission intended to conduct a thorough and fair investigation.[14] Nevertheless, when the SPA was asked by a U. S. Senate subcommittee which was investigating the FTC to evaluate its conduct in examining the association, Rhodes replied that, while the attitude of the examiners seemed fair, there was no way to predict the outcome of their report since "there is reason to believe that the examiners proceeded in the erroneous assumption that the association was endeavoring to conceal something from them. This was unjust, unfair and untrue."[15]

The first results of the Federal Trade Commission's investigations came in February, 1920, when the Department of Justice applied for a preliminary injunction against

158

the American Hardwood Manufacturers' Association and its members who had been actively involved in "open-price" activities. The accused were charged with "combining and conspiring together to suppress competition among themselves, and to enhance their selling prices . . . in restraint of interstate commerce."[16] The case against the hardware producers directly affected many southern piners who also produced hardwoods, and, of course, also posed an indirect threat to the activities of the Southern Pine Association.[17]

On March 16, 1920, a temporary injunction was granted by Judge John E. McCall of the Federal District Court of West Tennessee, who condemned the "open-competition" plan as an illegal restraint of trade. The Justice Department threatened to take legal action against statistical activities, and Attorney General A. Mitchell Palmer warned members of similar organizations to withdraw.[18] In October, the producers appealed their case to the Supreme Court, expecting a decision early in 1921.[19]

Southern Pine Association subscribers gathered for their annual meeting just after the injunction was issued. They heard John H. Lucas state that he could see nothing in the case which would apply to their organization. However, the Federal Trade Commission's agents had been actively at work in the records of the Southern Pine Association and its subscribers for weeks, and in 1921 and 1922 the FTC submitted three reports charging that through trade groups, including the SPA, the lumber industry was controlling prices and production, to the detriment of competition.[20]

The Southern Pine Association's optimism at the 1920 annual meeting proved to be unwarranted. By the time of the following year's session, the FTC investigations had resulted in an injunction suit by the government against the SPA and other defendants, including forty-eight subscribing Southern Pine Association corporations, seven other lumber-producing corporations, sixty-one individuals, and six trade newspapers, to stop the exchange of information which could contribute to price-fixing. The suit was filed in the Federal District Court of the Eastern District of Missouri charging violations of the Sherman Antitrust Act. The SPA board of directors immediately authorized John H. Lucas to employ as many associates as necessary to prepare the association's case. To cooperate with the lawyers the board formed a committee who included Stanley Horn, editor of the Southern Lumberman, representing the trade papers charged in the suit.[21]

At the association's annual meeting in April, President A. L. Clark testified that "neither your Directors, nor any one, at any meeting or at any other time or place, have ever in my presence or to my knowledge, discussed, connived or planned any agreement or movement to control or affect prices, production, running time, or curtailment, nor have I ever had knowledge of any such by anybody else, or for anybody else."[22] Judge John H. Lucas also reviewed the history of the association, attacking the agents and "those who assume to represent the Government that belongs to you and to me" and reiterating his belief that the SPA and its subscribers were innocent of any wrongdoing. Lucas's speech was frequently interrupted with applause. His final suggestion that the SPA re-elect its current officers as a demonstration that it had nothing to be ashamed of or to hide was greeted with a standing ovation.[23] The subscribers re-elected their directors with instructions to continue the existing officers in their positions and voted a special assessment of three cents per thousand feet on their lumber shipments for the remainder of 1921 to meet the legal expenses of fighting the government suit.[24] Lucas employed four additional lawyers, including former U. S. Senator Joseph W. Bailey of Dallas, Texas, to assist him in preparing the case.[25]

An ironic and probably not accidental factor in the Southern Pine Association injunction suit was the fact that it was filed before Federal Judge Charles B. Farris, who had rendered the decision in the Missouri Ouster Case against the Yellow Pine Manufacturers' Association. The Southern Pine Association and Judge Lucas believed that the suit had purposely been brought before Farris because of his unfavorable decision in the earlier case. However, Judge Farris refused to accept jurisdiction, and the case was transferred to the U. S. Court for the District of Kansas City.[26]

In June special agents of the Department of Justice requested permission to examine the association's records after the date the FTC's investigation was concluded in February, 1920, and the SPA board of directors agreed. The board also approved the payment of $12,500 to former Senator Joseph W. Bailey for his legal services, with an additional $12,500 to come if the action had to be appealed to the U. S. Supreme Court. At this time the association did not expect that its case would be heard until after the decision in the hardwood producers' case, which was set for reargument before the Supreme Court in October.[27]

The rehearing of the hardwood case took place on schedule in October, and on December 19, 1921, with Justices Brandeis, McKenna, and Holmes dissenting, the Supreme Court upheld the lower court's decision that the statistical activities and "open-competition" plan of the American Hardwood Manufacturers' Association constituted a combination in restraint of interstate commerce. The decision was attacked by Justice Brandeis as an encouragement of amalgamation in business, and by Justice Holmes as a violation of free speech. It was denounced by almost all the legal journals.[28]

John E. Rhodes quickly pointed out to his staff that the decision did not directly affect the Southern Pine Association injunction suit because the cases were not similar. Rhondes said that if after study it became apparent that the scope of the decision was as broad as some newspapers indicated, it might be necessary to amend the Sherman Antitrust Act, so that businessmen could legally pursue their activities. The secretary-manager was careful to note that "the Southern Pine Association has never conducted any work similar to the Open Competition Plan now enjoined, nor has it issued price lists, or undertaken to advise its subscribers concerning prices to be asked." Rhodes conceded that "the Association has compiled statistics of production, orders, and shipments, and stocks on hand similar to statistical publications of nearly 4,000 trade organizations in the United States."[29] Rhodes advised his subordinates that the association intended to continue its regular work "until our attorneys have conferred with Attorney General Daugherty, and decided to either ask him to go ahead with the suit, or agree to discontinue some of our statistics."[30] The secretary-manager's interpretation of the situation contrasted sharply with that of FTC attorney and examiner Walter B. Wooden, who said that "the decision will make the outcome of the Southern Pine case a foregone certainty." Wooden went on to state, "I should expect the Southern Pine Association to accept almost any sort of a consent decree and save themselves the expense of a contest, which would only serve to bring out how much farther that organization has gone than the Hardwood Association."[31]

The New South and the "New Competition"

Attorney General Harry Daugherty was delighted with
the decision against the hardwood manufacturers, observing
that "the ostensible object [of their association] was
competition, but the real object was the exact
opposite."[32] At this time, however, an open split was
beginning to appear within the ranks of the Harding
cabinet. In April, the President had recommended legislation to curtail the activities of trade associations on
the basis of information that the FTC attributed "the
failure to adjust consumers' costs to basic production
costs to the exchange of information by 'open price
associations,' which operate, evidently, within the law,
to the very great advantage of their members and equal
disadvantage to the consuming public." At the same time,
Secretary of Commerce Herbert Hoover was taking the position that "our trade associations must be encouraged and
supported if America is to hold her own."[33]
    Just when the Southern Pine Association was operating
under the threat of its own injunction suit and the
hardwood manufacturers were reaching the end of theirs,
the Secretary of Commerce was holding conferences in
Washington with representatives of the lumber industry
"for the purpose of working out some plan whereby statistics and information concerning production, stock,
consumption, etc., in the lumber industry, could be
gathered and made available to the public."[34] On the eve
of the decision in the hardwood case, Hoover addressed a
trade association and stated his belief "that the trade
associations have been unduly criticized, and that they do
contain in them a tremendous possibility, and, in fact,
the only avenue that I can see by which the Government can
get into contact with the trades in the mutual advancement
of some of our most fundamental interests. . . ."[35]
    The following year, Hoover pressed for rapprochement
with Daugherty, hoping to soften the administration's
antitrust position. Early in February, 1922, he inaugurated formal correspondence with Daugherty attempting to
get a firm statement with regard to the legality of a
number of trade association activities, including the
gathering and dissemination of statistics. Daugherty
refused to commit himself absolutely, noting that "it is
impossible to determine in advance just what the effect of
a plan when put into actual operation may be. This is
especially true with reference to trade associations,
whose members are vitally interested in advancing or, as
they term it, stabilizing prices, and who through the

medium of associations are brought into personal contact with each other." Daugherty concluded that "the expression of the view that the things enumerated by you, with the exceptions stated, may be done lawfully is only tentative. . . ."[36] The Attorney General did not even agree that statistical activities conducted through the Department of Commerce were legal until 1923.[37]

Nevertheless, the lumber industry chose to put a favorable light on Daugherty's letters to Hoover. Secretary-Manager Wilson Compton of the National Lumber Manufacturers' Association expressed his belief that trade associations could lawfully gather detailed information on production, orders, shipments, stocks, and prices from individual subscribers, but that this information could not be given to the public or distributed to the members, although general information based on compilations and averages of the same materials could be published.[38] John E. Rhodes informed his subscribers that "the Attorney-General, strongly emphasizing the value of trade associations . . . declared that the collection and dissemination of statistical information is not in itself a violation of the law."[39]

Meanwhile, the Southern Pine Association continued its friendly relationship with Hoover, kept close tabs on its own injunction suit, and rather than curtailing its program, began seriously to consider expanding its statistical facilities. In March, 1922, the board of directors authorized the creation of a committee to go to Washington, at Secretary Hoover's invitation, to consider methods by which the Department of Commerce could distribute statistical reports compiled by trade associations.[40] That same month, John H. Lucas met with Assistant Attorney General J. A. Fowler, who was in charge of the Southern Pine Association's case, and, on the basis of their discussion, predicted to the SPA's annual meeting that the case would be dismissed; he recommended that the SPA not discontinue any of its activities.[41] In fact, later in the year Lucas advised that it woudd be legal for the Southern Pine Association to expand its statistical exchanges in the South, and at the end of the year the SPA board authorized a plan for doing so.[42] In December, Judge Lucas reported to the association's board that the assistant attorney general had suggested that the SPA submit proposals for the issuance of a decree which would satisfactorily dispose of its case, and that the organization's attorneys were engaged in preparing them.[43]

The New South and the "New Competition"

As the discussions and negotiations concerning the
Southern Pine Association's injunction suit continued,
the SPA entered the middle 1920s fully cognizant of the
government's activities on other fronts.   In 1923 the
Supreme Court rendered a decision in the American
Linseed Oil Company case that followed the hardwood case
closely.[44]   As in the earlier case, the Southern Pine
Association concluded that there was very little in its
activities that would be affected.[45]   During 1923 and 1924
SPA lawyers and the Department of Justice conferred about
the possibility of a consent decree as a means of dis-
posing of the injunction suit.   The association would
admit to nothing in its activities that it considered
illegal and that it was willing to discontinue, so both
parties agreed that a trial would be necessary.[46]
In 1925 the legal climate changed considerably in both
the Department of Justice and the Supreme Court. Harry M.
Daugherty had been replaced at the Department of Justice
by Harlan Fiske Stone, whose appointment was lauded before
the SPA's mid-summer meeting as evidence that "the
Government is getting better and better all this time."[47]
The Supreme Court also showed a change of disposition in
its decisions in the Maple Flooring and First Cement cases
in June.   The decisions drastically changed the government's position on the "open-price" schemes.   In both
cases, the Court ruled that the statistical activities of
trade associations were not in themselves unreasonable
restraints on interstate commerce.   This meant that programs contributing to stability and uniformity of prices
were not necessarily illegal--a position closely akin to
that long expounded by Herbert Hoover.   In the wake of the
decisions the Justice Department joined Hoover in allowing
trade associations more latitude.[48]
The Southern Pine Association was encouraged by the
Supreme Court's decisions, and Joseph W. Bailey told the
mid-summer meeting that in light of the Maple Flooring
decision the Department of Justice would be wise to drop
its case against the association.[49] This was exactly what
it did the following year.[50] Ironically, Judge John H.
Lucas died on the eve of the final dismissal, and Bailey
praised his associate's activities as SPA counsel, conceding that while the Southern Pine Association had been
innocent of the charges leveled by the Department of
Justice, there had nevertheless been some activities by
individual association members "that might have been
fairly subject to criticism."   Bailey praised Lucas's

accomplishments in keeping the SPA isolated from the activities of some of its subscribers.

Former SPA Secretary-Manager H. C. Berckes later wrote that during the negotiations between the association and the government in connection with the case "there were other conferences of a confidential and classified character that are not reported. Therefore it is not possible to tell the whole story of the suit and its abatement."[51] Whatever the complete ramifications of the story, the SPA was legally safe for the remainder of the 1920s. Despite a brief examination of its records by an FTC examiner in 1927, the association could look confidently toward the refinement of its statistical activities as it approached the end of the decade, particularly with a proven friend of trade associations residing in the White House.

The Depression came. Hoover left. The new President was himself a former trade association executive, and the major early-New Deal depression-fighting agency, the National Recovery Administration, was built around trade associations. Their statistical activities, production controls, and price-fixing now had the open blessings of government. The SPA, as code agency for the southern pine industry, put its statistical services to good use.

The honeymoon was short-lived. The NRA died and the New Deal shifted toward a radically different attitude with regard to trade practices and the antitrust laws. The Southern Pine Association soon came under the scrutiny of the Department of Justice because of its statistical and other programs.

The SPA's difficulties resulted from the New Deal's general campaign to reform abuses in the construction industry and from Assistant Attorney General Thurman Arnold's efforts at the vigorous enforcement of the antitrust statutes. Among Arnold's first targets were the building and construction industries, and, in turn, the Southern Pine Association and other trade organizations in the lumber industry.[52] While applauding the government's investigation of the building industry, lumbermen were apprehensive about what might be in store for them. Colonel W. L. Greeley of the West Coast Lumbermen's Association defended the assistant attorney general as "thoroughly sincere: [and] devoted to free competition as the only effective protection against extensions of government regulations and control," but felt that Arnold was overly dramatic, prone to exaggeration, and extremely vocal in public appearances and statements—the sort of man who could give the industry a tremendous black eye.[53] Greeley's counterpart in the Southern Pine Association, H. C. Berckes, was even less charitable in discussing Arnold's motives and approach. According to Berckes, Arnold had set out to make "political capital." Not intent upon actually bringing the accused to trial, in Berckes's opinion Arnold was "using the tactics of publicity and harassment to bring about the acceptances of consent decrees."[54]

Arnold began his scrutiny of the Southern Pine Association on October 5, 1939, with the issuance by the federal district court in New Orleans of a subpoena duces tecum under which the Department of Justice was empowered to examine the files and records of the Southern Pine Association as part of its investigation of the building industry. A team of six special assistants to the attorney general, including future Supreme Court Justice Tom C. Clark, went through the records of the SPA and many of its subscribers with a fine-toothed comb.[55] Many firms whose records were not actually examined nevertheless came under the scrutiny of the Justice Department through their correspondence with firms whose offices actually were visited. The SPA's staff and advisers felt that the association's "skirts were clean and that the investigators would find little, if anything, about which they might make any worthwhile complaint."[56]

Despite the optimism of the southern pine manufacturers, it became apparent that the department felt that it had found sufficient evidence of production controls and price-fixing to get indictments against not only the Southern Pine Association but also a large number of its subscribers. The department's attorneys, agreed, however, that if the SPA and the firms which had participated in the questionable activities would enter into a consent decree, it would not work for widespread indictments. In line with established policy in such cases, the department would return an indictment against the Southern Pine Association as a corporation, but it would not refer to the SPA's officers, directors, or subscribers.57

The government's complaint, which was filed in the U. S. District Court for the Eastern District of Louisiana in New Orleans, listed as defendants the Southern Pine Association, the Southern Pine Lumber Exchange, the National Association of Commission Lumber Salesmen, and forty-one prominent southern pine lumber companies.

Statistics--The Heart of a Trade Association

According to the complaint, beginning on or about March 1, 1936, the defendants had engaged in a combination and conspiracy to restrain and monopolize the interstate trade in southern pine lumber through (1) fixing uniform, arbitrary, and noncompetitive prices; (2) curtailing and restricting the production of southern pine lumber; (3) maintaining and enforcing an agreed policy of distribution and thereby controlling the channels through which southern pine was distributed to consumers; and (4) formulating, promulgating, and administering grading rules and trade practices and promotional activities that served unjustly to exclude other firms from engaging in the southern pine trade and commerce.[58] The Department of Justice won a grand jury indictment of the Southern Pine Association and the other defendants along these general lines.[59]

Tom C. Clark, who directed most of the investigation and presented the case to the grand jury, also handled the negotiations with the Southern Pine Association after the indictment that led to a consent decree. H. C. Berckes later recalled that Clark had been "courteous and considerate" but had picked the names of the companies to be indicted almost at random. According to Berckes, "Mr. Clark went down the full list, picking the large and influential subscribers. When he had gotten a considerable number, he said, 'that's enough.' Those mills not indicted were gainers by default."[60] The Southern Pine Association's executive committee and board of directors decided, on February 14, 1940, to accept a consent decree and not formally fight the government's charges. The SPA did file an answer in the U. S. District Court in New Orleans denying and rebutting in detail the government's allegations.[61]

The Southern Pine Association's decision to enter a plea of nollo contendere to the indictment could have been divisive within the industry and among its subscribers. Many lumbermen were entirely convinced that they had done nothing wrong. The decision not to contest the indictment was reached through spirited consultations between the association's subscriber-officers, members of the SPA staff, and various lawyers and based on the belief that protracted litigation would hinder the SPA's programs and cause confusion and uncertainty among its subscribers and also that it might result in conviction and great expense.[62]

The New South and the "New Competition"

According to one of the association's lawyers, violations of the Sherman act were "so widespread and so patent . . . that lawyers were forced to the conclusion that a very, very large number of lumber manufacturing concerns and their officers might easily have been indicted and, upon a trial, easily convicted of this matter of swapping information and otherwise doing things that gave the Government the distinct, definite conviction that there had been agreements with respect to current prices of lumber, charged and to be charged, by people who were supposed to be, as a matter of law, competing with each other." The SPA counsel and other lawyers "were driven irresistibly to the conclusion that the best deal we could make in your [the SPA's] behalf was the best job and the best service that could be performed." In the counsel's view, "the Southern Pine Association 'took the rap' for a great number of lumber manufacturers and lumber manufacturing concerns" in the consent decree. He and his associates, he declared, were "fortunate in being able to keep out of the consent decree a very large number of manufacturers and manufacturing concerns which probably would have been included in an indictment had the wholesale indictment route been followed instead of this consent decree route."[63]

U. S. District Judge Wayne G. Borah signed the decree on February 21, 1940, in New Orleans. It included the names of the Southern Pine Association, the Southern Pine Lumber Exchange, and forty-one prominent southern pine manufacturing firms. The decree restrained the SPA and the other defendants from fixing prices, controlling production, and making agreements in relation to the sale of lumber products to any particular types or classes of trade. The association was specifically authorized to continue the compilation and dissemination of statistical information. Thus the SPA would continue to walk the antitrust tightrope so familiar to American trade associations, and its statistical facilities would be intact to help the industry, and the country, during the crises of World War II and the Korean conflict. The SPA's experiences with the courts and the federal government regarding its statistical activities provide one barometer of changing antitrust attitudes in twentieth-century America.

168

NOTES TO CHAPTER 5

1. "Outline of Work under Supervision of the Committees of the Southern Pine Association," Southern Pine Association Records, Box 39a (Louisiana State University Archives, Baton Rouge, La.). Collection hereafter cited as SPA Records.

2. Report of the Federal Trade Commission on Lumber Manufacturer's Trade Associations, Incorporating Reports of January 10, 1921, February 18, 1921, February 15, 1922 (Washington, D.C.: Government Printing Office, 1922), p. 57.

3. Ibid., pp. 58-59.

4. "Minutes of a Meeting of the Board of Directors of the Southern Pine Association Held at the Grunewald Hotel, New Orleans, La., Thursday, December 14, 1916," SPA Records, Box 70b, pp. 5-6.

5. James Boyd, "Philosophy of Price Structure," SPA Records, Box 77a, p. 9.

6. "Before the Federal Trade Commission, Conference with Representatives of the Yellow Pine Lumber Industry, Washington, D.C., October 30, 1917," SPA Records, Box 67a.

7. Report of FTC, p. 62.

8. R. C. Fraunberger, "Lumber Trade Associations: Their Economic and Social Significance (M. A. thesis, Temple University, 1951), pp. 15-16; Louis Galambos, Competition and Cooperation: The Emergence of a National Trade Association (Baltimore: Johns Hopkins University Press, 1966), pp. 66-67; Minita Westcott, "History of Trade Associations," American Trade Association Executives Journal, VII (Apr., 1956), 35; James W. Silver, "The Hardwood Producers Come of Age," Journal of Southern History, XXIII (Nov., 1957), 438; Robert F. Himmelberg, The Origins of the National Recovery Administration: Business, Government, and the Trade Association Issue, 1921-1933 (New York: Fordham University Press, 1976), pp. 5-7.

The New South and the "New Competition"

9. Galambos, Competition and Cooperation, pp. 80-81; Silver, "Hardwood Producers Come of Age," pp. 434-38. A detailed study of the conflicting attitudes within the Wilson administration concerning relaxation of the antitrust laws with regard to price-fixing is Robert F. Himmelberg, "Business, Antitrust Policy, and the Industrial Board of the Department of Commerce, 1919," Business History Review, XLII (Spring, 1968), 1-23. See also Robert D. Cuff, "A 'Dollar-a-Year Man' in Government: George N. Peek and the War Industries Board," Business History Review, XLI (Winter, 1967), 418-19; and Robert Sobel, The Age of Giant Corporations: A Microeconomic History of American Business, 1914-1970 (Westport, Conn.: Greenwood Press, 1972), pp. 27-30.

10. Silver, "Hardwood Producers Come of Age," p. 436.

11. "Minutes of a Meeting of the Board of Directors of the Southern Pine Association . . . June 16, 1919," SPA Records, Box 70b; "Lumber Summary, February 19, 1921," File 60-160-21, Records of the Department of Justice, RG 60, National Archives.

12. Silver, "Hardwood Producers Come of Age," p. 438. See also Himmelberg, Origins of the National Recovery Administration, p. 7.

13. Silver, "Hardwood Producers Come of Age," pp. 438-39.

14. "Minutes of a Meeting of the Board of Directors of the Southern Pine Association . . . December 5, 1919," SPA Records, Box 70b, pp. 2-5. It seems clear that the records of the association were carefully screened to remove any potentially damaging information before the FTC examiners began their work. "Memorandum on Proposed Action against Southern Pine Manufacturers," File 60-160-21, Records of the Department of Justice, RG 60, National Archives.

15. "Minutes of a Meeting of the Board of Directors of the Southern Pine Association . . . March 15, 1920," SPA Records, Box 70b, pp 2-5.

16. Silver, "Hardwood Producers Come of Age," p. 439.

17. H. C. Berckes, "The Pitch in Pine: A Story of the Traditions, Policies and Activities of the Southern Pine Industry and the Men Responsible for Them" (unpublished manuscript in possession of the author), pp. 86-87.

18. Galambos, Competition and Cooperation, p. 82; Silver, "Hardwood Producers Come of Age," pp. 443-44.

19. Silver, "Hardwood Producers Come of Age," pp. 444-46.

20. Report of the FTC, pp. 62-65, 70, 92-93, 130-31.

21. "Minutes of a Meeting of the Board of Directors of the Southern Pine Association . . . March 1, 1921," SPA Records, Box 70b. The Records of the Department of Justice, File 60-160-21, RG 60, National Archives, contain voluminous copies of materials relating to the suit, including records copied by the Federal Trade Commission from the files of various southern pine producers showing their efforts to control production and prices. These are found in the report titled, "Exchange and Criticism of Price Lists as a Factor in Price Maintenance."

22. A. L. Clark, "The Tide has Turned," in "Lumber Liquidates," SPA Records, Box 85b, p. 7. Clark's statement is at odds with information discovered by FTC examiners indicating that leaders of the association had on at least one occasion attended a "curtailment dinner" hosted by Edward Hines. "Memorandum on Proposed Action against Southern Pine Manufacturers," File 60-160-21, Records of the Department of Justice, RG 60, National Archives.

23. John H. Lucas, "The Contention of the Government," in "Lumber Liquidates," SPA Records, Box 85b, 29-34. John Henry Kirby also delivered a strong address at the meeting urging that the association actively pursue the case in the federal courts as a means of clearing the industry of all of the unjust charges which had been leveled at it down through the years.

24. "Lumber Liquidates," SPA Records, Box 85b, pp. 173, 175.

The New South and the "New Competition"

25. "Minutes of a Meeting of the Board of Directors of the Southern Pine Association . . . April 4, 1921," SPA Records, Box 70b.

26. Ibid. Faris actually disqualified himself because of an affidavit of prejudice against him which was filed by Charles S. Keith, Robert A. Long, and Captain J. B. White. See William J. Donovan to Vernon W. Van Fleet, Nov. 14, 1925, reproduced in U. S. Congress, Senate, Open-Price Trade Associations, 70th Cong., 2nd Sess., Senate Doc. 226 (Washington, D.C.: Government Printing Office, 1929), pp. 318-19. Also see telegram, Carroll, U. S. Attorney to Attorney General, Mar. 10, 1921, in Records of the Department of Justice, File 60-160-21, RG 60, National Archives, and other scattered correspondence and documents, including Keith's complaint, in the same file.

27. "Minutes of a Meeting of the Board of Directors of the Southern Pine Association . . . June 14, 1921," SPA Records, Box 70b. The size of Bailey's fee indicates the importance the SPA placed upon the injunction case and the faith it had in Bailey's abilities and contacts in political circles. At the time, Chief Counsel Lucas was on an annual $5,000 retainer and requested no additional salary for his services in connection with the injunction suit. "Minutes of a Meeting of the Board of Directors of the Southern Pine Association . . . April 4, 1921," SPA Records, Box 70b.

28. Silver, "Hardwood Producers Come of Age," pp. 447-49. For a discussion of the case and its background see H. Browning Carrott, "The Supreme Court and American Trade Associations, 1921-1925," Business History Review, XLIV (Autumn, 1970), 320-29.

29. Untitled, undated typewritten statement in SPA Records, Box 106.

30. John E. Rhodes to W. E. Gardner, Dec. 23, 1921, SPA Records, Box 106.

31. Walter B. Wooden to C. Stanley Thompson, Special Assistant to the Attorney General, Dec. 24, 1921, File 60-160-21, Records of the Department of Justice, RG 60, National Archives.

32. Silver, "Hardwood Producers Come of Age," p. 450.

33. Ibid., pp. 446-47. For a detailed discussion of Herbert Hoover's ideas and policies to promote the "New Era" through associational activities see Ellis W. Hawley, "Herbert Hoover, the Commerce Secretariat, and the Vision of an 'Associative State,' 1921-1928," Journal of American History, LXI (June, 1974), pp. 116-40. A detailed account of the debate between Hoover and Daugherty is included in Himmelberg, Origins of the National Recovery Administration, pp. 10-42. See also Joan Hoff Wilson, American Business and Foreign Policy, 1920-1933 (Lexington: University Press of Kentucky, 1971).

34. Southern Pine Association to Subscribers, June 24, 1921, Kurth Papers, Box 605 (Forest History Collections, Stephen F. Austin State University Library, Nacogdoches, Tex.).

35. "Extract from Speech by Secretary Hoover before Synthetic Organic Chemical Manufacturers' Association, October 28, 1921," in "Federal Court Approves Collection and Distribution of Trade Information," undated pamphlet published by the Southern Pine Association, SPA Records, Box 84b, p. 11.

36. The correspondence between Hoover and Daugherty was printed by the Chamber of Commerce of the United States. There are copies in the SPA Records, Box 106. The Hoover-Daugherty dialogue is discussed in Carrott, "Supreme Court and American Trade Associations," 329.

37. Galambos, Competition and Cooperation, p. 93-94.

38. "Trade Associations May Lawfully Compile and Publish General Economic Information," typewritten NLMA press release, Feb. 7, 1922, SPA Records, Box 106.

39. "Report of Secretary-Manager J. E. Rhodes," in "Protection for Buyers of Pine: Official Report of the Seventh Annual Meeting of the Subscribers to the Southern Pine Association, Held at Grunewald Hotel, New Orleans, March 28 and 29, 1922," SPA Records, Box 85b, p. 12.

40. "Minutes of a Meeting of the Board of Directors of the Southern Pine Association . . . March 27, 1922," SPA Records, Box 70b.

41. John H. Lucas, "Our Day in Court," in "Proceedings of the Seventh Annual Meeting of Subscribers to the Southern Pine Association . . . March 28 and 29, 1922," SPA Records, Box 70b, pp. 22-32.

42. John E. Rhodes to Harry T. Kendall, Nov. 29, 1922, SPA Records, Box 9a; "Minutes of a Meeting of the Board of Directors of the Southern Pine Association . . . December 13, 1922," SPA Records, Box 70b.

43. "Minutes of a Meeting of the Board of Directors of the Southern Pine Association . . . December 13, 1922," SPA Records, Box 70b.

44. Carrott, "Supreme Court and American Trade Associations," pp. 330-32.

45. "Activities of Southern Pine Association Compared with those of American Linseed Oil Co., et al. Through Armstrong Bureau of Related Industries as Outlined in Decision of U. S. Supreme Court," typewritten report in SPA Records, Box 106.

46. "Minutes of a Meeting of the Board of Directors of the Southern Pine Association . . . March 10, 1924," SPA Records, Box 70b; "Report of Chief Counsel," in "A New Era," SPA Records, Box 85b, pp. 38-39; A. T. Simpson, Assistant to the Attorney General, to H. N. Daugherty, Dec. 10, 1923, File 60-160-21, Records of the Department of Justice, RG 60, National Archives. The consent decree proposed by the Department of Justice would have totally eliminated the SPA's statistical activities. "In the District Court of the United States, Eastern District of Missouri, United States of America, Plaintiff v. Southern Pine Association and others, Defendants. Final Decree," File 60-160-21, Records of the Department of Justice, RG 60, National Archives.

47. "Proceedings of a Meeting of the Southern Pine Association . . . June 16, 1925," SPA Records, Box 68b, p. 13.

48. Galambos, Competition and Cooperation, pp. 99-100. Also see Carrott, "Supreme Court and American Trade Associations," pp. 332-38, and Hawley, "Herbert Hoover," p. 136. For the triumph of Hoover's approach and the departure of Daugherty, see Himmelberg, Origins of National Recovery Administration, pp. 43-53.

49. "Proceedings of a Meeting of the Southern Pine Association . . . June 16, 1925," SPA Records, Box 68b, p. 34.

50. "Proceedings of Eleventh Annual Meeting of the Subscribers to the Southern Pine Association . . . March 23, 24, 1926," SPA Records, Box 73b; John M. Collier, The First Fifty Years of the Southern Pine Association, 1915-1965 (New Orleans: Southern Pine Association, 1965), p. 78. See also William J. Donovan to Vernon W. Van Fleet, Nov. 14, 1925, reproduced in U. S. Congress, Senate, Open-Price Trade Associations, pp. 318-19.

51. Berckes, "Pitch in Pine," p. 93.

52. William E. Leuchtenburg, Franklin D. Roosevelt and the New Deal, 1932-1940 (New York: Harper Torchbook, 1963), p. 259. There is a brief account of Arnold's activities and the changing climate within the administration in Sobel, Age of Giant Corporations, pp. 112-20.

53. Ellis Lucia, Head Rig: The Story of the West Coast Lumber Industry (Portland, Ore.: Overland West Press, 1965), p. 200.

54. Berckes suggested that the Southern Pine Association could have successfully defended itself against Arnold's charges but chose not to because: "when an Association, no matter how innocent or successful in defending itself gets embroiled in law suits, its effectiveness is lost, its members resign through fear and there will remain no organization to carry on. Mr. Arnold knew this and he adopted that policy of Grand Jury investigations, indictments and threats and then offered the industry involved the expedient of a Consent Decree, a consent not to do things they were not doing anyway, to do things which suited the administration's socialist

175

thinking, and to remain under judicial scrutiny perpetually." Berckes, "Pitch in Pine," pp. 188-89.

55. Southern Pine Association to Subscribers, Feb. 21, 1940, SPA Records, Box 70a.

56. "Report of Counsel, J. H. Crooker," in "Proceedings of Southern Pine Association Twenty-Fifth Annual Meeting . . . 1940," SPA Records, Box 73b.

57. Southern Pine Association to Subscribers, Feb. 21, 1940, SPA Records, Box 70a.

58. There are mimeographed copies of the U. S. government's complaint against the Southern Pine Association and other defendants in SPA Records, Box 70a, and in File 60-160-21, Records of the Department of Justice, RG 60, National Archives. With regard to the association's inspection and grading activities, a special attorney of the Department of Justice charged that the SPA used grade-marking "as a means of combatting the competition of small mills, particularly those which engage in shipping direct to the consumer." He went on to say, "We have some evidence in the form of correspondence indicating that one of the principal objectives of the cooperative advertising campaigns [of] the Southern Pine Association . . . has been the direct restraint of such competition." He also said the department was interested in "the extent to which the inspection staff of the Southern Pine Association, represented to the public as disinterested technical experts who judge lumber impartially according to the grading rules, are actually trade promotion experts whose object is to advance the use of southern pine rather than other species and the use of the products of the Southern Pine Association member mills in particular." Finally, he said the department was interested in "the extent, if any, to which those inspectors who were stationed at principal marketing points such as New York, Detroit, and Chicago [were used] to check up on the prices at which the Southern Pine Association member mills were selling their products." Wallace Howland, Memorandum for Mr. Corwin D. Edwards, Nov. 9, 1939, File 60-160-21, Records of the Department of Justice, RG 60, National Archives.

59. There are mimeographed copies of the grand jury indictment in SPA Records, Box 70a, and in File 60-160-21, Records of the Department of Justice, RG 60, National Archives.

60. Berckes, "Pitch in Pine," p. 191.

61. Mimeographed copies of the Southern Pine Association's reply are in SPA Records, Box 70a, and File 60-160-21, Records of the Department of Justice, RG 60, National Archives.

62. Southern Pine Association to Subscribers, Feb. 21, 1940, SPA Records, Box 70a; Berckes, "Pitch in Pine," p. 193; "Report of Counsel, J. H. Crooker," in "Proceedings of Southern Pine Association Twenty-Fifth Annual Meeting . . . 1940," SPA Records, Box 73b.

63. According to SPA counsel, "the Government investigators did not include in that consent decree all of the lumber manufacturing concerns against which they had a showing of a violation of law. They did insist upon the large and responsible manufacturers, who, they said, would be representative of the Southern Pine industry." "Report of Counsel, J. H. Crooker," in "Proceedings of Southern Pine Association Twenty-Fifth Annual Meeting . . . 1940," SPA Records, Box 73b.

6

The Development of
Quality Standards, Advertising,
and Trade Promotion

The development and enforcement of quality standards are
among the most important trade association functions and
are closely related to advertising and trade promotion.
The consent decree which the SPA signed in 1940 focused on
the importance of quality standards by separating quality
inspection, certification, and marking from the SPA organization and making them available to all southern pine
manufacturers on an equal basis through an independent
agency. The important and critical point is that quality
enforcement and certification are important marketing
devices and can lead to a diminution of competition if
they are restricted to only a select group within an
industry. Within the southern pine industry, these
general activities were covered under the term grade-
marking.

In developing manufacturing and grading standards the
Southern Pine Association had a foundation to build upon--
the standards and procedures established by the old Yellow
Pine Manufacturers' Association. The actual work of the
SPA in this field, as in all others, was originally done
by an association department under the supervision of a
committee that acted through the secretary-manager.

The grading committee prescribed standard specifications for grading yellow pine lumber and, through the
association's inspection department, enforced them at its
subscribers' mills. In addition, it arbitrated disputes
over grades. The committee acted through seven subcommittees organized according to products. Each subcommittee
studied the problems falling within its particular area of

responsibility and made recommendations to the full committee. In making investigations, the subcommittees were authorized to visit the mills and yards of association subscribers and to solicit suggestions.[1]

The Yellow Pine Manufacturers' Association's grading rules were generally accepted in the industry prior to 1914, and when the SPA was organized it adopted and copyrighted the rules and changed them as necessary.[2] When a subcommittee of the grading committee, either on its own initiative or at the request of a subscriber, favored a change in the rules, it first consulted other interested subcommittees and then presented its proposal to the parent committee. The grading committee might then accept the change, subject to approval of the board of directors. Before acting, the board solicited the views of association subscribers and even of retail lumber dealers who were not subscribers.[3] The association was always concerned that the specifications and grading rules be accepted throughout the industry and thus copies of the rules and all changes were available to anyone who wanted them.[4]

Actual grading and inspection of southern pine lumber was done by a corps of inspectors, whose numbers varied between ten and twenty-five during the association's early years. The SPA hired many members of the old YPMA inspection staff after George K. Smith's abortive coup, and they formed the nucleus of an efficient inspection force. Heading the inspection and grading staff was a chief inspector who supervised activities. There was also an instructor of grades who trained association inspectors and conducted schools for the subscribers' graders at their mills. In order to check the effectiveness of its grading and inspection service, the association developed an elaborate system of records covering the performance of both its own inspectors and the graders at each mill.[5]

During 1915 and 1916, for example, serious hurricanes hit the Gulf Coast of Louisiana and East Texas. Much timber was downed, and heavy winds caused shakes or checks in the lumber manufactured from what remained. The association thus had to decide the amount of allowable wind shake in certain grades in the midst of opposition between those the storms had affected and those who had escaped their ravages. Intrafamily friction even emerged in cases where one mill of a large company was cutting wind-damaged timber and another was not. At one point the discussions became so heated that a recess was called and a twenty-four-hour cooling-off period instituted to allow mills of the same companies to adjust their differences before the entire grading committee reached a decision.[6]

According to Secretary-Manager John E. Rhodes, however, despite disputes and controversies during the SPA's first year of operation its grading committee "accomplished more . . . towards establishing a recognition of uniform grades for Southern Yellow Pine than has been done in any previous year. . . ." During the year, on the recommendation of the U. S. Forest Service's Forest Products Laboratory at the University of Wisconsin, the committee adopted a density rule which was copyrighted by the American Society for Testing Materials. The rule defined the relationship between the density and the strength of lumber. The committee also studied the test weights of timbers and other structural materials, the moisture content of southern pine, and kiln drying practices. All of these matters would be of continuing interest to the SPA, the consuming public, and the government.[7]

By 1917, the grading committee had facilitated lumber inspection by placing its subscribers' mills in eleven inspection districts. A system was worked out to improve the industry's quality standards. Association inspectors filed reports with each subscriber whose mills they visited and sometimes discussed their findings with the mill graders. The SPA awarded efficiency cards to graders demonstrating a high level of proficiency and, to assist them, it also reissued and distributed copies of its grading rules.[8] On the grading committee's recommendation, the board of directors also established an inspection department branch in the New York City area. It was expected that this office, by assuring that southern pine lumber sold in the vicinity met association specifications, would increase southern pine markets in New England and the middle Atlantic Coast area.[9]

The problem of industry grading standards was closely related to the desire of many industry leaders for the SPA to initiate a program of grade-marking to ensure the integrity of the stock and grades sold by association subscribers. SPA leaders also believed, of course, that grade-marking, or branding, lumber would increase association membership, because manufacturers who could not use the organization's grade-marks would be at a competitive disadvantage. Prior to the SPA's organization, many within the industry had practiced hammer-marking of

181

large timbers, but this did not bring protection to the users of items generally found in home and small construction.[10]

In January, 1916, the board of directors appointed a special committee on branding lumber to investigate and test branding machines and made a small appropriation to support its work. A month later, at the first annual SPA meeting, the chairman of the branding committee recommended that a branding program be adopted as rapidly as possible. In 1917, the committee had branding machines installed at two sawmills as an experiment. These machines proved unsatisfactory and, with the advent of World War I, the experiment was dropped. The quest for satisfactory grade-marking equipment and procedures was postponed until after the war.[11]

The difficulties of placing a grade-marking program in operation were not due solely to mechanical problems or World War I's interruption. Grade-marking was closely related to the matter of grading standards, and again internal divisions and factions hampered SPA efforts.[12] When the Forest Products Laboratory established a density basis for determining the strength of southern pine lumber, it triggered a controversy that complicated the effort to establish grading standards, side-tracked the grade-marking movement, provoked an effort to unseat the SPA's secretary-manager, and almost wrecked the SPA itself. It brought into the open differences between producers of two varieties of southern pine lumber—dense shortleaf and longleaf. The latter feared that the designation of dense shortleaf pine as being as strong as original growth longleaf would depress the value of their product.

For many years, the longleaf operators resisted the adoption of a southern pine density rule that would put dense shortleaf and longleaf on an equal basis, but the controversy went beyond the merits of the density rule. Longleaf mills held that they did not want the same grade-mark used on both longleaf and shortleaf, thus depreciating the premium price they received for their lumber. They believed their product so superior to shortleaf that it would not serve their interests to have an identical mark on the same grade of both varieties. This difference of opinion was finally resolved when disputes over the adoption of a density rule were settled, but, in the meantime, this and other difficulties, plus the interruption of World War I, impeded the establishment of a grade-marking program.[13]

The Development of Standards, Advertising, and Promotion

During the war, SPA grading and inspection activities were confined to furnishing inspectors for the lumber going into ships and cantonment construction. At the war's end, the Emergency Fleet Corporation was left with large stocks of surplus lumber at various shipyards in the East and South which it decided to sell. The Southern Pine Association furnished inspectors to tally and grade this lumber. By 1920 the association's standard specifications for southern pine lumber were recognized by virtually all American manufacturers and retailers, and they constituted the basis for the grades according to which most southern pine produced in this country was sold. However, while additional branding or grade-marking machinery was tested following the war, prior to 1920 no suitable method of marking lumber was discovered.

By the beginning of the 1920s, however, the SPA was embarking on new endeavors which would be of great significance in the area of grading and grade-marking. During 1920 and 1921, the association joined in discussions concerning national standardization sponsored by the National Lumber Manufacturers' Association. To meet consumer needs, the association consulted with special groups such as railroad car builders, agricultural implement companies, and retail dealers to establish appropriate grades.[14] The lumber producers believed that if they did not put their house in order the federal government would do it for them, and their thinking was shaped by the emergence of strong personalities who spearheaded the drives toward national lumber standards and consumer protection.

One of the industry's most important leaders in the movement for the proper grading of lumber was southern pine manufacturer Edward Hines of Chicago. Hines was a legendary figure of the early-twentieth-century lumber industry. He was constantly traveling around the country personally managing his vast interests in timberlands, mills, and wholesaling operations. A short, quick, little man with an aristocratic demeanor, he was tough-minded, imperious, and demanding. Hines detested the chaotic conditions in the industry and wanted immediate action to correct them. It was he who prodded the SPA board of directors into action in the matter of grade-marking in the southern pine industry.[15]

The war and its aftermath wrought havoc in the lumber industry's producing and marketing customs. Widespread were such practices as delivering lumber that failed to

183

meet specifications as to dimensions and grades as well as quantities. At first these practices were mainly limited to a few smaller operators, but the intense competition and hard times of the early 1920s made them more common among mills in financial difficulty, unethical wholesalers, and shady distributors and builders.[16]

Hines was deeply concerned about the situation, and early in 1922 he warned members of the SPA's grading committee that through these practices and the "insidious propaganda" of competitors the integrity of the association's lumber grades was being attacked. As a result, the SPA board was influenced to take up the problem.[17] On the eve of the association's annual meeting, the board discussed "the tendency which has become manifest during the past year to disregard the standard of grades for Southern Pine lumber as established by the association, and the extent to which such grades are being misrepresented and substituted." It reported to the association that: "the integrity of these grades and the good name of the Southern Pine industry can be safeguarded and protected if subscribers will adopt the practice of trade-marking their lumber and guaranteeing the quality thereof . . . [and] recommended that subscribers place in each car of lumber loaded by them a record of the contents covering both the grade and tally. . . ."[18]

` The annual meeting itself was organized around the theme "Protection for Buyers of Pine." Edward Hines strongly advocated grade-marking and standarization,[19] and manufacturers at the meeting rallied behind Hines and Secretary-Manager Rhodes by endorsing a special committee's recommendations of grade-marking and the placing of a tally card in each car of lumber loaded. The secretary-manager was instructed to poll the entire membership in regard to their willingness to grade-mark, with the recommendation that when 50 percent of them agreed to do so, the directors could "authorize the issuance of a list of such mills . . . and to furnish such list to all buyers of lumber."[20] However, despite this initial step, there were still internal squabbles over grade-marking and the mechanical difficulties that had to be solved.[21]

Southern Pine Association activities in grade-marking and standardization were not developing in a vacuum. Important events were transpiring in Washington, where Secretary of Commerce Herbert Hoover was embarking upon measures to promote standardization and efficiency in business and protection to consumers, with the cooperation of trade associations.[22] Hoover echoed the warnings of Edward Hines that if the industry failed to take measures to correct the chaotic conditions, the government would step in to end many of the nefarious practices. The Secretary of Commerce appealed for grading and inspection under the auspices of the lumber trade associations, with the ominous remark that "if you think it wiser . . . we could probably secure the enactment of a 'pure food law' in all building materials. I would rather see the trades themselves establish their own standards."[23]

The industry had actually been holding conferences for some time in an attempt to work toward the adoption of recognized national lumber standards, but it was not until the National Lumber Manufacturers' Association and other organizations of producers, distributors, and consumers sought the assistance of Secretary Hoover that the movement began to gain momentum. In working toward the institution and enforcement of national manufacturing standards, the associations believed that they were striking dangerously close to the federal antitrust statutes, and they felt more comfortable when Hoover came to their support.[24]

The lumbermen gathered in Chicago in April, 1922, under the leadership of the National Lumber Manufacturers' Association, in the first American lumber congress. The congress included representatives of associations of retailers and wholesalers as well as the producers' associations, and it approved the principle of grade-marking, which was also endorsed by the NLMA's directors and a number of wholesalers' and retailers' conventions.[25] The Southern Pine Association representatives' instructions indicated that the SPA was wary about the heralded cooperation between sections. The SPA board authorized its delegation to "commit the Southern Pine Association to the approval of such standards of sizes as may be recommended to the said Congress for universal adoption, provided that representatives of all associations participating in the said Congress are vested with like authority."[26] The SPA persistently felt that the western representatives came to the meetings without adequate authorization to commit their organizations to the decisions reached.

The West Coast Lumbermen's Association was having trouble resolving internal disagreements over grading, and this may have contributed to its reluctance to vest much authority in delegates sent to national lumber standards conferences. Furthermore, the WCLA during the early 1920s lacked the strong professional leadership the SPA enjoyed under Secretary-Manager John E. Rhodes and H. C. Berckes.[27] There was good reason for the WCLA's caution at the national conferences, however, for the southerners and westerners had very real differences over grading standards which could have seriously affected the financial structure of the industry.

After questions of terminology were dealt with, the basic difference between the sections was over the matter of standard sizes, and particularly what thickness a one-inch board should be when properly dressed on two sides. This matter, which Secretary Hoover later referred to as "the battle of the thirty-second," was the crux of the problem. At the time of the conferences there were two accepted dressed thicknesses for one-inch lumber in the United States—thirteen-sixteenths of an inch for lumber produced by eastern and southern producers and sold in eastern and southern markets, and three-fourths or twelve-sixteenths of an inch for lumber produced in the West.

The question of thicknesses had many ramifications. First, consumers obviously preferred thicker lumber, and in this they were backed by wholesalers, distributors, and the Forest Products Laboratory. The reasoning of the manufacturer was obviously different. The thicker the board the heavier, and the heavier the board the more expensive the transportation charges to get it to market.[28] The western manufacturers wanted the thinner standard in order to save on transportation charges, but they were also concerned because they shipped their lumber green, rather than running it through dry kilns, and since lumber shrinks, they wanted leeway in the sizes to allow for the uncertain amount of shrinkage that a trip across the continent might entail.[29] Finally, the smaller standard enabled a sawmill to cut its rough boards thinner, and thus get more footage out of its timber. When all of these factors are combined, the difficulties of compromise between the two sections are understandable.[30]

The first significant national meeting on lumber standards was the National Standardization Conference in Washington, D. C., in May, 1922. The conference attracted some 110 representatives of various organizations, including the Southern Pine Association, and was held under the auspices of the division of simplified practice of the National Bureau of Standards in the Department of

Commerce. The most important result of the meeting was the appointment of subcommittees to formulate the necessary standards in sizes and grades of lumber and the methods of interpreting and enforcing them.[31]

A second general conference in Chicago in July, 1922, created a central committee on lumber standards which included representatives of lumber manufacturers', wholesalers', and retailers' associations, the railway associations, the Association of Wood Using Industries, and the American Institute of Architects. The central committee in turn appointed a consulting committee on lumber standards which was an advisory body of technical experts from each of the large organizations represented at the conference. The consulting committee was to work out the technical aspects of standardization. The Southern Pine Association was represented on both the central committee and the consulting committee.[32]

As the Southern Pine Association entered 1923, there was much activity at both the regional and national levels in regard to grade-marking and standardization. The SPA's annual meeting heard the secretary-manager report that 72 percent of the subscribers had indicated their willingness to grade-mark when satisfactory mechanical devices were developed and that tests of one such machine were currently underway in several mills.[33] The subscribers were also addressed by a spokesman for the Department of Commerce, who was attending a number of lumbermen's meetings to emphasize Secretary Hoover's desire for the industry's self-regulation.[34]

The central committee met in Chicago again in June, 1923, and formulated definite American lumber standards. These standards were adopted at another Chicago meeting of the committee on October 31 and were then submitted to the Department of Commerce with a recommendation that the Secretary of Commerce convene a conference to take final action upon them. Secretary Hoover called a general conference of all interested groups in Washington on December 11 and 13, with about a hundred associations representing manufacturers, wholesales, retailers, consumers, architects, and contractors sending delegations. The conference adopted the new American Lumber Standards, which were promulgated by the Department of Commerce.[35] However, the squabbling was not over. Agreement had been reached only through the intervention of Secretary Hoover himself,[36] and there were still significant rumblings in some sectors of the lumber industry over the settlement.

The New South and the "New Competition"

Preliminary acceptance of the American Lumber Standards did not mean the subject was entirely closed. The delegates at the conferences could still be overruled by their parent bodies. The simplified practice recommendations and standardization decisions of the 1923 lumber conferences were also subject to continual revision and review by the central committee on lumber standards and subsequent general conferences. Various revisions of this sort were, in fact, undertaken periodically during the remainder of the 1920s.[37]

Apparently both the westerners and the southerners soon had some second thoughts about the agreement reached in December, 1923. The Southern Pine Association's annual meeting in the spring of 1924 featured reports on the progress of the American Lumber Standards, many of which seemed to be dedicated to removing the "misconception on the part of some of our subscribers and lumbermen generally as to this whole proposition." Chairman W. T. Murray presented the grading committee's report and noted that "a good many folks seemed to have the notion at first that Secretary Hoover called us on the carpet and told us to do something, that we must do, in the matter of simplification and standardization," and he reminded the subscribers that "you know that is not exactly true."[38] Secretary-Manager Wilson Compton of the National Lumber Manufacturers' Association also went to great lengths to refute the "uninformed and incorrect statement . . . sometimes made, in the South and elsewhere, that the present movement, for national lumber standards is an undertaking initiated by the Government and involving a measure of Government interference with the business affairs of the lumber industry."[39] Despite the obvious misgivings and distrust of some members, the Southern Pine Association's board of directors approved the grading committee's report on the standardization movement and instructed the secretary-manager to submit the matter to the semiannual meeting of subscribers in Memphis on June 27. Reiterating the decision made by the directors in March, the subscribers unanimously approved the actions taken. Thus when the American Lumber Standards officially went into effect on July 1, 1924, they had the approval of the SPA's grading committee, its board of directors, and its subscribers.[40]

The West Coast Lumbermen's Association had also pledged itself to support the American Lumber Standards, but the westerners seemed far more dissatisfied with the

decisions made. The president of the WCLA actually feared
for the organization's life because of threats by dissatisfied firms to pull out rather than accept the decisions
reached at the eastern conferences. Finally, after heated
conferences and disputes, WCLA subscribers agreed that
their association's new grading rules would be published
in accordance with the American Lumber Standards.[41]

While the negotiations over national standards were
proceeding during 1924, the Southern Pine Association was
also very much involved with the problem of grade-marking
within its own region. The association appeared to be on
the verge of finding a satisfactory marking device, and at
the annual meeting in the spring, subscribers approved the
institution of grade-marking on a voluntary basis under
the auspices of the association, which would lease
machines for the purpose.[42] Thus the Southern Pine
Association became the first organization of lumber manufacturers officially to adopt grade-marking.[43]

However, there was dissatisfaction over the fact that
the SPA was merely leasing the machines from the inventor
and manufacturer, and there was disappointment because the
entire process was moving so slowly. Once again Edward
Hines stepped in to bring about quicker action. As H. C.
Berckes later recalled, "We were playing around with it,
trying to get a machine to do it, and Edward Hines came in
with a whole table full of invoices. . . ." The invoices
demonstrated some of the fraudulent practices prevalent in
the industry. As Hines placed them before the board of
directors, he thundered, "This is something you can't play
with." As a result, "they immediately decided to go ahead
with the grade-marking by using a rubber stamp. . . ."[44]

The mere fact that SPA grade-marking was started did
not signify that the battle was over. During 1925 and
1926, the struggle both to get acceptance and compliance
with American Lumber Standards and to persuade SPA
subscribers to grade-mark continued. Both the Southern
Pine Association's board of directors and the subscribers
attending the annual meeting in March, 1925, adopted a
resolution endorsing grade-marking and recommending that
all subscribers begin to grade-mark immediately. They
also voted for a three cent per thousand feet assessment
for six months or less beginning March 1 to introduce and
advertise grade-marked lumber to the consuming public.[45]

By the middle of 1926, however, many SPA subscribers
were still not grade-marking, and others who claimed to be
continued to sell unmarked lumber upon request. Several

189

subscribers told of losing customers to firms which continued to fall in and out of the grade-marking camp, and a
mid-year trade extension meeting reached its most explo-
sive point when Edward Hines accused the non-markers of
cowardice and dishonesty.[46] On the following day, at
Hines's insistence, the SPA board of directors pledged
themselves individually to grade-mark their products, and
they appointed committees of directors and other important
subscribers in each SPA state to try to influence non-
markers to come into the fold.[47] The quality of grade-
marking was also an area of concern. SPA subscribers
were bluntly informed by their advertising counsel at the
1925 mid-summer meeting that he had seen some grade-marked
lumber in various cities that was "not any credit to you."
The major criticism was not the reliability of the grades,
but carelessness in applying the marks.[48]

Despite its members' reluctance to grade-mark their
products, the Southern Pine Association had an excellent
inspection program. In the 1920s the association maintained an experienced staff of about thirty lumber
inspectors.[49] SPA inspectors were constantly in the
field, and an official inspection was made at each mill
every thirty days. On the basis of this visit the mill
received a report indicating the amount inspected and the
accuracy of its graders. Besides inspectors acted as
instructors for graders at the individual mills and
assisted mill managers in bringing their plants into
conformity with the American Lumber Standards.[50] New
subscribers coming into the SPA generally showed a great
deal of improvement in the reliability of their grades as
a result of the help and criticism of association
inspectors.[51]

While the Southern Pine Association was attempting to
push grade-marking in its own region, it was also moving
toward full implementation of the American Lumber
Standards in its grading rules. In June, 1925, the SPA
grading committee revised the grading rules in accordance
with the national standards. This action was ratified by
the board and subscribers the same month, making the
Southern Pine Association the first association to revise
its rules in conformity with the standards.[52]

The association looked toward the concluding national
conferences on standardization, which were scheduled to
culminate in a final meeting in Washington during April,
1926, with some trepidation. The southerners were still
not convinced that other sections were entering the

meetings in good faith or were carrying out the decisions of the conferences. On the eve of the Washington conference, H. C. Berckes received a letter from one of his most influential subscribers complaining that many manufacturers and dealers were not supporting standardization. "I have heard a great many of the southern pine manufacturers express a great deal of dissatisfaction with the result of the Standardization Program," he wrote. "The members of the Southern Pine Association," he continued, "seem to be the only people who are in any way living up to the Standardization work, and even a great many southern pine manufacturers are not whole-heartedly supporting the movement." Berckes's correspondent warned that "those Southern Pine manufacturers who have been wholeheartedly supporting the Standardization Program and refusing to do business on anything except standard sizes and grades are becoming dissatisfied, because they feel that the net result will be a final loss of business to them."[53]

Despite the misgivings and mutual distrust of the southern and western lumbermen, the 1926 Chicago and Washington standardization conferences resulted in modification and at least temporary acceptance of the American Lumber Standards by both sides. The major crisis in national standardization had been passed for the moment, although there would be continued revisions and acrimony between sections. With this hurdle cleared the lumbermen could return to their respective territories and work on their own problems. For the southern pine manufacturers in the last years of the 1920s this meant continued debates over grade-marking, enlargement of the SPA's inspection activities, and the development of a movement to write moisture-content provisions into the association's grading rules.

During 1925, the association established the patterns which were to characterize grade-marking and standardization activities during the remainder of the 1920s. Early in the year, despite continued arguments and recriminations, the SPA board foreshadowed the action of subscribers in the annual meeting by reaffirming its advocacy of grade-marking, and it called on all subscribers to adopt this practice.[54] The first steps were also taken toward a further refinement in the grading rules when the SPA board created a special committee to study the question of moisture content in lumber.[55] The first concrete results of this project were to come the

following year. Finally, in order to enforce and popularize the association's grading activities, in 1927 the
SPA established inspection offices in Detroit and Chicago
in addition to one already existing in New York City.[56]

By placing inspectors in these areas, the Southern
Pine Association faced the danger that one of them could
be persuaded to submit false reports on claim inspections,
which could cost SPA subscribers a good deal of money. It
was possible that the inspectors, who generally came from
small sawmill town backgrounds in the South, might be
overwhelmed by the pleasures of the northern cities and
become vulnerable to the bribes or blandishments of
unscrupulous lumber purchasers. For this reason, the
Southern Pine Association's northern claims inspectors,
like those in the South, were frequently transferred from
location to location.[57]

In 1928 the question of moisture content dominated
grading and standardization matters both within the
Southern Pine Association and at the national level.
Secretary of Commerce Hoover called a general conference
of lumber producers, distributors, and consumers in May,
and a move to write moisture-content provisions into the
American Lumber Standards was one of the main topics of
conversation. For one rare moment there was apparently
peace and goodwill between southern and western producers.
Former Chief Forester William B. Greeley, newly employed
as secretary-manager of the West Coast Lumbermen's
Association, agreed with the idea of moisture-content
provisions, but called for more time to study the matter
at the mill level and determine what would be a reasonable
requirement which producers could not only support in good
faith but also fulfill. C. C. Sheppard, representing
the Southern Pine Association, seconded Greeley's motion,
which was accepted.[58]

The SPA's grading committee and board of directors
discussed the moisture-content provisions suggested for
the American Lumber Standards at the association's mid-
summer meeting. The board concluded that SPA subscribers
were currently shipping their lumber well within the
recommended limitations and ordered a thorough survey of
conditions in the southern pine field in order to come up
with concrete recommendations concerning maximum moisture
content for each grade and item of stock produced by
southern pine manufacturers.[59] In accordance with these
instructions, H. C. Berckes conferred with officials of
the Forest Products Laboratory, who agreed to undertake

a study of moisture content and drying practices at Southern Pine Association mills. Representative mills, east and west of the Mississippi River, large and small, longleaf and shortleaf, were studied by the laboratory with the assistance of five Southern Pine Association official mill inspectors.[60]

After the FPL study was completed, numerous meetings were held between Forest Products Laboratory representatives and the subscribers and staff of the Southern Pine Association. At the annual meeting in March, 1929, the grading committee discussed the survey and battled for five hours over a definition of dry lumber before writing moisture-content provisions into the Southern Pine Association's grading rules. Grading Committee Chairman W. T. Murray said he considered this the most important matter he had faced in over thirty years of grading committee work in various associations. Both the SPA's board of directors and its subscribers ratified the grading committee's action, thus taking another pioneering step forward and providing a fitting capstone to the grade-marking and standardization activities of the Southern Pine Association during the 1920s.[61]

During the early years of the 1930s the SPA maintained an "adequate and efficient" mill inspection service. During the same period, it initiated two programs to extend and improve inspection and grading services: first, in November, 1931, it decided to grant official Southern Pine Association grade-marking privileges to non-subscribing mills which would meet SPA standards and pay a fee for the service; and second, at the 1932 annual meeting, it wrote into the grading rules some distinctions between longleaf and shortleaf pine. This latter action was in line with a decision taken in the late 1920s to promote the species separately in certain cases and for some specific uses.[62]

Despite these efforts, in the early 1930s the grading committee chairman was deeply concerned about "half-hearted support of grade-marking and collateral activities." He reported that inferior products were being substituted for SPA grade-marked lumber and independent outside "inspection agencies" were furnishing their services to producers and distributors who wanted to market their lumber as "grade-marked" without meeting SPA standards.[63]

By the time the National Recovery Administration went into operation, the Southern Pine Association's staff had been cut in half, and mill inspections had been reduced from a monthly schedule to a two-month or longer one. The lumber code brought momentary improvement. It required species and grade-marking of all lumber, effective January 1, 1934. Thus a policy for which the Southern Pine Association had been struggling since the beginning of its existence became law. At the same time, the federal government purchased vast amounts of grade-marked lumber for its relief and recovery projects.[64]

As a consequence of these developments, the Southern Pine Association's inspection staff was greatly enlarged, regular monthly inspections of subscriber mills were reestablished, annual meetings for all inspectors to coordinate interpretation of grading rules were revised, inspection and trade promotion activities were coordinated, the study of moisture content and the characteristics of lumber shipped by southern pine mills was continued, and special inspection services in New York City and Washington were instituted to help satisfy the requirement for officially grade-marked lumber on all government contracts.[65] The SPA's efforts to serve the government were particularly noteworthy, for it was from this quarter and in the area of grading and inspection that the association encountered its last great crisis of the 1930s.

Beginning in 1931, the SPA made its grade-marking service available to nonsubscribers. The charge for certificate inspections was 50 percent higher for nonsubscribers than for SPA mills, "because of the necessity for including a proportion of the overhead, which is already borne by subscribers in the form of subscription fees."[66] During the NRA period and after, the federal government became a heavy user of grade-marked lumber, and by the late 1930s the Southern Pine Association had built up good will in some government circles because of its grade-marking activities. The Federal Housing Administration, for example, worked closely with the SPA and its inspectors.

However, during the NRA period there were complaints that Southern Pine Association inspectors gave preference to subscriber mills in scheduling their work, and as Grading Committee Chairman W. T. Murray said in 1938, the SPA was "constantly confronted with the ideas of some people that for the consumer's protection, the grading and inspection of all commodities should be a government function." It was largely to head off these criticisms,

The Development of Standards, Advertising, and Promotion

as well as to expand the practice of grade-marking, that the Southern Pine Association in 1939 removed the differential in charges between subscribers and non-subscribers for its inspection and grade-marking services. Unfortunately, from the SPA's point of view, this effort to disarm its critics was unsuccessful.[67]

The most significant portion of the consent decree which the SPA had to sign in 1940 as a result of Thurman Arnold and the New Deal's antitrust charges divorced grading and lumber inspection from the association. The key portion of the decree was the second section, which said:

> That the defendant, Southern Pine Association . . . shall accomplish a separation of all grading rules, standardization, inspection and grade-marking activities, on the one hand, from any and all other activities carried on by SPA, on the other hand. Said grading, inspection and grade-marking activities shall thereafter be carried on only by and through a separate and autonomous bureau of said SPA to be newly created and to be known and designated as Southern Pine Inspection Bureau. The services and activities of said Bureau will be at all times available on equal terms to all manufacturers of Southern Pine lumber without favor or discrimination and without any requirement for joining or otherwise subscribing to said SPA or to any other trade association, or supporting any service or activity other than those of grading, standardization, grade-marking and inspection to be carried on by the Bureau aforesaid.[68]

The leaders of the association and their legal advisers spent most of their time at a general industry meeting and the Southern Pine Association's annual meeting in March selling their decision to enter into a consent decree to SPA subscribers. The leader in this effort was Southern Pine Association President P. A. Bloomer of the Louisiana Long Leaf Lumber Company in Fisher, Louisiana. Bloomer, along with SPA attorney J. H. Crooker, emphasized that the SPA had not actually been convicted of anything, that there was nothing in the consent decree to interfere with the association's normal activities, that the arrangement was actually beneficial in illuminating what the SPA could and could not do, thereby enabling it to chart its future course more clearly, and, finally, that the establishment of the Southern Pine Inspection Bureau would actually strengthen the industry's grading and

195

inspection program. Bloomer told the subscribers that the industry had escaped the very real threat of having grading, inspection, and standardization activities taken over by the government.[69] H. C. Berckes later wrote that "tremendous credit for satisfying the lumbermen that their interests were being well watched, also for keeping them patient should go to Bloomer."[70]

The consent decree, as the Southern Pine Association was careful to point out, did little to change the normal operations of the industry. The Southern Pine Association paid a fine of $10,000, and the Southern Pine Inspection Bureau was set up as an autonomous organization with its own board of governors within the Southern Pine Association, but even in this case the original relationship was not greatly altered, and SPA Assistant Secretary-Manager Albert S. Boisfontaine simply moved over to the position of SPIB secretary-manager. One historian of the New Deal has written that, while Thurman Arnold "gave the antitrust drive a vigor it had not had at least since the Progressive era, he could claim few substantive gains."[71] The investigation and proceedings against the Southern Pine Association do not appear to have done much to embellish the assistant attorney general's record of accomplishments.

The activities of the Southern Pine Association in grading were closely related to its endeavors in advertising and trade promotion. Grade- and trade-marking were obviously the foundations for advertising the quality standards and uniformity of southern pine lumber and were crucial to the association's endeavors to retain its markets against the incursions of products from competing regions and substitute materials. Southern pine manufacturers, however, did not tend to be very consistent in their attitudes toward advertising. At times they emphasized advertising at the expense of all other SPA activities, while on other occasions they wished to eliminate advertising entirely as an economy measure. Naturally, the nature and intent of the association's promotional efforts also changed over the years.

Originally, there were three SPA agencies dealing with advertising—the trade promotion department and the trade extension and advertising committees. These bodies always worked closely together, and the trade extension and advertising committees were eventually consolidated.[72] The advertising committee had general supervision over SPA advertising campaigns, determining the products to be advertised and the potential markets at which advertisements were to be directed.[73]

The trade promotion department's main function was to support SPA advertising campaigns with direct-mail distributions designed to inform the lumber-consuming public of the advantages and uses of lumber produced by Southern Pine Association subscribers. The department also educated subscribers in the production of better lumber and helped retail lumber dealers develop better merchandising methods. The trade extension committee was responsible for research into new uses and markets for southern pine lumber. It was composed of the chairmen of subcommittees dealing with building construction, paving blocks, sales, lath and by-products, other kinds of wood and wood substitutes, new uses for yellow pine, substitutes for wood in railroad construction, fire prevention, and export sales. The committee's work was done primarily by consulting, construction, and paving engineers and other technical experts employed by the association's secretary-manager.[74]

During the early period of the SPA, the southern pine industry was primarily waging a defensive battle because of the incursions of other producing regions and substitute materials. Many, or perhaps most, industry figures did not visualize the extension of southern pine markets by the development of new uses for their product. The SPA's early endeavors in advertising and trade promotion may, therefore, seem quaint and even ludicrous to a later age, although they were deemed crucially important by contemporaries. During its formative years the association waged strenuous fights against laws and ordinances restricting or abolishing certain uses for lumber, for instance wooden sidewalks, curbs, shingles, and bridges. The SPA also fought the elimination of wooden railroad cars and vigorously pushed southern pine for the construction of wood cisterns, tanks, and silos. One of the most intensive efforts was designed to encourage the use of creosoted wooden blocks for paving streets.[75]

The decision to channel association promotional efforts through two separate committees reflected a division in industry thinking on these matters. Advertising through newspapers, trade journals, and national magazines intended for the general public was a rather new concept for the southern pine industry. While this sort of effort was widely practiced by firms with northern headquarters,

companies located strictly in the South with their officers generally on the scene of manufacturing operations
had traditionally favored promotion leaning toward
retailers, architects, engineers, contractors, specifiers,
and salesmen. They favored such devices as motion
pictures, traveling convention exhibits, promotional
literature, samples, souvenirs, and other direct-contact
techniques. While the two approaches were considered
complementary, each had strong advocates. Therefore, two
committees were organized--one for advertising and the
other for trade promotion.[76]

Both committees were quite active during the period
before U. S. entry into World War I. The advertising committee prepared and distributed to the public a wide
variety of pamphlets and leaflets and placed advertisements in many types of newspapers and trade journals, with
much of the emphasis on agricultural journals. The campaigns elicited considerable public interest, but the
advertising budget was cut drastically during the latter
part of the period because of the industry's economic
difficulties.[77] The trade extension committee concentrated
on the promotion of wooden pavements and silos and particularly emphasized efforts to win the favorable interest
of retail dealers and lumber salesmen. In fact, the
Trade Extension Committee sponsored a school of
salesmanship in 1916 which was well attended and became a
tradition in the industry. The committee led in organizing a Southern Pine Salesmen's Service Association to
encourage and assist salesmen in performing their work
more effectively.[78]

During the war, while building was restricted, the SPA
accumulated funds for the expected post-war economic
downturn, and by the conclusion of the armistice, it had
nearly $100,000 in its coffers for national advertising.
In 1919 the association decided that the best way to stimulate lumber consumption was to inaugurate a campaign to
promote home-building. This idea had several advantages:
there was a housing shortage because of the lack of civilian construction during the war, the plan fit neatly into
the association's efforts to encourage permanent settlement on southern cutover lands, and it would find a receptive market in returning servicemen. In addition, the
stimulation given the economy would help ease the absorption of the servicemen back into the civilian labor
market.

The Southern Pine Association called its undertaking the "Build a Home First" campaign, and early in 1919 the organization was asked by the United States Department of Commerce to participate in a similar national movement which became known as the "Build a Home" movement.[79] The SPA's advertising techniques ran the gamut from the preparation of lantern slides and handouts for newspapers through the preparation of publications of various sorts to the placing of paid advertisements in both specialized journals and national magazines directed to a general readership. The SPA also made a strong effort to increase the effectiveness of southern pine salesmen and prepared exhibits for display at various public functions.[80]

While the "Build a Home First" campaign was considered a success, the southern pine industry was still in trouble. Early in 1919, the SPA's committee on sales and distribution concluded "after reviewing all conditions, that manufacturers of substitute materials will make heavy inroads upon our markets." The committee made a long list of recommendations for meeting the challenge. These included the use of increased advertising, giving more attention to the needs of the industrial trade, intensifying efforts to penetrate foreign markets, and the introduction of "trade-marked" lumber.[81]

Southern pine lumbermen had been interested in the exploitation of foreign markets, and as much as 10 percent of their total production had gone outside the country. These markets had been disrupted by the war and were now threatened by competition from foreign lumber-producing nations with depressed labor conditions.[82] The association had long been active in the export trade field. When the SPA was organized, the board of directors created a subcommittee on export sales under its trade extension committee; and in 1915, the committee printed the association's grading rules in Spanish in order to facilitate trade in South America and the Caribbean.[83]

The association also undertook activities designed to increase southern pine sales abroad in the post-war period. After the war, the SPA sent a representative and an elaborate display to a trade exhibition in Paris and cooperated actively with the U. S. Department of Commerce's Bureau of Foreign and Domestic Commerce in sending four commissioners to Europe to study and assess the opportunities for American producers abroad. The SPA subscribed $10,000 to help meet the commissioners' expenses. The commissioners reported in 1919 that there were excellent possibilities in Europe for American producers, but that strong action was necessary since European states like Norway, Sweden, and Finland were themselves organizing to supply these markets.[84] To help develop that market, the Southern Pine Association in August, 1919, created an export inspection department to inspect and grade lumber in conformity with European specifications. Its services were offered to all southern pine exporters.[85] The association also attempted to familiarize Europeans more thoroughly with southern pine by placing publicity material in journals circulating among European importers. Illustrated articles on southern pine thus appeared in English, French, Spanish, Portuguese, Italian, and Greek publications. At the same time, the SPA did not neglect the South American and Caribbean markets.

Financial problems began to plague the SPA's advertising and trade promotional activities seriously in 1920, with the result that the operations of the trade extension committee had to be curtailed.[86] The association did, however, continue to participate in successful efforts to preserve preferential railroad rates on lumber shipments intended for foreign markets.[87] In addition, it advertised on a very limited scale in trade papers and the principal New Orleans newspapers, as well as in the Literary Digest and Collier's. The association's trade promotion department also furnished display and advertising materials to lumber dealers, but because of financial stringency was forced to begin charging for this service in April.[88] In 1921, expenditures for trade promotional activities were the lowest since the first year of the association's existence.[89] Furthermore, growing pressure on southern pine markets from West Coast fir producers began to make itself felt dramatically in the administrative and advertising activities of the association.

The contest between southern pine and fir was first evidenced in the competition to supply lumber for the construction of railroad cars and for the Atlantic seaboard trade. In July, 1922, the SPA board of directors appointed a special committee "for the purpose of investigating the extent to which fir lumber is displacing Southern Pine in the car material trade and the markets of the Atlantic seaboard."[90] Despite this concern and the appointment of a man to work specifically for increased railroad consumption of southern pine, 1922 was not a good year. At the end of the year, the SPA trade extension committee reported that, while the roads had purchased lumber for nearly two hundred thousand cars, only one-third was southern pine; the rest was fir. This was only about half of southern pine's normal share, which had been approximately 54 percent during the preceding decade. The committee reported that the decline was probably due to the lower cost of fir and in some cases to the inability of southern pine mills to furnish needed materials. Hoping to counteract the trend, the association placed advertisements in railroad journals and published and distributed technical materials extolling and demonstrating the use of southern pine for railroad car construction.[91]

Ironically, the southern pine manufacturers definitely believed that they had a superior product and that they had scientific proof of it. There was a question as to whether it was ethical to publicize this information and thereby implicitly downgrade their competitors' product.[92] The first major tests which seemed to indicate the superiority of southern pine over its competitors for certain structural uses were conducted by an association-employed consulting engineer, the New York City building authorities, the New York Lumber Trade Association, and Columbia University.[93] However, the SPA's internal struggle over whether this material should be used continued, with the West Coast interests joining uninvited into the fray.

Southern Pine Association advertising efforts during 1923 and 1924 concentrated on homebuilding and featured advertisements in national magazines such as Saturday Evening Post, American Magazine, Cosmopolitan, Good Housekeeping, and others.[94] However, expenditures were down from those of 1922 because of declining association revenues.[95] The board of directors pointed to the reduction in advertising and trade promotion revenues as one means of quieting the discontent of subscribers who were going to cut out within a relatively short period of time.

The Southern Pine Association's advertising expenditures were again reduced in 1925, but the SPA was shaken out of its lethargy in 1926 by the knowledge that for the first time in the twentieth century southern pine's share of the national softwood lumber market had fallen below 40 percent.[96] In addition, the SPA remained greatly concerned over the persistent and "considerable amount of misapprehension . . . regarding the continued availability of Southern Pine. . . ."[97] Southern piners strongly

believed that "the erroneous impression upon the part of
dealers, specifiers and consumers that the supply of
Southern Pine was fast disappearing and that they should
switch to fir" was being fostered by the westerners who
"encouraged this impression by the use of a slogan stating
that the West was 'America's Permanent Lumber Supply';
thus aiding and abetting the effort to read Southern Pine
out as a dependable source of supply."[98]

Of immediate importance in 1926, however, was the fact
that the western lumbermen had organized a mass meeting of
three to four hundred in Seattle and voted unanimously to
undertake a huge market extension campaign over a three-
year period at a minimum expense of $500,000.[99] The
Southern Pine Association responded promptly. The SPA
adopted a two-cent-per thousand-board-feet monthly voluntary fee to support trade extension work and authorized
the secretary-manager and president to negotiate a $50,000
loan if needed to subsidize these activities.[100] Much of
the campaign was carried out through popular national
magazines; it emphasized the idea that southern pine was
the "supreme structural wood of the world" and featured
its use in the construction of a bridge across Lake
Ponchartrain and in the concrete forms at Muscle
Shoals.[101]

The Southern Pine Association's advertising activities
in 1927 were dominated by three factors: the resolution
of differences between southern longleaf and shortleaf
producers, a strong surge of substitute materials which
joined western fir as threats to the southern pine
industry, and an advertising campaign predicated upon
Miami's experience in a devastating 1926 hurricane. The
longleaf and shortleaf people had long been bitter
enemies, arguing about the varying merits of their respective woods, and the longleaf producers had gone so far as
to organize the Longleaf Yellow Pine Association to promote their product.[102] By 1926, however, the two groups
were able to agree that the association would differen-
tiate between shortleaf and longleaf in its advertising
and literature.[103]

During 1927 the lumber industry generally, under the
leadership of the National Lumber Manufacturers' Association, inaugurated a million-dollar trade extension campaign to counteract the growing incursions of substitute
materials into traditional lumber markets. The program
emphasized a broad range of activities including research,

advertising, and publicity, as a result of which National
Secretary-Manager Wilson Compton reported that "for the
first time in a quarter-century lumber is measurably
holding its own in competition."[104] Nevertheless, what
the industry called the "new competition" was taking its
toll.[105] The Southern Pine Association's mid-summer
meeting emphasized the competition not only of Celotex and
other substitute materials, but also of fir. It was
reported that some leading southern pine consumers,
notably the Fisher Body Company, were switching to fir
because of their inability to obtain deliveries of good
southern pine. At the same time, the industry was losing
its grip on formerly large southern pine markets in major
northern cities such as Chicago, Detroit, and Kansas
City.[106]

The Southern Pine Association was not completely
satisfied with the idea of uniform campaigns in favor of
all wood species, and it was still plagued with internal
disagreements about the sort of approach to take in advertising its own product. During the year, representatives
of the SPA and the West Coast manufacturers met to
"discuss matters of common interest so that in advertising and trade extension work both groups may work to
the common interest of wood, and at the same time preserve
to each Association the right to extend its efforts in a
vigorous promotion of its individual wood."[107] The
meetings revealed only the difficulties of cooperation
between such highly competitive groups.[108]

The southern pine manufacturers believed they had
irrefutable evidence that their products, both longleaf
and shortleaf, were superior to the western species.
Studies conducted by the Forest Products Laboratory and
published in a Department of Agriculture bulletin showed
southern pine to be superior to its competitors in
strength, shock resistance, hardness, stiffness, and
working stresses and generally seemed to confirm the
conclusions of the previously mentioned SPA tests in New
York City.[109] The western interests objected to the use
of Forest Products Laboratory data in southern pine
advertising and urged that it be discontinued in the name
of interregional harmony. The southerners countered that
this data was in the best interest of consumers and that
the West had not been exactly honorable in advertising the
mistaken notion that the South would no longer be a
reliable timber supplier.

The New South and the "New Competition"

The last two years of the 1920s were marked by continued disputes between longleaf and shortleaf producers and concern about competition from western producers. There was increased attention to the influx of western woods into Atlantic seaboard markets via the Panama Canal. Southern pine manufacturers felt the growing West Coast competition in other markets besides the East. Of great concern was the loss of the market for oil derrick construction materials in the Southwest. While this was due in no small part to the introduction of steel derricks, it also resulted from the marketing of poorly manufactured southern pine, a factor which also helped to account for the loss of southern pine markets elsewhere.[110] The SPA bitterly protested plans of the National Lumber Manufacturers' Association to build a lumber derrick at the International Petroleum Exposition in 1929 using several different species of lumber, for it regarded this as an intrusion into a traditional southern pine field.[111]

Southern pine's competition with western producers was just as heated in foreign as in domestic markets. Consequently, in addition to various export associations organized by southern pine producers under the Webb-Pomerene Act, the SPA board decided in 1928 to designate $20,000 of its annual advertising budget to promote the use of southern pine in foreign countries.[112] This partially met the demands of the longleaf producers, who were most influential in the organization of export associations and were very concerned about markets abroad, particularly in the Caribbean.[113]

In addition to its loss of markets to the western producers and to substitutes, the southern pine industry was threatened near the end of the decade by foreign lumber which began to appear in the Atlantic seaboard markets. This lumber came primarily from Russia, which had reasserted its position as a leading lumber-exporting nation. Its appearance in American markets prompted a strong movement within the Southern Pine Association to put the organization on record as favoring a tariff on imported softwood lumber. By the end of the decade, a special association committee was working to secure southern congressional support for such legislation.[114]

In 1930 the SPA abandoned its costly advertising and trade promotion schemes, and at the same time, the field force was gradually dispersed.[115] However, fearing that competitors were augmenting their advertising facilities

204

The Development of Standards, Advertising, and Promotion

and forces for battles to come, in 1931 the association adopted a voluntary assessment of five cents per thousand feet to support advertising and trade promotion.[116]

During the early years of the 1930s promotional efforts shifted from advertising to maintenance of contacts among architects or specifiers and distributors of southern pine. In order to get by despite reductions in personnel, the SPA used members of its headquarters staff and inspection department for promotional work. In February, 1933, when association revenues sank to their lowest point ever, the SPA called upon its subscribers to support a voluntary two-and-one-half-cent-per thousand-feet fee to defray the cost of field inspectors and the maintenance of a "skeletonized" promotion department.[117]

In the latter part of 1933 and early 1934, promotional efforts were overshadowed by industry involvement in the New Deal recovery program, and advertising and related activities declined precipitously.[118] However, by the end of 1934 the SPA had a surplus of $67,000, and it began to look toward the expansion of promotional activities. As economic conditions began to improve in the late 1930s, the Southern Pine Association again began to expand its activities in such neglected fields as advertising and trade promotion.[119]

The renewed advertising and trade extension efforts were again directed against other producing sections and substitute materials. Emphasizing field work, the association had five field men engaged in trade promotion by late 1936.[120] One of their principal functions was to contact and encourage governmental agencies to purchase grade-marked southern pine.[121]

As the diplomatic situation in Europe worsened and the United States moved toward defense mobilization, the problem shifted from encouraging governmental purchases to stimulating the industry to meet the country's growing lumber needs. During the war, association advertising and promotional efforts were directed toward encouraging greater productivity among industry workers and driving home to the workers and the public the importance of southern pine in the construction of war machinery and facilities. The lumber that appeared in the civilian market often came from small operators with low quality standards, and by the latter part of the war the SPA was again becoming concerned with its more traditional advertising and trade promotion functions.

The New South and the "New Competition"

World War II conditions seriously damaged the industry's reputation. In October, 1944, J. Philip Boyd, director of the lumber and lumber products division of the War Production Board, told southern pine manufacturers of complaints reaching his office concerning wartime practices in the industry:

> I don't need to tell you fellows some of the practices that have been going on in the past year or more, not all of the mills but many mills have taken advantage of the situation to an extent that has hurt your whole industry in the minds of the buyers. These buyers did not come to you and tell you what they thought of you when you gave them something that they didn't want and shoved it down their throats, because they were afraid that you would cut them off from even that, but they did come to us in increasing numbers . . . it would have been a tragedy if, by these actions which can be very bluntly called greed in many cases, you should have offset all of the good things that you were trying to do on one hand by antagonizing the buyer on the other. Believe you me, I have had more than one big buyer, big user, of lumber tell me that if it was possible and when it was possible, at the first time he could do it, he was going to throw wood out of his plant completely and get hold of something else that he could depend on. We have had too many of those come into the War Board. You would be surprised at the testimonials that have come in along that line.[122]

The Southern Pine Association's correspondence from the distribution channels of the lumber trade supported Boyd's statement.[123]

To allay this discontent, to meet the competition of other materials, and to take advantage of the anticipated post-war housing and building boom, the board of directors unanimously approved an expanded trade promotion program. This program contemplated not only reforging close relationships with retailers, wholesalers, and commission men and advertising in an effort to offset the claims of competing materials, but also continuing SPA efforts to maintain the teaching of timber engineering in colleges and sponsoring research in areas such as glue laminating, chemical treatment, and other fields which might enlarge the market for southern pine.[124] In the research area, the Southern Pine Association's efforts were on a relatively

small scale and consisted mainly of cooperation with other
agencies, like universities, on such things as paint and
glue-lamination tests.[125] The situation confronting the
Southern Pine Association was exemplified by the fact that
while during the war it had been spending only about
$30,000 per year for advertising and trade promotion, the
radio program of one major substitute materials producer
cost over $800,000 annually! Obviously the association
had a lot of ground to cover.[126]

At the end of the war the SPA waged a struggle with
competitors on several fronts. In 1948 it launched a
multifaceted trade promotion campaign which carried it
into the 1950s and differed only in detail from earlier
advertising and promotional crusades.

Grade-marking, advertising, and trade promotion are
controversial trade association activities. The struggle
to develop quality controls and standards among southern
pine manufacturers is illustrative of the industry's
internal divisions. The consent decree episode of the
late 1930s reflects the critical eye which the government
and the public often focus on such association activities.
Advertising and trade promotion were less critical from
the public vantage point, but more divisive within the
industry.

Differences over advertising and trade promotion
strategies were very much a part of the Southern Pine
Association's experience from the beginning down to the
mid-1950s. There were also differences not only about the
types of advertising and trade promotion, but about the
percentages of the association's efforts and revenues
which should be channeled into this area. In the 1950s
such differences contributed to the ending of a long era
of SPA development and reflected changes that were trans-
forming the southern pine industry.

NOTES TO CHAPTER 6

1. "Outline of Work under Supervision of the Committees of the Southern Pine Association," John E. Rhodes
notebook, Southern Pine Association Records, Box 39a
(Louisiana State University Archives, Baton Rouge, La.).
Collection hereafter cited as SPA Records.

2. H. C. Berckes, "The Pitch in Pine: A Story of
Traditions, Policies and Activities of the Southern Pine

Industry and the Men Responsible for Them" (unpublished manuscript in possession of the author), p. 25; James Boyd, "Southern Pine Association Official Grades," SPA Records, Box 77a, p. 2.

3. "An Outline of Policies and Activities of the Southern Pine Association, 1915–1950," pamphlet published by the Southern Pine Association in 1950, SPA Records, Collection Prospects; "Outline of Work under Supervision of the Committees of the Southern Pine Association," SPA Records, Box 39a.

4. Boyd, "Southern Pine Association Official Grades," SPA Records, Box 77a, p. 4; "An Outline of Policies and Activities of the Southern Pine Association, 1915–1950," SPA Records, Box 39a.

5. Berckes, "Pitch in Pine," p. 25; "Lumber Awakes! Official Report of the First Annual Meeting of the Subscribers to the Southern Pine Association Held at Grunewald Hotel, New Orleans, Feb. 23, 24, 1916," SPA Records, Box 85b, p. 104.

6. Berckes, "Pitch in Pine," pp. 26–27.

7. "Lumber Awakes!," p. 22; Charles A. Nelson, "Born and Raised in Madison: The Forest Products Laboratory," Forest History, XI (July, 1967), 6–14.

8. "Pine and Patriotism: Official Report of the Third Annual Meeting of the Subscribers to the Southern Pine Association Held at Grunewald Hotel, New Orleans, Feb. 19, 20, 1918," SPA Records, Box 85b, pp. 152–53.

9. James Boyd, "On the Firing Line in the Inspection Department," SPA Records, Box 77a, p. 3.

10. Berckes, "Pitch in Pine," p. 117.

11. Ibid., p. 118; James Boyd, "Grade Marking of Southern Pine Lumber," SPA Records, Box 77a, pp. 1–2.

12. Berckes, "Pitch in Pine," p. 118.

13. Ibid., pp. 28, 118.

14. "Lumber Liquidates," SPA Records, Box 85b, p. 168; John E. Rhodes, "What the Southern Pine Association Has Done for the Industry and the Public," address before the sixth annual meeting, Southern Pine Association, Apr. 5-6, 1921, SPA Records, Box 84b.

15. Interview with H. C. Berckes, Jan. 24, 1968.

16. Berckes, "Pitch in Pine," p. 98.

17. "Minutes of the Meeting of the Grading Committee of the Southern Pine Association . . . February 11, 1922," SPA Records, Box 67b.

18. "Minutes of a Meeting of the Southern Pine Association Board of Directors . . . March 27, 1922," SPA Records, Box 70b.

19. Berckes, "Pitch in Pine," pp. 98-99.

20. "Minutes of a Meeting of the Southern Pine Association Board of Directors . . . March 27, 1922," SPA Records, Box 70b.

21. "Minutes of a Meeting of the Southern Pine Association Board of Directors . . . March 29, 1922," SPA Records, Box 70b.

22. Louis Galambos, Competition and Cooperation: The Emergence of a National Trade Association (Baltimore: Johns Hopkins University Press, 1966), p. 67. For Hoover's position on trade associations see U. S.; Department of Commerce, Tenth Annual Report of the Secretary of Commerce, 1922 (Washington, D.C.: Government Printing Office, 1922), pp. 29-32; Twelfth Annual Report of the Secretary of Commerce, 1924, pp. 22-24; Thirteenth Annual Report of the Secretary of Commerce, 1925, 10-27; and Fourteenth Annual Report of the Secretary of Commerce, 1926, 11-27.

23. Ralph W. Hidy, Frank Ernest Hill, and Allan Nevins, Timber and Men: The Weyerhaeuser Story (New York: Macmillan, 1963), p. 366.

24. Berckes, "Pitch in Pine," p. 100.

The New South and the "New Competition"

25. Hidy, Hill, and Nevins, Timber and Men, p. 366.

26. "Minutes of a Meeting of the Southern Pine
Association Board of Directors . . . March 27, 1922," SPA
Records, Box 70b.

27. Ellis Lucia, Head Rig: The Story of the West
Coast Lumber Industry (Portland, Ore.: Overland West
Press, 1965), pp. 148-49.

28. Berckes, "Pitch in Pine," p. 104.

29. Interviews with H. C. Berckes, Jan. 24, Feb. 10,
1968; Lucia, Head Rig, 112.

30. Berckes, "Pitch in Pine," p. 106.

31. James F. McNeil, "Results and Benefits of Applying
Simplified Practice to (Softwood) Lumber," SPA Records,
Box 39a; "Report of Grading Committee on National
Standardization Program, January 16, 1924," SPA Records,
37a.

32. McNeil, "Results and Benefits."

33. John E. Rhodes, "What the Association is Doing for
Southern Pine," in "Homes and Citizenship: Official Report
to the Eighth Annual Meeting of the Subscribers to the
Southern Pine Association, Held at Grunewald Hotel, New
Orleans, March 20 and 21, 1923," SPA Records, Box 85b,
pp. 20-21.

34. Hidy, Hill, and Nevins, Timber and Men, p. 366.

35. "Report of Grading Committee on National Standardization Program, January, 1924," SPA Records, Box 37a.

36. U. S. Department of Commerce, Bureau of Standards,
Lumber (fourth edition), Simplified Practice Recommenda-
tion R16-29 (Washington, D. C.: Government Printing
Office, 1929), p. 66.

37. McNeil, "Results and Benefits."

The Development of Standards, Advertising, and Promotion

38. W. T. Murray, "Lumber Standardization," in "A New Era," SPA Records, Box 85b, pp. 160-61.

39. Wilson Compton, "National Problems," in "A New Era," SPA Records, Box 85b, pp. 50-51. Compton read the correspondence with Herbert Hoover that had brought the Secretary of Commerce into the precedings.

40. "Minutes of a Meeting of the Southern Pine Association Board of Directors . . . March 10, 1924," SPA Records, Box 70b; John M. Collier, The First Fifty Years of the Southern Pine Association, 1915-1965 (New Orleans: Southern Pine Association, 1965), pp. 83-84.

41. Lucia, Head Rig, pp. 114-16.

42. "Minutes of a Meeting of the Southern Pine Association Board of Directors . . . March 10, 1924," SPA Records, Box 70b; C. C. Sheppard, "How to Make Grade-Marking Effective," in "A New Era," SPA Records, Box 85b, pp. 141-42, 146-49.

43. Collier, First Fifty Years, p. 83.

44. Interview with H. C. Berckes, Jan. 24, 1968. The SPA board of directors' report on their decision was somewhat more circumspect. See "Minutes of a Meeting of the Southern Pine Association Board of Directors . . . November 6, 1924," SPA Records, Box 70b. For the Lutcher and Moore Company's account of their pioneering efforts in grade-marking see Hamilton Pratt Easton, "The History of the Texas Lumbering Industry" (Ph.D. dissertation, University of Texas, 1947), pp. 396-97. According to H. C. Berckes, some operators also had opposed the machine-marking because of expense since they were close to cutting out, and in addition the longleaf producers were reluctant to mark their product with a grade that would also appear on shortleaf of the same grade. For another account of these proceedings see Berckes, "Pitch in Pine," pp. 124-27.

45. "Minutes of a Meeting of the Southern Pine Association . . . March 24 and 25, 1925," SPA Records, Box 73b.

The New South and the "New Competition"

46. "Transcript of the Proceedings of the Meeting of the Trade Extension Committee of the Southern Pine Association . . . July 21, 1926 . . .," SPA Records, Box 68b.

47. "Minutes of a Meeting of the Southern Pine Association Board of Directors . . . July 22, 1926," SPA Records, Box 70b; "Transcript of the Proceedings of the Meeting of the Southern Pine Association . . . July the 22nd, 1926 . . .," SPA Records, Box 68b.

48. "Proceedings of a Meeting of the Southern Pine Association . . . June 16, 1925," SPA Records, Box 68b.

49. H. C. Berckes, "A Decade of Service," SPA Records, Box 85b, p. 16.

50. Ibid, pp. 17-18.

51. Ibid., pp. 18-19.

52. "Minutes of a Meeting of the Southern Pine Association Board of Directors . . . June 16, 1925," SPA Records, Box 85b; "Proceedings of a Meeting of the Southern Pine Association . . . June 16, 1925," SPA Records, Box 85b.

53. Eli Wiener to H. C. Berckes, Apr. 8, 1926, Kurth Papers, Box 816 (Forest History Collection, Stephen F. Austin State University Library, Nacogdoches, Tex.).

54. "Minutes of a Meeting of the Southern Pine Association Board of Directors . . . March 23, 1927," SPA Records, Box 70b. The SPA estimated in 1927 that 67 percent of the total production of the association was grade-marked. See C. C. Sheppard, "The Status of Grade Marking," Lumber Trade Journal, Apr. 1, 1927, p. 25 (reprint in SPA Records, Box 74b.

55. "Minutes of a Joint Meeting of the Board of Directors and the Budget Committee of the Southern Pine Association . . . April 27, 1927," SPA Records, Box 70b.

56. "Minutes of a Meeting of the Grading Committee of the Southern Pine Association . . . March 21, 1927," SPA Records, Box 37a.

The Development of Standards, Advertising, and Promotion

57. Interview with H. C. Berckes, Aug. 10, 1968.

58. "Hearing before the General Conference of Lumber Producers, Distributors, and Consumers, May 3, 1928," SPA Records, Box 37a, pp. 41, 44-45, 47-48. Because of their past experiences and contact during the spring of 1928 with Colonel Greeley, the southern pine manufacturers looked forward to a better working relationship with the West Coast producers. Although the very real differences between the sections remained, the SPA felt that it had "made a step in advance, when the West Coast people employed Col. Greeley . . . Mr. Greeley is broad-minded and understands the whole situation, and when we have our conferences with him we are going further and getting on a better basis." "Minutes of the Meeting of Subscribers of the Southern Pine Association . . . June 20 and 21, 1928," SPA Records, Box 68b.

59. "Minutes of a Meeting of the Grading Committee of the Southern Pine Association . . . June 19, 1928," SPA Records, Box 37a; "Minutes of a Meeting of the Southern Pine Association Board of Directors . . . June 20, 1928," SPA Records, Box 70b.

60. "Minutes of a Meeting of the Grading Committee of the Southern Pine Association . . . November 8, 1929," SPA Records, Box 37a.

61. "Proceedings of Meeting of Grading Committee . . . March 25, 1929, Mr. W. T. Murray, Chairman, Presiding," SPA Records, Box 67b; "Murray on Relation of Grades to Markets," Lumber Trade Journal, Apr. 1, 1929, p. 28 (reprint in SPA Records, Box 74b); Collier, First Fifty Years, p. 95.

62. "Minutes of a Meeting of the Board of Directors of the Southern Pine Association . . . November 11, 1931," SPA Records, Box 70b; Southern Pine Association press release, Mar. 22, 1932, SPA Records, Box 9b.

63. W. T. Murray to L. O. Crosby, Jan. 13, 1933, SPA Records, Box 40a. Several pages of specific examples of these abuses are attached to Murray's letter. Further material concerning this problem is contained in the board of directors and grading committee minutes for Feb., 1933, in SPA Records, Box 70b.

The New South and the "New Competition"

64. Berckes, "Pitch in Pine," pp. 153, 170-71, 187-88.

65. Southern Pine Bulletin, I (Apr. 11, 1936), 6 (copy in SPA Records, Box 83b).

66. "The Whys and Wherefores Of Southern Pine Association Grade Marks and Certificates Of Inspections," SPA Records, Box 84b.

67. H. C. Berckes to J. F. Carter, Oct. 11, 1933, SPA Records, Box 40a; "Proceedings of Southern Pine Association Twenty-Third Annual Meeting . . . 1938," SPA Records, Box 73b; "Proceedings of Southern Pine Association Twenty-Fourth Annual Meeting . . . 1939," SPA Records, Box 73b.

68. "In the District Court of the United States for the Eastern District of Louisiana, New Orleans Division, Civil Action No. 275, United States of America, Plaintiff, versus Southern Pine Association, et al., Defendants," SPA Records, Box 39a.

69. "Proceedings of Southern Pine Association Twenty-Fifth Annual Meeting . . . 1940," SPA Records, Box 73b; "Proceedings of Industry-Wide Meeting of Southern Pine Manufacturers . . . March 29, 1940," SPA Records, Box 73b.

70. Berckes, "Pitch in Pine," p. 193.

71. William E. Leuchtenberg, Franklin D. Roosevelt and the New Deal, 1932-1940 (New York: Harper Torchbook, 1963), p. 260.

72. James Boyd, "Advertising," SPA Records, Box 77a, p. 2.

73. "Outline of Work under Supervision of the Committees of the Southern Pine Association," SPA Records, Box 39a.

74. James Boyd, "Trade Promotion," SPA Records, Box 77a, p. 1.

75. Berckes, "Pitch in Pine," pp. 42-43.

76. Ibid., pp. 44-45.

The Development of Standards, Advertising, and Promotion

77. "Statement of Expenses of the Advertising Department, Southern Pine Association, March 1, 1915 to January 28, 1916," SPA Records, Box 27b; W. H. Sullivan to Charles S. Keith, May 15, 1916, John Henry Kirby Papers, Box 222 (University of Houston Library, Houston, Tex.); "Annual Financial Statement, Expenses of Advertising Department for Year Feb. 1st, 1916 to Feb. 1st, 1917," SPA Records, Box 27b.

78. James Boyd, "Cooperation with Retail Lumber Dealers," SPA Records, Box 77a, p. 1; "School of Salesmanship," SPA Records, Box 68b, pp. 1, 2.

79. John E. Rhodes, "Activities of the Southern Pine Association," undated pamphlet published by the Southern Pine Association, SPA Records, Box 84b; Collier, First Fifty Years, p. 69.

80. Rhodes, "Activities of the Southern Pine Association," SPA Records, Box 84b; Collier, First Fifty Years, pp. 69-71.

81. "Report of Committee on Sales and Distribution of Southern Pine Association, February 24, 1919," SPA Records, Box 67a.

82. Berckes, "Pitch in Pine," p. 95.

83. "Lumber Awakes!," SPA Records, Box 85b, pp. 93, 133.

84. Ibid.; Rhodes, "Activities of the Southern Pine Association," SPA Records, Box 84b; Southern Pine Association to Subscribers, Nov. 27, 1918, SPA Records, Box 37a. For a brief discussion of the Wilson administration's promotion of trade association activities in the export field, see Gabriel Kolko, The Triumph of Conservatism: A Reinterpretation of American History, 1900-1916 (Chicago: Quadrangle, 1967. Orig. published, 1963, Free Press of Glencoe), pp. 275-76.

85. "Minutes of a Meeting of the Southern Pine Association Board of Directors . . . April 3, 1919," SPA Records, Box 67b, p. 6.

The New South and the "New Competition"

86. King H. Pullen, "Trade Extension Activities of the Association," in "Lumber Liquidates," SPA Records, Box 85b.

87. "Southern Organizations Minutes—1/12/20 Memphis," SPA Records, Box 67a; "Minutes of a Meeting of the Southern Pine Association Board of Directors . . . March 15, 1920," SPA Records, Box 70b.

88. "Lumber Liquidates," SPA Records, Box 85b, pp. 86, 88–92. The SPA was actually able to support the trade promotion department's payroll for the year from these revenues.

89. "Southern Pine Assocation Trade Promotion Expenses 1915–1946, Incl.," SPA Records, Box 12b.

90. "Minutes of a Meeting of the Southern Pine Association Board of Directors . . . July 7, 1922," SPA Records, Box 70b.

91. "Minutes of a Meeting of the Southern Pine Association Board of Directors . . . December 13, 1922," SPA Records, Box 70b.

92. Berckes, "Pitch in Pine," p. 135.

93. "Minutes of a Meeting of the Southern Pine Association Board of Directors . . . July 7, 1922," SPA Records, Box 70b; "Minutes of a Meeting of the Southern Pine Association Board of Directors . . . December 13, 1922," SPA Records, Box 70b.

94. King H. Pullen, "Advertising Southern Pine," Southern Lumberman, Dec. 20, 1924 (reprint in SPA Records, Box 84b).

95. "Southern Pine Association Trade Promotion Expenses 1915–1946, Incl.," SPA Records, Box 12b.

96. Collier, First Fifty Years, p. 89. Association advertising expenditures in 1925 totaled $108,175.95. "Southern Pine Association Trade Promotion Expenses 1915–1946, Incl.," SPA Records, Box 12b.

The Development of Standards, Advertising, and Promotion

97. E. J. Hurst, "Advertising and Trade Extension Activities," in "A Decade of Service," SPA Records, Box 85b.

98. Berckes, "Pitch in Pine," p. 135.

99. Lucia, Head Rig, p. 149.

100. "Minutes of a Meeting of the Southern Pine Association Board of Directors . . . March 22, 1926," SPA Records, Box 70b; "Minutes of a Meeting of the Southern Pine Association Board of Directors . . . July 22, 1926," SPA Records, Box 70b.

101. Collier, First Fifty Years, p. 89.

102. Berckes, "Pitch in Pine," pp. 136-37.

103. "Minutes of a Meeting of the Southern Pine Association Board of Directors . . . March 21, 1927," SPA Records, Box 70b.

104. Wilson Compton, "Lumber: An Old Industry and the New Competition," Harvard Business Review, X (Jan., 1932), 167.

105. Vernon H. Jensen, Lumber and Labor (New York: Farrar and Rinehart, 1945), pp. 25-26.

106. "Transcript of the Proceedings of the Mid-Summer Meeting of the Southern Pine Association . . . June 23, 1927," SPA Records, Box 68b.

107. "Minutes of a Meeting of the Southern Pine Association Board of Directors . . . October 5, 1927," SPA Records, Box 70b.

108. "Transcript of the Proceedings of the Trade Promotion Committee of the Southern Pine Association Meeting . . . June 22, 1927," SPA Records, Box 68b.

109. "Trade Promotion and Advertising Meeting," Lumber Trade Journal, July 1, 1927 (reprint in SPA Records, Box 74b).

110. "Minutes of Joint Meeting of Trade Promotion Committee and Advertising Committee of the Southern Pine Association . . . June 26, 1929; and of Midsummer Meeting of Subscribers, June 27, 1929," SPA Records, Box 68b; "Proceedings of the Meeting of the Southern Pine Association Held on December 10, 1929 . . . Hot Springs, Ark.," SPA Records, Box 68a. One leading southern pine manufacturer attributed much of the industry's marketing problem to the impact of the Panama Canal, arguing that because of the canal the Atlantic Coast market was lost, with the principal southern pine market then becoming the middle west. Elwood R. Maunder, comp., James Greeley McGowin--South Alabama Lumberman: The Recollections of His Family (Santa Cruz, Calif.: Forest History Society, 1972), pp. 36-37.

111. "Minutes of a Meeting of the Advertising and Trade Extension Committees of the Southern Pine Association . . . August 1, 1929," SPA Records, Box 70b.

112. "Minutes of a Meeting of the Southern Pine Association Board of Directors . . . March 26, 1928," SPA Records, Box 70b. There is an extended discussion of the Webb-Pomerene Act in Burton I. Kaufman, Efficiency and Expansion: Foreign Trade Organization in the Wilson Administration, 1913-1921 (Westport, Conn.: Greenwood Press, 1974).

113. Anson C. Goodyear to H. C. Berckes, June 4, 1928, SPA Records, Box 11b; "Proceedings of the Meeting of the Southern Pine Association Held on December 10, 1929 . . . Hot Springs, Ark.," SPA Records, Box 68a.

114. H. C. Berckes to Judge Wm. S. Bennet, Sept. 26, 1929, SPA Records, Box 37a; J. S. Farish to Berckes, Nov. 23, 1929, SPA Records, Box 27a; "Minutes of a Meeting of the Southern Pine Association Board of Directors . . . December 11, 1929," SPA Records, Box 70b; unaddressed circular from C. C. Sheppard intended for Southern Pine Association subscribers, Dec. 19, 1929, SPA Records, Box 37a.

115. "Mr. Berckes Talks to Subscribers," Lumber Trade Journal, Dec. 15, 1930, p. 37 (reprint in SPA Records, Box 74b).

The Development of Standards, Advertising, and Promotion

116. H. C. Berckes to C. C. Sheppard, May 9, 1931, SPA Records, Box 39b; "Minutes of a Meeting of the Board of Directors of the Southern Pine Association . . . March 25, 1931," SPA Records, Box 70b.

117. Southern Pine Association press release, Mar. 22, 1932, SPA Records, Box 9b; "Minutes of a Meeting of the Board of Directors of the Southern Pine Association . . . February 15, 1933," SPA Records, Box 70b.

118. "Southern Pine Association Trade Promotion Expenses 1915–1946, Incl.," SPA Records, Box 12b.

119. Berckes, "Pitch in Pine," p. 172.

120. "Report on Field Work to Trade Promotion Committee, W. H. O'Brien, November 11, 1936," SPA Records, Box 11b.

121. Southern Pine Association Press release, Mar. 29, 1937, SPA Records, Box 9a.

122. "Proceedings of a Meeting of the Southern Pine War Committee . . . October 26, 1944," SPA Records, Box 68a, pp. 8–9.

123. For examples of the dissatisfaction with the southern pine industry's treatment of wholesalers and retailers see H. W. Shepard to Southern Pine Association, Mar. 15, 1944, Everett H. Haines to Southern Pine Association, Feb. 23, 1944, and J. H. Austin to W. H. O'Brien, Feb. 15, 1944, all in SPA Records, Box 70a.

124. "Summary of Committee Recommendations Unanimously Approved by the Southern Pine Association Board of Directors, October 26, 1944," SPA Records, Box 70a.

125. "Minutes of a Meeting of the Board of Directors of the Southern Pine Association . . . October 26, 1944," SPA Records, Box 11a, p. 38; "Statement of Advertising and Trade Promotion Committee by W. H. O'Brien, Trade Promotion Manager . . . October 25, 1944," SPA Records, Box 11a, pp. 12–13.

126. "Or Else—Outline of Problems Facing Southern Pine Industry," SPA Records, Box 11a, p. 9.

An early meeting of the Southern Pine Association, possibly the first annual meeting in New Orleans in 1915

Charles S. Keith, first president of the SPA

John E. Rhodes, first secretary-manager of the SPA

John Barber White, an early leader of the southern lumber industry

John Henry Kirby, president of the National Lumber Manufacturers' Association, 1918-22

C. C. Sheppard, a bulwark of the
SPA during the 1930s and '40s

Henry E. Hardtner, a regional
leader in forest conservation

J. R. Bemis, who was deeply
involved in the restructuring
of the SPA in the mid-1950s

H. C. Berckes, longtime administrative leader of the SPA

Stanley Deas, H. C. Berckes, and Earl McGowin, two longtime SPA leaders and a prominent manufacturer

ulf Coast ports turned out ships constructed of southern pine for use in World War I

lear-cutting and dragging logs across young trees with steam skidders to reach
ailroad spurs helped create the industry's cutover land problems

Kirby Papers, University of Houston Library

John Henry Kirby became the focal point of the industry's World War I mobilization effort, as this cartoon from the *Houston Post* suggests

The SPA was a leader in the industry's war mobilization effort

A street scene in Bogalusa, La., a town that was built up around the Great Southern Lumber Company (ca. 1920)

Sawmill of the Great Southern Lumber Company, which claimed to be the world's largest at the time of construction in 1908 (ca. 1915)

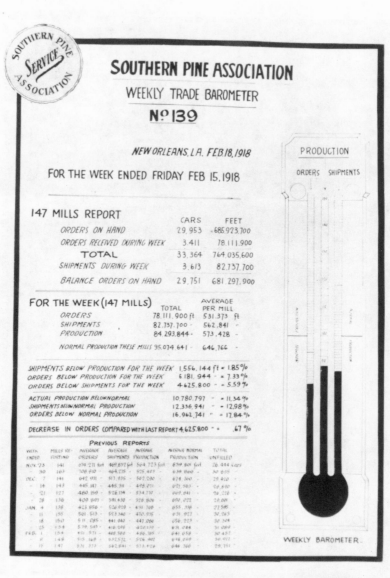

The "Weekly Trade Barometer," a major SPA statistical activity

7

The Transportation Struggle

Transportation was among the major concerns of the southern pine industry and thus of the SPA. The problem was not only that of getting the lumber to markets, but of getting it there cheaply enough that southern pine producers could compete effectively with other lumber regions and with various lumber substitutes. The problem was complicated by the fact that southern pine manufacturers were scattered across a broad geographical area and thus had different transportation needs and conditions.

SPA transportation interests were originally entrusted to a transportation committee and the traffic department. The committee consisted of three members, one representing subscribers east of the Mississippi River, another those west of the river outside of Arkansas, and the third those in Arkansas. Transportation committee decisions were subject to the approval of the board of directors, which kept under surveillance such matters as freight rates charged by common carriers, railroad car supply, bills of lading, freight claims, and the classification of lumber for shipment.[1] The committee's sectional composition reflected serious differences among subscribers that at times seemed to threaten the very life of the association.

The traffic department, which worked with and under the transportation committee, was headed by a traffic manager. He was appointed by the secretary-manager with the approval of the transportation committee and the board of directors. Although he had general supervision over all lumber traffic, his principal duty, like that of the committee, was to assure that the railroads maintained fair and equitable freight rates on southern pine lumber so that it could compete with products from other areas in common markets. There was also an assistant traffic manager who acted as coordinator of the department's varied activities. He reviewed the reports of the several state and federal rate-making bureaus and supervised the preparation of rate studies. The assistant traffic manager also handled routine correspondence.[2]

Transportation activities were important to the SPA's development, not only because of the problems handled, but also because of the men brought into the association to deal with them. Two individuals hired in an almost haphazard fashion to work with transportation matters during the SPA's earliest days remained to become undoubtedly the most significant career employees during a long span of Southern Pine Association history.

The first of these was A. G. T. Moore, who toiled for almost four decades as traffic manager and then as head of the association's conservation activities. Like most of the SPA staff, Moore was a native New Orleanian. He was trained in transportation rate work while in the employ of the Louisville and Nashville Railroad, where he began as an office boy. After learning the intricacies of rate-making and the rate structure, Moore moved into a job as assistant rate clerk and traffic manager with the New Orleans Board of Trade. He eventually left the board of trade and spent some time as secretary of the chamber of commerce in Gainesville, Florida, before returning to Crescent City. He applied for a job as SPA traffic manager and was hired by John E. Rhodes, who then ordered Moore to "go get somebody" to assist with his work.[3]

Moore did not have to look far to find his assistant. His choice was H. C. Berckes, who had also worked for the board of trade. Berckes's humble beginning with the SPA did not give any indication that he was destined eventually to become its highest professional officer. Berckes was also a native of New Orleans. He was descended from a Protestant German family which had settled originally in the vicinity of Buffalo, New York, and had emigrated to New Orleans after the Civil War. Upon finishing high school, Berckes went to work for the New Orleans Board of Trade and worked for that organization from 1910 to 1915. During his tenure with the board of trade, Berckes worked as a stenographer and rate clerk, but he spent his evenings learning all he could about transportation and the railroad rate structure. After joining the Southern Pine Association, he attended night classes at the Tulane College of Commerce.[4]

The beginnings of SPA transportation work were rather inauspicious. It, together with grading rules and some old equipment, represented the only observable direct tie with the old Yellow Pine Manufacturers' Association. At the time of its demise, the YPMA had been working on the preparation of a transportation rate book, but this activity naturally stopped after the Missouri Ouster Case. By this time the YPMA had built a formidable file of freight rate tariffs which was brought to New Orleans from Missouri and used by the SPA in compiling its first rate book.[5]

The yellow pine industry's development was intimately related to the extension of railroad lines into the South. The somewhat haphazard way in which this penetration took place is at least partially responsible for the chaotic and confusing railroad rate structure in the South, as, indeed, in the rest of the nation.[6] By the time the Southern Pine Association came into existence, the outlines of the southern freight rate structure were established, the movement toward consolidation of southern roads into comprehensive rail systems was well underway, and the framework of the federal regulatory mechanism was established. However, the SPA had to operate in the oft-confusing world of rate making described by one observer as "a highly developed science of relativity." According to one work on the southern rate structure, understanding this environment entails a knowledge of five terms: classification, classification territory, rate territory, class rates, and commodity rates.[7]

Classification refers to the grouping of similar items in terms of physical composition, value, or competitive relationship into one "rating" or "classification" group, thereby permitting a single scale of charges for many different articles and eliminating the need for individual rates for each article moved. The determination of an article's classification depends on tradition, competition, the cost of handling due to bulk and weight, ability to bear costs, liability to damage, and the rates on competing goods. In the early days before pooling arrangements, consolidations, and federal regulation, each railroad made up its own classification. There was no attempt at uniformity. One early railroad published its rates under five headings: "heavy goods," "light goods," "case goods," "logs," and "whiskey." Gradually the practice developed of giving a single key rate to first class in the several classifications or territories with other classes as percentages of the first-class rate.[8]

The United States is divided into three major classification territories – "Official," "Southern," and "Western." The "Official" classification covers the area north of the Ohio River and a line running from Cincinnati through West Virginia to Norfolk, Virginia, and east of the Mississippi River and a line running from the head of Lake Michigan through Milwaukee to the Illinois state line. The "Southern" classification territory covers the area south of the Official and east of the Mississippi River. The area west of the Official and Southern areas is included in the "Western" classification territory. Thus Southern Pine Association subscribers came from two different classification territories – Western and Southern. The territories evolved from arrangements made by the railroads during the nineteenth century and were made official with the approval of the Interstate Commerce Commission in 1919. There are differences in the ratings given in each territory, and an article given a certain rating in one territory may receive a completely different rating in another.[9]

As if the matter of classification were not enough, the country is also divided into five rate territories in which first-class rates are established at different levels. This means that goods having the same classification move at different rates in the several rate territories. The five rate territories include the "Official," "Southern," "Southwestern," "Eastern Trunk Line," and "Mountain Pacific." For movements between the territories, the rates are blended to arrive at a through rate with no single scale determining the rates between any two territories.[10] Again the SPA's subscribers operated in two territories – Southern and Southwestern. The fact that the Southern Pine Association's subscribers fell into different classification and rate territories divided by the Mississippi River complicated the tasks of the transportation department and at times threatened the continuance of the association's transportation work, if not the SPA itself. Remembering early hectic traffic endeavors, H. C. Berckes remarked, "Like we always said, God, if only the Mississippi River had dried up we'd be all right."[11]

The South has generally suffered from higher rates than the other classification and rate territories. However, it has been difficult to demand redress, because the southern disadvantage is primarily due to higher class rates, and the class rate structure does not control the entire movement of goods in southern and interterritorial commerce. Class rates are designed to cover the needs of the occasional shipper and the shippers of high-cost products. Producers who ship frequently or who ship large quantities of a product may find class rates prohibitive. These people may, through consultation with the railroads, litigation before the Interstate Commerce Commission, or threats to ship their goods by other means, receive special rates which are exceptions to the class rate structure. These changes in the basic rate structure are called commodity rates, and they are generally given to shippers producing heavier or less valuable goods which would be unable to bear the costs imposed by the regular class rate structure.[12] More than 95 percent of all freight traffic throughout the country moves on such exceptions to the class rate structure, and lumber is among the materials shipped under commodity rates. In fact, the South has generally had lower commodity rates than other areas on a number of important raw materials, such as brick, fertilizer, coke, lime, logs, lumber, pig iron, pulpwood, sand, gravel, crushed stone and slag, iron and steel scrap, and iron ore. According to many critics, this has helped to impose and retain the mantle of raw extractive material production upon the South.[13]

Within the rate system and structure outlined above, the Southern Pine Association carried out its activities on behalf of the varied transportation interests of its subscribers. These activities centered around attempts to fight actions by the railroads which would have directly injured the interests of Southern pine producers or aided their competitors from other lumber-producing sections and the manufacturers of substitute materials. Naturally, the main focus of association activity was upon direct negotiation with the carriers themselves whenever possible and presentation of the Southern Pine Association's position before the Interstate Commerce Commission and other federal agencies if necessary. The SPA seemed continually at odds with the railroads during much of its existence, and this seems to have been true of lumber associations in other areas as well. In fact, one of the major reasons behind the formation of many lumber trade organizations was the manufacturers' concern over transportation.[14] However, the Southern Pine Association was in a more precarious situation than most due to the fact that

225

extremely powerful subscribers were located in different rate and classification territories and thus did not always have identical interests.

The rate structure became crucial to the southern pine industry as production outstripped the needs of local markets. The completion of the railroads and the consolidation of the southern rail and water systems permitted southern pine to enter northern markets, where it immediately encountered competition from other producing sections. In the early days of the industry Missouri producers made no attempt to send their products east of the Mississippi River, confining their marketing to St. Louis and the western territory. However, the development of yellow pine lumbering in Arkansas, especially after 1888, brought penetration into Official territory in Illinois and Indiana. Large-scale yellow pine production east of the Mississippi, in Georgia, Mississippi, Alabama, and the Carolinas, started about the same time, but this area's distribution was confined primarily to the Atlantic seaboard and the eastern part of the country, while the producers west of the Mississippi River monopolized the Illinois and Indiana markets.[15] By the turn of the twentieth century, southern pine was marketed throughout the entire nation east of the Rocky Mountains with approximately 10 percent of the annual production going into the export trade.[16]

By the time the SPA was organized, however, southern pine producers were facing not only the rate problems within their own sections but also the competition of other kinds of lumber and substitutes for their national markets, thus giving them an intense concern for the rate structure in other sections. The development that shaped the transportation and marketing conflicts of the association's early history was the opening of the Panama Canal in 1914. With the opening of the canal, lumber from the West Coast began to move via water to the East Coast, where it gradually replaced southern pine.

The principal western competition came from fir, and some members of the association and its staff came to believe the railroads were actively supporting the expansion of the western fir markets. According to this point of view, the transcontinentals persistently pushed the interests of the western producers, while southern railroads and intermediate and final destination carriers in the North tended to ignore the interests of southern pine because of the erroneous belief that the southern pine

region, like earlier great producing regions, would soon
be cut out. SPA leaders who accepted this interpretation
believed the association should vigorously oppose any
reduction of rates from the West Coast unless they were
matched by corresponding concessions to southern
producers.

However, there were others who did not enthusiastically support SPA efforts to keep the fir producers out of
southern pine markets. At times, these individuals were
active in the upper echelons of association affairs.
Their motives were mixed. Some were men who had invested
in western operations as their southern holdings became
depleted and thus had a foot in both camps; their presence complicated SPA activities in a number of areas and
sometimes threatened to bring the entire association's
structure tumbling down. Others believed that competition
between the various lumber-producing regions should be
deemphasized in the interest of national industry resistance to the inroads of substitute materials. Many of
these men were sincere nationalists who believed there
should be a common bond and cooperation among producers of
all species. Others were probably what their detractors
considered them to be – men with "ambitions for personal
preference and reputation in National affairs. . . ."[17]
The SPA staff was often involved in this and other disputes within the association's ranks.

Association Traffic Manager A. G. T. Moore and his
assistant, H. C. Berckes, were caught in the middle of
one of these controversies in the very early days of the
new SPA's existence. The clash was between producers
east and west of the Mississippi with production facilities in the Southern and Southwestern rate territories,
respectively. Perhaps the most important basing point for
southern pine producers was Cairo, Illinois, which was the
standard for the entrance of southern lumber into Official
territory via other Ohio River crossings at Evansville,
Louisville, and Cincinnati.[18] Eastern producers had a
two-cent rate advantage over their western counterparts on
shipments to Cairo. At one of the first SPA meetings,
John Henry Kirby rose and said, "I recommend that the
Traffic Department try to get the two-cent differential
taken off." Immediately, W. L. Sullivan, manager of the
powerful Great Southern Lumber Company operation at
Bogalusa, Louisiana, sprang to his feet and bellowed, "If
you do that, we're out of the association." In an atmosphere charged with tension, Kirby shouted back, "If you

don't do it, we're out." The change would have amounted to approximately fifty dollars per car, and two of the industry's most powerful firms with the influence to lead entire sections out of the SPA were standing in heated confrontation. In the crisis John E. Rhodes took the chair from President Charles S. Keith and quickly adjourned the meeting for lunch. "So they went and had lunch and talked a little, and they came back and they agreed that they'd abolish the Traffic Department . . . they'd keep us . . . and Mr. Rhodes . . . and Mr. Moore . . . , but if any traffic matters came up on which they'd be in unanimous agreement we would handle it. So we got back in, and little by little a whole big Traffic Department was back again."[19] The traffic department was thus allowed to continue its day-to-day activities at least until the SPA's first important transportation case could be resolved.[20]

This case came up soon after the department's creation in 1915. It concerned one of the most important transportation issues ever to face the lumber industry, the railroad freight rates on rough and finished lumber. The case grew out of two decisions by the Interstate Commerce Commission in 1913 and 1915 stating that existing freight rates on lumber and lumber products were discriminatory in treating rough and finished products alike. The commission invited the carriers to prepare a new schedule of rates removing this discrimination by distinguishing between lumber in its several stages of processing.[21] The railroads formed a classification committee which submitted to the ICC a revised plan for the classification of lumber freight rates providing for the levying of higher charges on dressed lumber than on rough. The plan also proposed that when two or more items of lumber and lumber products were shipped in one car the charge for the entire shipment should be computed at the rate fixed for the item with the highest classification.

The Southern Pine Association was one of the first lumber organizations to protest the proposed reclassification plan. It charged that the plan would result in increased freight costs on southern pine lumber, up to 20 percent on certain shipments and an average of 5 percent overall.[22] The SPA questioned whether the roads had properly interpreted the commission's wishes and expressed the opinion that, should rates on finished lumber be raised, those on rough lumber ought to be correspondingly reduced.[23] The association and other lumber interests filed a formal complaint against the new rate proposals.

The Transportation Struggle

On July 15, 1915, the Interstate Commerce Commission opened an investigation of lumber freight rates and classification throughout the United States. It sent questionnaires covering the effects of the proposed rate changes to the Southern Pine Association and other interested organizations. While preparing a reply to this questionnaire, the SPA decided to join the National Lumber Manufacturers' Association and others in the industry to fight the reclassification plan.[24] These organizations took the position that there should be no change in lumber freight rate classifications and authorized the president of the National Lumber Manufacturers' Association to appoint a special committee to represent them before the Interstate Commerce Commission. This group was known as the national executive committee and represented twenty-eight organizations, including the Southern Pine Association, with an annual production of nearly seventeen billion board feet of lumber.[25]

In addition to its cooperation with other lumber organizations, the Southern Pine Association had its own six-man reclassification committee appointed by the board of directors to take care of southern pine interests during the ICC investigation. The SPA and seven other organizations also employed an attorney who worked with the reclassification committee and the traffic manager in handling the case.[26] All of their efforts were successful, for in 1919, after extended hearings, the Interstate Commerce Commission rejected the carriers' reclassification plan.[27]

Although the reclassification case was the most important single matter the transportation committee and the traffic department faced in 1915, they were involved in other activities. For example, they complained to the ICC about the practice of some shippers who used so-called "transit" cars as rolling warehouses rather than delivering their contents as quickly as possible and freeing the cars for use by other shippers. They also advocated the retention and strict enforcement of reconsignment charges on all shippers who detained cars for the purpose of reconsigning their shipments and did what they could to assure an adequate car supply for SPA subscribers. The transportation committee further sought a greater freight allowance from the carriers for the car stakes and dunnage provided by its shipper-subscribers. The reconsignment penalty was the subject of controversy for a number of years, but due to the continued support of the Southern Pine Association

and other lumber organizations, it was retained. The
question of freight allowances for dunnage and car stakes
also remained alive for a long time, with the SPA insisting
that it was too low and the railroads holding that it was
too high.[28]

Other early transportation activities of the association included the maintenance of complete files of lumber
tariffs, Interstate Commerce Commission decisions, and
other pertinent data, and the publication of rate books,
which gave the lumber freight rates from every southern
sawmill shipping point to all destinations in southern
pine consuming territory. The association also continued
successfully to oppose the efforts of other species to
invade long-time southern pine markets through changes or
advantages in the rate structure. The SPA thus established an efficient traffic program and was well equipped
to handle the transportation difficulties brought about by
World War I.[29]

Shortages and tie-ups in the nation's transportation
system were serious impediments which interfered with the
southern pine industry's activities during the war. The
major problem was the shortage of railroad cars that first
developed nationally in 1916 and continued throughout
1917, until the creation of the Railroad Administration.[30]
In 1916, the car shortage became one of the main concerns
of the Southern Pine Association's transportation committee.[31] In the interest of car conservation and transportation efficiency, the association urged its subscribers
to load their cars heavily to utilize space more fully.[32]
The SPA's traffic department was generally quite effective
in helping the industry secure adequate car supplies to
move the most critically needed material during the war,
but transportation continued to be one of the southern
pine industry's major difficulties in meeting the
nation's wartime lumber needs.[33]

During the 1920s the SPA concentrated on efforts to
protect its subscribers' markets from incursions of
western lumber and to guarantee that southern producers
obtained sufficient railroad cars to transport their
products. During the decade the association made a fundamental change in transportation policy in the hope of
preserving traditional southern pine markets. Because of
the increasing competition between sections and the
corresponding importance of traffic matters, the SPA's
traffic department grew from one man to seven by the
latter part of the 1920s.[34]

230

The Transportation Struggle

The Southern Pine Association's strong efforts to maintain its own rates and preserve the' existing rate relationships between southern and western producers dominated the early 1920s. There were no attempts to resist or protest rate reductions from other producing sections so long as the existing relationships were maintained through corresponding southern reductions. However, it became obvious that the railroads were far more attentive to the needs of the western industry than the southern pine region, which was regarded as being in the last stages of its existence as a major producing area. Southern railroads did not seem fully to realize the possibility that the southern pine region could continue to produce on a permanent basis, and they appeared blithely unaware of the growing threat of truck transportation to their virtual monopoly of the southern lumber-carrying trade.[35]

Not all SPA subscribers supported efforts to maintain existing rate relationships between southern and western producers. Those operators who had interests in the West believed strongly that the old SPA policy of nonresistance to rate changes should be continued. It was only after lengthy discussions and much recrimination between those subscribers with western operations and "a band of 'National-minded' individuals" and those with purely southern interests that the Southern Pine Association and its transportation committee secured the right to work vigorously for the preservation of southern pine markets.[36]

Although seeking to protect its subscribers, the SPA hoped to maintain amicable relationships with the National Lumber Manufacturers' Association, West Coast producers, and the railroads. The SPA's board nevertheless declared that it would be "unalterably opposed to any advance in freight carrying charges on lumber which will alter or disturb the differentials now existing between the rates on Southern Yellow Pine and those other competing woods and building materials."[37] It authorized the transportation committee in fighting to maintain those relationships and, "to take such steps with the carriers or the Interstate Commerce Commission as the Committee may deem necessary. . . ."[38]

However, having taken the position that it was more effective to work with the railroads than against them, the SPA attempted to settle disputes through conferences with the roads and their agents rather than by going immediately to the Interstate Commerce Commission for redress.

The New South and the "New Competition"

By the middle 1920s the SPA's traffic manager was convinced that this method was succeeding and that the railroads were taking a more cooperative attitude in attempting to find workable solutions.[39] That they should do so was understandable, for an important part of the southern carriers' cargo was lumber, amounting on one major southern road to nearly 16 percent of annual freight revenues.[40]

The railroads sought to remove the SPA complaints by increasing efficiency in car handling, improving facilities for carrying heavy traffic, establishing American Railway Association district offices throughout the country to handle regional problems, and organizing regional advisory boards composed of shippers.[41] The Southern Pine Association and its subscribers were heavily represented on these boards. The southern piners were quite pleased with the performance of the carriers and withdrew their plans to go to the federal government for redress.[42]

As the SPA entered the second half of the 1920s, general transportation policies were spelled out and redefined. So the transportation committee and traffic department could take concerted action on behalf of all subscribers, the transportation committee defined the proper rate relationships between producers east and west of the Mississippi River to their various marketing areas and pledged itself to maintaining these relationships. The committee agreed not to oppose rate reductions from either producing section, but said that after the reduced rates were published it would work for the restoration of the proper relationship.[43]

With this internal matter decided, the Southern Pine Association moved toward fundamental reevaluation of its position regarding freight rates in other producing regions. In 1926, in the face of increasing penetration of middle-western and eastern markets by West Coast producers, the SPA's board of directors accepted the transportation committee's recommendation that the association, if necessary, should "oppose before the carriers, or rate regulatory agencies, reductions in rates or ask cancellation of lower competitive rates than are enjoyed by Southern Pine which will operate unequally or unjustly against the Southern Pine Industry."[44] The SPA deviated somewhat from this policy in 1927 when the board resolved that while the transportation committee and traffic department should work to preserve southern pine's position in freight relationships, they should not oppose reductions from other sections "unless discrimination be alleged."[45]

However, by the end of the decade the association remained sufficiently alarmed that the board decided unanimously that the SPA could no longer continue its policy of permitting freight rate reductions from competing lumber producing territories without protest. The board instructed the association to oppose competitors' applications for rate reductions into southern pine marketing territories, and the SPA closed out the decade by successfully resisting certain rate reductions from the Pacific Coast into Central Freight Association territory in the Midwest.[46]

The association's transportation efforts during the 1930's followed the same lines as during the previous decade: contacts with southern carriers and appearances before governmental agencies to ensure that southern pine producers would not be outmaneuvered on the matter of freight rates by their western rivals or the producers of substitute materials. Since lumber moved on commodity rather than class rates, the SPA did not become involved in the great crusade of the 1930s to remove class rate discrimination against the South, but its transportation department kept a close watch on developments so that any attempt to bring lumber into the class rate system could be defeated. Under the leadership of Traffic Manager A. G. T. Moore, the interests of southern pine producers were zealously guarded, and the SPA approached World War II with a battle-tested and smoothly functioning traffic department.[47]

The war brought the expected transportation shortages and difficulties, which were intensified or aggravated by the fact that the southern pine industry was beginning to experience a major change in transportation patterns. By the end of the war, the SPA was encountering not only the old perennial problems, but also some markedly new difficulties in the transportation field. In the post-war period railroad freight costs climbed progressively higher, and the Southern Pine Association was concerned lest its western competitors should obtain rate reductions that would disturb the relationship between the two sections. The SPA was also wary about possible efforts by the rail systems to compensate for reductions in class rates by increasing southern commodity rates. The association, therefore, was very conscious of the need to

convince the railroads that southern pine would be a
long-lived industry and that it would be in their best
interests to cultivate the southern lumbermen's good
will.[48]

From 1937 to 1948 the southern pine manufacturers
gained an eleven-and-one-half-cent-per-hundred-pounds
advantage on West Coast producers on shipments to the
important market of Chicago. This meant a sales advantage of approximately three dollars per thousand feet on
lumber items sold in the Chicago market, which was considered typical of the entire Official territory. The SPA
believed that southerners were "fully entitled" to this
advantage "by virtue of our shorter haul and lower transportation cost factors." The SPA, however, conceded that
westerners "seem to feel they have suffered a real disadvantage," and the transportation committee and department were on guard against possible attempts at readjust-
ment. In fact, the committee advised subscribers of "the
necessity of their letting us know at once of any rumors
or proposals of intended rate reductions from the West
Coast to any part of our common consuming territory."[49]

The industry's attention was not concentrated exclusively on the railroad situation. There was a good deal
of concern about possible inroads by competitors into
southern pine territories via water and truck, or varying
combinations of water-truck-rail shipments. The growing
importance of motor trucks in transporting lumber led the
SPA in 1947 to begin collecting and interpreting statistics on motor transport.[50] By 1950 the preliminary
results of Southern Pine Association studies on industry
transportation patterns were in – and they were a revela-
tion. The traffic department's studies showed that the
mills surveyed reported that about 43 percent of their
monthly shipments were almost evenly divided between
interstate and intrastate traffic. Furthermore, some
mills were using their own trucks as well as those of common carriers, customers, and itinerants. The department
reported that some trucks were traveling as far as 1,200
miles from the mill, and it concluded that "distance no
longer can be considered a factor as to how far Southern
Pine lumber may be trucked at reasonable costs." The
department also noted that "in almost every case, those
resorting to truck shipments report it is because of high
rail freight costs." The department was determined to use
the threat of truck shipments to persuade the railroads to
reduce their rates.[51] The SPA's traffic department was

thus fighting for the protection of its industry's interests by compiling information and statistics for both presentation to the carriers and appearances before the Interstate Commerce Commission. Ironically, this effort was to be weakened, not by the opposition of the association and industry's antagonists, but by upheaval within the ranks of the SPA itself.

The SPA did a generally effective job in promoting and protecting the transportation interests of an industry which had serious internal divisions on the issue. By the mid-1950s, however, conditions in the southern pine industry were rapidly changing. There was a decided shift from rail toward trucks to carry southern pine to market, and some industry leaders were no longer sure that the SPA's extensive transportation activities were worth the cost. Conflicts over this, as well as other matters, contributed to the major changes in personnel and functions which the Southern Pine Association experienced in mid-decade.

NOTES TO CHAPTER 7

1. Albert S. Boisfontaine, "The Southern Pine Association in Retrospect: Seventeen Years of Trail Blazing in the Trade Association Field," Southern Lumberman, CXLIV (Dec., 1931), 109.

2. "An Outline of Policies and Activities of the Southern Pine Association, 1915-1950," Southern Pine Association Records, Collection Prospects (Louisiana State University Archives, Baton Rouge, La.) Collection hereafter cited as SPA Records.

3. Interview with H. C. Berckes, Jan. 24, 1968.

4. The material on the early life of H. C. Berckes is taken from interviews with Mr. Berckes on Jan. 24 and Feb. 10, 1968.

5. Interviews with H. C. Berckes, Jan. 24 and Feb. 10, 1968.

6. The standard sources for the story of the southern rate structure are William H. Joubert, Southern Freight

The New South and the "New Competition"

Rates in Transition (Gainesville: University of Florida Press, 1949); Robert A. Lively, The South in Action: A Sectional Crusade against Freight Rate Discrimination (Chapel Hill: University of North Carolina Press, 1949); and David M. Potter, "The Historical Development of Eastern-Southern Freight Rate Relationships," Law and Contemporary Problems, XII (1947), 416-99.

7. Lively, South in Action, p. 3.

8. Ibid., pp. 3-4.

9. Ibid., pp. 4-6; Potter, "Historical Development," p. 417.

10. Lively, South in Action, pp. 6, 8; Potter, "Historical Development," p. 417; C. Vann Woodward, Origins of the New South 1877-1913 (Baton Rouge: Louisiana State University Press, 1951), pp. 312-13.

11. Interview with H. C. Berckes, Jan. 24, 1968.

12. Potter, "Historical Development," p. 417.

13. Samuel P. Hays, The Response to Industrialism: 1885-1914 (Chicago: University of Chicago Press, 1957), p. 128; Lively, South in Action, pp. 10-14; George Brown Tindall, The Emergence of the New South, 1913-1945 (Baton Rouge: Louisiana State University Press, 1967), pp. 600-601; Woodward, Origins of the New South, pp. 314-15.

14. R. C. Fraunberger, "Lumber Trade Associations: Their Economic and Social Significance" (M.A. Thesis, Temple University, 1951), pp. 35, 39, 81.

15. Ibid.

16. H. C. Berckes, "The Pitch in Pine: A Story of the Traditions, Policies and Activities of the Southern Pine Industry and the Men Responsible for Them" (unpublished manuscript in possession of the author), p. 47.

17. Ibid., p. 49.

18. James Boyd, "Fifty Years in the Southern Pine Industry," Southern Lumberman, CXLIV (Dec., 1931), 62.

19. Interview with H. C. Berckes, Jan. 24, 1968.

20. "Meeting of the Transportation Committee of the Southern Pine Association, April 18, 1916," SPA Records, Box 67a.

21. Eastern Wheel Manufacturers' Association et. al. v. Alabama and Vicksburg Railway Company et. al. 27 I.C.C. Reports 382 (1913); Anson, Gilkey and Hurd Company et. al. v. Southern Pacific Company et. al., 33 I.C.C. Reports 342 (1915).

22. James Boyd, "Transportation; Greatest Medium for Industry and Consumer," SPA Records, Box 77a, p. 7.

23. "Official Report of Proceedings of Mass Meeting of Subscribers of the Southern Pine Association Held at Blackstone Hotel, Chicago, Illinois, July 14, 1915," SPA Records, Box 736, pp. 12–13.

24. "Lumber Awakes! Official Report of the First Annual Meeting of the Subscribers to the Southern Pine Association Held at Grunewald Hotel, New Orleans, Feb. 23, 24, 1916." SPA Records, Box 85b, p. 161.

25. Ibid.

26. Ibid.

27. Boyd, "Transportation; Greatest Medium for Industry and Consumer," SPA Records, Box 77a, p. 7.

28. "Minutes of a Meeting of the Board of Directors of the Soutern Pine Association Held in the Lumbermen's Club, Memphis, Tennessee, Friday, February 26th, 1915," SPA Records, Box 70b, p. 5.

29. "Minutes of a Meeting of the Board of Directors of the Southern Pine Association Held at the Gayoso Hotel, Memphis, Tennessee, Tuesday, April 18th, 1916," SPA Records, Box 67a, p. 3; "Minutes of the Transportation Committee of the Southern Pine Association Held October 30th, 1916, at the Congress Hotel, Chicago, Illinois," SPA Records, Box 67a, p. 5.

The New South and the "New Competition"

30. George Soule, Prosperity Decade: From War to Depression, 1917–1929 (New York: Holt, Rinehart and Winston, 1947), pp. 33–34.

31. "Minutes of a Meeting of the Board of Directors of the Southern Pine Association Held at the Gayoso Hotel, Memphis, Tennessee, Tuesday, April 18th, 1916," SPA Records, Box 67a, p. 3.

32. "War Activities Of The Southern Pine Association," SPA Records, Box 84b, p. 30.

, 33. Berckes, "Pitch in Pine," p. 72.

34. Lumber Trade Journal, XCI (Apr. 1, 1927), 36.

35. Berckes, "Pitch in Pine," pp. 47–48.

36. Ibid., p. 48.

37. "Minutes of a Meeting of the Board of Directors of the Southern Pine Association . . . Mar. 15, 1920," SPA Records, Box 70b.

38. "Lumber Liquidates: Official Report of the Sixth Annual Meeting of the Subscribers to the Southern Pine Association Held at Grunewald Hotel, New Orleans, April 5, 6, 1921," SPA Records, Box 85b, p. 152.

39. Southern Pine Association to The Transportation Committee, March 24, 1921, SPA Records, Box 67a; A. G. T. Moore, "The Quick Turn-Over and Right Price of Transportation," in "A New Era: Official Report of the Ninth Annual Meeting of the Subscribers to the Southern Pine Association, Held at Roosevelt Hotel, New Orleans, March 11 and 12, 1924," SPA Records, Box 85b, pp. 91–93; A. G. T. Moore, "Carriers and Commerce--The Arteries and Life Blood of the Nation," Southern Lumberman, Dec. 20, 1924 (reprint in SPA Records, Box 84b).

40. C. H. Markham, "Transportation Today and Tomorrow," in "A Decade of Service: Official Report of the Tenth Annual Meeting of the Subscribers to the Southern Pine Association, Held at Roosevelt Hotel, New Orleans, March 24 and 25, 1925," SPA Records, Box 85b, pp. 42–43. Markham was president of the Illinois Central Railroad.

The Transportation Struggle

41. Moore, "The Quick Turn-Over and Right Price of Transportation," SPA Records, Box 85b, pp. 95-96.

42. R. H. Aishton, "The American Ways," in "A New Era," SPA Records, Box 85b, pp. 77-79; "Proceedings of the Fifth Meeting of the Southeast Shippers' Regional Advisory Board, American Railway Association Car Service Division . . . March 19, 1924," SPA Records, Box 67a; E. A. Frost, "Report of Transportation Committee," in "A Decade of Service," SPA Records, Box 85b, p. 199.

43. Frost, "Report of Transportation Committee," SPA Records, Box 85b, p. 209.

44. "Minutes of a Meeting of the Board of Directors of the Southern Pine Association . . . June 23, 1927," SPA Records, Box 85b.

45. "Minutes of a Meeting of the Board of Directors of the Southern Pine Association . . . June 23, 1927," SPA Records, Box 85b.

46. "Minutes of a Meeting of the Board of Directors of the Southern Pine Association . . . January 30, 1929," SPA Records, Box 85b; "Report of Secretary-Manager H. C. Berckes," and "Supplemental Report of Mr. Berckes Covering Association Activities," both in Lumber Trade Journal Apr. 1, 1929 (reprint in SPA Records, Box 74b).

47. "Statement on Traffic and Transportation By Eli Wiener, Chairman, Transportation Committee, Southern Pine Association," SPA Records, Box 9a; "Freight Rate Problems of the Southern Pine Industry, Annual Report to the Transportation Committee, by A. G. T. Moore," SPA Records, Box 9a.

48. Ellis Lucia, Head Rig: Story of the West Coast Lumber Industry (Portland, Ore.: Overland West Press, 1965), pp. 125-27; "Eli Wiener, Chairman, Transportation Committee, Report to Executive Committee, January 31, 1946," SPA Records, Box 9a; "Southern Pine Association, Activities of Traffic Department, Annual Report of A. G. T. Moore, Traffic Manager, to Transportation Committee Meeting, May 8, 1946," SPA Records, Box 9a.

The New South and the "New Competition"

49. "A. G. T. Moore, Traffic Manager, Annual Report, April 6, 1949," SPA Records, Box 10a.

50. Southern Pine Association press release, Mar. 22, 1947, SPA Records, Box 10a.

51. "Joint Meeting SPA Board of Directors and Southern Pine Industry Committee . . . January 25 and 26, 1950," SPA Records, Box 70a.

8

The Conservation Struggle

Forestry and conservation were among the most significant concerns of the southern pine industry and the SPA. The association was probably somewhat ahead of the industry generally in its recognition of the regrowth potential of southern forests and its advocacy of sustained-yield operations. During its formative years, however, neither the SPA nor the industry did much of significance in this area. Almost from the beginning the SPA committees dealt with the problems of cutover lands and forestry, but there were no major developments until after World War I.

The subject of cutover lands was intimately related to such other industry concerns as forestry and conservation and the transition from the age of large mills to a period of small-mill domination. Denuded lands were becoming a matter of concern when the SPA was organized, and by the 1920s there was a devastated area of some 1 million acres in the coastal plain from South Carolina to Texas, with a total of about 156 million cutover acres in the South as a whole.[1] Timber resources in many parts of the South were being exhausted, leaving a residue of abandoned towns and unemployed workers. The characteristic "solution" to these related problems was to bring the land into agricultural production, for which it was often poorly suited, and to place the workers on the land.[2]

The condition of Southern cutover lands varied. Some, where selective cutting procedures had been followed, still contained a fairly extensive growth of timber. Others had been more thoroughly denuded, without, however, disturbing the saplings and small trees. Some cutover lands had not only been denuded of mature trees, but also

241

of most of the small trees. Many areas which had been logged after the turn of the century were cleared of almost all of their trees because felled logs had been dragged across the ground to railroad spurs by steam-powered skidders. By the early twentieth century, however, a few southern lumbermen were becoming concerned about the preservation and proper utilization of the area's timber resources.

The Southern Pine Association became the first organization of its kind to study these problems seriously.[3] In 1916, it organized a cutover land committee to determine the areas of cutover lands, to find the best means for their utilization, with the aid of state and federal agricultural agencies, and to organize state associations of owners of idle lands. The association also directed its committee to organize a conference of interested parties to discuss ways and means of furthering the utilization of cutover lands.[4] In general, one of three courses of action could be followed: (1) where the destruction of the timber had been so extensive that a second commercial cut was unlikely, the land could be converted to non-forest uses, such as grazing or farming; (2) where only moderate measures were needed to develop the timber still standing, simple forestry practices could be applied; and (3) where full crops of high-quality timber were desired, extensive reforestation programs could be undertaken.[5]

The first cutover land conference sponsored by the Southern Pine Association was held in April, 1917, and acting on resolutions adopted at the conference, the SPA cutover land committee, with the association's financial support, took the lead in forming the Southern Cut-Over Land Association.[6] Chartered in 1917, this organization served as a clearinghouse of information on cutover lands. The data came from SPA members and from federal and state agencies. The Cut-Over Land Association sponsored and published scientific studies on the utilization of such lands.[7]

However, while understanding the idea behind selling cutover lands for agricultural development, some lumbermen doubted the value of the approach. Henry Hardtner of Louisiana's Urania Lumber Company, one of the industry's great pioneers in reforestation, referred to the 1917 cutover land conference as "a big scheme to try to sell land that was not worth while for agriculture at all." Hardtner later said that the entire plan was "just a skin

game to fool people in the north and west, to think that
they could make a whole lot of money out of poor lands."[8]
    Despite the opposition of some lumbermen to trying to
convert cutover lands to grazing land, most southern pine
manufacturers, with the support of the railroads, promoted
the idea.[9] The railroad companies encouraged settlement
on cutover lands in order to replace lost timber-hauling
revenues with freight charges on agricultural products,
and the lumber firms were anxious both to get their cutover lands off the tax rolls and to bring in a new popu-
lation that would consume the products of remaining
mills.[10] The development of agriculture on cutover lands
would also, of course, provide a solution to the problem
of workers stranded by the lumber industry's western
migration.[11] The Southern Pine Association expected the
migration of settlers not only from the northern states
but also from war-ravaged areas in Europe. Returning
American soldiers were also regarded as likely settlers,
and they afforded southern lumbermen the luxury of dis-
posing of unwanted property and performing a "patriotic"
service at the same time.[12] Although Henry Hardtner's
pioneering reforestation program at Urania was mentioned
at the first cutover land conference, reforestation was
apparently not considered seriously, and Hardtner later
recalled ironically that "you didn't hear any of them
talking about putting timber back on the land did you?"[13]
    Meanwhile, despite the pessimism of some SPA offi-
cials, the southern lumber industry's giants moved to
dispose of their cutover lands. For example, the Kirby
Lumber Company's affiliate, the Houston Oil Company,
transferred some eight million acres of land in East Texas
and Louisiana to the Southwestern Settlement and Development Company, which planned to subdivide the tract and
sell it as farms.[14] A similar approach was that of the
Long-Bell Lumber Company, which set up a subsidiary called
the Long-Bell Farm Land Corporation. This body sold a
sizable amount of land, but was plagued with an extremely
high percentage of repossessions and passed on to the
state of Louisiana a considerable problem in tax delinquencies and defaults.[15] This experience seems to justify
historian Vernon Jensen's view that "the encouragement of
people . . . to settle on the cut-over lands heaped tragedy on tragedy."[16]
    In dealing with the cutover land problem, the SPA
cooperated closely with the Southern Settlement and
Development Organization established by a 1912 conference

of southern governors in Baltimore. The organization was supported by many southern railroads, businessmen, and landowners in its advocacy of "a general program of economic development and informational service for corporations interested in the region." It emphasized the establishment of subsidiary state development boards, which was also one of the SPA's major endeavors in dealing with the cutover land situation in 1919.[17]

The Southern Pine Association and lumber interests in the South were the major forces, along with the Southern Settlement and Development Organization, behind the organization of the various state development bodies. The general purposes of these organizations varied, ranging from advocacy of all facets of agriculture through working for various kinds of improved community facilities and the attraction of settlers from other areas.[18] While lumber interests were expected to provide the financial backbone of such organizations, an effort was made to get a broad basis of support from all sectors of the community in order to avoid the "suspicion on the part of some that this was another scheme for selling cutover land and was being pushed with that end in view. . . ."[19] For this reason the Southern Pine Association, although allowing one of its officers to serve as a director of the Southern Settlement and Development Organization, refrained from open affiliation with efforts to organize landowners and community development associations at the state and local level.[20]

The association did, however, contribute both money and the services of its staff to the organizations. It announced that the Mississippi organization, which was patterned after similar bodies along the Atlantic seaboard, would be a prototype for organizations of this kind to be established in other Southern Pine Association states.[21] The SPA's position was summarized by an individual who was authorized to speak for the association at meetings to organize a Louisiana state landowners' organization in the following manner:

> The Southern Pine Association is interested in the agricultural development of this State in all its phases so that contentment and prosperity and right living will come to the farmers of the State in such a way that they will be delighted to be farmers in Louisiana, and by this condition of affairs attract the attention of citizens of other States to want to

own and operate farms near such a contented people, and by this indirect process the members of the Southern Pine Association will dispose of their holdings in the State of Louisiana.[22]

The SPA vigorously fought any and all intimations that the idle lands of the South were not suitable for diversified agriculture. The association provided $10,000 for the National Research Council to undertake a scientific study of the possibilities of cutover timberlands in the South, and by late 1920 fieldwork was in progress under the direction of Austin Cary of the U. S. Forest Service. Cary was known as an advocate of the possibilities of second-growth timber in the South, and the fact that the Southern Pine Association and Secretary-Manager Rhodes supported Cary's work was a significant indicator that strict reliance upon agriculture to solve the problem of cutover lands might be losing some of its appeal in the SPA.[23]

Continuing its efforts to bring settlers to the South, however, in 1920 the cutover land committee worked with the U. S. Department of the Interior to attempt to persuade Congress to enact legislation designed to induce World War I veterans, and other persons as well, to occupy southern cutover lands. The committee hoped that the development of settlements in the South through the encouragement of such legislation would advertise the desirability of these lands to the rest of the nation and attract additional immigrants.[24]

Despite the hope of many southern lumbermen that they could dispose of their cutover lands by converting them to cattle ranges and farms, other members of the industry and government officials were beginning to believe in the regenerative powers of the southern forests. While the cutover land problem was still very much in evidence at the end of the 1920s, and although the plight of people stranded on such lands remained conspicuous during the Great Depression,[25] the first real strides toward the salvation of Dixie's piney woods through conservation and reforestation were initiated during the post-war period.

The struggle for enlightened conservation and forestry policies in the southern pine industry depended not upon convincing lumbermen of their obligation to future generations or the general welfare, but upon showing them that conservation and better forestry practices were economically feasible and in their own interest. The Southern Pine Association, along with noted industry

245

pioneers like Henry Hardtner, was in the forefront of
what was thus primarily an educational campaign.

Of course, as an organization whose continued existence depended upon the support of its subscribers, the
SPA could not dictate, but only persuade. Furthermore,
the association and its industry could and did not support
some of the forestry measures proposed nationally by members of what one might term the "Gifford Pinchot School"
of forestry and conservation. Southern pine conservation
leaders believed in forestry for profit on private
holdings rather than in governmental takeover of actual
and potential timber lands, and they believed that government had a responsibility to make it feasible for the private owner to practice good forest management through
equitable tax laws and the provision of technical and
administrative assistance in dealing with matters such as
forest fires. In general, the experience of the Southern
Pine Association in dealing with the forestry and conservation questions during the early years of its existence
seems to reinforce the suggestions of historians who have
urged students of conservation, and indeed of Progressivism in general, to abandon their preoccupation with
moralizing and concentrate on the "hard" side of reform--
the activities of scientific planners and economically
motivated businessmen of vision and the battles against
regressive taxation and apathetic communities and
governments.[26]

When the Southern Pine Association came into existence
in late 1914, the national conservation movement was
strong, particularly in the East. The South was not in
the mainstream of conservation thought. However, there
were enlightened men in the southern pine industry and the
SPA who were anticipating, and sometimes working for, the
implementation of advanced forestry policies in their
region both at the governmental level and on their own
properties. Although the famous national leaders and the
focal point of attention in the conservation movement were
centered in the North, East, and West, some of the most
important experimentation in the fields and on private
tracts was taking place in the southern pine region.

The most perceptive leader of early southern pine
forestry efforts was Henry Hardtner, president of
Louisiana's Urania Lumber Company, who became known as the
"father of forestry in the South." Hardtner became concerned about the constant cries of "timber famine" in the
early twentieth century and the devastation of the gently

rolling pine forests of central Louisiana.[27] He had faith in the regenerative powers of southern pine land and, beginning around 1903 or 1904, began to investigate growing timber rather than merely harvesting it.

Hardtner was one of the first southern lumbermen to seek the advice and assistance of the U. S. Forest Service in instituting and experimenting with practical reforestation measures on his own lands. In fact, as early as 1904 and 1905 Hardtner began to purchase cutover lands, a dramatic demonstration of his belief in their reproductive powers. In 1909, Hardtner pioneered in initiating forest fire protection for his lands. The fame of the Urania reforestation and fire protection experiments began to grow, and it was largely through Hardtner's efforts that the state of Louisiana organized a conservation department in 1908, which he served for four years as chairman. The Urania Lumber Company was the first organization to place its forest land under a timber conservation or reforestation contract with the state, and its operations in central Louisiana became a mecca for southerners who were becoming interested in the possibilities of reforestation.

The Urania experiments also attracted national attention, and over the years Hardtner developed a close association with the Yale University Forestry School, which conducted both experiments and field classes on his properties.[28] For the most part, however, Hardtner's efforts were ignored and rather generally ridiculed. This is not to say that other southern pine companies were not experimenting with reforestation. The Kirby Lumber Company and the Lutcher and Moore firm, both operating in Texas and Louisiana, undertook some reforestation work in the early twentieth century.[29] However, most of the other companies' efforts were desultory.[30]

The obstacles in the way of successful and profitable private reforestation were many. The industry was built on credit, and its operations from the time of its migration to the South were based on the concept of cut out and move on. Vast expansion was undertaken on loans at from 6 to 8 percent interest, with heavy annual obligations to be met. Even during times of depressed prices and overproduction, therefore, it was considered more practical to continue to operate at full steam and at least cover part of the overhead rather than shut down completely and have the facilities devoured by fixed obligations. One observer reported, in the early twentieth century, that as much as $2.00 on every thousand

board feet had to be applied to bonded indebtness. Under
these circumstances, the mills often continued to run
night and day in order to meet their obligations.[31]

Another major obstacle was taxation--the tendency of
states and local governmental units to tax the lumber companies as heavily as they could on the ground that the
industry was depleting an irreplaceable natural resource
and should be required to lend heavy support to government
before it moved on and left the area denuded. In many
cases, lumber companies were the only large economic units
in their areas, and while this gave the owners and managers positions of unquestioned leadership in their
communities, it also resulted in heavy financial burdens.
Furthermore, taxation policies often penalized a company
which tried to introduce sustained yield or permanency
into its operations. John Henry Kirby, for example,
believed that "the greatest obstacle in the way [of
reforestation] is taxation."[32] Although members of the
industry presented various proposals, their basic desire
was for lower property taxes on land set aside for
reforestation. Among the most commonly suggested tax
reforms were the levying of some sort of severance tax and
taxing the land at its value at time of purchase rather
than according to its worth as reforestation progressed.

Finally, the constant danger of fire was a major
obstacle in the path of successful reforestation and sustained-yield management on southern pine lands. While
professional opinion varied in regard to the value of
controlled burning of pine lands as a means of removing
possible timber for uncontrolled conflagrations and to
help thin out overly seeded areas, there was general
agreement that fires when the trees were seedlings and
the time-honored practice of "woods-burning" by the populace of the southern pine woods were major impediments to
improved woods practices.[33] One of the private conservationists' major tasks, then, would be to persuade government to accept at least partial responsibility for fire
protection on private timber lands.

Ignorance of the regenerative powers and physical
properties of southern pine trees also helped to prevent
the implementation of sustained-yield operations on most
southern pine lands. Many lumbermen simply did not know
how long it took to grow trees. They tended to believe
that it was far too long to make reforestation of their
denuded lands profitable. It is not too surprising that
when one prominent East Texas firm applied for a loan in

the late nineteenth century, offering a mortgage on its timber lands in western Louisiana as collateral, the application was rejected with the advice that the land was "a liability, not an asset, because it was so heavily timbered and could not easily be cultivated!"[34] Henry Hardtner helped to overcome this and other obstacles by the practical demonstration on his own lands of the feasibility of reforestation and by the spirit he generated, despite ridicule and criticism, within the southern lumber industry and the SPA.

Although most southern lumbermen generally viewed the cutting out of their operations as inevitable, the Southern Pine Association did not concentrate all of its activities concerning denuded lands on settlement and agricultural schemes. When the association was created, a forestry committee was organized, and it began to gather and interpret statistical information that would be needed before a sensible and comprehensive conservation and forestry policy could be developed. The committee was, therefore, to sponsor surveys to determine just how much standing timber remained in the southern pine belt, codify the existing forestry legislation of the southern states, investigate the taxation situation, and attempt to determine means of utilizing lower-grade timber to help cut down the drain on forest resources.[35] As the SPA grew in size and influence, association staff members tried to steer its subscribers and the industry as a whole toward more enlightened forest practices.

During 1914 and 1915, as the SPA was being organized, the U. S. Forest Service examined conditions in the nation's troubled lumber industry. The objective of the study was to "obtain and place before the public in a constructive way the essential facts regarding this industry and their bearing upon forest conservation."[36] The conclusions of the Forest Service investigations were published in a series of Department of Agriculture bulletins.

By the time these studies were under way, Gifford Pinchot, the white knight of the American conservation movement, had almost abandoned his original hope that enlightened conservation practices could be brought about through voluntary cooperation between government and private landowners. During and after the Theodore Roosevelt administration, Pinchot had been gradually drifting toward a belief that only strong government control or, better yet, government ownership of the forests would make

249

conservation feasible. Pinchot had come completely to distrust the private interests and would soon advocate "public ownership, or such public control as will amount to giving the people of the country . . . the benefit of public ownership."[37] Pinchot was predicting the exhaustion of American timber resources in thirty to thirty-five years.[38]

A quite different point of view was presented in one of the bulletins published as a result of the 1914-15 surveys. The author was William B. Greeley, at the time an assistant forester. Although originally one of Pinchot's disciples, Greeley had gradually become convinced that the failure of private lumbermen to undertake meaningful conservation measures was not always due to their basic character defects or wickedness, but simply to the fact that the lumber industry was suffering from some chronic economic maladies and that enlightened forestry practices had not been accepted by the industry as economically feasible. Greeley believed that the industry was suffering from high interest rates, inefficient production techniques and equipment, increasing transportation costs, and erratic taxation policies. Feeling that the situation could be salvaged only through the cooperative efforts of state and federal governments and private landowners, Greeley proposed a program built around three major points: extension of state and national forests, equitable taxation policies, and systematic forest products research.[39]

Greeley's analysis was published with the blessing of his superior, Chief Forester Henry S. Graves, who continued to support the idea of cooperation between government and private interests. Before its publication, Graves sent the report with a covering letter to Gifford Pinchot, explaining that it had been purposely written in a sympathetic manner so that the "lumbermen who read . . . [it] will be impressed by its fairness."[40] Pinchot registered a strong protest against publication of the document and publicly categorized Greeley's effort as a "whitewash of destructive lumbering."[41] As an enlightened forestry advocate who had demonstrated his concern for the plight of the lumbermen, Greeley had, however, opened lines of communication between the industry and government, and as the schism in conservation ranks developed, there was no doubt that the leaders and conservation-minded subscribers of the Southern Pine Association were squarely in the Greeley camp.

The Conservation Struggle

With the advent of World War I and an increased drain on America's timber resources, there developed an intensified concern to find solutions to such forestry problems as correct cutting practices, the efficacy of controlled burning, the best methods of fighting wood pests, and the actual growth rate of trees. By the end of the war, forestry opinion could be divided into three categories: (1) the "radical school," led by Pinchot and dedicated to the ideas of public ownership of forests or its equivalent, the depravity of the lumbermen, and the pliability of the Forest Service; (2) the "moderate school," represented by people like Graves and Greeley, many government administrators, and enlightened lumbermen, who believed in "reasonable government regulation, steady utilization of government timber, and broad cooperation in reforestation"; and (3) "diehard old-school lumbermen who resented all government activity."[42] As the competing forces moved toward confrontation at the war's end, the Southern Pine Association would be squarely in the camp of the "moderate school."

During and following World War I, U. S. Forest Service personnel came south to promote improved forestry practices. However, it was not until the end of the war that emphasis shifted from production to the conservation of the nation's remaining timber resources. By late 1919 and early 1920, wholesale and retail lumber prices were soaring, and the nation was again roused by cries of timber famine. Virtually everyone agreed that some sort of new federal legislation was needed to promote systematic conservation and reforestation, but how should this be accomplished? William B. Greeley and Chief Forester Henry S. Graves continued to favor cooperation between governments and private individuals, while the supporters of Gifford Pinchot argued strongly for federal control and increased or even full government forest ownership.[43]

In 1919 Graves started a drive to draw up minimum requirements for the establishment of approved methods of forestry practice. To arouse public interest in a national forestry policy, conferences were held throughout the country and interested citizens and organizations were invited to make suggestions.[44] A southern forestry conference was held in Jacksonville, Florida, with SPA Secretary-Manager John E. Rhodes serving as co-chairman. Rhodes stressed his personal interest in forestry and said that, while he had always believed it would eventually be possible to interest lumbermen in practical forestry,

"forestry in a general way has not been possible . . .
because the economic conditions have not been developed
to a point which makes it profitable. In fact, unless a
thing is profitable it is impossible to interest men in
it." Rhodes concluded, however, that he believed
"conditions are now developing which will make it possible
to interest lumbermen in forestry, particularly in the
south."[45]

In the spring of 1920, Chief Forester Graves was
succeeded by William B. Greeley, who continued the campaign of his predecessor with his own emphasis on cooperative forestry. However, by this time Gifford Pinchot was
openly in the fray once again, serving as head of the
Committee for the Application of Forestry of the Society
of American Foresters.[46] Pinchot opened headquarters in
Washington and garnered influential support from various
quarters, and in November, 1919, his committee submitted
its report embodying Pinchot's hope for strong governmental action to force improved forestry practices on private
lands.[47]

Both sides picked up impressive support and came up
with legislative programs which were debated on the floor
of Congress. Pinchot's recommendations were placed
before Congress in May, 1920, in the form of a bill submitted by his friend Senator Arthur Capper of Kansas.[48]
However, a poll conducted earlier by the Society of
American Foresters to ascertain the opinion of professional foresters toward the Pinchot report, on which the
Capper bill was based, had indicated overwhelming
opposition, and neither the Wilson administration nor
the Republican leadership in Congress accepted the
proposals.[49]

Strangely enough, Senator Capper had also sponsored a
successful resolution which instructed the Secretary of
Agriculture to investigate reports "that the forest
resources of the United States are being rapidly depleted,
and that the situation is already serious and will soon
become critical."[50] The report resulting from this
resolution, which acknowledged the depletion of timber but
advocated the Graves-Greeley solutions, was submitted to
Congress by then-Chief Forester Greeley on June 1, 1920.[51]
The pro-Greeley forces organized a National Forestry
Program Committee, which assisted in formulating a bill
embodying the Greeley program that was placed before the
Congress by Representative Bertrand E. Snell.[52] The
battle lines were now formally drawn.

252

As the two sides were nearing open conflict, John E. Rhodes was keeping his subscribers informed about the Forest Service's conferences and advocating that the industry formulate a coherent forestry policy and work toward cooperative conservation efforts with the state and federal governments. Rhodes warned that "if the industry is not prepared to meet the issue squarely as it is now being agitated, and in a spirit of helpful cooperation, we cannot avoid the consequences of radical public views on the subject. . . ."[53]

At the same time, other significant events were transpiring in southern pine conservation circles. Early in 1920, the Southern Pine Association's board of directors voted to contribute almost ten thousand dollars to support a three-year survey of timber resources and the rate of growth in the southern pine area to be undertaken by the forestry committee of the National Research Council. This activity was pushed by Rhodes, and the fieldwork was to be conducted by the Forest Service's Austin Cary.[54]

During the summer of 1920, one of the giant firms in the southern pine industry swung into line behind the advocates of conservation, reforestation, and sustained yield. In May, at the invitation of Henry Hardtner, the officials of the Great Southern Lumber Company of Bogalusa, Louisiana, visited the operations of the Urania Lumber Company to get a first-hand look at the experiments being carried on there. Impressed by what he saw, Colonel W. L. Sullivan, general-manager of the Great Southern, announced to the New Orleans press on his way back to Bogalusa that his company was planning to begin a comprehensive reforestation and conservation program. It is almost impossible to over-estimate the importance of the change in outlook of this influential firm.[55]

In 1921 the Southern Pine Association took a definite position in regard to the proposed federal forestry measures, which were by now called the Capper and Snell-McCormick bills. In June the SPA forestry committee submitted a long report to the board of directors that approved the general principles of the Snell Bill and urged the industry to cooperate with federal and state agencies wherever practicable in implementing improved forestry practices.[56] On October 19, 1921, the SPA issued a declaration of its forestry policy, which generally endorsed the principle of the Snell-McCormick bill.[57]

Not all of those in the southern pine industry supported or approved of the association's position. Some

of the industry's leading figures, including notably the
SPA's first president, Charles S. Keith, opposed all
federal forestry legislation as representing a threat to
private property rights. At a special SPA subscribers'
meeting in Memphis at the end of the year, the delegates
heard both the Capper and Snell-McCormick bills described
as unconstitutional.[58] However, dominant sentiment in
the industry was probably summed up at Memphis by
Secretary-Manager Rhodes, who said that while "lumbermen
up to this time have opposed any sort of forestry legislation," they were now "willing to accept the Snell bill,
for if they do not accept that, they will have to accept
the Capper bill."[59]

For the time being, the matter of national forestry
legislation was at a stalemate. As it became clear after
hearings on the Snell bill in January, 1921, and January,
1922, that there was a deadlock between the forces favoring federal regulation and those favoring state regulation
and cooperation, the bill was dropped. In February, 1923,
Representative John D. Clarke of New York introduced two
substitute measures which helped to keep interest in the
matter alive, although they were not acted upon.
Similarly, the Capper bill went through several stages of
evolution without any concrete results.[60] In fact, in
1922 the chairman of the SPA's forestry committee cava-
lierly refused to spend time discussing the Capper bill
because, he said, it "has not been seriously considered by
Congress, and does not appear that it is likely to
be. . . ."[61]

The Southern Pine Association continued to support the
Snell-McCormick bill, and when the House of Representatives Committee on Agriculture and Forestry conducted a
hearing in January, 1922, the SPA sent six representatives, including Secretary-Manager Rhodes, to testify. In
addition, John Henry Kirby, in his capacity as president
of the National Lumber Manufacturers' Association, was in
attendance.[62] The southern lumbermen did not limit their
concern merely to favoring the Snell or Greeley approach.
The SPA's forestry committee reported that it felt "that
not enough attention has been given to the part which the
states can play in solving the forestry question," and it
argued that "if forestry is to be practiced upon a scale
sufficiently large to meet the needs of the future for an
extensive supply of timber, the State and Federal governments must undertake it." The committee believed that
lumbermen should be willing to sell their denuded lands at

reasonable prices to the government and should work to
create favorable public sentiment toward such activities,
and it concluded that it was unfair to expect private landowners to provide fire protection for their standing
timber.[63]

Again, the Urania Lumber Company's Henry J. Hardtner
was a courageous dissenter. Hardtner, at the SPA's
seventh annual meeting in 1922, thundered that he was not
practicing forestry as a philanthropist and that "as to
being a Governmental problem, I do not agree with any man
in this hall in trying to shove this responsibility off on
the Federal Government, or the State Government."[64]
Hardtner did, however, call on the lumbermen to "ask the
state and the nation to fix a reasonable tax rate on your
lands. . . . Put it up to the Government, show your good
faith, tell the Government that you will do these things—
'We are willing to do it, but we can't do it until you
make it possible for us to do it.'"[65] Nevertheless, at
the end of the year the forestry committee "expressed the
view that the southern states should be encouraged to
engage in forestry as a state function, purchasing for
that purpose areas of cutover lands more suitable for tree
growth than agricultural development which the present
owners should be willing to exchange for long term bonds
at present assessed valuation for such lands"[66] On a
more practical level, the association appropriated $5,000
for a study of state forestry legislation.[67]

In the spring of 1923, subscribers at the Southern
Pine Association annual meeting heard a report on forestry
which indicated that a growing number of people in the
South favored acquisition by the states of idle lands
suitable for forest growth, and they were told that the
Senate's select committee on reforestation would be visiting New Orleans.[68] The committee toured the country
during 1923, and its report singled out fire and taxes as
the two greatest causes of deforestation but recommended
that the federal government attempt no direct regulation.
Among its specific recommendations were the extension of
public forest ownership and encouragement of private
reforestation. The report also urged that the government
extend its cooperation to include the protection of all
state and private forests. The committee's recommendations were included in bills introduced in the Senate by
Senator Charles L. McNary and in the House by Representative John D. Clarke.[69] Congress passed the Clarke-McNary
Act on June 7, 1925, despite Pinchot's opposition. It

provided for federal-state cooperation in protecting forests but failed to provide for government regulation of timber cutting.[70]

Members of the Southern Pine Association meeting in their 1924 annual session in New Orleans heard the Clarke-McNary bill praised by Secretary-Manager Wilson Compton of the National Lumber Manufacturers' Association as a measure which proposed "an economic solution" to the problem of reforestation as opposed to the "political solution" of the Capper-Pinchot bill.[71] Compton concluded that "if the action of the lumber industry is wisely guided it will support progress now along the McNary-Clarke lines and not further encourage political experimentation along the Pinchot lines."[72] Compton's feelings were echoed by John L. Kaul, chairman of the SPA forestry committee, who said that "this bill represents a definite and valuable step forward . . ."[73]

By the end of 1924, some southern pine industry spokesmen felt that valuable steps toward the perpetuation of southern forests and the southern lumber industry had been taken through various government and private activities. Writing in the Southern Lumberman in late 1924, Berckes optimistically stated that "when one considers the present amount of standing timber and the increased attention that is being devoted to reforestation by both state and federal governments and private land owners, there is every reason to believe that the life of the southern pine industry will be prolonged indefinitely."[74] The article singled out a number of southern lumber firms which had inaugurated comprehensive reforestation and protection programs and emphasized that:

> As the various southern states come to recognize the public's share of the responsibility in the matter of providing a permanent and adequate supply of timber for future generations and enact laws providing for proper co-operation with private land owners in the matter of fire protection and suppression and in adjustment of taxation on forest property so that private timber land owners can grow trees without bearing a tax burden that would make the enterprise financially disastrous, it is believed there will be much greater development in the forestry movement throughout the South.[75]

The association estimated in 1924 that there were some 212 billion board feet of pine timber remaining in the southern states, counting both timber stands being logged by existing firms and others of varying sizes and types, including second growth on cutover lands.[76]

As the Southern Pine Association entered the second half of the decade, its emphasis was on cooperation between private and public agencies and individuals interested in improved forest practices and conservation and on more complete utilization of forest products to help counteract the scarcity of timber. In March the board of directors approved the recommendations of the National Conference on Utilization of Forest Products which had been held in November, 1924, in Washington, D. C., under the auspices of the Secretary of Agriculture. To carry out its endorsement in a practical manner, the SPA board authorized the secretary-manager to undertake the organization of mill managers' and superintendents' associations in each of the southern pine-producing states to "consider at regular meetings, mechanical and manufacturing problems in the industry, to devise ways and means for improving the methods and processes of lumber manufacturing and handling and to secure the thorough utilization of forest material."[77]

The remainder of the 1920s saw the Southern Pine Association working to implement and foster good forestry practices and attitudes among its subscribers and the citizens of the South generally and attempting to counteract some of the popular misconceptions about the southern timber supply. Gifford Pinchot, leaving the governorship of Pennsylvania in early 1927, was one of the prime forces in keeping the cry of timber famine before the public in the late 1920s, as he continued to work toward his goal of direct federal regulation of private forests.[78] The SPA was particularly incensed about these charges, because their competitors from the West Coast fir regions were in some cases mounting campaigns to sell lumber in the South and were hitting vigorously on the theme that the southern pine forests were nearly depleted. This struggle with the western producers became increasingly important as the 1920s progressed.[79]

The Southern Pine Association also maintained its interest in the progress of federal forestry legislation during the latter 1920s. During 1925 and 1926, a special committee of the Society of American Foresters conducted a study of the current state of forest research. Earle H. Clapp, chief of the Branch of Research of the U. S. Forest Service, wrote the committee's report, which was published in 1926 by the American Tree Association for the SAF. The report was the basis of the McSweeney-McNary Act, first proposed in Congress in 1927 by Representative John R. McSweeney of Ohio and finally enacted into law on May 22, 1928. The act was based on the cooperative principle and provided a broad charter for forestry research. It established a ten-year program that included the establishment of a system of forest and range experiment stations, expanded research in forest products and inaugurated a nationwide survey of forest resources and national requirements.[80] The SPA strongly endorsed the McSweeney-McNary bill, and the board of directors strongly urged individual subscribers to "write to their respective senators and congressmen urging their support of this legislation."[81] After the passage of the act, Secretary of Agriculture W. M. Jardine expressed his "personal appreciation and that of the department" for "the great help which you and your association rendered in support of this measure."[82]

The association's efforts to educate its subscribers and the southern populace about sound woods practices were carried out in conjunction with the southern education project of the American Forestry Association between 1928 and 1930. Much of the financial support for this campaign was provided by the southern pine industry. The major emphasis of the program was upon fire prevention, and the message was taken to the residents of the southern piney woods through motion pictures, speeches, and exhibits.[83] The association itself "embarked upon an ambitious educational forestry program among the mill towns," and its subscribers in many cases sponsored and conducted local forest fire prevention programs. In addition, the SPA prepared "educational press matter as well as suggested speeches to be delivered before civic clubs, schools and public meetings."[84]

In assessing the record of the Southern Pine Association in the fields of forestry and conservation during the 1920s, it can perhaps be said that the educational efforts came closest to achieving real success. This success was not, furthermore, only in the area of convincing the inhabitants of the piney woods that woods-burning was not a good thing. Rather, the real educational success was in convincing at least a few of the lumbermen themselves that sustained-yield operations or controlled cutting and reforestation could be a sound investment and in persuading a number of state governments and national governmental leaders that cooperation between private industry and public agencies could lead to an improvement in the general welfare. Remarkable strides were made in the implementation of advanced forestry techniques on private holdings in the South, notably at Urania and Bogalusa; there were marked steps forward in the establishment of state forestry programs in many of the southern states; and the southern pine industry lined up consistently on the winning side during the 1920s as significant national forestry legislation was enacted. Perhaps the biggest step forward was made by turning the minds of southern lumber operators away from the panaceas of agricultural settlement or abandonment to dispose of their cutover lands and toward a growing realization of the regenerative powers of the southern forests. However, according to a man who spent much of his career as a professional forester in the south: ". . . the 20's showed some advance in better forest management on private lands but far from enough to warrant any warmth of enthusiasm among the foresters and economists pulling for it from the side lines. And such progress as there had been was conspicuously absent from the ranks of the small landowners."[85]

Furthermore, while the Southern Pine Association could consider itself in good company in that it supported the policies of the U. S. Forest Service and Chief Forester William B. Greeley, which were generally endorsed by the Society of American Foresters during the 1920s, there was, of course, another side to the story. Gifford Pinchot continued to agitate for stronger federal action during the latter part of the decade and considered both the Forest Service's Greeley and the Society of American Foresters to be under the evil influence of an exploitive lumber industry. Pinchot believed that, except for a few isolated instances, the industry was not making an honest attempt to reform.[86] It has been suggested that the clamor raised by Pinchot and his followers actually goaded the lumbermen into some conservation activities in order to forestall increased federal regulation; this view certainly seems to be at least partially true judging from the remarks of several SPA spokesmen. It is interesting that only four years later the lumber industry itself wrote a provision into its code under the National Recovery Administration requiring cutting methods that would provide a new crop of trees.

The southern pine industry's forestry and conservation activities during the 1930s were strongly influenced by its experience under the Lumber Code. In fact, the

The New South and the "New Competition"

Southern Pine Association's experience with the code was a major factor in propelling the organization into continuing efforts to bring about enlightened forestry practices in the southern piney woods.

Article X, which dealt with forestry and conservation, was supposedly the only part of the Lumber Code in which President Roosevelt expressed real interest, and it has been described as the only part that "finished stronger than it began."[87] H. C. Berckes anticipated Roosevelt's interest in this subject. As early as December, 1932, Berckes noted that FDR was "forestry-minded" and predicted that "with a man like President-elect Franklin D. Roosevelt at the head of our federal government, a better opportunity than ever before will exist to bring about the complete utilization of southern lands."[88] According to Berckes, the President pushed in exactly this direction by requesting that the lumber industry code include provisions for perpetuation of the forests. "While the President proposed this," said Berckes, "there is no doubt that he was reminded and needled by the ardent and dedicated conservationists including the U. S. Forest Service." Therefore, the conservation article of the code was characterized by the SPA leader as "a token of good faith the industry had to pay for its opportunities of self-regulation."[89]

Article X pledged the lumber industry to implement measures for conservation and sustained production, after the convening of conferences with the Secretary of Agriculture and other officials to draw up supplements to the lumber code.[90] The Secretary of Agriculture called such a conference in October, 1933, and the Southern Pine Division immediately began to gather facts for the preparation of acceptable forest practices provisions. The division held sixteen meetings during November to gather local information and discuss the forest conservation program. In the meantime, the Southern Pine Division appointed a conservation committee chaired by Henry Hardtner, "the father of forestry in the South." During late 1933 and the first days of 1934, a tentative forest conservation code evolved, and a national forestry conference in Washington at the end of January resulted in a formal amendment to the Lumber Code providing for forest conservation; it was approved by President Roosevelt on March 23.[91]

As part of the Forest Conservation Code the President approved Schedule C, which provided for a "well-organized program for sustained production in the forest . . . stressing fire, insect and disease prevention, reforestation, adequate slash disposal, selective logging, and sustained yield."[92] The Southern Pine Division held an industry code conference to deal with this and other matters in New Orleans on April 4 and 5, 1934, and the conservation committee submitted rules of forest practice to the general session of several hundred lumbermen. The members voiced unanimous approval of these rules, and the Southern Pine Division became the first to file its rules of forest practice in compliance with Article X and its forestry supplement.

The Forest Conservation Code and rules of forest practice became effective in the Southern Pine Division on June 1, 1934. These rules contained fire protection measures, specified the number of trees to be left per acre after logging operations in order to assure regeneration, and attempted to spur the implementation of sustained-yield operations. To help with their implementation and administration, the Southern Pine Association established a Department of Conservation which was originally staffed by a manager and a research forester.[93]

Although the Southern Pine Division and the SPA conscientiously attempted to act within the spirit of Article X, they were not reluctant to suggest that the public and government should do their part to make forestry and conservation on private lands both possible and effective. Some consistent SPA notes were sounded by the association's conservation committee chairman, Henry Hardtner, in an address before the National Forestry Conference in January, 1934, when he called for more equitable state and local taxation on growing timber; more funds for fire protection programs carried out jointly by the state and national governments and by private owners; and federal loans for private forest owners to enable them to maintain and protect their trees during the growing cycle, with the land to serve as security for the loans and repayment to come at the time the timber was cut.[94]

By June 1, 1934, the Forest Conservation Code and rules of forest practice required by Article X were in effect on the operations of all southern pine sawmills, and on July 5 the SPA Department of Conservation certified three companies in Alabama, Arkansas, and Louisiana as the industry's first "sustained-yield" operations. Under the Lumber Code, firms which qualified as sustained-yield operations were given special privileges, including

The New South and the "New Competition"

notably 10 percent increases in production allotments.[95] By the end of 1934, six southern pine manufacturers were certified as conducting sustained-yield operations.[96] They were the only southern pine firms so certified at the time of the Lumber Code's death, although there were several others whose operations were on a sustained-yield basis but had not been so certified. However, most southern pine operations had not reached a sustained-yield basis of operations.[97]

The year 1935 brought the death not only of the Lumber Code but also of Henry Hardtner, the leading southern apostle of enlightened forestry and conservation practices. However, the influence of both the code and the man would live on in the Southern Pine Association's forestry and conservation efforts. At the code conferences and SPA annual meeting in March, on the eve of the NRA's demise, the board approved a conservation committee resolution calling for the continuation of the association's department of conservation and its work regardless of the fate of the Lumber Code. In fact, as H. C. Berckes later wrote, "When the entire NRA Act was declared unconstitutional . . . Article X lingered on and through all legitimate and practical means formed the nucleus of the present successful forestry efforts."[98]

While the Southern Pine Association continued its forestry and conservation efforts during the remainder of the 1930s and into the World War II period, it opposed one aspect of the conservation movement favored by some national leaders—the acquisition of additional forest land by government. The conflict over government land acquisition agitated the entire forestry profession, the lumber industry, and the ranks of the Roosevelt administration during the late 1930s. In part, it involved a struggle by the Department of the Interior to secure the transfer of the Forest Service from the Department of Agriculture to Interior. The President wavered in his position, but finally supported the retention of the status quo, to the extreme consternation of Harold Ickes. The Forest Service and the Department of Agriculture favored the multiple-use concept of forest management, with the national forests being used for economic as well as recreational activities, while Ickes favored the conversion of forests into national parks where the emphasis would be purely upon recreational use, with large-scale federal acquisition a part of the program. In the 1930s, however, the Forest Service reverted to its earlier policy

262

The Conservation Struggle

of lambasting the lumber industry, and it too recommended additional forest acquisitions. The Southern Pine Association was opposed to the transfer of the Forest Service, but did not find the service's advocacy of additional public land ownership much, if any, more favorable than the plans of Ickes and the Department of Interior. The SPA consistently held that public land acquisition should be confined to areas of low productivity which were unsuited for private forest ownership and management.[99] This attitude had clearly changed since the early 1920s when the SPA's emphasis was strongly upon disposition of the lands to private citizens or to the government.

Further attention was focused on the problem of land ownership and use by the joint committee on forestry, created by Congress in 1938 to study the ownership and management of forest lands in the United States. The committee conducted investigations and held hearings during 1939 and 1940 before presenting a report in 1941 in which it recommended increased public ownership of timber lands. In statements before this body the SPA stuck to its standard positions regarding forestry, conservation, and land ownership. However, the total impact of governmental activities in the area of forestry and conservation during the 1930s, which ranged from the NRA through the joint committee, did spur the Southern Pine Association into renewed interest in these matters, if only to avoid public criticism and possible takeovers of private lands. Thus during the latter part of the decade the SPA continued its forestry and conservation efforts and, hoping to improve the industry's image, attempted to publicize these activities. It entered World War II, which would bring significant drains on the nation's timber supply and renewed public conservation measures, with a wary eye focused on the agencies and officials of the national government.[100]

One federal agency became a center of controversy early in the war. During 1942 the southern pine manufacturers and other lumbermen became involved in a running dispute with the U. S. Forest Service. In June Acting Chief Forester Earle H. Clapp presented a scheme for increasing the production of lumber, called the forest products service plan, for the consideration of the War Production Board. The plan basically contemplated the allocation to the Forest Service of a revolving fund of $100 million from the Commodity Credit Corporation to be used to purchase, produce, store, and sell forest products

and to provide funds to enable small producers to obtain
credit, markets, and transportation. The original proposal was to be carried out by an executive order and would
give the Forest Service authority to take over plant facilities and acquire timber. There was a heated outcry from
the lumber industry, including the agencies of the
southern pine area. They argued that the forest products
service plan was simply another scheme of the advocates of
publicly controlled cutting practices; that it would
encourage government competition with private enterprise;
that it was based on an exaggerated and pessimistic estimate of the industry's timber supply, forest practices,
and performance; that the credit needs of small producers
could be met adequately from existing sources; and that
the government would do better if it would help existing
producers by better coordination of government lumber
usage and by easing the supply and labor problems of the
industry. Despite internal disagreements, the plan
received the support of the War Industries Board and got
to the desk of the President, where it continued to come
under heavy opposition until it was finally dropped.
Under the impact of declining production in 1943, however,
parts of the program were put into effect in spite of the
lumber industry's continued strong resistance.[101]

During World War II the SPA's forestry and conservation position remained the same as it had been during the
prewar years--with the southern pine manufacturers
opposing increased federal and state regulations and advocating private forestry and conservation efforts as a
means of forestalling governmental action. By 1944 one of
the SPA's more progressive subscribers complained to H. C.
Berckes about this essentially negative approach, noting
that he could not "justify for myself the promotion of
better forestry practices on the sole basis of nullifying
federal arguments for regulation." Berckes's reply illu-
minates the awkward situation of an employee who endeavors
to lead his employers in new directions: "I agree with
what you say, especially in regard to a positive attitude
on forestry," lamented the secretary-manager, "but you
know that many of our people still feel that we must continue to wage a running battle with Federal, and even
state, officials."[102]

Among the association's forestry and conservation
efforts during the war was the extension of the tree farms
program into the southern pine woods. The tree farms
movement originated in 1941 when the lumber, pulp, paper,

and plywood industries formed the American Forest Products Industries to encourage better forestry practices and tree growing and to conduct public relations for the member industries. One of the AFPI's major activities was a program under which timberland owners who practiced proper forest management principles and placed their property on a sustained-yield basis could apply to the organization for certification as a tree farm.[103] As a writer in the Journal of Forestry explained, "Tree farms mean adequate forest protection, efficient cutting practices, necessary artificial reforestation and good wood utilization."[104]

The tree farms movement, it was hoped, would not only benefit the industry by helping to preserve its timber supply, it would also eliminate much of the popular disdain for the lumber industry which had been engendered by the old cries of timber famine. In addition, it would blunt the campaigns of the Gifford Pinchot followers for public regulation of forests. According to one leading study of the industry, "by forming lands into tree farms, lumbermen could show the public that they were devoting themselves to the nation's welfare," and "the plan to turn privately owned forest land into tree farms would be not only sound business but also excellent public relations."[105]

Although the tree farms program was first put into operation in Washington and Oregon, by 1942 it was under way in the South. Introduced by Stanley Horn of The Southern Lumberman at the request of the AFPI, the program started in Alabama with immediate plans for its extension into Arkansas and thence into other southern states. According to Horn, the SPA took "a very active and interested part in supporting the movement in the South and in helping it get started in each of the states where we have taken any steps so far."[106] The program's adoption was facilitated by the fact that numerous southern pine firms were already practicing various forms of enlightened forestry or sustained-yield activities.[107]

By late 1944, the SPA had taken over the southern tree farms program from the AFPI. By this time, the program was operating in Alabama, Arkansas, Mississippi, North Carolina, and Texas, with requests on file to extend it to Georgia, Louisiana, Tennessee, and Virginia. Some 565 landowners with holdings ranging from 10 to 230,000 acres had been recognized as tree farmers, and there were some 5,783,461 acres under the tree farms program in the South.[108] To determine the most suitable means of handling the system, the SPA tested various methods of operation, ranging from association financing for the general overhead expenses to the employment of an SPA forester who devoted all of his time to the tree farms project. The Southern Pine Association also financed extension of the program into North Carolina, Mississippi, and Texas and contributed the association forester's services for planning and development. The SPA contemplated extending the tree farm system to all twelve southern states.[109]

While the southern pine industry was working toward the improvement of its forestry and conservation practices, the federal government was also active in this field. In 1944 alone, Congress passed four measures described as "desirable" by the chairman of the Southern Pine War Committee's legislation and taxation subcommittee. The first of these was a law which provided for the establishment of a federally sponsored, cooperative sustained-yield program entirely on federal land and also in cooperation with private individuals and state or local authorities. Second was an amendment of the Clarke-McNary Act of 1924 providing increased federal funds for cooperative forest fire control activities with the states. The third act was the timber tax amendment to the Internal Revenue Code, which allowed lumbermen to treat income from the sale of timber as a capital gain in computing federal income taxes. Previously, an owner who sold his standing timber had the excess of its market value over its historical cost taxed at capital gain rates, while the owner who cut his own timber had been required to treat the excess of market value over historical cost as ordinary income, subject to regular income tax rates, and, in the case of corporations, to excess-profits tax rates. This inequity was now removed. The fourth act of Congress provided funds for the completion of a national survey of forest resources.[110] Thus, with a more favorable federal legislative framework and growing public and industry awareness of the possibilities of conservation and sustained yield, the southern pine industry could look forward to the postwar period with confidence and the expectation of progress in forestry and conservation.

In the postwar period forestry and conservation were closely related to the southern pine industry's transportation concerns. While superficially most dissimilar, they were tied together by the SPA's need to convince southern railroads that the piney woods were being managed on a sustained-yield basis and that the industry was therefore permanent.

Transportation costs were not, however, the only factor pushing the SPA into forestry and conservation activities. Much of the association's work was still designed to prevent the development of government regulation of practices on privately owned timber lands. The pressure for increased governmental activity was compounded by the heavy toll of the nation's forests taken by World War II and the emergence of national labor unions as strong proponents of federal regulation. As Southern Pine Association Assistant Secretary-Manager Stanley P. Deas saw the situation immediately after the end of the war, "the heavy cutting of our forests to meet the tremendous war demands is now being used as the basis for expanded propaganda by proponents of federal regulation . . . the C.I.O. is now carrying the same torch . . . openly asking for federal control of your forests." Deas concluded ominously that "the cold, hard fact is . . . we cannot relax our efforts for self-government in forestry."[111]

The SPA saw three major forestry issues facing the industry: federal forest land acquisition, public forest regulation, and public forest management service. These issues were combined in an omnibus forestry bill introduced in the House of Representatives by Frank E. Hook of Michigan in 1946. The measure ignored state administrations entirely, while empowering the Secretary of Agriculture to regulate private forest operations by direct federal action.[112] It was strongly and successfully opposed by the Southern Pine Association.[113]

In opoosing the Hook bill, the SPA reiterated its longstanding policy regarding forest regulation:

(1) That the place for publicly owned forests is in areas of low productivity or otherwise unsuited to private ownership and management, and that any program of public forest acquisition in Southern states that may be proposed by any public agency should be formulated only after due representation has been afforded the forest industries.

(2) That, whenever there shall be presented specific cutting regulations which, after voluntary trial by the Lumber Industry, have been proved practical and desirable, we would then be willing to consider the incorporation of such rules of forest practice in the statutes of the respective Southern states.[114]

The New South and the "New Competition"

The SPA's emphasis on state action supports the statement of former Chief Forester and Secretary-Manager of the West Coast Lumbermen's Association William B. Greeley that "public regulation under state administration is favored by many people as a means of forestalling or showing there is no necessity for, the exercise of Federal police power over private forestry."[115]

The latter part of 1946 brought the meeting of an American Forest Congress, sponsored by the American Forestry Association, to consider the nation's postwar forestry problems. It was the first such gathering since President Theodore Roosevelt's widely publicized American Forest Congress of 1905. The meeting came on the heels of separate but complementary surveys of the nation's forests conducted by the AFA and the U. S. Forest Service. The surveys showed that the country's forest growing stock was inadequate and poorly distributed; in terms of board-foot volume, cutting was exceeding growth by about 50 percent; the management of private forests was on the whole, despite some conspicuous exceptions, much less satisfactory than that of those in public ownership; and the key to better forestry rested in improved management of small nonindustrial holdings which made up three-fourths of the total area of privately owned commercial forest land.[116] The Southern Pine Association was represented at the congress and presented a comprehensive forest conservation policy statement. The association seemed most impressed by the proceedings and believed that the forestry and conservation situation now boiled down to a choice between private or governmental control of cutting practices, with the public demanding effective action and willing to support whichever method could be proved to be better.

At the SPA's annual meeting in 1947, some subscribers were concerned that the association was not paying enough attention to the forestry problem. There was a consensus that in order to upgrade the industry's performance in forestry and conservation it would be necessary to inaugurate a comprehensive program of education and cooperation with small operators and timber owners who were chronically slow in initiating new methods. The Southern Pine Association planned a broad program of publicity to convince the public that private industry was concerned about effectively safeguarding the nation's timber supply.[117]

Conditions in the industry varied widely. The association sent out questionnaires to its subscribers, and of those reporting, 77.7 percent owned forest land, with an average acreage of 57,064 per company. Most purchased at least some stumpage from small landowners. The survey showed a much greater tendency toward destructive cutting practices on privately owned, noncompany lands, thus pointing up the need for the education and indoctrination of small landowners in profitable and proper methods of forest management.[118] As part of the effort to bring private interests of all kinds into the campaign for enlightened forestry and conservation, the SPA invited representatives of the pulp and paper industry to address the 1948 annual meeting in the hope of laying the groundwork for cooperation between the South's two most significant wood-using industries.[119]

During the meeting, William B. Greeley told the Dixie lumbermen that "in the South you are far ahead of the Northwest in utilizing what your forests grow." Greeley noted the cooperation between lumbermen and the pulp and paper industry and stated that the old production rivalry between southern and western lumbermen had been diverted to the "far more constructive fields of forest management and utilization, and I have flown here from Puget Sound to tell you that the South is in the lead." Citing the statistics of the U. S. Forest Service, Greeley stated that eighty-six forest operations in the southern states were operating on a sustained-yield basis and that these operations constituted some 61 percent of the larger forest holdings in the South.[120]

By 1948 the accomplishments of the Southern Pine Association and its subscribers were impressive. The tree farms program was well under way, covering eight states and including some 1,046 certified tree farms with a total of over nine and one-half million acres. By the end of 1948, the association had spent over $12,000 on tree farms, and only Louisiana and Oklahoma remained outside the program. The SPA still considered fire the primary forestry problem of the South, and action to prevent and control fires was being undertaken in cooperation with federal and state agencies. During 1947 alone, over seven million dollars were expended in Dixie to control fire, and by the middle of 1948 organized protection was provided for 54 percent of the total state and private forest land in the South. Less intensive protection, primarily in the form of education, was utilized on an additional 11 percent of the forests, leaving some 35,500,000 acres of private forest land without any organized form of protection. A more positive set of statistics showed the

South leading the nation in forest land under management programs, with most large landowners doing a respectable job of managing their forests. The forest reappraisal survey of 1945-46 had shown that approximately 72 percent of the large landholdings were utilizing enlightened cutting practices. However, only a small percentage of total southern forest lands were held in lots of over 50,000 acres. Over 73 percent, or 122,000,000 acres, were controlled by some 1,650,000 owners of fewer than 5,000 acres each, and the reappraisal classified 74 percent of the cutting practices on these holdings as poor or destructive. During 1948, the Southern Pine Association was pushing for improvement of these figures, conducting a forest planting survey, and providing technical assistance in the formation of seedling nurseries. In addition, it furnished technical advice to numerous subscribers with regard to their individual forestry problems and programs, and it was working toward the establishment of demonstration cutting areas to publicize the wisdom of growing trees.[121]

While the tree farms program and other forestry and conservation activities continued to grow, one of the healthiest signs for the future was the development of southern state tree nurseries. In 1948 nearly 170 million seedlings were produced and distributed from nineteen southern state nurseries, almost twice the number produced the previous year, and the lumber industry alone purchased some 22,400,00 of them. That same year, it grew over two and two-thirds million seedlings in company nurseries or purchased them from other sources. During 1949, 122 lumber manufacturers in twelve southern states reforested over 28,000 acres of company-owned lands. Of these, 62 manufacturers were SPA subscribers, who planted 85 percent of the total figure. The upward trend continued in 1950, and by the time of the 1951-52 planting season the number of state nurseries in the South had increased to twenty-one, while 20 percent of their seedling production went to the lumber industry. During the season the lumber companies planted over 39,250,000 seedlings from state nurseries, plus an additional 6 million grown in company nurseries or acquired elsewhere. The industry planted 52,291 acres of company lands and distributed over one million trees for planting by farmers.[122] As a result of the efforts of the Southern Pine Association and other interested parties, by 1952 southern pine sawtimber growth was exceeding harvest and mortality by 22 percent. The southern pine industry seemed finally to have achieved a permanent basis and the old fears of a "timber famine" should by this time have been largely discredited.[123]

However, as President E. O. Lightsey told the 1952 annual meeting, while the southern pine manufacturers had "made great strides toward self-government in forestry and in the management of our own affairs," the industry still faced "the threat of federal regulation."[124] The specter of increased federal control over private forest holdings was constant throughout this period, and the efforts of the SPA and Southern Pine Industry Committee to resist them were paramount in the industry's second phase of forestry and conservation activities.

The first federal regulatory measure in this period was a timber control bill drawn up at the suggestion of the Forest Service and introduced in the Senate by Clinton Anderson of New Mexico on May 10, 1949. It allowed the Secretary of Agriculture, in the absence of federally approved state action, to impose a program of improved forest practices regulations on privately owned forest lands. In the case of approved state plans, the federal government would provide matching funds to help finance the program. The Southern Pine Association, SPIC, and other lumber interests bitterly and successfully fought this proposal duirng 1949 and into the 1950s.

Among other legislation proposed was the Granger bill, which originally called for amendments to the Clarke-McNary Act providing substantially increased federal funds for forest fire control, forest nurseries and planting, forestry education, and forest management services for landowners and operators. This bill was strongly opposed by the SPA, SPIC, NLMA, and other regional associations, but was finally passed with amendments and the deletion of the forest management section. The Southern Pine Associ-ation opposed this legislation on the grounds that it was dangerous to private control and constituted an unwar-ranted extension of federal powers. As a matter of economy, the association also unsuccessfully opposed a 1949 act which increased the appropriation for the nation-wide forest survey authorized by the McSweeney-McNary Act of 1928, as amended in 1944. Along the same line, the SPA unsuccessfully voiced its reservations about the Coopera-tive Forest Management Act of August 25, 1950, which authorized an annual appropriation of $2,500,000 to enable the Secretary of Agriculture to cooperate with state

271

foresters to provide technical services to private forest landowners and operators and processors of primary forest products. The association's concern was that the legislation would pave the way for further expansion of the U. S. Forest Service into forest management on private lands. In fact, the Southern Pine Association, or its leaders, by this time seemed to have become obsessed with the fear that all of the events of this period, in other areas as well as conservation and forestry, were part of a vaguely defined plot or conspiracy to overwhelm the private enterprise system.[125]

This pervasive concern about government seems to have been a characteristic of southern pine manufacturers throughout the existence of the SPA. At times it undoubtedly blurred their vision and led to unenlightened or even reactionary attitudes and policies. It should be noted, however, that the southern pine producers were quite willing to use the government when it was to their advantage.

In the area of forestry and conservation, for example, during the early years following World War I they were anxious for the government to take over their cutover lands, or at least to help unload them on unsuspecting purchasers. When the manufacturers became convinced that a sustained yield was economically feasible, they lobbied for government assistance in the form of tax breaks, fire protection, etc. Some still hoped, also, that the government would take over those lands which were unsuitable for private development.

The Southern Pine Association was in the vanguard of industry thinking in coming to recognize and promote the sustained-yield approach. It promoted enlightened forestry and conservation practices, for instance, selective cutting, as practical, businesslike measures. However, whether out of the sincere convictions of its leaders and staff people or as a matter of expediency, the SPA shared and conveyed its industry's strongly anti-government biases.

NOTES TO CHAPTER 8

1. George Brown Tindall, The Emergence of the New South, 1913-1945 (Baton Rouge: Louisiana State University Press, 1967), p. 82. For a brief look into the

conservation attitudes of southern pine producers in the early twentieth century see, Philip P. Wells, "Philip P. Wells in the Forest Service Law Office," Journal of Forest History, XVI (Apr., 1972), 26-27.

2. Vernon H. Jensen, Lumber and Labor (New York: Farrar and Rinehart, 1945), p. 85.

3. Albert S. Boisfontaine, "The Southern Pine Association in Retrospect: Seventeen Years of Trail Blazing in the Trade Association Field," Southern Lumberman, CXLIV (Dec., 1931), 111.

4. "Prospectus: Incorporation, By-Laws, Departments," pamphlet published by the Southern Pine Association in 1925, Southern Pine Association Records,, Collection Prospects, p. 6 (Louisiana State University Archives, Baton Rouge, La.) Collection hereafter cited as SPA Records.

5. W. G. Wahlenberg, Longleaf Pine: Its Use, Ecology, Regeneration, Protection, Growth, and Management (Washington, D.C.: Charles Lathrop Pack Forestry Foundation, 1946), pp. 16, 46.

6. James Boyd, "Cut-Over Lands," SPA Records, Box 77a, p. 5.

7. "Prospectus, Incorporation, By-Laws, Purposes: Southern Cut-Over Land Association," SPA Records, Box 67a.

8. "Proceedings of Meeting of Southern Foresters Held in the Office of the Commissioner of Conservation of the State of Louisiana, at New Orleans, Louisiana, on January 18 and 19, 1918," SPA Records, Box X-69.

9. The ironic thing about the entire scheme was that it had already been tried in the Great Lakes states and found wanting. Lucile Kane, "Selling Cut-Over Lands in Wisconsin," Business History Review, XXVIII (Sept., 1954), 236-48; Stanley Todd Lowry, "Henry Hardtner, Pioneer in Southern Forestry: An Analysis of the Economic Bases of His Reforestation Program" (M.A. thesis, Louisiana State University, 1956), p. 59; Anna C. Burns, "Henry E. Hardtner, Louisiana's First Conservationist," Journal of Forest History, XXII (Apr., 1978), 78-85.

The New South and the "New Competition"

10. "Minutes of a Meeting of the Board of Directors of the Southern Pine Association . . . December 14, 1916," SPA Records, Box 70b; Jensen, Lumber and Labor, p. 64; "Lumber Awakes! Official Report of the First Annual Meeting of the Subscribers to the Southern Pine Association Held at Grunewald Hotel, New Orleans, Feb. 23-24, 1916," SPA Records, Box 85b, p. 64.

11. "Minutes of a Meeting of the Board of Directors of the Southern Pine Association . . . December 14, 1916," SPA Records, Box 70b; Jensen, Lumber and Labor, p. 85.

12. Southern Pine Association to Subscribers, Oct. 25, 1918, Kurth Papers, Box 489 (Forest History Collection, Stephen F. Austin State University Library, Nacogdoches, Tex.).

13. Lowry, "Henry Hardtner," pp. 59, 64.

14. "Houston Oil Company Sold Their Cut-Over Land," Gult Coast Lumberman, IV (Sept. 1, 1916), 28.

15. Helene King, "The Economic History of the Long-Bell Lumber Company" (M.A. thesis, Louisiana State University, 1936), p. 18; Lowry, "Henry Hardtner," pp. 59-60.

16. Jensen, Lumber and Labor, p. 64.

17. Tindall, Emergence of the New South, pp. 128-29.

18. "State-Wide Activities of a State-Wide Organization, Mississippi Landowners Association," SPA Records, Box 37b. The cover of this pamphlet lists the organization's objectives as better living conditions, better schools, farm ownership, better roads, enlargement of the livestock industry, propagation of grass and forage crops, extensive drainage, utilization of the twenty-million acres of idle land in Mississippi, and land settlement.

19. H. E. Blakeslee to A. G. T. Moore, Nov. 18, 1919, SPA Records, Box 37b.

20. John E. Rhodes to Frank G. Wisner, Sept. 23, 1919, SPA Records, Box 37b.

21. Southern Pine Association to Subscribers, Oct. 9, 1919, SPA Records, Box 37b.

22. L. L. Squires to A. G. T. Moore, Dec. 5, 1919, SPA Records, Box 37b.

23. "Scientific Southern Survey," Lumber, Nov. 8, 1920, p. 27 (clipping in SPA Records, Box 66b).

24. "Lumber Liquidates," SPA Records, Box 85b, pp. 147-48.

25. Jensen, Lumber and Labor, p. 85; Lowry, "Henry Hardtner," p. 60. For the experiences of one firm with reforestation (beginning in the mid-1930s) see Elwood R. Maunder, comp., James Greeley McGowin--South Alabama Lumberman: The Recollections of His Family (Santa Cruz, Calif.: Forest History Society, 1977), passim.

26. Cogent arguments along these general lines are advanced in Samuel P. Hays, The Response to Industrialism: 1885-1914 (Chicago: University of Chicago Press, 1957); Gabriel Kolko, The Triumph of Conservatism: A Reinterpretation of American History, 1900-1916 (New York: Free Press, 1963); Robert H. Wiebe, Businessmen and Reform: A Study of the Progressive Movement (Cambridge, Mass.: Harvard University Press, 1962); Samuel P. Hays, Conservation and the Gospel of Efficiency: The Progressive Conservation Movement, 1890-1920 (Cambridge, Mass.: Harvard University Press, 1959); Paul W. Glad, "Progressives and the Business Culture of the 1920's," Journal of American History, LIII (June, 1966), 79-80; and Thomas LeDuc, "The Historiography of Conservation," Forest History, IX (Oct., 1965), 23-28.

27. Predictions that the country was going to experience a timber famine were constantly made by conservationists. In 1930 the prospect of such a famine for the nation was foreseen by a member of the U. S. Bureau of Forestry and by the redoubtable Gifford Pinchot. A similar prediction for the South in particular was delivered by the president of the Mississippi Valley Lumbermen's Association. Jo Dent Hodge, "Lumbering in Laurel at the Turn of the Century" (M.A. thesis, University of Mississippi, 1966), pp. 35-37. Many southern pine lumbermen believed the predictions, and in

1903 two of the industry's giants, R. A. Long and John Henry Kirby, predicted that the timber of East Texas would be gone in twenty-five years. James William Martin, "History of Forest Conservation in Texas 1900-1935" (M.A. thesis, Stephen F. Austin State College, 1966), p. 34. Long "forecast that at the current rate of consumption present long-leaf yellow pine stands would be exhausted long before a second crop could be produced to take its place. He called for foresters and lumbermen to join hands to lick this problem." Hodge, "Lumbering in Laurel," p. 37.

28. "Henry E. Hardtner," Journal of Forestry, XXXIII (Oct., 1935), 885; Lowry, "Henry Hardtner," 31.

29. Hamilton Pratt Easton, "The History of the Texas Lumbering Industry" (Ph.D. dissertation, University of Texas, 1947), pp. 124-25, 236, 432-33.

30. R. C. Fraunberger says that "prior to the depression of the 1930's there was not any great trend toward stabilization of the industry through the practice of forestry." R. C. Fraunberger, "Lumber Trade Associations: Their Economic and Social Significance" (M.A. thesis, Temple University, 1951), p. 87. It should be noted, however, that companies with large timber supplies were much better situated to develop enlightened forestry policies than were those that more or less were forced to buy and utilize small tracts of timber as they went along. See Maunder, James Greeley McGowin, pp. 56-57.

31. Lowry, "Henry Hardtner," pp. 21-22.

32. R. S. Nowlin, "Economic Development of the Kirby Lumber Company of Houston, Texas" (M.A. thesis, George Peabody College for Teachers, 1930), p. 86. For a brief summary of the relationship between taxation and reforestation see Harold K. Steen, The U.S. Forest Service: A History (Seattle: University of Washington Press, 1976), pp. 190-91.

33. For example, in 1935 Hardtner, Austin Cary of the U.S. Forest Service, and other practical and professional foresters expressed varying opinions about the efficacy and possible methods of controlled woods burning. Both Hardtner and Cary acknowledged that they had in some ways

changed their views about controlled burning over the years as they had learned more about its effects at various times of the year and under differing conditions on different varieties and sizes of pines. Journal of Forestry, XXXIII (Mar., 1935) (reprint in SPA Records, Box 84b). Natives of the southern pine region had a long tradition of woods burning which was variously motivated. Some burned just for maliciousness, some out of resentment of the social and economic domination of the large lumber companies, and others because they believed that burning improved the range for the grazing of livestock. The problem in all of these cases was the fact that the burning was uncontrolled and often devastated the lumbermen's pine stocks at the wrong stage of the growth cycle.

34. Easton, "History of Texas Lumbering," p. 125.

35. "Outline of Work under Supervision of the Committees of the Southern Pine Association," John E. Rhodes's notebook, SPA Records, Box 39a.

36. William B. Greeley, Some Public and Economic Aspects of the Lumber Industry, Part I of Studies of the Lumber Industry. U.S. Department of Agriculture, Report No. 114. (Washington, D.C.: Government Printing Office, 1917). For a detailed examination of the Forest Service see Steen, U.S. Forest Service.

37. Ralph W. Hidy, Frank Ernest Hill, and Allan Nevins, Timber and Men: The Weyerhaeuser Story (New York: Macmillan, 1963), p. 377. For a brief look at Pinchot's attitudes regarding transportation and other natural resources see Glad, "Progressives and Business Culture," pp. 82–83.

38. William B. Greeley, Forests and Men (Garden City, N.Y.: Doubleday, 1951), p.69.

39. George T. Morgan Jr., William B. Greeley A Practical Forester, 1879–1955 (St. Paul, Minn: Forest History Society, 1961), pp. 32–36. Between 1900 and 1935 the head of the Forest Service was called Forester, instead of Chief. Therefore while it is technically correct that Greeley was an assistant forester, in fact he was one of several assistant chiefs.

40. Ibid., p. 37.

41. Greeley, Forests and Men, p. 118. The correspondence between Pinchot and Graves is quoted in Morgan, William B. Greeley, p. 37.

42. Hidy, Hill, and Nevins, Timber and Men, p. 379.

43. Ibid., p. 386.

44. Morgan, William B. Greeley, p. 39.

45. Ibid., p. 54.

46. Ibid., p. 39.

47. Ibid.; Hidy, Hill, and Nevins, Timber and Men, p. 386.

48. Martin Nelson McGeary, Gifford Pinchot, Forester-Politician (Princeton, N.J.: Princeton University Press, 1960), p. 330; Morgan, William B. Greeley, p. 45; Hidy, Hill, and Nevins, Timber and Men, p. 386.

49. Hidy, Hill, and Nevins, Timber and Men, p. 386; Morgan, William B. Greeley, p. 41.

50. Morgan, William B. Greeley, p. 41.

51. Ibid.

52. Hidy, Hill, and Nevins, Timber and Men, p. 387.

53. "Association Activities; Report of Secretary-Manager J.E. Rhodes Submitted to the Board of Directors of the Southern Pine Association, at Chicago, Ill., June 16, 1919," SPA Records, Box 84b, pp. 63-64.

54. "Minutes of a Meeting of the Board of Directors of the Southern Pine Association . . . March 15 and 18, 1920," SPA Records, Box 70b; Lumber, Nov. 8, 1920, p. 25 (clipping in SPA Records, Box 60b). See also Elwood Maunder, comp., Voices from the South: Recollections of Four Foresters (Santa Cruz, Calif.: Forest History Society, 1977), pp. 116-20.

55. J. Walter Myers, Jr., Opportunities Unlimited: The Story of Our Southern Forests (Chicago: Illinois Central Railroad, 1950), p. 53.

56. "Minutes of a Meeting of the Board of Directors of the Southern Pine Association . . . June 14, 1921," SPA Records, Box 70b.

57. "Minutes of a Meeting of the Board of Directors of the Southern Pine Association . . . October 19, 1921," SPA Records, Box 70b.

58. "Minutes of the Meeting of the Southern Pine Association . . . December 15th, 1921," SPA Records, Box 73b; "Memorandum of Proceedings of a Special Meeting of Subscribers to the Southern Pine Association . . . Memphis, Tenn., Thursday, December 15, 1921," SPA Records, Box 68b.

59. "Minutes of the Meeting of the Southern Pine Association Held in the Convention Room, Gayoso Hotel, December 15th, 1921," SPA Records, Box 73b.

60. Samuel Trask Dana, Forest and Range Policy, Its Development in the United States (New York: McGraw-Hill, 1956), pp. 216-17.

61. John L. Kaul, "The Lumbermen's Interest in Forestry," in "Protection for Buyers of Pine: Official Report of the Seventh Annual Meeting of the Subscribers to the Southern Pine Association Held at Grunewald Hotel, New Orleans, March 28 and 29, 1922," SPA Records, Box 85b, p. 136.

62. Ibid., pp. 136-37.

63. Ibid., p. 138.

64. "Proceedings of the Seventh Annual Meeting of Subscribers to the Southern Pine Association . . . March 28 and 29, 1922," SPA Records, Box 73b, p. 85.

65. Ibid., p. 87.

The New South and the "New Competition"

66. "Minutes of a Meeting of the Board of Directors of the Southern Pine Assoiciation . . . December 13, 1922," SPA Records, Box 70b.

67. "Minutes of a Meeting of the Board of Directors of the Southern Pine Association . . . March 27, 1922," "Minutes of a Meeting of the Board of Directors of the Southern Pine Association . . . July 7, 1922," and "Minutes of a Meeting of the Board of Directors of the Southern Pine Association . . . August 10, 1922," all in SPA Records, Box 70b.

68. "What the Association Is Doing for Southern Pine," in "Homes and Citizenship: Official Report of the Eighth Annual Meeting of the Subscribers to the Southern Pine Association, Held at Gruenewald Hotel, New Orleans, March 20 and 21, 1923," SPA Records, Box 85b, p. 32.

69. Dana, Forest and Range Policy, pp. 220-21; William B. Greeley, Forest Policy (New York: McGraw-Hill, 1953), p. 181.

70. McGeary, Gifford Pinchot, p. 331. For a detailed summary of the bill see Dana, Forest and Range Policy, pp. 221-24. As the struggle over legislation and between the Pinchot and Greeley programs developed, Pinchot came to regard Greeley as "a pawn of the lumbering interests." McGeary, Gifford Pinchot, p. 331.

71. Wilson Compton, "National Problems," in "A New Era: Official Report of the Ninth Annual Meeting of the Subscribers to the Southern Pine Association Held at Roosevelt Hotel, New Orleans, March 11 and 12, 1924," SPA Records, Box 85b, 46.

72. Ibid., p. 50.

73. "Report of Forestry Committee," in "A New Era," SPA Records, Box 85b, p. 66.

74. H. C. Berckes, "Trend of Southern Pine Production and Supply," Southern Lumberman, Dec. 20, 1924 (reprint in SPA Records, Box 84b).

75. Ibid.

76. "Pine Timber Stand and Pine Lumber Production in the Southern States as of the Year 1924," SPA Records, Box 39a.

77. "Minutes of a Meeting of the Board of Directors of the Southern Pine Association . . . March 23, 1925," SPA Records, Box 70b.

78. McGeary, Gifford Pinchot, p. 333.

79. "Minutes of a Meeting of the Board of Directors of the Southern Pine Association . . . March 23, 1925," SPA Records, Box 70b.

80. Dana, Forest and Range Policy, pp. 225-26.

81. "Minutes of a Meeting of the Board of Directors of the Southern Pine Association . . . January 11, 1928," SPA Records, Box 70b.

82. "Proceedings of Fourteenth Annual Meeting Southern Pine Association, March 25, 26, 27, 1929, Roosevelt Hotel, New Orleans, Louisiana," Lumber Trade Journal Apr. 1, 1929 (reprint in SPA Records, Box 74b).

83. Q. T. Hardtner, "Progress of Private Forestry in the South—Reflections of a Southern Pine Manufacturer." Paper presented at 37th annual meeting of the Southern Pine Association in New Orleans, April 8, 1952 (copy in SPA Records, Box 68a).

84. "Proceedings of Fourteenth Annual Meeting Southern Pine Association, March 25, 26, 27, 1929," SPA Records, Box 74b.

85. Inman F. Eldredge, "Forty Years of Forestry on Private Lands in the South," paper presented at 37th Annual Meeting of the Southern Pine Association in New Orleans, April 8, 1952 (copy in SPA Records, Box 68a). Additional information on the rise of forestry in the southern pine region may be found in Robert S. Maxwell, "The Impact of Forestry on the Gulf South," Forest History, XVII (Apr., 1973), 31-35; and Robert S. Maxwell, "One Man's Legacy: W. Goodrich Jones and Texas Conservation," Southwestern Historical Quarterly, LXXVIII (1974), 355-80.

The New South and the "New Competition"

86. McGeary, Gifford Pinchot, pp. 333-36.

87. Greeley, Forests and Men, p. 134; Hidy, Hill, and Nevins, Timber and Men, pp. 494-95.

88. Southern Pine Association circular, Dec. 10, 1932, SPA Records, Box X-66, p. 1.

89. Herbert C. Berckes, "The Pitch in Pine: A Story of the Traditions, Policies, and Activities of the Southern Pine Industry and the Men Responsible for Them" (unpublished manuscript in possession of the author), p. 164. Secretary-Manager William B. Greeley of the West Coast Lumbermen's Association recalled the origins of Article X somewhat differently. According to Greeley, when the lumbermen were conferring and drawing up their code he had pointed out that "President Roosevelt is almost certain to want something in this code on forestry. Let's beat him to the draw. It will help us get the rest." Greeley said that his argument carried the day and that he was "commissioned to draft a clause which would commit the industry to a reasonable program of forest conservation." Greeley, Forests and Men, 134.

90. Southern Pine Division Code Bulletin, I (Jan. 4, 1934) (copy in SPA Records, Box 103b).

91. "Administration of the Lumber Code in the Southern Pine Division," SPA Records, Box 103b.

92. Hidy, Hill, and Nevins, Timber and Men, 495.

93. Southern Pine Division Code Bulletin, I (Jan. 4, 1934); "Administration of the Lumber Code in the Southern Pine Division," SPA Records, Box 103b. See also Maunder, Voices from the South, pp. 163-64, 166.

94. "The Public's Responsibility to the Cause of Forestry, Address by Harry [sic] E. Hardtner, Chairman, Conservation Committee, Southern Pine Association . . . before Forestry Conference, Washington, D.C., January 25, 1934," reprint published by the Southern Pine Association, SPA Records, Box X-68, p. 3.

95. Southern Pine Association press release, June 26, 1934, SPA Records, Box X-68; Southern Pine Association press release, July 5, 1934, SPA Records, Box 103a.

96. Southern Pine Association press release, Dec. 1, 1934, SPA Records, Box X-68, p. 3.

97. "Southern Pine Timber Holdings as of December 31, 1915," SPA Records, Box X-70, p. 5.

98. Southern Pine Division Code Bulletin, I (Mar. 20, 1935) (copy in SPA Records, Box 103b); "Henry E. Hardtner," pp. 885-86; Berckes, "Pitch in Pine," p. 164.

99. A. G. T. Moore, "The Lumberman as a Constructive Factor in Conservation," Southern Pine Division Code Bulletin, I (Mar. 20, 1935), 18-21; "Meeting of Conservation Committee Southern Pine Association . . . Twenty-Third Annual Meeting . . . 1938," SPA Records, Box 73b, pp. 31-32; "Report of A. G. T. Moore, Manager, Department of Conservation," SPA Records, Box 9a; Hidy, Hill, and Nevins, Timber and Men," 444-45; Richard Polenberg, "The Great Conservation Contest," Forest History, X (Jan., 1967), 13-23.

100. Hidy, Hill, and Nevins, Timber and Men, pp. 444-45, 501; "Meeting of Conservation Committee Southern Pine Association . . . March 29, 1937," SPA Records, Box 9a; "Proceedings of Southern Pine Association Twenty-Third Annual Meeting . . . 1938," SPA Records, Box 73b; A. G. T. Moore, "Southern Pine: The South's Greatest Agricultural Crop . . . Statement Filed on Behalf of Southern Pine Association, New Orleans, La., with the Joint Committee on Forestry of the Congress of the United States, at Hearing Washington, D.C., beginning January 16, 1940," SPA Records, Box 70a.

101. Hidy, Hill, and Nevins, Timber and Men, p. 460. There are numerous circulars, newspaper clippings, letters, and other materials relative to the forest products service plan and later related legislation in SPA Records, Boxes 52b, 94a, and 94b.

102. P. F. Watzek to H. C. Berckes, Sept. 5, 1944, SPA Records, Box 11b; Berckes to Watzek, Sept. 7, 1944, SPA Records, Box 11b.

103. Hidy, Hill, and Nevins, Timber and Men, p. 505; "Proceedings of Meeting of the Southern Pine War Committee . . . October 26, 1944," SPA Records, Box 68a, p. 39. The American Forest Products Industries was created as a subsidiary of the National Lumber Manufactuers Association in 1932.

104. Hidy, Hill, and Nevins, Timber and Men, p. 505.

105. Ibid., pp. 505-6.

106. "Proceedings of Twenty-Seventh Annual Meeting of the Southern Pine Association, March 25 and 26, 1942," SPA Records, Box 73b, pp. 79-89.

107. For descriptions of these programs on the lands of the various southern pine operations see "Proceedings of Meeting of Conservation Committee, New Orleans, Louisiana, March 13, 1941," SPA Records, Box 73b.

108. "Forestry Provides the Future, Report of W. C. Hammerle, Ass'n Forester, at the Conservation Committee Meeting . . . October 25, 1944," SPA Records, Box 11a, p. 3.

109. Ibid., p. 4; "Statement Tree Farms Sub-Committee, Presented by N. F. McGowin, Acting Chairman, at the Conservation Committee Meeting . . . October 25, 1944," SPA Records, Box 11a; "Summary of Committee Recommendations Unanimously Approved by the Southern Pine Association Board of Directors, October 26, 1944," SPA Records, Box 70a.

110. "Statement Legislation and Taxation Subcommittee, Presented by P. A. Bloomer, Chairman, at the Conservation Committee Meeting . . . Oct. 25, 1944," SPA Records, Box 11a; Hidy, Hill, and Nevins, Timber and Men, pp. 506-7.

111. S. P. Deas, "Lumberman, What of Tomorrow?," mimeographed speech, SPA Records; Box 11a; Hidy, Hill, and Nevins, Timber and Men, pp. 506-7.

112. "Forestry Omnibus Bill, H. R. 6221--Hook," SPA Records; Box 11a; Greeley, Forest Policy, p. 244.

113. "H. M. Seaman, Chairman, Conservation Committee, Report to the Board of Directors--Southern Pine Association, May 10, 1946," SPA Records, Box 10b.

114. Ibid.

115. Greeley, Forest Policy, p. 244.

116. Dana, Forest and Range Policy, pp. 295-96.

117. "Minutes of a Meeting of the Conservation Committee of the Southern Pine Association . . . March 19, 1947," SPA Records, Box 10b; "Script for Panel Discussion, Wednesday, March 19, 1947," SPA Records, Box 10b, pp. 8-10; W. C. Hammerle to H. C. Berckes, Jan. 8, 1947, SPA Records, Box 12b; "Forest Conservation Policy Statement of the Southern Pine Association, Presented to American Forest Congress, October 9, 10 & 11, 1946 . . . ," SPA Records, Box 52a.

118. W. C. Hammerle to H. C. Berckes, Jan. 8, 1947, SPA Records, Box 12b.

119. Southern Pine Association Press Release, Apr. 10, 1948, SPA Records, Box 10b.

120. "Proceedings of Meeting of Subscribers to the Southern Pine Association and Southern Pine Industry Committee . . . April 8 and 9, 1948," SPA Records, Box 74a, pp. 64-65.

121. "Annual Report Forest Conservation Department, Southern Pine Association, W. C. Hammerle, Forester, April 7, 1948," SPA Records, Box 10b; H. C. Berckes to H. M. Seaman, Nov. 3, 1948, SPA Records, Box 70a. The industry's strides in moving toward enlightened forestry and conservation policies were lauded in a reflective mood by SPA President Q. T. Hardtner, a member of the famous pioneering family in southern forestry, who said during the 1948 annual meeting that the "steady and sure progress through the years toward a permanent Southern Pine Industry and the reflection of this belief by my fellow subscribers" was "the fulfillment of a dream come true."

The New South and the "New Competition"

"Presidential Addres Q. T. Hardtner, 33rd Annual Convention, New Orleans, April 7, 8, and 9, 1948," SPA Records, Box 10b.

122. "Annual Report Forest Conservation Department-Southern Pine Association, W. C. Hammerle, Forester, April 6, 1949," SPA Records, Box 10a; "Forest Conservation," mimeographed report, SPA Records, Box 12a; Southern Pine Association Press Release, Aug. 9, 1950, SPA Records, Box 53a; Southern Pine Association to Subscribers, Aug. 9, 1951, SPA Records, Box 53a.

123. John M. Collier, The First Fifty Years of the Southern Pine Association, 1915-1965 (New Orleans: Southern Pine Association, 1965), pp. 158-59.

124. "Proceedings of Thirty-Seventh Annual Convention of the Southern Pine Association and Industry-Wide Meeting under the Auspices of Southern Pine Industry Committee . . . April 7, 8 and 9, 1952," SPA Records, Box 68a.

125. "Q. T. Hardtner, Chairman, Conservation Committee, Forestry Legislation," SPA Records, Box 12a; "Timber Saving Forest Conservationists Prepare a New Push to Curb Tree Cutting," Wall Street Journal, May 11, 1949; "Forest Conservation," mimeographed report, SPA Records, Box 12a; H. C. Berckes to Southern Pine Industry Committee, Oct. 27, 1949, SPA Records, Box 70a; "Statement of Southern Pine Association . . . on H. R. 2001, 81st Congress, First Session," SPA Records, Box 10a; "Statement of Southern Pine Association . . . on H. R. 2296, 81st Congress, First Session," SPA Records, Box 10a; Southern Pine Association to George Fuller, Feb. 3, 1950, SPA Records, Box 50a; H. C. Berckes to R. M. Eagle, May 24, 1949, SPA Records, Box 12a; Berckes to C. C. Sheppard, May 21, 1949, SPA Records, Box 12a; Dana, Forest and Range Policy, pp. 419-21.

9

The "Labor Problem"

From the beginning of large-scale lumbering in the southern pine woods laboring conditions were far from ideal. Early in the twentieth century toilers in the mills and camps of the southern pine region reached a point of desperation that placed them on a collision course with the industry's paternalistic and obstinate lumber barons.

Both the Southern Pine Association and the Yellow Pine Manufacturers' Association, its immediate predecessor as the industry's leading trade association, were intimately involved in the region's labor turmoil. Surviving records indicate that the YPMA and the SPA worked closely with the Southern Lumber Operators' Association, formed in 1906, which was an employers' association in the purest and simplest meaning of the term. The sole reason for its birth and continued existence was to serve as a vehicle of opposition to unionization. The YPMA and the SPA worked closely with the SLOA during the pre-World War I labor turmoil.[1]

The Operators' Association outlived the YPMA and its relationship with the Southern Pine Association was not as open, but it seems clear that the groups cooperated in certain areas. The Operators' Association performed a valuable service for both the YPMA and the SPA—it allowed them to keep their skirts relatively clean from the violence which was often involved in labor conflicts. Therefore, the trade associations could maintain a respectable image in the community and with the government while their members attained their objectives in the labor field through the less respectable Operators' Association. The

287

SLOA continued to exist and provide such a service for the SPA until the time of the New Deal.[2]

Given its background of trouble with discontented workers, it is not surprising that the southern pine industry encountered serious labor problems during World War I as it endeavored to cooperate with government agencies and to provide lumber for the war effort. During the war the southern pine industry was constantly plagued by labor shortages resulting from the drifting of lumber workers into southern urban centers to find more lucrative occupations opened to them by wartime labor shortages and from the migration of blacks out of the South to work in northern defense industries. Furthermore, the lumber industry was not considered by the government to be a "priority" industry. The labor priorities section of the War Industries Board issued its first labor priorities order on September 17, 1918, and omitted lumber from the list, because the order's "chief purpose was . . . to procure an automatic flow of fuel and transportation service. . . . Lumber . . . was not on the preference list because it was intended to discourage long hauls of that commodity for the use of civilians and to promote the use of wood as fuel." Nonetheless, there was a military need for some kinds of lumber, and the loss of lumber workers to other occupations was viewed with alarm by some government officials.[3]

The industry itself seemed to have mixed opinions regarding the labor situation during the war's early stages. Those present at the SPA's annual meeting in New Orleans in late February, 1918, heard a warning from the secretary-manager of the West Coast Lumbermen's Association that the industry in that area was facing severe labor troubles because of "continued agitation on the part of official Washington . . . socialistic professors, speculators in philosophy, theorists having poetical ideas of political economy and . . . ex-walking delegates from mineworkers' unions. . . ." He predicted the adoption of an eight-hour day by many operators, possibly by government order, and reported that in his section lumber wages were higher than those in shipyards.[4] SPA President Charles S. Keith seemed to share the same fears for the southern pine region, conceding that "we have a labor problem to contend with," but he strongly condemned any effort to establish government wage requirements, either maximum or minimum, and he bitterly attacked the eight-hour day as "seditious and treacherous. . . ."[5]

The "Labor Problem"

Two months later, however, War Industries Board Lumber Administrator John Henry Kirby described the industry's labor situation as "fair" and reported that "though somewhat short handed in a few instances, plants generally are running full time, and all government work is being turned out promptly." Kirby estimated an average labor shortage of 17 percent, because the draft, shipyards, and other occupations were siphoning off the industry's labor supply. He said that southern pine mills were continuing to run on an "open shop" basis and operating ten hours a day, with only a few plants maintaining night shifts. In order to meet the problem of labor shortages, lumbermen were offering increased pay and other inducements, and "in some cases negro women are being employed to do light tasks about mills." Kirby concluded that the manufacturers did not "anticipate any serious difficulties in maintaining operations during the present year" and that the territory was "practically free of labor trouble."[6]

Kirby viewed conditions differently than other leaders in the industry. In late 1917, the leading trade journal in Kirby's own region said, "According to general reports, there is more labor trouble at the mills of the south at the present time than ever before." The journal ascribed the trouble to the short labor supply caused by the war, saying that the shortage gave more than usual force to the laborers, and it reported several strikes in progress and others "fomenting."[7] By March, 1918, the Gulf Coast Lumberman was reporting the employment of the first woman sawmill engineer in the history of the Texas lumber industry, and by the middle of the summer a special industry committee, in a letter to the War Industries Board, noted "a serious labor shortage" and said that constant advances in wages were "not sufficient to overcome the effect of the draft and the competition for labor by shipyards and other war industries."[8]

Labor shortages were common in the southern lumber industry through the end of the war and into the postwar period. To deal with this condition, the mills in some cases hired workers from new sources and increased their wages to more competitive levels.[9] The major activity on an industry-wide basis was a Southern Pine Association attempt to increase the productivity of laborers by an extensive campaign featuring speaking tours of returned soldiers, who visited the mills and logging camps and attempted to arouse the patriotic ardor and productivity

The New South and the "New Competition"

of the personnel.[10]   Despite such efforts, however, labor shortages hampered the southern pine industry's war efforts, and the labor situation appeared bleak indeed as the industry looked toward the postwar period.

The labor shortage of the southern pine industry continued well into the twenties. Many workers left lumbering to work in other industries in the South, but the most serious labor difficulty was a great exodus of blacks to better jobs and living conditions above the Mason and Dixon line. The southern pine industry and the SPA led in trying to stop this labor drain, often acting in conjunction with the Southern Lumber Operators' Association. Labor problems were compounded when some blacks and whites attempted unionization of the "peaceful" southern lumber industry. On at least one occasion, these efforts culminated in violence comparable to that of the earlier Graybow incident.

Black migration out of the South became a matter of major concern to southern lumbermen and other employers on the eve of World War I and intensified during and after the conflict. The movement had been developing since the end of the Civil War, and it was not entirely unprecedented.[11] The movement during and after World War I was prompted, as before, by bad conditions in the South and expectations of a better life in the North, but the movement was accelerated because of the comparative ease of obtaining traveling money and jobs in the North. Again, as before, southern employers revealed their concern over the migration.[12]

Near the end of World War I, the Southern Lumber Operators' Association conducted an investigation of the labor situation in the pine woods. It attributed the exodus of black laborers to "labor agents who are establishing headquarters in an endeavor to organize the negroes to go north."[13] To combat the problem, the Operators' Association recommended that its members circulate among their black employees the Negro Advocate, a magazine published at Fordyce, Arkansas, by Milton Hampton, a black minister. The association assured the lumbermen that Hampton's publication would "keep the colored laborers of the South satisfied with their conditions . . . advise against the exodus of neighbors . . . and elevate their morals. . . ." The Negro Advocate was published from approximately 1917 to 1922, with some subsidization from the lumber operators, who were assured by the Operators' Association that "its articles and editorials will be closely scrutinized by this office."[14]

290

The "Labor Problem"

In keeping with its subscribers' awakening interest in the subject, in May, 1918, the SPA established a committee on industrial relations, with jurisdiction over all questions relating to labor or employee relations. The SPA board also suggested to its subscribers that they advance the wages of sawmill laborers in proportion to any increase in prices the government was willing to pay for southern pine lumber.[15]

In addition to its other activities, the SPA engaged an investigator to make a comprehensive survey of the labor situation in the industry. His report, completed in August, found a general improvement in the working conditions and wages of both blacks and whites in the industry and commented that southern pine manufacturers took a "more generous view of the Negro than is general in the South," although they still believed that the only way to handle a black was to "keep him broke." The fact that the lumber industry was unorganized was attributed to racial antagonism between whites and Negroes, but the report warned that unionization was inevitable and advised the industry to prepare for its advent. The report optimistically stated that there was a sincere desire on the part of both labor and management for improved relations and concluded that "the time has arrived for a more enlightened program."[16]

The report's generally rosy portrayal of labor conditions and the possibilities of peaceful organization in the industry was not supported by other reports of the same period or by actual events. A state government report on lumbering conditions in Louisiana, an important Southern Pine Association state, found "conditions of employment at a very low ebb and practically every labor law on the statutes being violated."[17] Furthermore, there was no real indication that the industry was willing to accept unionization. The Southern Pine Association had watched the IWW activities in the West Coast industry during the war with great anxiety and disapproval, and it strongly opposed unionization and labor's desire for a short working day. The year following the war there was a violent confrontation between a biracial movement to organize laborers and the Great Southern Lumber Company of Bogalusa, Louisiana, which provided emphatic evidence of the southern pine industry's opposition to unions. This episode differed only in detail from the earlier struggle at Graybow.[18]

The New South and the "New Competition"

The Bogalusa conflict originated in 1919 out of an attempt by two American Federation of Labor unions, the United Brotherhood of Carpenters and Joiners of America and the International Timber Workers Union, to organize the employees of the Great Southern Lumber Company, which was the world's largest lumber manufacturer and at times a powerful voice in the Southern Pine Association. Existing labor dissatisfaction was intensified by increased rents in the company town during the early part of the year. The AFL was successful in organizing a sawyers' and filers' union (which was taken over by the carpenters), a regular carpenters' local, and a timberworkers' union. The three unions organized a central trades assembly with the head of the carpenters' union, Lum Williams, as president and began a campaign to organize all lumberworkers in the area, including blacks. The effort to recruit Negroes, who were organized in a segregated local, was spearheaded by Sol Dacus, the black vice-president of the local. The union effort was fought by a pro-company citizens' committee, the Self-Preservation and Loyalty League (SPLL), which was apparently motivated in part by anger over the union efforts to organize both blacks and whites, and by the company itself, which instituted a lockout in September, 1919. Some members of the SPLL were appointed deputy sheriffs and harassed union members; others pillaged Dacus's house on several occasions. After about two months of the lockout members of the citizens' committee allegedly killed Lum Williams and three other union men. Those charged with the murder were acquitted. The loss of Williams doomed the organizational effort.[19]

In 1919 both the SPA and the Southern Lumber Operators' Association began a strong effort to stem the continuing Negro migration out of the South. The two organizations joined in urging industry support of the Negro Advocate, which the SPA said would "attempt to overcome" the "vast amount of sensational and revolutionary reading matter" contained in "papers published in the North for circulation among the colored people of the South. . . ."[20] On the recommendation of M. L. Alexander of the Southern Lumber Operators' Association, the Southern Pine Association contributed five hundred dollars to the Negro Advocate in February. By the end of the year the SPA had endorsed the entire program of the SLOA and had authorized the employment at its own expense of two men to solicit members for the Operators' Association.[21]

The "Labor Problem"

The SPA's postwar activities went beyond this effort to keep the Negroes contented and in the South. The association actually tried to reverse the flow of labor and bring southern blacks living in the North back to their old homes and jobs. By early 1919, the SPA was interested in the "surplus of idle colored labor in the North, particularly in the larger cities," and solicited information from its subscribers concerning their labor needs. The association received suggestions that it employ a man in Chicago to assist in the return of blacks to the South and noted that "the great majority of idle negroes now in the North are unable to pay their transportation. . . ."[22] By the end of May, the SPA reported that there were "approximately 10,000 negroes in Chicago at the present time, about 73% of whom are non-residents," and it stated that "a surprising number of these negroes have at some time in the past been employed in the saw mills and woods in the Southern States." The association advised that "colored common labor can be gotten together on short notice and signed up for work in the South," and it noted that there were no federal or Illinois state laws prohibiting the recruitment of such workers. The SPA also cited the willingness of "the railroads radiating from Chicago to the South . . . to render every possible assistance in encouraging the transportation of colored labor . . . and in endeavoring to see that the parties are kept together to destination."[23]

In June, the SPA board of directors authorized Secretary-Manager Rhodes to "prepare and submit to subscribers a plan for an assessment of 1 cent a thousand on their shipments, for the purpose of conducting propaganda to show colored workmen that it is to their best interests to return and to remain in the South." The fund was also to be used to pay railroad transportation charges back to the South with the understanding that "those firms which employ them shall not charge them for their railroad fares."[24] At the end of the month, the association advised its subscribers that plans were being carried forward in conjunction with the Southern Lumber Operators' Association to bring about the return of Negro labor. The plan was to open employment offices in one or more northern cities, beginning with Chicago. Each prospective employer was to guarantee "to pay the transportation of the number of men supplied, with the understanding that not more than 50 cents per day as reimbursement for transportation, shall be deducted from the wages to be paid them, and that if they remain at least six months, their fares will be returned to them." It outlined details to ensure that all laborers embarking for the southern mills would arrive there. The entire project was to be supervised by the SPA's committee on industrial relations.[25]

Early in July the SPA actually established an employment office in a Negro section of Chicago under the direction of a white man from the area who was supposedly familiar with the northern labor market. The office survived only until the end of August, but the reasons for its closing are unclear. Years later, a former SPA official attributed it to the fact that the labor agent was caught up in the Chicago riot of late July during "The Red Summer" of 1919.[26] At any rate, because of unsettled racial and working conditions in Chicago and because many blacks were returning to the South, the SPA's secretary-manager advised his board of directors in August that association subscribers were reporting a sufficient labor supply. He noted that by the middle of August forty-five subscribers had contributed $1,818.22 to the special fund to conduct the work in Chicago. On the basis of this report, the board directed that the association's labor office be closed as of August 31 and that its expenses be paid out of the SPA's general fund, with the special contributions to be retained for "such further disposition as the Directors may hereafter determine."[27] The Southern Pine Association estimated that its employment bureau had been instrumental in returning some eight hundred experienced millworkers to jobs in the South.[28]

The employment bureau's success and the achievement of a satisfactory labor supply in the southern pine industry proved short-lived, and by the spring of 1920 the SPA was again concerned about the Negro exodus. Secretary-Manager John E. Rhodes reported to the SPA board of directors that this resulted from the activities of "labor agents . . . actively at work among the sawmills and logging camps. . . ." Some of the nation's largest corporations, including the Goodyear Rubber Company and the Aluminum Company of America, he advised, were actively recruiting southern laborers, both black and white. Rhodes hinted at the necessity for more forceful measures to stop the labor outflow by pointing out that "few of the Southern states have laws preventing the recruiting and shipping of labor to other states, although all states require employment agents to obtain licenses." He added that some local officials were "taking vigorous steps to compel every able-bodied man to work, threatening to send those who do not to jail or work on the country roads as prisoners." "This," said Rhodes approvingly, "is beginning to force a good many idle negroes back to the camps in Florida, Georgia, and Alabama." He concluded that the continued movement of Negroes to the North would "have a detrimental effect upon the production of lumber," and he advised that "every effort should be made to stop the movement."[29] By early June, the SPA's director of safety and industrial relations was urging southern pine-producing states to enact legislation "prohibiting the exportation of labor outside the confines of the State."[30] The Southern Lumber Operators' Association continued to urge support of the Negro Advocate in order to counteract the influence of "quite a number of VICIOUS Negro Magazines and Newspapers being freely circulated amongst the negroes throughout the South for the purpose of creating Race prejudice and inducing negroes to go North."[31]

Despite the "get tough" policies of the southern pine industry and the South generally, the migration of the labor force continued. A survey of its subscribers conducted by the SPA in May, 1923, revealed that the exodus of Negro labor was most serious in Mississippi, Arkansas, and Alabama, where the situation was "quite serious in a number of communities." Mills in Texas and Louisiana had not yet been seriously affected, "altho," it was reported, "the situation in these two states is likely to become aggravated."[32]

Although the SPA's analysis of the situation in 1923 gave the old standard reasons for Negro emigration—the activities of labor agents, the glittering promises of the North—there seemed to be a realization on the part of some mill owners that the South was not a paradise for blacks. Several SPA subscribers reported that "persecutions, brow-beating and bulldozing by petit officers, who profit by arrests, is the cause of much dissatisfaction among negro labor in various localities."[33] Even though most mill operators held the traditional southern white view of the Negro,[34] the SPA survey revealed a widespread conviction within the industry that Negroes were valuable to the South, necessary to the operation of the southern pine industry, and suffering from many undesirable and even intolerable conditions. Frequently mentioned suggestions for improving the blacks' lot offered by SPA subscribers were "providing of better housing and living

conditions for the colored labor, increased school
facilities, fair wages and protection for the negroes
against unscrupulous officers of the law."[35]

For the most part southern lumberman and others during
the middle of the 1920s sought to fight the migration of
the Negro by "showing him that his welfare lies in the
South."[36] As earlier, much of this effort was undertaken
by supporting "safe" Negro publications and spokesmen.
Typical of such publications was a newspaper called the
National Negro Voice, edited and published in New Orleans
by a black named R. A. Flynn. Flynn's paper was endorsed
by the Southern Lumber Operators' Association as a "conservative Negro newspaper" that would counterbalance the
influence of "a number of radical negro publications
freely distributed throughout the South which tend to
breed Race hatred and discontent."[37] Flynn wrote in the
first issue: "It shall be the policy of this paper: To
show the Southland in its true light relative to its
treatment of the colored citizenry—as against misleading
and erroneous propaganda which would have the North and
the world believe that the Negro has no opportunities in
the South for racial betterment and that his state,
therein, is but slightly higher than that of slaves in
actual bondage."[38]

The newspaper was filled with articles counseling
Negroes against the lure of the North.[39] Such propaganda
was not very effective. As one black in Chicago was
reported to have said when questioned about race riots
there, "If I've got to be killed, I would rather be killed
by my friends."[40]

Not all of the southern lumber operators' energy was
expended on propaganda. As the 1920s wore on some lumbermen apparently made attempts to improve conditions for
their workers. The National Negro Voice carried accounts
of the improved facilities and services being offered
workers in southern lumbering towns.[41] Although these
stories were undoubtedly exaggerated, the Southern Lumber
Operators' Association reports on conditions at its
members' mills indicated that conditions had improved. A
report on what was probably a typical large mill town in
East Texas stated, "The houses furnished employees are in
the best of repair and rentals very low. The store prices
are reasonable and in fact labor has every reason to be
loyal as everything is done in reason and fair treatment
to make them comfortable and satisfied. No reports of any

organized movement or agitation was found nor is there any friction between white and colored labor."[42] The operators generally seemed to believe that they were doing a great deal to make conditions in the lumber camps and mills of the South more attractive. As one prominent operator declared, "We have tried to make it a more livable place—the sawmill—and we have worked with an idea of making a more contented crew, and I believe we have all accomplished a great deal along that line."[43] However, the situation undoubtedly varied widely from mill to mill, and the smaller mills probably lagged behind their larger competitors in the improvement of their facilities.[44]

While conditions in some southern lumber mill towns may have improved during the 1920s, mill wages continued to be lower and hours longer than in other sections of the country. Furthermore, southern lumber operations were slow to improve safety standards.[45] The attitude toward such matters in the South continued to be one of "apathy and indifference," and accidents were unnecessarily frequent.[46] The SPA in 1918 established a committee on safety which supervised a department of safety. The department did little more than prepare educational and graphic materials to indoctrinate the subscribers' employees in the use of proper safety precautions and compile statistics showing the number of men employed in each lumbering operation and the number of accidents and deaths for workers in each category.[47]

The department of safety was reorganized in 1919 and began to prepare files of information on standard safety specifications and safety codes approved by insurance companies, rating bureaus, and state boards, as well as catalogues of the manufacturers of safety appliances and first-aid materials. It also accumulated a file of all safety laws in the country and kept copies of the constitutions, by-laws, and reports of many employee benefit associations established in other industries.[48]

The rationale for safety work was very clear to Secretary-Manager Rhodes, who noted "first . . . the humanitarian phase, and second, the fact of the Southern lumber industry being identified with movements of this kind, because the Southern lumbermen were beginning to be severely criticized by safety men and others because of their apparent indifference in this regard. . . ."[49] Many individual companies apparently became convinced that comprehensive safety programs could save money through reductions in insurance premiums and increased efficiency.[50] However, despite reports that its subscribers were reducing the number of man-hours lost due to accidents, and despite the obvious public relations benefits in making the industry more attractive to labor, the Southern Pine Association's safety activities were discontinued in 1921 for financial reasons.[51]

The Southern Pine Association and its industry encountered a continuing series of labor problems during the postwar era and they failed to resolve them satisfactorily. Problems of labor shortages and inefficiency were still prominent as the SPA approached the 1930s, and, as the SPA's secretary-manager later wrote, labor conditions in the industry and the ever-present threat of unionization "more or less simmered until the Depression. . . ."[52]

The simmer warmed to a boil as a result of the new labor regulations promulgated under the National Recovery Administration. In the southern piney woods the inclusion of Section 7(a) of the National Industrial Recovery Act had not prompted any major efforts at union organization, but the adoption of minimum wages and maximum hour provisions, while not intended to change traditional interregional patterns, had in at least some cases increased southern lumbering wages significantly and at a much faster rate than in the western lumber industry. The Southern Pine Association had fought efforts to impose compulsory restrictions upon the hours of labor before the passage of the NIRA, and the organization struggled vigorously and successfully to protect southern wage differentials in the negotiations which led to the formulation of the NRA codes. Nevertheless, the widespread violations of NRA wage and hour provisions signify that many southern lumbermen had not been convinced by their NRA experience that they could live with such regulations, and the Southern Pine Association was a supporter of the Southern States Industrial Council which was organized in 1933 partly to defend the South against alleged discrimination in the form of higher wages imposed from the outside.[53]

On June 27, 1935, an event of great significance for basically nonunionized industries like the southern pine industry occurred when the national labor relations bill emerged from Congress and was signed into law by President Roosevelt on July 5. The bill had been pushed originally by Senator Robert Wagner of New York, and only belatedly won the support of the President. The ease with which it moved through Congress amazed even its staunch supporters. The Southern Pine Association, although certainly not in favor of the act's guarantee of the right of collective bargaining, surprisingly made no attempt to fight the measure. H. C. Berckes later attributed the measure to "new Dealers" and "distressed labor and their unions" who were "'sitting pretty' in Washington and . . . making the most of their position." "The Southern Pine industry was scarcely organized by Union labor and gave scant attention to the implications of the Wagner Act and little support to those opposing this legislation," Berckes recalled. Thus the Southern Pine Association seems to have accepted, at the time of the Wagner Act's passage, the idea of a close New Deal-big labor alignment, which was not yet strictly speaking true.[54]

After a lull in the development of significant activity on the labor front, during which the Southern Pine Association reestablished an office in Washington to strengthen its contacts and relations "in connection with legislation, trade promotion, and cooordination with the work of the National Lumber Manufacturers," the SPA avidly watched stirrings toward new labor legislation, but this time not as a passive observer.[55] The next step came early in 1937 in the wake of the Supreme Court's decisions upholding state minimum wage laws and the Wagner Act. Secretary of Labor Frances Perkins, with the assistance of Grace Abbott, the former head of the Children's Bureau, prepared a wages and hours measure which was introduced in the Senate by Hugo Black of Alabama and in the House by William P. Connery, Jr., on May 24.[56]

On the eve of the impending fight over the new proposal, H. C. Berckes reported to his subscribers the general context and environment within which the struggle would be conducted. He noted first that in the course of widespread contacts with business leaders, "I was surprised to find that the attitude of so many industrialists and businessmen had changed from what it was last year. They seem to accept very readily many of the ideas for wage-and-hour legislation and other measures for business regulation." Berckes further noted ominously that "many were also pessimistic regarding labor developments, and I could find very little sympathy among a number of those contacted toward our problem in the South." Berckes summarized the situation in order to prepare his subscribers for the coming battle:

The New South and the "New Competition"

Frankly, I have found most of these businessmen anticipating a larger degree of influence by labor in their business, and the attitude of many of them would not be appreciated by the members of our industry. Much of this comes from the fact that there is plenty of agitation with respect to the necessity for curbing the trend of industry southward. A great many industrialists in the North, and especially politicians, believe that the South has an undue advantage and that labor is being sweated to the extent of destroying entire Northern industrial communities, which are already moving South because of wage differentials and agitation from foreign labor elements in the North.

Many of the arguments that are being advanced for New Deal legislation are based on this premise. There is no doubt but that Southern industry will be sorely tried this spring and summer, and if wage-and-hour legislation and licensing bills are passed, undue pressure will be used without consideration of the underlying economic conditions which make for the difference between Northern and Southern labor.   For the Southern Pine industry we are doing all we can in gathering information so as to be in a position to again present our case.[57]

The wages and hours bill, although complex, basically provided for Congress to establish minimum wages and maximum hours and for an independent, five-man, presidentially appointed labor board that would be given power to conduct hearings and then increase minimum standards in cases where collective bargaining had been attempted and had failed. It also contained a measure outlawing child labor involved in interstate commerce.[58] The measure was introduced in a Congress that was increasingly divided by the court-packing scheme, by a leadership contest in the Senate, and by growing sectional animosities.   Strong opposition from the South, which centered around simple objections to government control over business and the fear of losing the competitive advantages of lower wage scales, was spearheaded outside Congress by the Southern Pine Association.

One southern lumberman, a prominent SPA subscriber, estimated that the frequently mentioned possible minimum base figures of a forty-hour week and a forty-cent per hour wage would raise lumber costs from eight to twelve dollars per thousand feet and allow the highly mechanized

western lumber industry to trample their southern
competitors underfoot.[59] The Southern Pine Association's
subscribers discussed the situation at their annual
meeting in March and heard Berckes describe the impending
legislation as "by far the most important question facing
our industry. . . ." Berckes conceded the inevitability
of such legislation and counseled the industry to dedicate
its efforts to a defense of southern wage and hour
differentials.[60]

Convinced that the wages and hours proposal constituted a threat to the entire southern lumber industry, the
Southern Pine Association organized a mass meeting of
manufacturers of all species, which was not limited to SPA
subscribers. This session was held in New Orleans on June
4, and out of the discussions emerged the Southern Pine
Industry Committee, which led the fight against the
Black-Connery proposals. The organization was to serve as
a propaganda and pressure group, it was organized
throughout the South, and it in effect served as the
Southern Pine Association's alter ego for lobbying and
pressure tactics.[61]

It was immediately apparent that the Black-Connery
bill would face strong opposition in both the House and
Senate as members of the Congress responded to their own
instincts and the outraged protestations of opponents
within their constituencies. In the South, the Southern
Pine Industry Committee produced reams of material
pointing out why the legislation must be defeated. These
materials ranged from a reprint of a column from the
Washington Daily News, "One Man's Opinion," by the now-
embittered Hugh S. Johnson, in which the old NRA administrator warned that "the South had better wake up . . .
pronto or it will find itself sold down the river to a
renewal of some of its problems of reconstruction days,"
to a pamphlet modestly entitled "27 Reasons Why The Black
Fair Labor Standards Bill Should Be Defeated."[62] The SPIC
also circulated copies of various newspaper editorials and
cartoons and of speeches by various political and public
figures. Toward the end of 1937, as the fight continued
in the House of Representatives, the committee produced a
sixty-five-page pamphlet that constituted "A Compendium of
Arguments and Opinions against Federal Wage and Hour
Legislation, as Expressed by Senators, Congressmen,
Economists, Industrialists, Labor Leaders, Agricultural-
ists, Newspapers, Publicists, and Informed Individuals in
Many Fields."[63]

The New South and the "New Competition"

The Southern Pine Industry Committee and SPA also tried to galvanize public opinion and attempted to influence the actions of congressmen through other standard techniques of political persuasion and pressure. According to H. C. Berckes:

> . . . in the immense work through the Southern Pine Industry Committee we kept the individual Congressman or Senator advised of what was going on by his particular constituents by mail. And if there were hearings, we sent those constituents to be witnesses, while I, as Secretary–Manager . . . appeared before many committees. But we always tried to get a lumberman from those regions to appear before the Congressional committee and tell his story. . . . We let committees feel that they were getting the story direct from the man himself, and not from an advocate. While I was a registered lobbyist I did little lobbying myself. Very seldom did I go see a Congressman or a Senator about a piece of legislation or about any condition within the industry unless they called upon me, and if they did, I would always send or write to them this information by their own constituents. We found that to be a wonderful way of handling it.[64]

By the middle of the summer of 1937, the activities of the SPA, SPIC, and other opponents of the Black–Connery legislation seemed to be having a powerful impact on the people of the South. Senator Black was warned that the bill's opponents were making heavy inroads among his own constituents in Alabama, with "the worst offenders of all against industrial decency in this state—the lumbermen—. . . doing most of the agitating."[65] According to Tindall, "The clamor of the bill's opponents gave an impression of general hostility in the region," while on the other hand the Gallup Poll "recorded Southerners as 51 percent favorable to minimum wage legislation in December, 1935; 56 percent in May, 1937, and again in May, 1938."[66]

In the meantime, joint hearings on the bill were held by House and Senate committees headed by Black and Connery in June. After opposition to the original bill from both southerners and, surprisingly, the leaders of both the AFL and the CIO, early in July the Senate committee reported out a revised bill which was somewhat more in line with labor's demands. After a bitter floor debate which reflected the growing sectional and philosophical split in Democratic ranks, the Senate approved the revised bill.[67]

The "Labor Problem"

The fight then shifted to the House, where the bill was strongly opposed by conservative southerners and Republicans who bottled it up in the Rules Committee. The measure finally reached the floor on December 2, 1937, by means of a discharge petition, only to be recommitted to committee on December 17, partially as a result of AFL President William Green's reconsideration of the administration's version of the bill.[68] H. C. Berckes later recalled that in considering strategy the bill's opponents had believed "it seemed the better part of wisdom to keep the legislation in the . . . Rules Committee of the House . . . and it was hoped that with returning prosperity and sanity the proposed legislation would be dropped."[69]

However, the battle was rejoined in 1938. The southern pine manufacturers and their representatives found "the going was a little rougher than in the two former sessions of Congress," although they still had "a fair hope that the bill could be defeated by a narrow margin in the House, or talked to death in the Senate." According to Berckes, "the pressure from the opposition never ceased," and "Senators and Representatives were constantly pressured to 'hold the line.'"[70] The forms of pressure have been graphically described by Berckes, who estimated that the southern pine industry's expenditures in opposing the bill reached $200,000 annually at the peak of the campaign, "not including the expenses of many of its leading lumbermen who paid their own expenses in attending meetings, hearings, and broadcasting the messages."[71] To direct this tremendous financial outlay, southern lumbermen had "a strong representative Industry Committee," and "the use of the facilities and staff of the Southern Pine Association."[72]

In Berckes's words:

> The work of organization was broad and intense. Wherever opposition to the Act was discerned there contact was made and organization effected. More than three thousand associations and groups were consolidated into a working entity. Its work centered in the Southern Pine Offices in Washington and New Orleans where all information regarding the legislation was analyzed, printed and disseminated. . . . Data was prepared for submission to Congressional Committees, not only by Southern Pine lumbermen, but by others called as witnesses.

303

The New South and the "New Competition"

Not only were the groups kept informed but the meaning, intent and purposes of the law were set forth in advertising, speeches, pamphlets, letters, wires, and circulars to the public, businessmen, farmers, bankers, educators and to legislators, federal and state. Addresses were made before civic groups, women's clubs, etc., and on the radio.

Newspapers, magazines and trade paper comments, news stories, editorials and cartoons became voluminous. The Southern Pine Industry Committee culled this material and regularly issued a tabloid-size publication reproducing with permission, some of the most impressive cartoons and editorials. This showed the thousands of news agencies, groups and individuals that they were not alone in their opposition, thereby strengthening their determination and increasing their activity.[73]

Ironically, the factors that upset all of the calculations and efforts of the southern opponents of the bill originated in the South. In January, 1938, Alabama's Lister Hill won the Senate seat vacated when Hugo Black was appointed to the Supreme Court in a campaign in which he supported the wages and hours bill. In May, in an even more resounding triumph, Claude Pepper won the Florida Democratic primary contest for a Senate seat by defeating a bitterly anti-New Deal, anti-wages and hours bill congressman. These victories seemed to demonstrate that the southern electorate was not overwhelmingly opposed to wages and hours legislation, as many supposed spokesmen for the section such as the Southern Pine Association and the Southern Pine Industry Committee had so stridently claimed. The victories were also ominous warnings to congressmen facing the 1938 election of the still-potent influence of Franklin Delano Roosevelt. Three days after the Florida primary, members of the House almost trampled one another in their rush to sign a discharge petition to again bring the minimum wage bill out of committee for the consideration of the House. On May 24 the bill passed by a more than three to one margin.[74]

After differences between the House and Senate versions of the bill, including the provisions for regional differentials, were reconciled in the conference committee, the measure was passed. The President signed the Fair Labor Standards Act on June 25, 1938. The act placed administration of the law under one man in the

Labor Department, who would confer with advisory industry committees. No minimum wage rate was to be fixed on a purely regional basis, but the advisory boards were to consider in their deliberations the transportation, living, and production costs which shaped competitive conditions. The ultimate objective was a forty-hour week and a minimum hourly wage of forty cents, to be achieved gradually, starting with a forty-four-hour week in October, 1938, to be reduced by two hours in each of the next two years; and with a minimum wage starting at twenty-five cents and rising to forty over a seven-year period.[75]

Since the wage and hours administrator could advance the rates ahead of schedule upon the recommendation of the industry committees, the Southern Pine Industry Committee remained very much concerned with the matter of wages and hours. Furthermore, according to H. C. Berckes, "there was the contemplation (fully realized later) that Congress would adjust the minimum wage as conditions indicated--up always, of course, but never down."[76] In July, 1938, the beginning wage rate in the lumber industry was lower than the twenty-five-cent minimum for 43 percent of the common laborers in southern sawmills. Some lumbermen closed their mills instead of attempting to comply with the legislation, and of the thirty to fifty thousand employees laid off in the month following the effective date of the law about 90 percent were concentrated in a few southern industries, including lumbering.[77]

The Southern Pine Industry Committee continued to disseminate material attacking the Fair Labor Standards Act and its administration. The SPIC also circulated a mimeographed newsletter, entitled "Wage-Hour Law News Notes," to keep the industry informed of the latest developments.[78] Among the major criticisms the southern pine manufacturers leveled was the charge that enforcement of the wage and hour provisions was lax and, in addition, that selection of the industry committees appointed to advise the wages and hours administrator was heavily dominated by Secretary of Labor Frances Perkins and that these committees were biased against the South.[79]

The Southern Pine Association and its industry remained dissatisfied with the administration of the Fair Labor Standards Act through the rest of the 1930s and continued to try to protect their interests through the Southern Pine Industry Committee. Near the end of the decade, however, the immediate problems posed by the new wages and hours requirements were overshadowed by the nation's drift toward war and the growing prosperity coming to the southern pine industry through its participation in the defense effort. The techniques and legislative and administrative experience acquired by the SPIC would nevertheless be valuable assets to the industry and SPA in their extensive contacts with the federal government during World War II. They would also stand the southern lumbermen in good stead when the old civilian problems returned in the war's aftermath.

Labor shortages were among the southern pine industry's most serious problems during World War II. The Southern Pine War Committee sponsored a manufacturers' clinic in New Orleans in June, 1942, to gather information on it, as well as other matters, for presentation before the War Production Board and Office of Price Administration officials.[80] The basic problem stemmed from the induction of men into the military and the drift of laborers away from lumbering, particularly toward the high-paying defense construction and defense industries, among them the shipyards of the Gulf and South Atlantic coasts and the military cantonments in the South.[81] The SPWC's clinic unearthed abundant evidence of the labor shortage in the southern pine woods. H. C. Berckes advised the lumbermen that the government was cognizant of the problems and that there was "a very distinct movement going on in Washington to have some relief for skilled labor for the sawmills."[82]

The New Orleans meeting brought numerous cries of pain from lumbermen who were feeling both the economic and the cultural shock of changing labor conditions. One employer incredulously noted the transformation brought about by the new defense industries: "A nigger that I raised--I was quite proud of the nigger, I thought he was pretty smart--come by with a check for $92 for a week's work." "That's more than I make," lamented the manufacturer.[83] Another discussed bitterly the impact of a defense project near his plant and company town:

> . . . they sent a labor truck to the plant. Talking in our sawmill language, I was so damned mad I wanted to go outside. Niggers we raised and that have been there to the third generation--before the third generation was born--we have been operating there forty years; we have been their doctors, lawyers, nurses and everything; we are bankers and everything else

for them; and they go down there and work for those people because they are paid 55 cents and 50 cents-- and they live in our houses, and we furnish water and light. I've seen these niggers eat canned peaches that we don't even have ourselves. They have raised the standard of living down there--and I don't see where Paul McNutt is going to come in; I don't know.[84]

A common complaint was voiced somewhat later by an Arkansas producer who noted that his operation had "green lumber all over the yard because we are short the necessary men to stack it" and further that on the government camp construction sites in his state "they pay the men more than we can afford to pay and the men claim they don't have to work half as hard at the camps as they do at the lumber plants."[85]

By the latter part of 1942 the industry's labor problem attracted government attention. In September, 1942, the War Manpower Commission classified the major forest industries as essential. Paul V. McNutt, chairman of the commission, issued a "freeze order" or employment stabilization plan in twelve western states, including the important southern pine-producing state of Texas. The order prohibited workers employed in logging and lumbering in those states from seeking employment in other industries. McNutt threatened to issue similar orders for other parts of the nation if necessary.[86] Toward the end of the year the War Production Board's chairman, Donald Nelson, instructed the industry to implement a forty-eight-hour week wherever possible; the Selective Service Board provided draft deferment eligibility to workers in forestry, logging, and lumbering; and the War Labor Board approved sizable wage increases.[87]

The seriousness of the labor situation in the southern pine woods was reflected in H. C. Berckes's testimony before Harry S. Truman's special senate committee to investigate the national defense program on November 24, 1942. The SPA secretary-manager pointed out that a study made in August by the War Production Board, based upon some 597 southern pine mills with an estimated 40 percent of the industry's total production, showed that on January 1, 1942, they employed 53,826 wage earners, but by July 31, this figure had declined to 51,620, with a labor turnover of 37 percent. During this seven-month period, 19,703 workers left the southern pine industry, with 63 percent going to such other employers as shipyards,

307

war-construction projects, and railroads, in pursuit of higher wages; 15 percent entering the military; and 22 percent leaving for various other reasons. Of the 17,497 workers added to the payrolls during this period, many were older men and formerly part-time and unemployed workers who were generally inexperienced and undependable. Absenteeism was an increasingly acute problem.[88]

In the meantime, drastic measures were being utilized to deal with the industry's labor shortage. This problem was the major topic of discussion in February as southern pine producers convened in New Orleans for a conference with government representatives.[89] A War Manpower Commission representative explained the services and new programs of the commission and the U. S. Employment Service told the lumbermen that an arrangement had been worked out with the Gulf Coast shipyards whereby the yards would no longer employ a worker transferring from another essential industry "unless he has a very special case," and recommended "planned utilization of the remaining labor supply, especially of older men, and if possible, of women."[90] The plea for cooperation with the U. S. Employment Service in at least some cases fell on deaf ears. "And we are told to go to the . . . United States Employment Agencies," bellowed one prominent lumberman. "The men in charge of them are very gracious, they seem eager to help you, but the class of men they have to offer you, they would be in your way. You could afford to pay them money to stay away." This man believed much of the labor difficulty stemmed from government projects paying "excessive wages." The Louisianian noted ironically that "if some of these experts can tell us how to get men to swamp and cut down the trees during the hot summer months, they will go far in solving our problems."[91] Others in the meeting echoed virtually the same sentiments.[92]

Two months later, in April, 1943, the Southern Pine War Committee met with the Southern Hardwood Industry War Committee to review the defense situation. Spokesmen from various parts of the southern pine belt focused again on labor as the major problem. An Alabama manufacturer reported a meeting between a lumberman from his state and a government representative who asked the lumberman if he would like to recover laborers who had drifted to the Gulf Coast for higher pay and received the frustrated retort, "No, I can't do anything with them now, after they have been to the shipyards." Spokesmen from Arkansas and Oklahoma bemoaned labor raids from West Coast defense industries, and one Arkansas producer noted that "we have colonies of Negroes located in California" and added that out of 454 men lost by his company between January 1 and April 1, only 45 were drafted. A Floridian listed the usual complaints, including the loss of labor to defense industries, but added a new note--the raiding of female lumber employees. "They are now picking up these women, taking them to the airfields and other camps and working them in the places where they have worked soldiers, cleaning up the quarters and running the laundries, and they give them about $25 a week," he noted. From a town of some three thousand inhabitants, he estimated, approximately 150 to 175 women were being transported twenty miles daily to work at an airfield. A Louisiana producer chimed in that his efforts to put women to work had been foiled after about eight or ten had started, when "they had a chance to go to the laundries as mentioned and they quit their jobs and went to the laundries because it was easier work." Reports from other parts of the southern pine woods were similarly pessimistic.[93]

To deal with the labor problem, the southern pine industry, beginning in 1942 and continuing through the end of the war took several extraordinary measures. It requested draft deferments for key employees and received excellent cooperation from local draft boards. It also employed "men with one arm, one leg, one eye, and men with other physical handicaps, who normally wouldn't be considered as proper material for sawmill labor."[94] The industry's experience was not significantly different from that of sawmills on the West Coast which found themselves recruiting "women, old men, teen-agers, interned Italian seamen, physically disabled men, malaria convalescents, and even two college professors."[95] In the southern piney woods, however, there were two labor developments which were especially interesting--the use of female laborers and the use of prisoners of war. The utilization of women in southern lumbering had been extremely rare before World War II, and it was not until 1942 that reports of their entry into Dixie's lumber industry became common. During 1943, as the labor shortage became more acute, females began to fill formerly all-male jobs, and by the middle of the year they were working in operations throughout the South as moulders, edgers, cut-off and rip-saw loaders, checkers, bundlers, resaw roller operators, graders, janitors, planing machine operators, and in other capacities. A Southern Pine War Committee survey conducted

The New South and the "New Competition"

from June 29 to July 12, 1943, and covering thirty-four
mills in Alabama, Arkansas, Florida, Louisiana, Mississippi, Oklahoma, and Texas, found twenty-five mills
employing 797 females. Of these, 441 were white and 356
black, and they performed twenty-eight different kinds of
jobs. The committee noted that there were several hundred
additional women employed in other southern lumber plants.
     According to the SPWC report, many of the women came
from families with other members working in the industry,
many were performing both household chores and their lumbering duties, and many saw their employment as a temporary thing to assist their families and help win the
war. One supposedly typical female lumber worker was a
veritable Pauline Bunyan, who "in addition to working 48
hours a week felling trees . . . kept house for her husband and seven children, a step-brother and a boarder,
milked two cows night and morning, made butter for the
family and attended to other household duties with the
help of her older children." According to the Southern
Pine War Committee, this woman's truly fortunate husband
"indicated she was as capable as a man." The committee
said that the managers of lumber plants surveyed "are of
the general opinion that the women employees give practically the same satisfactory service, and display practically the same efficiency on the jobs as men workers;
that the women were quick to learn their jobs . . . are
enthusiastic and conscientious about their work. . . ."[96]
Despite raids from other defense industries, women had by
the end of 1943 become valuable contributors to the
southern pine war effort.
     The utilization of prisoner of war labor in the
southern pine and other industries during World War II was
in many ways more interesting than the concurrent influx
of females. By the latter part of 1943, there were
163,706 German and Italian prisoners interned in the
United States. Their numbers reached a peak of 425,806 by
the end of June, 1945. Not all of these prisoners,
however, were eligible for labor in the United States. By
the terms of the Geneva Convention of 1929, only privates
could be required to perform labor, and they could not be
forced to work at jobs that were dangerous, unhealthful,
or of direct military applicability.[97] The major use of
prisoners during World War II was in their own camps and
in other military installations, but a few small groups
were made available to private employers before the end of
1943.[98]

The "Labor Problem"

The fundamental policies regarding prisoner of war labor were worked out by August, 1943, and most non-military aspects of the problem were delegated to the War Manpower Commission. In response to a request by a private employer for prisoner of war workers, the commission made an investigation and, if it found civilian labor to be unavailable, certified the employer's need for prisoners. The commission also determined the conditions and terms of employment. Matters relating to interpretation of the Geneva Convention and security were handled by the War Department. Prisoners were available only in cases where there was a dearth of other workers, and the procedure for obtaining POW laborers was for the employer to file a request through the U. S. Employment Service in which he agreed not to discriminate against the prisoners, to pay them the prevailing wage rates, and to provide suitable working conditions.[99] In the final analysis, however, the local labor supply was not so important in allocating the prisoners as was the existence in certain industries of strong labor unions which strongly opposed their use. In lumbering, prisoners were more extensively utilized in the Southeast and in Maine than on the Pacific Coast, where there were fairly effective labor organizations.[100]

The preliminary stages of the first mass transfer of prisoners to America came in August, 1942, when the British government requested the United States to intern some 150,000 British-captured prisoners of war in order to relieve overtaxed facilities in England. The Joint Chiefs of Staff agreed and initiated plans for the construction of facilities for the prisoners and for their employment. The original plans, submitted in September, 1942, by the Provost Marshal General, called for the distribution of approximately 75 percent of the first batch of some fifty thousand prisoners to the unused camps in the Southwest that had originally been planned for the housing of enemy aliens. The PMG also planned to house prisoners in temporary housing on military installations, some of which finally became permanent. The second group of 100,000 prisoners was expected to be interned in the South and Southwest. By late 1942, there were numerous camps completed or under construction which would house prisoners in areas within range of southern pine operations.[101]

The first Southern Pine Association or SPWC contact with the prisoner of war system came in June, 1943, when

311

The New South and the "New Competition"

field man C. N. Gould called on the Eighth Service Command
Headquarters in Dallas to investigate the availability of
prisoners for employment in the southern pine industry.
Gould reported to the SPWC that the only war prisoners
within the Eighth Service Command who were then near
enough to the belt to be utilized were at Huntsville and
Sherman, Texas, and at Fort Smith, Arkansas. However,
there was a possibility that camps at Leesville and
Ruston, Louisiana, would soon be occupied by prisoners.[102]
While Gould was conferring with Eighth Service Command
Headquarters, another SPWC representative was talking with
representatives of the Fourth Corps Area Service Command
in Atlanta, and by early June these efforts were successful in securing some fifty war prisoners for employment by
southern pine manufacturers in Georgia.[103] By the latter
part of July, one Texas company was using fifteen prisoners from the Huntsville Internment Camp.[104]
     During the summer of 1943, Southern Pine War Committee
field men visited numerous manufacturers and conferred
with camp commanders and government officials regarding
the use of prisoners in the southern pine industry. They
found all three groups generally favorable toward the
idea, but rather vague about the procedures to be
followed. Of the lumber operators who gave a definite
response, an overwhelming majority, by a ratio of approximately fifteen to one, indicated that they would be
willing to use the POWs.[105]
     Despite widespread interest in the use of POWs and the
growing numbers of prisoners in the United States, the
industry did not make effective use of such labor. The
pulpwood and lumbering industries used a total of only
165,743 man-months of POW labor from June, 1944, to
August, 1945.[106] Apparently, the industry had difficulty
in making arrangements to obtain these workers from the
government.[107]
     Labor problems continued during the last full year of
the war. Producers were complaining of manpower shortages
and that their wartime laborers were far less efficient
than the prewar ones. Concerning the composition of the
labor force, 388 operations reported that only 520, or 2.8
percent were women; 256, or 1.3 percent prisoners of war;
and 164, or .9 percent, Hondurans. Although many operations apparently wanted war prisoners and resented it when
they were taken from them for other work, the comment of a
Texas producer reflected the general assessment of the
prisoners' performances: "The first month they seemed

good, but inexperienced; the last month they were impossible."[108]

Late in 1944 the SPA called a special two-day meeting in New Orleans to deal with anticipated postwar problems. A major topic of discussion was labor relations. During the war there had been attempts by the American Federation of Labor and the Congress of Industrial Organizations to unionize the southern lumber industry. Although they had little success, their efforts could be interpreted as a portent of things to come and led to the establishment of an SPA labor relations department.[109] The labor relations committee reported that it anticipated further organizational efforts. It portrayed the SPA's role as that of an information-providing organization which would maintain an educational and information service for its subscribers so they could enter labor negotiations fully aware of their rights and existing labor conditions. The SPA was not to enter into negotiations between an employer and his employees, and it was not to concern itself with the establishment of an industry-wide labor policy. However, the committee's report recommended and the SPA board approved a wide-ranging program of labor activities, including the establishment of a labor relations bulletin service to report and interpret legislation, regulations, and executive orders concerning labor matters; the publication of a labor news sheet; the conducting of surveys to determine industry practices regarding sick leave, holidays and holiday pay, bonuses, and similar matters; the institution of an industry-wide wage survey and job classification study; and the gathering and compilation of statistical material.[110]

By the end of the war the association's expanded program of labor relations was primarily concerned with providing subscribers the information they would need if and when they became involved in negotiations with groups attempting to unionize their operations. By the middle of 1945, some thirty southern pine operations were unionized, and the SPA reported that as many mills had been organized in the last eighteen months as in the preceding twelve years, with union agents working actively and effectively in the southern pine territory.[111] "Both the CIO and the AFL have stated, in print, that the lumber industry in the South is going to be organized," editorialized a leading southern trade journal, "and don't try to kid yourself. Just as sure as there are pine trees in Georgia, the

313

unions are going to step up their activities in the South, and within five to ten years, every lumber operation of any size is going to have to face the issue."[112] The Southern Pine Association made every effort to see that manufacturers were informed and prepared.

The labor problem was extremely important to southern pine producers because of the low degree of mechanization in the industry and the low productivity of southern lumber workers compared with those in other sections. During the war, the SPA had been interested in new mechanical developments, such as the use of power saws by woods workers, and as the conflict neared its end H. C. Berckes began to promote a program of mechanical efficiency so that producers could initiate "more skillful mechanized lumber operations" which would enable them to "compete in future markets and continue to pay the high labor rates that we are now paying." Berckes noted that the SPA had been "working with manufacturers of sawmill machinery and equipment, many of whom are engaged in the development of new ideas for improved manufacture and increased efficiency in the production of Southern lumber."[113]

The main objection to such an SPA program arose from the fact that many producers were small with operations of an uncertain duration, and they thus hesitated to spend money for expensive equipment.[114] However, an advocate of a mechanical efficiency program agreed:

> We must all have the very best equipment that can be had, equipment that will increase the production per man hour in order to enable us to obtain a greater production with shorter hours and at the same time equip us to meet the wage schedule that we will hereafter be forced to pay.
> The lack of such equipment made it most difficult. . . . Our plants were scheduled for long hours and low production due to the fact that we were all operating antiquated machinery. . . . There is no question but that the $1.25 negro is no longer available, and we held on to him too long. Instead of installing machinery to do the work, we always undertook to do it putting in another cheap negro.[115]

At its October meeting, the SPA staff announced the development of services to combat high manufacturing costs through research into mechanization or mechanical efficiency and by furnishing lists of available used machinery and equipment to association subscribers. The SPA called upon the manufacturers to exchange ideas through and cooperate with the program.[116] The SPA's mechanical efficiency committee was revitalized to develop these activities. It seemed to be the consensus of the meeting that improved mechanical efficiency would be the industry's greatest need at the war's end.[117]

The problems of scarcity of labor and its low productivity remained matters of great concern in the industry after the end of the war. This was particularly true because of the possibility of federal legislation to increase wages and labor union efforts to organize the southern lumber industry. The question of labor legislation was handled primarily by the Southern Pine Industry Committee, while the SPA's Labor Information Service was responsible for keeping subscribers informed of labor conditions and of their rights and obligations with regard to labor organizations. Neither the LIS nor the SPA took any official position on the introduction of unions into any particular operation or into the South generally. While it is obvious that SPA staff members were not favorably disposed toward union organizations, the SPA and LIS remained officially neutral, and some southern pine manufacturers actually felt that "the Association may be conditioning the minds of the operators to make them receptive to unionization."[118] On the other hand officers of the International Woodworkers of America reported to their membership that "the Southern lumber operators through the Southern Pine Association and other trade associations are putting up a solid front in resisting our demands for higher wages and better working conditions."[119]

The battle for the organization of southern industries got under way in the spring of 1946, when the CIO announced its plan to mount a million-dollar campaign, called "Operation Dixie," to organize some 1,500,000 nonunion workers, with heavy concentration on the key industries of textile manufacturing and lumbering. The campaign was headquartered in Atlanta and was led by Van A. Bittner. Assistant to the president of the United Steel Workers and a close confident of CIO President Phillip Murray, Bittner was respected and feared for his previous efforts at leading organizational drives in the meatpacking and steel industrees. The CIO's effort was to be biracial and directed at the entire South, and while concentrating on textiles and lumbering it was to include such other industries as furniture, clothing, rubber, oil, chemicals, packing houses, and various white-collar

fields. The union planned initially to put some two
hundred full-time organizers in the field, and in order to
head off resentment and charges of "outside agitation"
hoped to sprinkle its organizational staff heavily with
native southerners and veterans.[120]

Responding to the threat of the CIO drive, which he
termed "just another seasonal March wind," the AFL's
southern representative, George L. Googe, pointed out that
his organization would continue to spend $2,500,000 and
utilize 300 field organizers in the South annually. An
operation of this scale, he noted, "is considered merely a
normal function of the Federation." Googe placed the
AFL's southern membership at the time at 1,800,000
including 390,000 Negroes. His organization, he declared,
contemplated a campaign in the South to increase wages,
working standards, and political activity by workers.
Announcing that the AFL was "adequately prepared for the
next excursion of the CIO's Politico–Communist organizations and their fellow travelers into the South," Googe
dismissed the southern activities of the rival union: "We
have had the experience of seeing Sidney Hillman and the
CIO Politico–Communists raise large slush funds and broad-
cast to the World that they were going to organize all
Southern wage earners and revolutionize the people of the
Southern States. But the net result has been sporadic
raids upon AFL Unions, picnic junkets of Northern radicals
and a motley crew of parlorpink intellectuals squandering
funds and bestirring hatred to the trade union movement as
a whole."[121]

Approximately a month later, however, the AFL
announced its own southern membership drive with a goal of
one million new members. In that drive, Googe boasted,
unlike the CIO the AFL would not be "compelled to call
upon Northern Communists or broken down left wingers from
New York and the West to carry on our campaign in the
South."[122] In May, AFL delegates meeting in Asheville,
North Carolina, heard their leaders, including President
William Green and Secretary-Treasurer George Meany,
attempt to pin the charge of Communist domination on the
CIO, pledge that the AFL's membership drive and activities
would be conducted without regard to race or color, and
warn southern businessmen that they faced inevitable
unionization and should choose between the AFL or its
radical rival. Like the CIO, the AFL announced its inten-
tion to use local residents as organizers.[123]

While they wanted no labor organization at all, the southern pine industry preferred the AFL to the CIO. Probably reflecting the opinion of many, one prominent subscriber labeled the CIO's activities as "un-American" and charged that "it is a Russian organization; and, possibly back of it all is the undertaking to create all of the chaos they can in our country to weaken and break us down to where the industry of this country will be so handicapped with the confusion now being created that the Communists will have their opportunity, through the support of Russia, to accomplish in the United States what they are seeking to accomplish in all countries."[124]

Many southern pine manufacturers saw resistance as useless. As one prominent lumberman put it, "I don't think there is anything we in the Southern Pine Industry can do to combat it . . . all we can do is to hope that the CIO and other unions will not be successful in our individual plants. Unionization, however, seems to be on the move, and I don't think it can be stopped."[125] A Missouri lumberman summed up the general attitude most succinctly: "It seems we will have to make a choice of two evils, whether we are to have the C.I.O.-P.A.C- communistically inclined, come into the south and stir up race trouble, or whether we will go along with the more conservative A.F.L., which I believe will be more reasonable in their efforts to organize, and of course will fight the C.I.O. in any way they can."[126]

Union activity was a major topic at the SPA's 1946 annual meeting. "Neither this industry, your Committee, nor the Southern Pine Association can take any concerted action to forestall unionization. It is the law of the land under the Wagner Act and we will proceed lawfully," wrote H. C. Berckes, "but there is no necessity for the members of our industry acting and thinking 'in the dark' to negotiate collective bargaining agreements without sufficient economic data and full instructions in regard to management's rights and obligations."[127] Accordingly, as the unions moved into the field during 1946, the SPA and its Labor Information Service continued to gather information and to channel it to subscribers through circulars, bulletins, the "Collective Bargaining Contract Clause Manual," and personal contacts.

Both the AFL and the CIO talked optimistically during 1946, but their progress was not as dramatic as the advance ballyhoo might have led one to expect. In fact, the announced goals of one million new members for each union were probably simply part of the organizations' propaganda efforts. Not long after the campaign started, a CIO official was reported to have said that 250,000 new members would have been a reasonable goal for his organization, while an AFL leader laughingly said that the federation's target had been "set in Washington."[128] Both organizations seemingly spent as much time attacking one another as they did the industries they were attempting to organize, with the AFL pursuing the theme that their opponents were tinged with Communism and the CIO alleging collusion between the American Federation of Labor and the employers. The CIO's established policy of organizing both blacks and whites in the same unions also exposed it to the charge of race-mixing. Bittner had a strong anti-Communist reputation, and he surrounded himself with a staff that was calculated to take the teeth out of that charge. He also loudly repudiated the proffered assistance of a New York organization called "Help Organize the South," which was led by black Congressman Adam Clayton Powell. The CIO drive was billed as an effort of, by, and for southerners.[129]

Despite Bittner's reputation and actions, the charges of Communism made against the CIO were enthusiastically picked up by businessmen and the conservative community of the southern pine woods. The Southern Pine Association's mimeographed publication "Labor News Items" in August, 1946, passed along the titillating news that the AFL's George Googe had issued a list of Communist-dominated international unions, including naturally the CIO-affiliated International Woodworkers of America. While noting that Bittner had denied that any of his organizers were Communists, the SPA newsletter suggested somewhat vaguely and ominously that "even though officers of the international union may not be Communists, many of their locals are dominated by those who are, and the reverse may be true."[130]

During the same period, a circular of the Southern States Industrial Council, which listed prominent Southern Pine Association subscriber C. C. Sheppard as a member of the executive committee, lambasted the CIO's southern campaign in language which clearly anticipated the McCarthy era. The CIO and its political action committee were accused of planning to "establish political control over the nation and to supplant our democratic institutions with centralized federal control, patterned on Communist concepts." "If these people should be successful in their efforts," the circular predicted, "the free Southern workman will become the serf of the Communist-CIO-PAC leaders, his working hours will be filled with fear for existence, and his sleep made miserable by dreams of the horrors that fill his heart and mind." As for southern blacks, the circular reported:

> One of the most pitiful, and at the same time most dangerous features of this drive to organize the South is the way the Negroes are being misled and used by these Communist groups. By advocating a system of social and economic equality, and by arousing racial ill-will and hatred between the White and Negro races, these people are promising the Negro an earthly Utopia which they know they cannot deliver, and which they really have no intention of attempting to deliver. . . .
>
> I predict that the ones who will suffer most from the abortive efforts of this group of carpet-baggers will be the Negro who permits himself to be used in this unholy effort. He will have no friends among his own race, and certainly he will have none among the Whites. Perhaps his Communist friends will take care of him by "liquidation," as they have so many others they could no longer use.[131]

By the end of 1946, despite optimistic statements from the AFL and CIO, it was apparent that both organizations were lagging far behind their anticipated goals, although the CIO particularly was making some gains in the southern lumber industry. According to the SPA's Labor Information Service, by October the CIO had organized thirty-two southern lumber operations, while the AFL had organized ten.[132] According to SPA statistics, during all of 1946 there were 106 National Labor Relations elections in the southern lumber industry, with the CIO winning 71, the AFL 14, and independent unions 2. The Southern Pine Association estimated that 150 or more operations were unionized, with the CIO being the region's dominant labor organization.[133]

While disappointed with the 1946 efforts, the CIO's Van A. Bittner promised that his work would be carried on with renewed vigor during the next year. He noted that his 250 organizers in the field were composed of 85 percent southerners and 75 percent veterans.[134] The need for battle-tested organizers was pointed up in Bittner's charges toward the end of the year that seventeen CIO

319

organizers and members had been assaulted, some in lumbering areas, since the beginning of "Operation Dixie."[135] According to Bittner, "One of the worst things about this situation is that law enforcement officers in some towns are working in close collusion with employers or have become suddenly blind to the beating of organizers and union members."[136]

Despite the problems of 1946, it was to be the peak year for both the AFL and CIO membership drives. The internecine warfare and other factors which had hampered the two unions' activities in 1946 continued in 1947, now accompanied by a strengthening of the employers' legal position with the passage of the Taft-Hartley Act over the veto of President Truman on June 23. One CIO spokesman noted that employers were resisting collective bargaining and charged that "they seem to think that labor unions are going to be legislated out of the picture and that they can return to the old open sweat shop conditions that the workers are fighting so hard to eliminate from industry."[137]

There was one significant change in union tactics during 1947. Both the AFL and the CIO dropped their emphasis on using native southerners and military veterans as organizers. Apparently part of the blame for the poor showing of the unions during 1946 was placed on the inexperience of the original organizational staffs, and therefore they were replaced with experienced and tough-minded northern organizers from the steel, coal, and automotive industries.[138] Part of the difficulty of the original organizers may be seen in H. C. Berckes's recollection that "because of past experience, timidity or caution, union organizers did not push violently in their work. They approached the employers more cooperatively, and were met with a similar attitude," recalled Berckes. "Some of the organizers were taken on fishing and hunting trips, were otherwise profitably entertained and usually left the South with little progress being made in their organizing efforts."[139] Despite the use of more professional personnel in 1947, the results were meager. Business Week, in assessing "Operation Dixie" near the end of the year, said that "the glamor had worn off; the trappings were tarnished."[140] The SPA Labor Information Service's statistics showed that during the year there had been only seventy-three NLRB elections in the southern lumber industry, with forty-nine union victories--twenty-nine for the CIO and twenty for the AFL.[141]

With only brief exceptions, organizing efforts in southern lumbering continued to decline in intensity and importance down to the middle-1950s. Finally, in 1953 the CIO officially terminated "Operation Dixie" in the wake of the death of President Phillip Murray in 1952 and the subsequent reordering of the union's structure. Although there were conflicting opinions about the manner in which the drive had been handled and the degree of success attained, there can be little question that the CIO effort in the South had been disappointing.[142] The AFL had begun to curtail its activities as early as the spring of 1947.[143]

The results of NLRB elections during this period reflected the downward trend of union organizing activity. The number of elections progressively declined from sixty-three in 1948 to twenty-nine in 1949 and twenty-one in 1950. In 1951 there was a brief resurgence with forty-five elections held, but this number declined to thirty-four in 1952. During the period, the unions won approximately 136 elections, with the CIO enjoying much more success than the AFL.[144] The Southern Pine Association attributed the unions' failure to five factors:

(1) the small size and wide scattering of individual operators; (2) management had been well informed and knew how to deal effectively with the situation; and (3) employers spoiled one union argument by raising wages and giving other benefits voluntarily; (4) the 75 cents FLSA minimum wage in January 1950 made union promises of wage increases, their principal argument for unionization, fall flat; and (5) the cost of organizing and negotiating a collective bargaining agreement in many operations exceeded the per capita return the parent union could hope to collect from the organized workers.[145]

There was a steady increase in wage rates for southern lumber workers from 1946 to 1953, but it is debatable whether this was due to the influence of unions or to the rise in minimum wage levels imposed by federal wage and hours legislation. Statistics compiled by the Labor Department's Bureau of Labor Statistics for the years from 1938 through 1953 indicate that the southern lumber industry, utilizing a high percentage of relatively unskilled laborers, had a high concentration of workers laboring at or slightly above the prevailing minimum wage levels. The bureau concluded that "during the past 15 years the general trend of average hourly earnings in this industry has paralleled changes in minimum wage legislation."[146] While the presence of labor unions in neighboring plants may have influenced nonunion operations to increase their wages in an attempt to prevent organization, it is nevertheless true that the average hourly rate differential between union and nonunion workers in southern lumber mills in the post-World War II decade was relatively small.[147]

The Southern Pine Association during this period maintained its Labor Information Service and continued its policy of strict noninvolvement in personal negotiations between subscribers and unions. The association's distaste for unions was clear, but there is no evidence that it acted in anything approaching the manner of the old Southern Lumber Operators' Association. This change was partly because by the 1940s and 1950s the industry no longer enjoyed the homogeneity of opinion with regard to organized labor that it once had. As a spokesman for the Labor Information Service committee noted in 1948, "While there is no record that any Southern lumber producer has cordially welcomed a labor union at his plant, it is a fact that many employers believe that, if their workers want a union to represent them, that is the workers' business and the employers will deal with them as long as they are reasonable." "On the other side of the fence," he continued, "there are lumber producers who think that hysterical labor unions organized by outside professionals do not bring benefits either to their own members or to the companies, and therefore, an all-out effort should be made to resist their entry into a plant."[148] The same speaker attempted to allay the fears of some subscribers "that the operation of a labor information program would create a reputation for the Association as an anti-labor, union-busting group. . . ."[149] If the SPA did not acquire this reputation, it was not because of any lack of effort on the part of the unions, specifically the CIO. As the fortunes of "Operation Dixie" declined, there was a tendency among CIO spokesmen to single out the Southern Pine Association as a major villain. During a 1949 CIO organizing campaign at the Southern Pine Lumber Company in Diboll, Texas, union handouts featured cartoons which portrayed the Southern Pine Association as responsible for wage cuts, and union speakers described the SPA as a "big owners' union."[150] In 1951, Carl Winn, secretary-treasurer of the International Woodworkers of America, at

a Washington, North Carolina, Labor Day celebration,
accused "the lumberman's association" of the "damnable
practice" of "playing the workers in one mill against the
workers in another." He went on to charge that "the
Southern Pine Association supports the individual operator
financially when his workers strike to try to force a
decent contract."[151] Manager P. C. Gaffney of the Southern
Pine Association Labor Information Service angrily branded
Winn's remarks as "typical of the inflammatory remarks
that are endlessly made by professional union people for
the purpose of creating a cleavage between management and
employees," and, he observed, "as the intensity of a [sic]
organizing campaign increases, or as the solidity of a
union diminishes, so generally does a respect for the
truth decline."[152]

Anti-union charges were made against the SPA all
during "Operation Dixie." In 1951, for example, the
southern representative for the IWA-CIO cited his organization's accomplishments "despite the fact that the
Southern Pine Association is fighting our union with every
weapon at its command," and in 1953 the CIO's regional
director for Mississippi and Louisiana charged that the
SPA had been "set up principally as an employers' 'Union'
to prevent employees from gaining the rights of organized
labor. . . ."[153] Although it is true that the Southern
Pine Association, its staff, and its subscribers were by
no means admirers of labor unions, there is nothing in the
association's open records during the period to justify
charges that it intervened directly in labor conflicts or
in any way acted like the older type of employers'
association. It did, however, exert strong efforts on
behalf of legislation that was anti-organized labor in
tenor, and it consistently supported conservative governmental activities and legislation throughout the post-
World War II period, as, in fact, it had done since its
inception. These activities were not carried out by the
SPA or its Labor Relations Service as such, but by a
series of committees under various names which supposedly
represented the entire industry but were actually dominated by SPA manufacturers and served by the SPA staff.
In the postwar period, the most important of these committees in dealing with labor matters, as well as other
legislation, was the Southern Pine Industry Committee.

The Southern Pine Industry Committee, as noted
earlier, was formed in 1937 to carry out the industry's
unsuccessful fight against passage of the Fair Labor

Standards Act. During World War II the SPIC was inactive, and the SPA shifted its support to the Southern Pine Emergency Defense Committee and the Southern Pine War Committee. At the war's end, the SPWC was still in existence, but it was not considered appropriate for this organization, which had functioned supposedly as a representative of all the southern pine industry and been designed to facilitate the government's war effort, to enter into the many partisan issues which would almost inevitably find the southern lumbermen at odds with the federal government. Therefore, in January, 1946, the SPWC and the old SPIC were liquidated and their functions absorbed by a temporary organization called the Joint Emergency Committee for the Southern Pine Industry.

In May the JEC was succeeded by a new, permanent Southern Pine Industry Committee. It was to represent the entire industry and to be supported by voluntary contributions from both SPA subscribers and nonsubscribers.[154] It was contemplated that the committee would represent the industry before the OPA and work for higher price ceilings and for the abolition of the agency; maintain liaison with the Civilian Production Administration through a Washington office; operate as a lobby to influence legislation, particularly in the fields of forestry and labor; and generally act as an information-gathering and disseminating agency for the southern pine industry.[155]

The Southern Pine Industry Committee was registered under the Regulation of Lobbying Act of 1946, but generally did not have its staff members lobby in person on Capitol Hill. The southern pine manufacturers, furthermore, were very careful to keep the SPIC and the SPA separate and distinct. As a SPA staff member described the setup in 1952, "the Southern Pine Association gets into Legislation only after the laws have been passed, whether it is labor laws, tax laws or any other kind. After the legislation is on the Statute books, then the Association will pass out information to its subscribers and there isn't any chance for a conflict with the provisions of the anti-lobbying Act." "On the other hand," he continued, "the Southern Pine Industry Committee has been the agency which has carried on relations with the government departments, and more especially, has dealt with Congress on legislation."[156]

SPIC Secretary H. C. Berckes later recalled that "the Industry Committee availed itself very little of any direct approaches to Congressmen and Senators. It gladly appeared before Congressional Committees and spoke for the industry there. It also supplied economic data when requested to do so by Congressmen and Senators." "When the effect of any legislation was felt by the members of an industry the Industry Committee urged those members affected to write to their Representatives and Senators frankly and fully as to how they would be affected individually," wrote Berckes. "Congressmen and Senators wanted that type of information from their constituents; not the harangues of paid lobbyists or representatives, nor to receive scores of form letters or stereotyped objections. The Southern Pine Industry Committee continued this 'grass roots' approach insistently and its standing and reputation was enhanced thereby."[157]

In addition to its activities in informing its own contributors and assisting their efforts in influencing lawmakers and administrators, the SPIC maintained close relationships with other organizations and produced a flood of circulars, advertising copy, pamphlets, news releases, and other materials designed to build up support for the industry's position on various issues.

One major area of postwar labor concern was the constant pressure for increases in the minimum wage levels established by the Fair Labor Standards Act. This pressure came from organized labor, some northern manufacturers, and other interests who were concerned about the impact of low southern wages on industries and workers in other sections. As noted earlier, the old Southern Pine Industry Committee had fought unsuccessfully against passage of the first wages and hours law in 1938, which had established an original minimum hourly wage of twenty-five cents, rising on a gradual basis to forty cents in February, 1944. As the minimum level had risen, average wages in the southern pine industry had tended to increase, remaining slightly above the legal minimum levels. Under the impact of World War II, in October, 1946, wages in the industry rose to an average of sixty-four cents an hour, far above the minimum level, and reached sixty-nine cents by late 1949. However, the southern pine industry strongly resisted efforts to revise the minimum, which nevertheless were successful in 1949, with a seventy-five cent minimum becoming effective on January 25, 1950.[158]

While denying industry opposition to higher wages, the SPIC offered several arguments against raising the minimum wage. These generally stressed the predominance in the industry of small producing units which had a high percentage of unskilled workers and little mechanization, and were, therefore, characterized by relatively low labor productivity and high labor costs. Increased labor costs could not be overcome by the small mills through mechanization, because of the transitory nature of these mills and their low capitalization. Furthermore, mills which were selling in interstate trade, and were thus affected by the federal wage requirements, were often in direct competition with mills in intrastate commerce having lower wage scales. In addition to its economic arguments, the SPIC questioned the right of the federal government to establish a wage structure and bemoaned the growth of government control and the trend toward a "collectivist" society.[159]

With the victory of Harry Truman in the 1948 presidential election and the replacement of the "do-nothing, good for nothing" conservative-dominated 80th Congress by a new Congress in which the Democrats controlled both houses, the Southern Pine Industry Committee correctly anticipated upward revision of the minimum wage. As H. C. Berckes saw the situation, "The pressure will be very strong now for an increase in the minimum wage, and, to a level higher than that which a Republican Congress might have recommended . . . we will have to conduct a stronger fight to get necessary amendments to the Wages and Hours Law that will eliminate time-and-a-half for overtime, define regular rate of pay, and clarify administrative provisions and procedure . . . it will be only through the conservative Southern Democrats in Congress plus the returning Republicans who were sympathetic to overhauling the Wage and Hour Law, that any relief can be secured."[160]

The Southern Pine Industry Committee met in January, 1949, to map a strategy for the campaign against wage and hour revisions. Convinced that more strenuous activity would be needed, it voted unanimously to request all manufacturers to contribute an additional five cents per thousand feet of production, in addition to the usual six-cent voluntary fee, to support the expenses of the intensified fight. The committee members were informed that some 46,542 pieces of SPIC wages-hours literature had been ordered and distributed by 135 cooperating industrial and trade organizations, chambers of commerce, and individuals.[161] In addition, on February 4, 1949, four witnesses for the SPIC testified before the House Committee on Education and Labor.[162] During the last six months of its intensive fight against the measure, the SPIC spent some $40,000, of which $30,000 had been contributed by SPA

subscribers and $10,000 by others who "had a keen interest
in our fight but a distant relation to our Southern Pine
Industry."[163]   Despite   the   SPIC's   efforts,   the   81st
Congress passed, and, on October 26, President Truman
signed, the Fair Labor Standards Amendments of 1949, which
raised   the   minimum   wage   level   to   seventy-five   cents,
effective January 25, 1950. On November 1, 1949, the SPIC
published and began to distribute the text of the wage-
hour law revision with explanations of sections which
would   be   particularly   significant   for   southern   pine
manufacturers.[164]

During   the   early   postwar   years,   the   Southern   Pine
Industry Committee also became deeply involved in efforts
to amend or eliminate that old bete noire of industry, the
Wagner Act.   The path was smoothed by the postwar
resurgence of conservatism and anti-New Dealism which had
been demonstrated in the 1946 Congressional elections when
the Republicans won control of both houses of Congress.
Writing from Washington, in March H. C. Berckes suggested
to SPIC Chairman C. C.   Sheppard that his committee would
have to consider revision of the Wagner Act.   Berckes
bemoaned the "tendency on the part of business and other
witnesses to be on the defensive and take a negative
approach to labor   legislation" and submitted for future
consideration by the committee "a simple, rough outline of
an approach which seems strong."[165]

Berckes's proposed "Memorandum on Labor Legislation"
bore a striking resemblance to the emerging Taft-Hartley
Act and was a clear exposition of the SPA leader's personal views in regard to organized labor.   According to
the memorandum:

> Outlawing the "closed shop" is a negative approach
> to a problem that should be handled more positively.
> The issue is a man's "right to work." It might be held
> that this right, is not an absolute one, but it can be
> regulated just as the "right to strike."
> A "closed shop" is actually an agreement through
> conspiracy (bargaining if you prefer) to bar a man
> from work, all other factors notwithstanding, because
> he does not belong to a particular union.   That act,
> not by the judgment of a single individual, but by
> conspiracy, infringes upon a man's constitutional
> right to "life, liberty, and the pursuit of happi-
> ness." It is also a blot upon a free labor movement.

The New South and the "New Competition"

Industry-wide bargaining is also a conspiracy; it is the restraint of trade on a scale that could bring national disaster to our economy, if not carefully watched. By an industry-wide bargaining agreement between one labor union and all units in one industry, a product that is vitally necessary could be curtailed in volume, distributed unfairly, and costs projected so high as to be ruinous to users and consumers of the product.

Mass-picketing and some of the evils thereof should be subjected to a "highwayman's act." The evils and the methods are the same. In mass-picketing two or more men conspire, use force or through joint efforts infringe upon a man's "right-to-work," to his use of the public highways and streets.

None of the above would be tolerated if indulged in by two or more business organizations or by non-union citizens. The evils are the result of class regulation, piecemeal as well.

The logical solution of all of these problems can only be arrived at through the principle of equal justice under law. The application of anti-trust laws, conspiracy laws, and restraint of trade laws should apply alike to all citizens.[166]

Returning to New Orleans, on March 18 Berckes discussed proposals to amend the Wagner Act and his memorandum to C. C. Sheppard with the SPIC. The following day the SPIC instructed the secretary to "participate with other organizations in the effort to secure at the present session of Congress amendments to the Wagner Act and other remedial legislation that would cure the abuses in employee-employer relations. . . ."[167] With the strong support of the Southern Pine Industry Committee and like-minded organizations, the Hartley bill passed the House in the spring. After modifications, the measure emerged from the Senate in June, 1947, as the Taft-Hartley bill. It was vetoed by President Truman, but was promptly passed over his veto. The measure, which organized labor liked to call the "slave labor" act, outlawed the closed shop, revived government injunctions as a means of dealing with labor disputes, and through Section 14b enabled states to pass "right-to-work" laws outlawing the requirement of union membership as a condition of employment. The Southern Pine Association and SPIC were pleased with the law. Although a speaker at the association's annual

328

meeting declared, "The Taft-Hartley Law is not too strong; it's not strong enough," southern pine organizations dedicated much of their efforts in following years to ensuring that the law remained on the statute books without modification.[168]

The southern pine industry and the SPA thus entered the 1950s with precisely the same sort of labor attitudes and activities they had demonstrated prior to World War I and even earlier. Their techniques were somewhat more sophisticated, and there were some differences of opinion among the manufacturers which contributed to the changes in leadership and structure that came to the association during the decade. It is striking, however, how strongly and consistently anti-labor they had been throughout their existence.

The pine manufacturers had generally failed to resolve their labor problems satisfactorily. The World War I problem of labor migration to other sections continued through the 1930s and 1940s. Employers continued to resist unionization, and management efforts to improve conditions for workers in the industry so that they would remain contented in the South were piecemeal at best. Housing conditions continued to be generally wretched, and prior to the New Deal hours were long, wages low, and safety programs virtually nonexistent. Industry spokesmen who talked about "contented workers" and "good laboring conditions" in the southern pine woods were either less than candid or were victims of their own delusions. During the 1930s and 1940s the lumbermen continued to fight every effort to upgrade their workers' conditions, and the late 1940s and early 1950s saw them struggling mightily to prevent unionization.

The attitudes of these lumbermen are important, since they were generally powerful, respected figures in their communities and regions, and they therefore provide a revealing insight into southern attitudes toward social and economic issues. The attitudes of these manufacturers and their trade association reflect the adamant anti-labor and anti-union attitudes that have characterized the economic and social leaders of the "New South" in general.

NOTES TO CHAPTER 9

1. James E. Fickle, "The Louisiana-Texas Lumber War of 1911-1921," Louisiana History, XVI (Winter, 1975), 59-85.

The New South and the "New Competition"

See also Merl E. Reed, "Lumberjacks and Longshoremen: The
I.W.W. in Louisiana," Labor History, XIII (Winter, 1972),
41-59.

2. The background of these developments and references
to other sources may be found in James E. Fickle,
"Management Looks at the 'Labor Problem': The Southern
Pine Industry during World War I and the Postwar Era,"
Journal of Southern History, XL (Feb., 1974), 61-63.
There are scattered materials relating to the Southern
Lumber Operators' Association in the Temple Industries
Records, Box 94 (Forest History Collections, Stephen F.
Austin State Library, Nacogdoches, Tex.).

3. Grosvenor B. Clarkson, Industrial America in the
World War: The Strategy behind the Lines, 1917-1918
(Boston: Houghton Mifflin, 1923), 291-92. Bernard M.
Baruch, American Industry in the War: A Report of the War
Industries Board (Washington, D.C.: Government Printing
Office, 1921) p. 90, gives essentially the same explana-
tion for lumber's exclusion from the priority list. As
early as August, 1917, the SPA was complaining about labor
shortages and attempting to secure exemptions from mili-
tary service for sawmill workers. Southern Pine Associa-
tion to F. W. Dunham, Aug. 15, 1917, R. E. Wood Memorandum
for Admiral Capps, Aug. 16, 1917, Wood to W. C. McGowan,
Aug. 16, 1917, all in Records of the U. S. Shipping Board,
Construction Division, General File, RG 32, National
Archives, Washington, D.C.

4. "Pine and Patriotism," Southern Pine Association
Records, Box 85b, pp. 139-40 (Louisiana State University
Archives, Baton Rouge, La.). Collection hereafter cited
as SPA Records.

5. Ibid., p. 20.

6. John Henry Kirby to Charles Piez, May 16, 1918,
John Henry Kirby Papers, Box 144 (University of Houston
Library, Houston, Tex.) Collection hereafter cited as
Kirby Papers.

7. "Labor Troubles at Saw Mills," Gulf Coast
Lumberman, V (Oct. 15, 1917), 49.

330

8. "Women for Sawmill Engineers," Gulf Coast Lumberman, V (Mar. 15, 1918), 40; John Henry Kirby, R. A. Long, and F. W. Stevens to Members of the War Industries Board, July 3, 1918, Kirby Papers, Box 144.

9. A mill manager of the Sabine Tram Company in East Texas later reported that his company never employed Negroes until 1917-18, when it employed both blacks and Mexicans because of the war labor shortage. Hamilton Pratt Easton, "The History of the Texas Lumbering Industry" (Ph.D. dissertation, University of Texas, 1947), p. 268. Ruth Allen in her study of East Texas lumber workers says that the World War I labor shortage "seems to have had little effect upon wages paid in Texas. . . ." Ruth A. Allen, East Texas Lumber Workers: An Economic and Social Picture, 1870-1950 (Austin: University of Texas Press, 1961), p. 70.

10. "Lumber Liquidates: Official Report of the Sixth Annual Meeting of the Subscribers to the Southern Pine Assocation Held at Grunewald Hotel, New Orleans, April 5, 6, 1921," SPA Records, Box 85b, p. 27.

11. The story of this earlier migration is treated in Walter L. Fleming, "'Pap' Singleton, the Moses of the Colored Exodus," American Journal of Sociology, XV (July, 1909), 61-82; Roy Garvin, "Benjamin or 'Pap' Singleton and His Followers," Journal of Negro History, XXXIII (Spring, 1971), 39-52; Morgan D. Peoples, "'Kansas Fever' in North Louisiana," Louisiana History, XI (Spring, 1970), 121-35; John G. Van Deusen, "The Exodus of 1879," Journal of Negro History, XXI (Apr., 1936), 111-29; and Arna Bontemps and Jack Conroy, Anyplace but Here (New York: Hill and Wang, 1966), pp. 53-71.

12. For a brief account of the causes and development of the "Great Migration" of Negroes out of the South see George Brown Tindall, The Emergence of the New South, 1913-1945 (Baton Rouge: Louisiana State University Press, 1967), pp. 146-50; and William M. Tuttle, Jr., Race Riot: Chicago in the Red Summer of 1919 (New York: Antheneum, 1970), pp 78-84.

13. Southern Lumber Operators' Association to All Members, Mar. 3, 1917, John Henry Kirby Papers, Box 221.

14. Southern Lumber Operators' Association to All Members, Nov. 5, 1918, Kurth Papers, Box 489 (Forest History Collections, Stephen F. Austin State University Library, Nacogdoches, Tex.).

15. "Minutes of a Meeting of the Board of Directors of the Southern Pine Association . . . June 16, 1919," SPA Records, Box 70b.

16. "Special Report on Industrial Conditions in the Mills and Logging Camps of the Southern Pine Association," SPA Records, Box 67b.

17. Ninth Biennial Report of the Bureau of Statistics of Labor of the State of Louisiana, 1916-1918, pp. 96, 124-34, quoted in Vernon H. Jensen, Lumber and Labor (New York: Farrar & Rinehart, 1945), pp. 79-80. More favorable descriptions of conditions in the industry can be found in Jo Dent Hodge, "Lumbering in Laurel at the Turn of the Centry" (M. A. thesis, University of Mississippi, 1966), pp. 51-54; and George A. Stokes, "Lumbering in Southwest Louisiana: A Study of the Industry as a Culturo-Geographic Factor" (Ph.D. dissertation, Louisiana State University, 1954), pp. 42-43, 60-62, 65-66.

18. The story of the Bogalusa events is recounted briefly in Jensen, Lumber and Labor, pp. 91-94; Huey Latham, Jr., "A Comparison of Union Organization in Two Southern Paper Mills" (M. A. thesis, Louisiana State University, 1962), pp. 28-35; F. Ray Marshall, Labor in the South (Cambridge, Mass.: Harvard University Press, 1967), pp. 99-100; and Charlotte Todes, Labor and Lumber (New York: International Publishers, 1931), pp. 174-77.

19. Fickle, "Management Looks at the 'Labor Problem,'" pp. 68-69.

20. Southern Pine Association to San Augustine County Lumber Company, Apr. 22, 1919, Kurth Papers, Box 505.

21. Interview with H. C. Berckes, Jan. 24, 1968; "Minutes of a Meeting of the Board of Directors of the Southern Pine Association . . . June 16, 1919," SPA Records, Box 70b; "Minutes of a Meeting of the Board of Directors of the Southern Pine Association . . . December 5, 1919," SPA Records, Box 70b.

22. Southern Pine Association to Subscribers, May 15, 1919, Kurth Papers, Box 516.

23. Southern Pine Association to Subscribers, May 28, 1919, Kurth Papers, Box 516.

24. "Minutes of a Meeting of the Board of Directors of the Southern Pine Association . . . June 16, 1919," SPA Records, Box 70b.

25. Southern Pine Association to Angelina County Lumber Co., June 30, 1919, Kurth Papers, Box 516.

26. Interview with H. C. Berckes, Jan. 24, 1968. For a discussion of Chicago in the "Red Summer" see Tuttle, Race Riot.

27. "Minutes of a Meeting of the Board of Directors of the Southern Pine Association . . . Aug. 20, 1919," SPA Records, Box 70b; "Minutes of a Meeting of the Board of Directors of the Southern Pine Association . . . December 5, 1919," SPA Records, Box 70b.

28. "Lumber Liquidates: Official Report of the Sixth Annual Meeting of the Subscribers to the Southern Pine Association held at Grunewald Hotel, New Orleans," SPA Records, Box 85b, p. 26.

29. John E. Rhodes to the Board of Directors, May 4, 1920, Kurth Papers, Box 549. For information on the devices utilized to impede the outflow of southern labor see Leo Alilunas, "Statutory Means of Impeding Emigration of the Negro," Journal of Negro History, XXII (Apr., 1937), 148-62; Henderson H. Donald, "The Negro Migration of 1916-1918," Journal of Negro History, VI (Oct., 1921), 425-27; and Tindall, Emergence of the New South, pp. 148-49. The activities of local officials with regard to idle laborers remaining in the South, as mentioned above in the letter from John E. Rhodes to the SPA Board of Directors, often resulted in gross miscarriages of justice with regard to both white and black laborers. In some cases, as Vernon Jensen points out in Lumber and Labor (p. 85), "both Negro and white laborers were . . . arrested and fined and imprisoned for no offense at all, or simply for being out of a job. Afterward, an employer would appear and pay the fine on the condition that the debt would be

worked out." In one such case in the early 1920s a prominent Southern Pine Association subscriber was exposed to
the glare of unfavorable national publicity because of the
violent death of a young white laborer bound over to hard
labor in one of the company's lumber camps by local officials acting in league with the manufacturer. An
interesting account of this macabre story is found in N.
Gordon Carper, "The Convict-Lease System in Florida,
1866-1923" (Ph.D. dissertation, Florida State University,
1964), pp. 330-80.

30. W. Graham Cole to George R. Christie, June 5, 1920,
Kurth Papers, Box 561.

31. Southern Lumber Operators' Association to Members,
June 10, 1920, Kurth Papers, Box 549.

32. "Report On the Exodus of South's Negro Labor," SPA
Records, Box 93a.

33. Ibid.

34. For example, one subscriber replied to the SPA
questionnaire: "It is also my experience that the negro
if let alone is satisfied and happy in his 'Shack' that
while to us appears a poor meager outfit to call a home,
yet it is a home to him and he prefers it to more com-
modious surroundings. The average mill negro 'Wants but
little here below nor wants that little long.' He don't
want any thing to hold him back when he gets ready [to]
vacate between suns. So I have found that the negro don't
want any house or furniture that will hinder his migration process when he imagines the place is too hot for him
or too cold. In my opinion the wages offered North are
simply an opportunity for the negro to accept in a case of
imagined emergency on account of the advertised exploits
of the Ku-Klux-Klan in the South; which he (the negro)
considers a menace to his tranquil pleasures of 'Crap-
shooting and bootlegging and escapades with his women
folks.' There has been too much said about the K.K.K. for
the Southern negro to appreciate and stay satisfied on the
job when fancy offers and 'transportation free' is offered
by the fellow 'Up north.' A negro enjoys a ride even [if]
it be a free one to the jail or the penitentiary." Q. D.
Sauls to John E. Rhodes, SPA Records, Box 93a. A folder
entitled "Labor Going North" in this box of the SPA

Records contains the replies to the association's questionnaire, which reveal a wide variety of reactions to the status of Negroes in the South.

35. "Labor Report for Mr. Berckes, June 15, 1923," SPA Records, Box 93a.

36. "A Decade of Service: Official Report of the Tenth Annual Meeting of the Subscribers to the Southern Pine Association Held at Roosevelt Hotel, New Orleans, March 24 and 25, 1925," SPA Records, Box 85b, p. 40.

37. Southern Lumber Operators' Association circular, Oct. 6, 1925, Kurth Papers, Box 795.

38. National Negro Voice (New Orleans), Jan. 1, 1924.

39. Ibid. A series of full-page advertisements with cartoon portrayals of contrasting conditions in North and South pointing out the advantages and opportunities for blacks in Dixie appeared during 1923 in the New Orleans States as part of "A Series of Frank Talks and Presentations of Facts to the Colored Race by Prominent Leaders Thereof."

40. Dewey H. Palmer, "Moving North: Migration of Negroes during World War I," Phylon, XXVIII (Spring, 1967), 60.

41. "Lumber Plants or Mills," National Negro Voice (New Orleans), Oct. 3, 1925.

42. "Inspection Report Southern Lumber Operators' Association," Kurth Papers, Box 803.

43. "Proceedings of Joint Meeting of Alabama, East Texas, Louisiana, Mississippi-East Louisiana and Tri-State Sawmill Managers' Associations Held at Roosevelt Hotel, New Orleans, March 22, 1926," SPA Records, Box 686.

44. Jensen, Lumber and Labor, pp. 80-81. For a management description of conditions in an Alabama mill town, see Elwood R. Maunder, comp., James Greeley McGowin—South Alabama Lumberman: The Recollections of His Family (Santa Cruz, California: Forest History Society, 1977).

The New South and the "New Competition"

45. Allen, East Texas Lumber Workers, pp. 79-82; Jensen, Lumber and Labor, pp. 81-83.

46. Jensen, Lumber and Labor, p. 83.

47. John E. Rhodes, "What Southern Pine Mills Are Doing to Reduce Personal Injuries," SPA Records, Box 46b, pp. 1, 2, 4.

48. "Safe-Guarding the Workman: A Report of the Activities of the Safety Department, Southern Pine Association, for the Year 1919," SPA Records, Box 46b.

49. "Proceedings of Fifth Annual Convention of Southern Pine Association . . . March 16-18, 1920," SPA Records, Box 73b, p. 232.

50. "The Dollar Side of Safety," in "Proceedings of Joint Meeting of Alabama, East Texas, Louisiana, Mississippi-East Louisiana and Tri-State Sawmill Managers' Associations . . . March 22, 1926," SPA Records,, Box 68b, pp. 67-69.

51. Untitled report in folder entitled "Safety First Literature," SPA Records, Box 46b; "Minutes of a Meeting of the Board of Directors of the Southern Pine Association . . . April 4, 1921" SPA Records, Box 70b, p. 3.

52. H. C. Berckes, "The Pitch in Pine: A Story of the Traditions, Policies and Activities of the Southern Pine Industry and the Men Responsible for Them" (unpublished manuscript in possession of the author), p. 235.

53. The Times Picayune (New Orleans), Mar. 31, 1933, p. 6; "Pine Men Oppose Bill To Restrict Hours of Labor," The Four L Lumber News, XIII (Apr. 15, 1931), 4; C. C. Sheppard, "Wages and Hours of Labor in the South: Statement in Behalf of the Southern Lumber Industry before National Industrial Recovery Administrator . . . July 20, 1933," SPA Records, Box H-35; Tindall, Emergence of the New South, pp. 444-45, 522.

54. Berckes, "Pitch in Pine," p. 174; William E. Leuchtenburg, Franklin D. Roosevelt and the New Deal, 1932-1940 (New York: Harper Torchbook, 1963), pp. 150-52; James T. Patterson, Congressional Conservatism and the New

Deal: The Growth of the Conservative Coalition in Congress, 1933-1939 (Lexington: University of Kentucky Press, 1967), p. 183.

55. Southern Pine Bulletin, I (Oct. 15, 1935) (copy in SPA Records, Box 83b).

56. Tindall, Emergence of the New South, p. 533.

57. H. C. Berckes to E. L. Kurth, Feb. 24, 1934, SPA Records, Box 9a. This letter was mimeographed and circulated among the SPA subscribers. The association viewed President Roosevelt's court-packing scheme as a means of guaranteeing that legislation such as the proposed wages and hours measure would be approved by the Supreme Court and thus opposed it, as it did other New Deal proposals, on the grounds that the association was defending the "American system of government." Berckes did seem to rather accurately portray northern opinion. For an example see Jay Franklin's "We, the People" column in The Evening Star (Washington, D.C.), Feb. 23, 1937.

58. Patterson, Congressional Conservatism and the New Deal, p. 149.

59. J. L. Camp, Jr., to Sam F. Hobbs, June 28, 1937, quoted in Tindall, Emergence of the New South, p. 533.

60. "Address of H. C. Berckes, Secretary-Manager, Southern Pine Association, at the Annual Meeting of the Southern Pine Association . . .," Supplement to Southern Pine Bulletin, I (Apr. 8, 1937) (copy in SPA Records, Box 83b).

61. Berckes, "Pitch in Pine," pp. 175-76; James Boyd, "Gross Darkness—Then Comes Dawn," SPA Records, Box 77a, pp. 57-58; Tindall, Emergence of the New South, pp. 533-34. An interesting note is the fact that the western lumber industry, whose competition the southerners deeply feared, cooperated with the SPIC and Southern Pine Association's fight against the wages and hours measure. For a brief discussion of this matter see Berckes, "Pitch in Pine," pp. 177-78.

62. Both of these items are in the SPA Records, Box 93a.

63. "Effects Of Black-Connery Wage and Hour Bill upon Labor, Farmer, Consumer, Manufacturer, American System . . .," pamphlet published by Southern Pine Industry Committee, SPA Records, Box 137b; "The Black-Connery Wage and Hour Bill: An Address by Hon. E. E. Cox, U. S. Congressman from Georgia, before Southern States Industrial Council, Nashville, Tennessee, November 4, 1937," reprint published by Southern Pine Industry Committee, SPA Records, Box 93a.

64. Interview with H. C. Berckes, Aug. 10, 1968.

65. Charles B. Crow to Hugo L. Black, July 20, 1937, quoted in Tindall, Emergence of the New South, p. 534.

66. Tindall, Emergence of the New South, p. 534.

67. Leuchtenburg, Roosevelt and the New Deal, p. 261; Patterson, Congressional Conservatism and the New Deal, pp. 149-54.

68. Leuchtenburg, Roosevelt and the New Deal, pp. 261-62; Patterson, Congressional Conservatism and the New Deal, pp. 193-96.

69. Berckes, "Pitch in Pine," p. 182.

70. Ibid.

71. Ibid., p. 181.

72. Ibid., p. 179.

73. Ibid., p. 180.

74. Leuchtenburg, Roosevelt and the New Deal, p. 262; Patterson, Congressional Conservatism and the New Deal, pp. 242-45; Tindall, Emergence of the New South, p. 535.

75. Leuchtenburg, Roosevelt and the New Deal, p. 262; Patterson, Congressional Conservatism and the New Deal, pp. 245-56; Tindall, Emergence of the New South, pp. 535-36.

76. Berckes, "Pitch in Pine," p. 183.

77. Tindall, Emergence of the New South, p. 536.

78. For examples of the material circulated by the Southern Pine Industry Committee against the Fair Labor Standards Act see SPA Records, Boxes 80a and 63. Copies of the SPIC's "Wage-Hour Law News Notes" are in SPA Records, Box X-66, p. 1.

79. "Proceedings of Meeting of Southern Pine Association . . . November 28, 1939," SPA Records, Box 68a.

80. "Proceedings of Clinic Held under the Auspices of Southern Pine War Committee . . . June 3, 1942," SPA Records, Box 68a, p. 46.

81. Ralph W. Hidy, Frank Ernest Hill, and Allan Nevins, Timber and Men: The Weyerhauser Story (New York: Macmillan, 1963), pp. 460-61.

82. "Proceedings of Clinic Held under Auspices of Southern Pine War Committee . . . June 3, 1942," SPA Records, Box 68a, p. 47.

83. Ibid.

84. Ibid.

85. W. J. Yost to H. C. Berckes, Sept. 4, 1942, SPA Records, Box 75b.

86. Allen, East Texas Lumber Workers, p. 83; Hidy, Hill, and Nevins, Timber and Men, p. 461; Paul V. McNutt to All Loggers and Workers in Sawmills, Planning Mills, and Veneer and Plywood Plants, Sept. 15, 1942, SPA Records, Box 75a.

87. Hidy, Hill, and Nevins, Timber and Men, p. 461; Southern Pine War Committee, "War Bulletin," XLVII (Sept. 16, 1942), LXXIV (Feb. 28, 1943), both in SPA Records, Box 75a; Southern Pine War Committee to Southern Pine Manufacturers, Mar. 1, 1943, SPA Records, Box 75a.

88. "Southern Pine and Its Production, Statement by H. C. Berckes . . . November 24, 1942," SPA Records, Box 90a, p. 3.

89. Robert C. Weaver, "Negro Labor since 1929," *Journal of Negro History*, XXV (Jan., 1950), 35-36. Because of the large number of Negroes employed in southern lumber mills and camps, the migration of the blacks was naturally a major conversational subject, and the comments of Chairman C. C. Sheppard of the Southern Pine War committee probably summed up the feelings and experiences of many lumbermen. "I would like to call the attention of those Government representatives to one movement that is now starting in our section of the country," said Sheppard, and the Louisianian noted that "some of our Negro labor is leaving our plant and going north to higher-rated jobs around Detroit and Chicago. Last Sunday, there were six of them loaded into one automobile and started north." Sheppard remembered that "we had a lot of that during the first World War," and he warned that "we are not troubled just by the shipyards paying higher wages and taking our labor, we are troubled with other industries, war industries; we are troubled with the paper mills taking them, and many of the war industries located North and East--shell loading plants and all those operations." "Proceedings of Joint Industry-Wide Conference of the Southern Pine War Committee and the Southern Hardwood Industry War Committee . . . February 19, 1943," SPA Records, Box 68a, p. 73.

90. "Proceedings of Joint Industry-Wide Conference of the Southern Pine War Committee and the Southern Hardwood Industry War Committee . . . February 19, 1943," SPA Records, Box 68a, pp 42-48.

91. Ibid., p. 70.

92. Ibid., pp. 71-72, 75-76.

93. "Proceedings of Joint Meeting of Southern Pine War Committee and Southern Hardwood Industry War Committee . . . April 14, 1943," SPA Records, Box 74b, pp. 3-19.

94. "Proceedings of Joint Industry-Wide Conference of the Southern Pine War Committee and the Southern Hardwood Industry War Committee . . . February 19, 1943," SPA Records, Box 68a, p. 67.

95. Hidy, Hill, and Nevins, *Timber and Men*, p. 462.

96. "Women Workers in South's Lumber Industry: Report of a Survey of Lumber Manufacturing Plants in Portions of Seven States—Alabama, Arkansas, Florida, Louisiana, Mississippi, Oklahoma, and Texas. Conducted by Southern Pine War Committee, New Orleans, La.," SPA Records, Box 82a.

97. Bryan Fairchild and Jonathan Grossman, The Army and Industrial Manpower (Washington, D. C.: Government Printing Office, 1959), p. 189.

98. Ibid., p. 190.

99. Ibid., pp. 191-92.

100. Ibid., p. 193.

101. George G. Lewis and John Mewha, History of Prisoner of War Utilization by the United States Army, 1776-1945, Department of Army Pamphlet 20-213 (Washington, D.C.: Government Printing Office, 1955), pp. 83-86. Pages 84 and 85 of this work contain a list of the plants completed and under construction, which shows their capacities.

102. "Daily Report, C. N. Gould, June 11, 1943," SPA Records, Box 52a.

103. Southern Pine War Committee to Abrams Brothers Lumber Company, June 12, 1943, SPA Records, Box 87a.

104. "Daily Report, C. N. Gould, July 31, 1943," SPA Records, Box 52a. On August 2, 1943, Gould visited the plant of the Hall Bros. Lumber Company in Huntsville, Texas, which was using seventeen prisoners of war, and reported that after three weeks of working the prisoners the proprietors of the firm were quite pleased with the results. One of the owners remarked that he "wouldn't take a thousand dollars for what we have done with these prisoners already, because it has put us back into normal production which we had been unable to do otherwise." Ibid.

105. Reports of these field visits are in SPA Records, Box 52a.

The New South and the "New Competition"

106. Lewis and Mewha, _Prisoner_ _of_ _War_ _Utilization_, pp. 125-26.

107. H. C. Berckes to C. C. Sheppard, Apr. 12, 1944, SPA Records, Box 91a.

108. "Southern Pine War Committee, New Orleans, Louisiana, Report on Operating Conditions In Southern Pine Industry: Analysis of Questionnaire Released by Southern Pine War Committee, January 29, 1945 . . .," mimeographed report, SPA Records, Box 76a, pp. 1, 2, 9.

109. R. C. Fraunberger, "Lumber Trade Associations: Their Economic and Social Significance" (M. A. thesis, Temple University, 1951), p. 122; Jensen, _Lumber_ _and_ _Labor_, pp. 283-84; "Minutes of a Meeting of the Board of Directors of the Southern Pine Association . . . September 16, 1943," SPA Records, Box 75a.

110. "Minutes of a Meeting of the Board of Directors of the Southern Pine Association . . . October 26, 1944," SPA Records, Box 11a, pp. 44-51.

111. "Meeting the Problems of the Southern Pine Industry," SPA Records, Box 84a, pp. 13-17.

112. Richard Ben Wand, "Lumber's Labor Problem," _Southern_ _Lumber_ _Journal_, XLIX (Aug. 10, 1945).

113. H. C. Berckes to Paul T. Sanderson, July 21, 1944, SPA Records, Box 42a.

114. As one critic of the proposed SPA effort put it, "Frankly I don't think the Association can expect to make much headway in mechanization in the Southern Pine Industry as 90% of the mills in the South are very small and somewhat uncertain in their operations and will not be in postiion to spend much money on modernizing." E. L. Kurth to H. C. Berckes, July 24, 1944, SPA Records, Box 42a.

115. L. O. Crosby to H. C. Berckes, July 26, 1944, SPA Records, Box 42a.

116. "Minutes of a Meeting of the Board of Directors of the Southern Pine Association . . . October 26, 1944," SPA Records, Box 11a, 46.

117. John M. Collier, The First Fifty Years of the Southern Pine Association, 1915-1965 (New Orleans: Southern Pine Assocation, 1965), p. 135.

118. Southern Pine Association to C. T. Parsons, Sept. 24, 1946, SPA Records, Box L.I.S. 42.

119. "Excerpt from Officers' Report to the 12th Annual Constitutional Convention of the International Woodworkers of America," SPA Records, Box L.I.S. 11.

120. Milton MacKaye, "The CIO Invades Dixie," Saturday Evening Post, July 20, 1946, p. 12; "CIO Organizers Drive to Unionize 1,500,000 Workers In South," Washington Star, Mar. 17, 1946; Doris Lockerman, "CIO Drive Will Seek to Organize 1,500,000," Atlanta Constitution, Mar. 20, 1946; "'Invasion' of South by C.I.O. Due Soon," Little Rock Arkansas Democrat, Apr. 17, 1946. The story of "Operation Dixie" is outlined in Marshall, Labor in the South, pp. 246-69.

121. Doris Lockerman, "'Just Another Season March Wind' Googe Says of CIO Plans in South," Atlanta Constitution, Mar. 22, 1946.

122. "AFL to Contest CIO Dixie Drive, Counterattack Launched by Rival Group," Times-Picayune (New Orleans), Apr. 26, 1946.

123. Chris A. Mathisen, "AFL Says 'Home Town Boys' Will Organize South," Washington Star, May 12, 1946; Louis Stark, "AFL Warns South of 'Radicals,' Green in Opening Organizing Drive, Says It Helps Area to Fight 'Communist Forces,'" New York Times, May 12, 1946.

124. L. O. Crosby to H. C. Berckes, Mar. 20, 1946, SPA Records, Box L.I.S. 42.

125. Arthur Temple to H. C. Berckes, Mar. 20, 1946, SPA Records, Box L.I.S. 42.

126. C. F. McKnight to H. C. Berckes, June 5, 1946, SPA Records, Box L.I.S. 42.

127. H. C. Berckes to C. C. Sheppard, Apr. 4, 1946, SPA Records, Box 9a.

128. Max Hall, "Labor Drives to Organize, AFL and CIO Simply Are Asking More Than They Expect to Get," New Orleans States, May 27, 1946.

129. "C.I.O Launches Organizing Drive, 'Operation Dixie,'" Business Week, Apr. 27, 1946, p. 92; "CIO Drives in South Pushed by Bittner, Neither Klan Nor 'Back-Door Agreements' Can Stop It, He Tells Steel Workers," New York Times, May 16, 1946; "Operation Dixie Acquires Southern Accent," Business Week, May 18, 1946; MacKaye, "The CIO Invades Dixie," pp. 12, 94.

130. "Labor News Items," no. 20 (Aug. 21, 1946) (copy in SPA Records, Box L.I.S. 42).

131. Remmie L. Arnold to the Employers of the South, Apr. 29, 1946, SPA Records, Box L.I.S. 42. The mood of the "establishment" in areas directly affected by the CIO's drive was reflected in a Monroe, Louisiana, newspaper editorial celebrating the union's failure to organize prominent southern pine operations in nearby Clarks and Urania, as the publication pulled out all stops in describing the union's "carpetbagging chicanery," "seductive propositions," "ignominious record," "rotten policies and pernicious doctrines," "despicable examples," "vicious mask of deceit and hypocrisy," "disgusting obstinancy," "spurious facade," and "malevolent and revolting designs." "The C.I.O. Retreats," Monroe Morning World, Nov. 3, 1946.

132. "CIO Leading in Race to Unionize Southern Lumber Industry," Southern Lumber Journal, Oct. 1946 (reprint in SPA Records, Box L.I.S. 42).

133. Robert M. Moore and Nichelson E. Buchwalter, "Collective Bargaining in the Southern Lumber Industry," Southern Lumberman, July 15, 1952 (reprint in SPA Records, Box L.I.S. 11).

134. Mark Temple, "CIO Out to Beat South's 'Industrial Tyranny,' Bittner Speaks at Convention, Resolution Condemns Injunction," _Atlanta Journal_, Nov. 21, 1946.

135. "Union Organizers Beaten Is Charge," _Times-Picayune_ (New Orleans), Sept. 29, 1946.

136. "CIO Organizers Assaulted in Anti-Union Conspiracy," _International Woodworker_, Oct. 2, 1946.

137. "Botkins Warns of Anti-Labor Drive Effect," _International Woodworker_, June 18, 1947.

138. John Mebane, "Unionizing Dixie, Southern Drive Stalls," _Wall Street Journal_, Jan. 22, 1947.

139. Berckes, "Pitch in Pine," p. 236.

140. "Operation Dixie Slows Up," _Business Week_, Oct. 25, 1947, pp. 19-20.

141. Moore and Buchwalter, "Collective Bargaining in the Southern Lumber Industry."

142. Marshall, _Labor in the South_, pp. 263-69.

143. Ibid.

144. The available figures on elections and results are not entirely consistent. Those cited are taken from Moore and Buchwalter, "Collective Bargaining in the Southern Lumber Industry" and from A. E. Broadle to Stanley P. Deas, July 14, 1953, SPA Records, Box L.I.S. 11.

145. A. E. Broadle to Stanley P. Deas, July 14, 1953, SPA Records, Box L.I.S. 11.

146. U. S. Department of Labor, "Wage Structure, Southern Lumber Industry, April, 1953," Bureau of Labor Standards Report No. 45 (Nov. 2, 1953), mimeographed report (copy in SPA Records, Box 146b).

147. "Average Hourly Straight-Time Rates For Common Labor, Union Vs. Non-Union--October 1, 1951," confidential mimeographed report, SPA Records, Box L.I.S. 10. This

The New South and the "New Competition"

report, covering mills in ten southern pine states, shows an average hourly wage differential of only .046 cents between union and non-union mills.

148. "Proceedings of Meeting of Subscribers to the Southern Pine Association and Southern Pine Industry Committee . . . April 8 and 9, 1948," SPA Records, Box 74a, pp. 69-70.

149. Ibid., p. 70.

150. Arthur Temple, Jr., to John G. Curren, May 11, 1949, SPA Records, Box L.I.S. 11; "Two Unions Stand Alone in Fight Against Pay Cuts" (CIO leaflet), SPA Records, Box L.I.S. 31.

151. "Strong Union, Area Negotiations Is Answer, Carolina Workers Told," International Woodworker, Sept. 12, 1951.

152. P. C. Gaffney to L. W. Morgan, Oct. 9, 1951, SPA Records, Box L.I.S. 11. In a previous letter to Gaffney, Morgan had written that as a member of the SPA's board of directors, "I don't recall seeing any such disbursement shown on the trial balance which I have seen. This only goes to show how unreliable and careless with the truth the organizers can get." Morgan to Gaffney, Sept. 28, 1951, SPA Records, Box L.I.S. 11.

153. "Organize Is Theme at Portsmouth," International Woodworker, Aug. 22, 1951; "Southern Pine Meet Draws 23 Locals," International Woodworker, Feb. 25, 1953.

154. "Minutes of a Joint Meeting of the Southern Pine War Committee and the Southern Pine Industry Committee . . . January 30, 1946," SPA Records, Box 9a; Minutes of a Meeting of the Board of Directors of the Southern Pine Association . . . May 10, 1946," SPA Records, Box 10b.

155. "What Your Money Buys When You Support the Joint Emergency Committee for the Southern Pine Industry," typewritten report, SPA Records, Box 9a. This report, prepared for the industry's May 9, 1946, mass meeting, represents the functions of the SPIC as well as the JEC, for in reality there was little difference between the two organizations.

346

156. "Proceedings of the Younger Men's Conference of the Southern Pine Association . . . November 21-22, 1952," SPA Records, Box 68a, p. 123.

157. Berckes, "Pitch in Pine," p. 270.

158. U. S. Department of Labor, "Wage Structure, Southern Lumber Industry, April, 1953," SPA Records, Box 146b, p. 1.

159. Typical examples of this approach are a speech by J. H. Ballew of the Southern States Industrial Council delivered to a meeting of southern pine manufacturers in New Orleans on September 6, 1945, and published and distributed in pamphlet form by the SPIC under the title "Dangers of Impending Legislation to Southern Industry" (copy in SPA Records, Box 93b) and a booklet entitled "Effects of Wages and Hours upon the Southern Pine Industry," published by the Southern Pine Industry Committee in November, 1945. The material in this booklet was prepared for presentation to the Committee on Education and Labor of the U. S. Senate and to the Labor Committee of the U. S. House of Representatives, which were considering amendments to the Fair Labor Standards Act of 1938. There is a copy of this booklet in SPA Records, Box 93a. As Vice-Chairman Tom DeWeese expressed it in a paper delivered before a meeting of the SPIC on March 18, 1947, "A statutory minimum wage is the first step toward a controlled economy." DeWeese also hit some other major objections to the proposed wages-hours measures, including the provisions for higher pay rates for overtime work or work in excess of forty hours per week, which the southern pine industry felt were unfair to logging operations because of the uncertainties and weather difficulties which might make it necessary for a crew to work far less than forty hours one week and far more the next and the lack of enforcement of the existing legislation that had been a chronic weakness of federal regulation of the southern pine industry since the time of the National Recovery Administration. Tom DeWeese, "The Effects of the Wage-Hour Law," SPA Records, Box 9a.

160. H. C. Berckes to C. C. Sheppard, Nov. 3, 1948, SPA Records, Box 70a.

161. "Minutes of a Meeting of the Southern Pine Industry Committee . . . January 25, 1949," SPA Records, Box 12a.

162. "Southern Pine Industry's Position on the Wage-Hour Law, Presented in Statements by R. M. Eagle, Carmona, Texas, Arthur Temple, Jr., Diboll, Texas, G. C. Rogers, Brunswick, Georgia, J. M. Higgins, Thorsby, Alabama, in Behalf of the Southern Pine Industry Committee before the Committee on Education and Labor of the House of Representatives, February 4, 1949," SPA Records, Box 72b.

163. H. C. Berckes to Southern Pine Industry Committee, Oct. 27, 1949, SPA Records, Box 70a.

164. "Text of the Wage-Hour Law (as Revised) and Explanation of Sections of Particular Interest to Southern Pine Manufacturers," SPA Records, Box 12a.

165. H. C. Berckes to C. C. Sheppard, March 6, 1947, SPA Records, Box 55b.

166. "Memorandum on Labor Legislation," attached to ibid.

167. "Minutes of a Meeting of the Southern Pine Industry Committee . . . March 19, 1947," SPA Records, Box 9a. A mimeographed copy of Berckes's March 18 statement to the committee is stapled to these minutes.

168. This comment on the Taft-Hartley Act was part of a speech by Irving G. McCann, who was former counsel of the Committee on Education and Labor of the U. S. House of Representatives. "Southern Pine Meeting Held in New Orleans," Southern Lumberman, Apr. 15, 1949 (reprint in SPA Records, Box 10a).

10

Mobilization for World War II

The important role played by the southern pine industry
during the World War II mobilization effort belied the
opinion of many lumber producers articulated in 1939 by
Secretary-Manager Wilson Compton of the National Lumber
Manufacturers' Association who stated that "lumber is not
a war industry."[1] In fact, the Southern Pine Association
and its industry were heavily involved in the national
mobilization effort long before the war began.

While the beginnings of full-scale formal warfare in
Europe came after Hitler's invasion of Poland in the fall
of 1939, it was not until early 1940, when the British
government placed large orders for aircraft lumber, that
the American lumber industry began to feel the impact of
military needs.[2] In the meantime, the Roosevelt Administration had been attempting to create administrative
machinery to direct a defense or mobilization effort. The
first step was the establishment of the War Resources
Board in September, 1939. This board drew up recommendations that were ignored by the President, and it was
succeeded by the Office for Emergency Management, created
on May 25, 1940, and the National Defense Advisory
Commission, which was appointed on May 29 of the same
year. The commission theoretically served as an advisor
to the Council of National Defense which had been formed
during World War I and was now revived, but in fact it
formulated and carried out policy. The National Defense
Advisory Commission included a lumber group within its
industrial materials division, but it did not initially
anticipate a shortage of wood products.[3]

The New South and the "New Competition"

As early as June, 1940, the Southern Pine Association offered its assistance to the War Department, the National Defense Advisory Commission, and other agencies. As the intensity of mobilization began to build, the SPA augmented its staff, kept the industry informed about government lumber requirements, offered its services to government contractors, and reopened its Washington office to keep in closer touch with events. During the summer of 1940, the tempo of this work gradually increased, until in the fall Southern Pine Association leaders called an industry-wide meeting in New Orleans to organize the entire industry, rather than simply the SPA, for full participation in the defense program.[4] By September, the U. S. government had become the country's largest lumber consumer, and in that month it ordered two billion board feet for the construction of cantonments; southern producers were asked to furnish most of the material.[5]

At the New Orleans meeting the defense situation was explained by a number of speakers, including SPA officials and Wilson Compton of the NLMA. Industry members and the Southern Pine Association "voted unanimously to forgive and forget its quarrel with President Roosevelt and his New Deal policies, and to rally the whole Southern pine industry with all its resources to support the emergency of national defense."[6] To do this the lumbermen formed the Southern Pine Emergency Defense Committee, composed of one manufacturer from each southern pine-producing state and chaired by C. C. Sheppard of the Louisiana Central Lumber Company in Clarks, Louisiana. The committee's name was later appropriately changed to Southern Pine War Committee.

The SPEDC met for the first time during the New Orleans meeting and recommended that the entire industry voluntarily assume the financial burden of the war activities which had been borne since the beginning of June by the Southern Pine Association. The lumbermen agreed to a voluntary assessment of three cents per thousand feet on shipments to support the work of the Southern Pine Emergency Defense Committee. They also voted unanimously to supply the government complete information on all aspects of the industry except prices and adopted a resolution pledging complete cooperation with the defense program. The lumbermen believed that the industry had sufficient facilities and raw materials to meet government needs but that stocks were depleted because of prevailing low prices. All producers were urged by the

350

speakers to give priority to government orders. The mood of the meeting was set by SPEDC Chairman C. C. Sheppard's pledge to the government that "this industry is going to make good on the job of delivering this material" and his admonition to lumbermen to "deliver the goods . . . not with the idea of trying to pinch out the last dollar that we can prevail upon the Government . . . to pay."[7] Thus, fifteen months before Pearl Harbor the Southern Pine Association had established the basic structure which would carry the industry through the defense and war experience.

The first step in the SPEDC's effort was to mail a questionnaire to 2,800 southern pine manufacturers asking them to estimate the amounts of various lumber items they could furnish for defense. On the basis of this information, the committee prepared three-month forecasts of the industry's defense capacity which were supplied to the National Defense Advisory Commission to help in planning the mobilization effort.[8] The Emergency Defense Committee also operated as a liaison between lumbermen and contractors on government projects. The federal government relaxed lumber specifications to permit the use of a wider range of species, lower grades, and wood with higher moisture content, and the Southern Pine Inspection Bureau attempted to speed the granting of grade-marking privileges to producers supplying government projects.[9]

Concern about the international situation and enthusiasm for the mobilization effort did not, however, bring an end to problems on the home front, either civilian or governmental. During the early phase of the defense drive, Southern Pine Association subscribers were intensely concerned about the possible inroads of other species and substitute materials in the government's mobilization effort. These threats were actively resisted, and the SPA viewed the defense program as an excellent opportunity to renew old acquaintances and demonstrate lumber's possibilities and uses to new contacts among engineering and architectural firms. At the SPA's annual meeting in March, the board voted funds for an expanded trade promotion program, and in July the association embarked on a campaign which doubled the organization's expenditures in that area. The fields open to lumber producers dramatically widened during this period, as frame prefabricated buildings and wooden beams came into use, cheaper grades were converted into boxes and crates, wood was utilized for buildings ranging from giant airplane hangers to defense housing, and wood was used in British and American aircraft.[10]

However, despite the myriad of new possibilities for using wood and generally good relations with government officials, the southern pine industry was running into heavy criticism from some quarters in official Washington. The most vigorous and controversial came from Leon Henderson, who was serving as defense commissioner in charge of price stabilization. Henderson had strongly criticized the lumber industry, and the southern pine industry in particular, during 1940 because of steadily rising prices which he attributed to the attempt of lumbermen to capitalize on the government's defense needs. Henderson's charges created quite a stir in the industry, and on January 23, 1941, the fiery New Dealer appeared before an industry-wide meeting in Washington and angrily chastised the lumbermen. President M. L. Fleishel of the National Lumber Manufacturers' Association, a prominent southern pine manufacturer, presented the industry's point of view. Lumber producers, particularly in the South, attributed rising price levels to the impact of wages and hours legislation, the tremendous lumber demand created by government programs, and the government's lack of coordination in buying lumber. The lumbermen believed Henderson acted unfairly and boorishly at the meeting, and he charged that he had not been properly informed of the framework and organization of the session. Regardless of the validity of the charges and countercharges, Henderson had the upper hand in the battle for public opinion. Drew Pearson's "Washington Merry-Go-Round" gloried in Henderson's performance and industry leaders decided not to continue the controversy in the press. Furthermore, Henderson's warnings of probable future governmental controls over prices and production sounded ominous to an industry that had not yet outlived its disenchantment with the National Recovery Administration.[11]

In April the industry's fears were realized when President Roosevelt established the Office of Price Administration and Civilian Supply. By fall, ceiling prices imposed on southern pine lumber had aroused wide opposition in the industry.[12] Nevertheless, its leaders participated in a conference of some sixty or seventy southern pine leaders, including manufacturers, wholesalers, and commission men, which was called by Leon Henderson to discuss prices and advise the government. After the government's price schedule was announced in

August, federal officials proved willing to meet and talk with the lumbermen about modifications or exemptions from the prices which were to go into effect on September 5. At a meeting held in New Orleans on August 30, more than six hundred lumbermen conferred with Peter A. Stone, price executive of the lumber and buildings materials section of the Office of Price Administration and Civilian Supply. Stone promised to convey their views on lumber prices to the proper officials, and it appeared that the channels of communication between the industry and government would remain open for fruitful negotiations.[13] Prices were not the only area of controversy between the southern lumbermen and the government. There were also reports on the shipment of green lumber, cheating on grades, and overbidding on government contracts during 1940.[14]

All of the earlier accomplishments and difficulties of the southern pine industry paled when Japanese bombs struck Pearl Harbor on December 7, 1941. SPA President Earl M. McGowin immediately sent a telegram to President Roosevelt pledging the association's unqualified support, and on December 12 the Southern Pine Emergency Defense Committee and the SPA executive committee met jointly in New Orleans and adopted a resolution to expand the industry's efforts in the crisis.[15]

During the first year of actual warfare, modifications were made in the southern pine industry's defense structure. One of the changes was merely semantic--on March 27, 1942, the Southern Pine Emergency Defense Committee became the Southern Pine War Committee.[16] During the year, another change of sorts was made in the war committee's support when the SPA's executive committee voted that the SPA would absorb its subscribers' contribution to the war committee out of the association's general subscription fee.[17] Facilities were established in the SPA's offices to provide rapid contact between industry members and the government and for the reproduction and dissemination of government orders, rules, and regulations.[18]

As the nation plunged deeper into war, the realization dawned in Washington that lumber was not an inexhaustible resource and that its use had to be regulated. The industry was soon governed by a maze of regulations, beginning with War Production Board Ruling L-21 of May 13, 1942, which restricted the use of softwood construction lumber for nonmilitary purposes. The ruling

was amended on July 10 and was superseded on August 27 by
Conservation Order M-208, which introduced detailed
priority ratings on lumber and controls on specific
grades. There were also additions, adjustments, amendments, and supplements to the government's price ceilings
and efforts to eliminate a shortage in railroad cars
through a "maximum loading order" issued by the Office of
Defense Transportation.[19]

During that year the government also moved toward
centralization of its purchasing efforts, and the men who
were to be most influential in lumber procurement emerged.
In the summer of 1942, J. Philip Boyd left the
Weyerhaeuser Sales Company to become chairman of the
lumber committee of the Army and Navy Munitions Board and,
then, in January, 1943, director of the Lumber and Lumber
Products Division of the War Production Board. H. C.
Berckes found Boyd to be capable and fair, although he
"may have represented the West Coast viewpoint a little
bit more than ours. . . ."[20] To centralize purchasing for
the Army, Navy, and other service branches, a central procurement agency under the auspices of the U. S. Corps of
Engineers became active under the direction of Colonel F.
G. Sherrill. It cooperated with Boyd's Lumber and Lumber
Products Division. Berckes had an excellent relationship
with Sherrill and later praised the colonel's performance
and his abilities.[21]

By the middle of 1942, the problems which were to
hamper the southern pine industry's war production had
become clear. The most important seemed to be securing
tires and an adequate labor supply. During a Southern
Pine Emergency Defense Committee meeting at the beginning
of the year, the major topic of discussion was the tire
shortage. By World War II, over 90 percent of southern
logging and lumbering was done on rubber-tired vehicles,
and an adequate supply of tires was obviously essential.
These were similar but less serious difficulties and shortages in other supply and equipment areas.[22]

The production of southern pine lumber actually fell
during the war, despite the industry's and the government's talk about meeting the nation's wartime needs. By
late 1943, southern pine production was 17 percent behind
a similar period in 1942, and there had been a 10 percent
production decline during 1942. Stocks on hand and
unfilled orders reflected a serious fall in production.[23]
According to a survey of some three hundred producers
representing approximately 30 percent of southern pine

production in the middle of 1943, the leading difficulties were manpower shortages, of which 93 percent complained; inability to secure timber, which bothered 80 percent; problems connected with the government's regulations on prices and wages, cited by 53 percent; and troubles with priorities, which bothered 49 percent. A sizeable number of producers believed their difficulties were increasing.[24]

The industry made a poor production record despite a Southern Pine War Committee drive for maximum production during 1943. The committee sponsored meetings to discuss production problems throughout the southern pine district; they were attended by government representatives and some twelve hundred manufacturers.[25] The committee also sent out field men to consult with both manufacturers and representatives of government agencies in an effort to remove production impediments. These men were in effect roving troubleshooters.[26]

By April, 1943, the problems of the lumber industry had attracted national attention. In April the small business committee of the House of Representatives began an investigation of the industry. According to a Forest Service estimate, that spring some nine thousand of the nation's thirty-one thousand sawmills were closed because of various wartime problems, and the committee was inundated with complaints about the lumber situation and particularly the small mills. The committee appointed a subcommittee which held a hearing in Washington at which the department chiefs of various federal agencies charged with lumber matters and H. C. Berckes, secretary of the Southern Pine War Committee, testified.[27] Berckes stated that he believed that about a thousand small southern pine mills were out of production, and he emphasized the lack of coordination between government agencies concerned with lumber and timber problems. He also stressed the industry's chronic labor shortage.[28]

Because of complaints by Berckes and other witnesses, the House small business committee recommended the creation of an interagency committee to coordinate the efforts of federal agencies dealing with the lumber program As a result of the efforts of the committee and Donald M. Nelson, chairman of the War Production Board, the log and lumber policy committee was created. Its members included the director of the Lumber and Lumber Products Division of the War Production Board; the price executive of the lumber branch of the Office of Price

Administration; a public member of the National War Labor
Board; the director of the bureau of placement of the War
Manpower Commission; the chief of the materials and equip-
ment branch, Office of the Chief of Engineers, Engineers
Corps, War Department; and an assistant chief of the
Forest Service, U. S. Department of Agriculture.[29]

The House small business committee hearing elicited
from federal officials the first public admission that
there was a shortage of lumber for national defense. The
committee's chief investigator also mentioned simmering
disputes within the industry between factions inside and
outside the associations.[30] These two matters began to
hit the newspapers in late summer. In his "Washington
Merry-Go Round" column, Drew Pearson alleged that there
was dissension within the ranks of government agencies and
reported that "serious charges have been made that big
lumber dealers are throttling smaller mills, and that Gen.
Eugene Reybold, chief of army engineers, has played into
the big lumber dealers' hands." Pearson declared that
Reybold had "issued orders that Army purchases must come
only from the lumber associations, which comprise the big
mills. . . ." He singled out the Southern Pine Association for special criticism: "In the South, for instance,
about 750 mills belong to the Southern Pine Association,
one of the most powerful lumber associations, while 15,000
small Southern mills do not belong. The Southern Pine
Association was prosecuted by the Justice Department for
monopolistic practices and was forced to sign a consent
decree. Nevertheless, Army engineers have ruled that Army
lumber purchased in the South must come from the Southern
Pine Association, thus leaving 15,000 smaller mills out
in the cold."[31]

Pearson's articles prompted the small business committee to schedule another hearing to investigate the
charges, and the SPA was advised that it could send a
representative to defend itself.[32] The hearing was held
on October 11 and 12 before Congressmen Estes Kefauver of
Tennessee and J. W. Robinson of Utah and the committee's
chief investigator. The sessions were concerned not only
with the charges that the Corps of Engineers was limiting
its purchases to members of recognized lumber associations
and ignoring smaller producers, but also with complaints
that former Weyerhaeuser employee J. Philip Boyd, as
director of the Lumber and Lumber Products Division of the
War Production Board, was favoring his old company and
that the southern lumber industry was lagging behind other

sections in meeting its defense obligations. They covered, besides, the policies and procedures of the Office of Price Administration and the chronic manpower problem, particularly in the southern lumber industry. Among the many witnesses who testified were H. C. Berckes and Albert S. Boisfontaine of the southern pine industry.[33] Berckes's testimony consisted primarily of a rehash of the industry's problems and accomplishments and an account of the services performed by the SPWC for all producers, large and small. At Berckes's suggestion, the committee agreed to hold hearings and conferences in the South to examine the problems of the southern lumber industry.

In anticipation of the committee's visit, critics of the SPA and its related organizations began to voice their complaints. One of the most vocal was Secretary W. W. Findley of the West Side Lumber Association, an organization of Arkansas lumber producers. As early as June, 1943, Findley charged in a letter to Chairman Wright Patman of the House select committee on small business that "the Southern Pine War Committee and the Southern Pine Association have very little standing with sixty percent of the lumber producing operators of the United States." "We have found in the past twenty years of dealing with the Lumber Industry of Arkansas . . . that the Southern Pine Association has been a detriment to the sixty percent of the producing area," said Findley. The Arkansan concluded by once more reminding Patman "that the Southern Pine Association, the Southern Pine War Committee, Mr. C. C. Shepherd [sic] and Mr. Berckes do not represent the majority of the Lumber Industries as they have specifically stated in testimony before your committee."[34]

On November 8, Findley reiterated to the Patman committee his allegation that the SPA and SPID did not represent the industry, and he included a lengthy collection of criticisms of the SPIB's structure and activities. "If at the proposed hearing of this committee in New Orleans, men are to be called on to testify as to the situation in all its phases that have heretofore been called upon by the committee and whose efforts so far have not borne any fruit as regards increased production or anything else favorable to the war effort," concluded Findley, "the hearing in New Orleans will be of no benefit in securing increased production of lumber and naturally we feel that the expense attendant upon a trip to New Orleans, the loss of time away from producing properties where the management is essential and most essential at the present time, will be a waste of effort."[35]

The hearings brought the entire House committee on small business, rather than simply the subcommittee on lumber matters which had previously been handling these problems, to the Crescent City. The log and lumber policy committee also held meetings, as did the Southern Pine War Committee, and all southern pine producers were invited to testify. Some seven hundred members of the industry came to New Orleans, and about thirty appeared before the committee. The lumbermen blamed much of the industry's difficulties on government policies and cited the usual long list of production impediments.[36]

W. W. Findley did not repeat his charges of November 8 during his testimony, and anyway the SPA had answered them in a lengthy letter to Wright Patman before the hearings began.[37] The most significant development stemming from the hearings was an announcement by J. Philip Boyd, director of the Lumber and Lumber Products Division of the War Production Board, that the southern pine industry would be placed under a limitation order similar to that under which the western industry was already operating. The purpose of the order was to ensure that lumber production would be channeled into the hands of the government and military. This announcement represented the WPB's response to a challenge to its authority from Colonel Fred G. Sherrill of the Central Procuring Agency, who had sent a telegram to southern lumbermen demanding an extra 25 percent of their production for his agency. The colonel's action sparked the WPB into action and stimulated southern pine production momentarily. It also placated western producers who believed the southern pine industry was not carrying its portion of the war burden.[38] Nevertheless, the southern pine industry's performance during 1943 was disappointing.

The situation at the end of 1943 was summarized by the House committee on small business in an interim report to Congress on January 13, 1944. According to the committee, the southern pine industry's production fell from approximately 11,750,000,000 board feet in 1942 to no more than 9,500,000,000 feet in 1943, a decline of approximately 30 percent compared with a drop of only about 8 percent in the Pacific Northwest. The committee reported that, as of December 31, 1943, the Corps of Engineers needed more than a quarter of a billion feet of southern pine which it had been unable to locate and acquire. It reiterated the list of impediments to lumber production, including the manpower shortage, low wage scales, low price ceilings, equipment shortages, excessive freight rates, complexity or confusion of some federal regulations, lack of harmony within the industry, and the fear of postwar competition from substitute products. It pointed out that because of less mechanization it took more man-hours to produce lumber in the South than in the West, thus making the labor situation more critical. The committee concluded that "the industry as a whole should be commended for its ability to produce as much lumber as it has produced in 1943 in the face of this admitted manpower shortage and other obstacles. . . ."[39]

Although the industry had a poor record, the SPA had worked hard to increase production. One of its major endeavors was in assisting the War Department to organize and conduct a six-week "Army Salute to Wood Caravan," which was designed to boost morale among lumber workers. The caravan consisted of 375 officers and men with nearly one hundred pieces of motorized military equipment. It traveled more than four thousand miles through the South and presented programs at forty locations before an estimated combined audience of 191,500 people. It also conducted rallies in thirty-two lumber plants before over twelve thousand sawmill workers.[40]

The last full year of World War II, 1944, saw the Southern Pine Association and its industry continuing to struggle with the problems of wartime production. Lumber of all types was by this time a critical material. It was in fact more critical than steel, and "reversing the previous pattern, steel was now used instead of wood in Army cars, truck bodies, railroad cars, and furniture! Both logging and lumber went on the Production Urgency List."[41] The urgency of the situation was compounded by the imminence of the invasion of France and the concomitant need for crating and boxing lumber to package munitions and supplies.[42] As J. Philip Boyd saw the situation, "The war requirements are mounting steadily and at this moment the amount of Southern Pine lumber going to the war is not sufficient to maintain war activities."[43]

The government's solution to these problems came on March 22, 1944, with the issuance of Order L-335 which established comprehensive lumber controls to be effective during the third quarter of 1944. The order provided the coordination in purchasing and distribution for civilian

agencies which had been effected by the services since the
middle of 1942.[44] Many lumbermen found the order, which
defined priorities for supplying lumber to various
agencies, confusing. Therefore, Boyd attempted to make
the order clear and acceptable through circulars and a
series of regional meetings.[45] When he appeared before
the southern pine manufacturers in the latter part of the
year, Boyd descrrbed Order L-335, "which some of you have
cussed," as "a decided success."[46] Boyd said that
"within thirty days after the 1st of August . . . [it] had
pretty well straightened out the procurement of not only
the war agencies themselves, but all of the supporting
activities of the war." The order, he declared, had produced a "leveling out of responsibility among all producers as to the war needs themselves," and war requirements
were "being spread over this entire lumber industry, east,
west, north, and south, and not on a few people who have
been bearing the burden for the past three years."[47]

Nevertheless, the situation in the southern pine
industry was not good. Production again took a decided
drop, with the total for the year amounting to only
8,007,000,000 board feet, a decline of nearly two billion
feet from the previous year.[48] Returns from a Southern
Pine War Committee questionnaire in January, 1945, showed
that the chronic problems of producers remained. Of those
replying, 97 percent reported manpower difficulties, 77.8
percent had equipment problems, 37.3 percent complained of
government controls, 33 percent were experiencing difficulties in obtaining timber, and 11.1 percent had been
hampered by weather conditions.[49]

Despite its unimpressive performance, the Southern
Pine Association was honored on August 31, 1944, when
Secretary of Commerce Jesse Jones, chairman of the jury of
awards of the American Trade Association Executives,
announced that the SPA had won the 1943-44 national cham-
pionship among large national trade associations for its
cooperative services to businessmen and its comprehensive
efforts in the mobilization and war production programs.
In the words of the committee, "The award was granted
because of the highly successful mobilization program of
some 3,000 lumber producers and mill owners in 10 southern
states, from Virginia to Texas, by this association."[50]

The final year of World War II found the southern pine
industry continuing to struggle with the problems which
had plagued wartime production efforts and marshaling its
forces for the period of postwar adjustment. Even with

victory in Europe imminent in the late spring of 1945,
tight government controls were maintained and War
Production Board orders affecting lumber were retained.
The army, however, sent no more lumber to Europe after
April, and by the end of June controls were relaxed. The
demand for military lumber continued to decline during the
summer, and finally in mid-August the War Production Board
revised lumber control Order L-335 to permit lumber to be
sold virtually without restrictions. The order was
finally annulled on September 30, and on October 15 the
government removed all limits on new construction, leaving
lumbermen subject to no controls other than the OPA price
regulations.[51] The production trend for 1945 continued
downward, with a decline of 8 percent from 1944. During
the same period, there was a drop of about 7 percent in
the available stockpile of southern pine. These figures
boded ill for the prospect of supplying the pent-up lumber
demand that the war's end could bring.[52]

The end of World War II thus found the Southern Pine
Association and its industry in a somewhat contradictory
position. They had been praised on a number of occasions
for contributions to the defense effort, but had also come
under heavy criticism and had, in fact, not produced lumber in the quantity desired. The association had received
recognition and enhanced its stature in the industry
through its role as the industry's spokesman in dealing
with the government, but it also became the focal point
for both industry and public dissatisfaction with lumber
conditions. Emerging from World War II with a mixed
record, the Southern Pine Association and its industry
faced stiff challenges in the postwar period. The
approaching decade promised to be a period of great change
which would allow no respite to reflect on the glories or
failures of the past.

NOTES TO CHAPTER 10

1. Ralph W. Hidy, Frank Ernest Hill, and Allan Nevins,
Timber and Men: The Weyerhaeuser Story (New York:
Macmillan, 1963), p. 451.

2. Ibid., p. 451-52. There is a detailed discussion of
mobilization planning, the activities of the Nye Committee, and the origins of the "military-industrial complex"

The New South and the "New Competition"

in Paul A. C. Koistinen, "The 'Industrial-Military Complex' in Historical Perspective: The Interwar Years," _Journal of American History_, LVI (Mar., 1970), 823-39. Also see Robert Sobel, _The Age of Giant Corporations: A Microeconomic History of American Business, 1914-1970_ (Westport, Conn.: Greenwood, 1972), pp. 153-77.

3. Bruce Catton, _The War Lords of Washington_ (New York: Harcourt, Brace, 1948), pp. 101-103; Hidy, Hill, and Nevins, _Timber and Men_, p. 452; Broadus Mitchell, _Depression Decade: From New Era through New Deal, 1929-1941_ (New York: Holt, Rinehart and Winston, 1947), p. 373. For a brief summary of the administrative structure of American mobilization see Mitchell, _Depression Decade_, pp. 372-74.

4. H. C. Berckes to P. A. Bloomer, Sept. 12, 1940, Southern Pine Association Records, Box 75a (Louisiana State University Archives, Baton Rouge, La.). Collection hereafter cited as SPA Records.

5. Hidy, Hill, and Nevins, _Timber and Men_, p. 452.

6. _Times-Picayune_ (New Orleans), Sept. 21, 1940.

7. Southern Pine Association Press Release, Sept. 20, 1940, SPA Records, Box 75a; Southern Pine Emergency Defense Committee to All Southern Pine Manufacturers, Sept. 23, 1940, SPA Records, Box 87b; "Minutes of a Meeting of the Southern Pine Emergency Defense Committee . . . September 20, 1940," SPA Records, Box 75a; "Southern Pine Industry Meeting Called by Southern Pine Association . . . September 20, 1940," SPA Records, Box 75a; pp. 64, 66.

8. "Remarks of Assistant Secretary," in "Southern Pine Emergency Defense Committee, Proceedings of Industry-Wide Meeting . . . March 14, 1941," SPA Records, Box 9a, p. 32.

9. John M. Collier, _The First Fifty Years of the Southern Pine Association, 1915-1965_ (New Orleans: Southern Pine Association, 1965), p. 155; Hidy, Hill, and Nevins, _Timber and Men_, p. 455.

10. Arthur Temple, "A Defense Program for Southern Pine," pamphlet in SPA Records, Box 83a. This pamphlet is a printed version of a speech delivered by Temple at the July 17, 1941, meeting of the SPA in New Orleans. Hidy,

Hill, and Nevins, Timber and Men, pp. 454-55; "Proceedings of 26th Annual Meeting Southern Pine Association, March 13-14, 1941, and the Industry-Wide Meeting of Southern Pine Emergency Defense Committee, March 14, 1941," SPA Records, Box 73b, pp. 17-18, 21.

11. "Statement of M. L. Fleishel, Chairman Lumber and Timber Products Defense Committee, Willard Hotel, January 23, 1941," SPA Records, Box 76a; "Stenographic Record of Meeting," SPA Records, Box 76a; "Proceedings of 26th Annual Meeting Southern Pine Association, March 13-14, 1941, and Industry-Wide Meeting of Southern Pine Emergency Defense Committee, March 14, 1941," SPA Records, Box 73b, pp. 23-24. The strong opinions and sharp recollections of this encounter with Henderson as recalled by the SPA's former secretary-manager are contained in Herbert C. Berckes, "The Pitch in Pine: A Story of the Traditions, Policies and Activities of the Southern Pine Industry and the Men Responsible for Them" (unpublished manuscript in possession of the author), pp. 185-87.

12. Mitchell, Depression Decade, pp. 382-83; "Summary of Letters and Wires Received Pertaining to Price Schedule No. 19," SPA Records, Box 75a.

13. "Transcript of Meeting of the Southern Pine Emergency Defense Committee . . . August 30, 1941," SPA Records, Box 68a; Southern Pine Association Press Releases, September 1, 1941, and August 30, 1941, SPA Records, Box 75a.

14. "Proceedings of 26th Annual Meeting Southern Pine Association, March 13-14, 1941, and Industry-Wide Meeting of Southern Pine Emergency Defense Committee, March 14, 1941," SPA Records, Box 73b, 33.

15. Collier, The First Fifty Years, p. 119.

16. "Minutes of a Meeting of the Southern Pine Emergency Defense Committee . . . March 27, 1949," SPA Records, Box 75a.

17. H. C. Berckes to C. C. Sheppard, Sept. 2, 1942, SPA Records, Box 75b; "Minutes of a Meeting of the Southern Pine War Committee . . . September 29, 1942," SPA Records, Box 75a.

18. "Southern Pine At War," SPA Records, Box 81a, pp. 4-5.

19. Hidy, Hill, and Nevins, Timber and Men, pp. 458-59; Southern Pine War Committee, "War Bulletin," XXXII (May 13, 1942) and XXXIII (May 28, 1942), SPA Records, Box 75a.

20. Hidy, Hill, and Nevins, Timber and Men, p. 459; interview with H. C. Berckes, Feb. 10, 1968.

21. Hidy, Hill and Nevins, Timber and Men, p. 460; interview with H. C. Berckes, Feb. 10, 1968.

22. "Southern Pine Emergency Defense Committee . . . January 9, 1942 . . .," typewritten transcript, SPA Records, Box 68a; "Southern Pine and Its Production, Statement by H. C. Berckes, Secretary, Southern Pine War Committee before Special Senate Committee to Investigate the National Defense Program, Hon. Harry S. Truman, Chairman, Washington, D.C., November 24, 1942," SPA Records, Box 90a, pp. 4-5.

23. "Statement Filed by Southern Pine Industry Committee on Behalf of Southern Pine Industry before Industry Committee No. 64 for Logging, Lumber and Timber and Related Products . . . August 30, 1943," SPA Records, Box 90a, pp. 4.7.

24. Ibid., p. 28.

25. "Statement by C. C. Sheppard, Chairman, Southern Pine War Committee, Wednesday, April 14, 1943," SPA Records, Box 75b.

26. "Field-Work," typewritten report, SPA Records, Box 75b.

27. "The Problems of the Lumber Industry in 1943, First Interim Report from The Committee on Small Business, House of Representataives, Pursuant to H. Res. 18, a Resolution Creating a Select Committee on Small Business of the House of Representatives and Defining Its Powers and Duties" (Washington, D.C.: Government Printing Office, 1943), pp. 1-2, committee print in SPA Records, Box 88a.

28. "Statement of H. C. Berckes, Secretary and Manager of the Southern Pine Association, and Also Secretary of the Southern Pine War Committee," in "Hearings before the Select Committee to Conduct a Study and Investigation of the National Defense Program in Its Relation to Small Business in the United States, House of Representatives, Seventy-Eighth Congress, First Session on H. Res. 18, a Resolution Authorizing an Investigation of the National Defense Program in its Relation to Small Business, May 21, 1943, Part 12" (Washington, D.C.: Government Printing Office, 1943), pp. 755-67, unrevised copy in SPA Records, Box 121a.

29. "Problems Of The Lumber Industry In 1943," p. 2.

30. Ibid., pp. 5, 14.

31. Drew Pearson, "Washington Merry-Go-Round," _Times Picayune_ (New Orleans), Aug. 15, 1943.

32. Dan W. Eastwood to Oliver O. Bright, Sept. 13, 1943, SPA Records, Box 88a.

33. "Hearings before The Select Committee to Conduct a Study and Investigation of the National Defense Program in Its Relation to Small Business in the United States, House of Representatives, Seventy-Eighth Congress, First Session on H. Res. 18, a Resolution Authorizing an Investigation of the National Defense Program in its Relation to Small Business, October 11 and 12, 1943, Part 22" (Washington, D.C.: Government Printing Office, 1943), unrevised copy in SPA Records, Box 88a.

34. W. W. Findley to Wright Patman, June 25, 1943, SPA Records, Box 88b.

35. W. W. Findley to Wright Patman, Nov. 8, 1943, SPA Records, Box 88b.

36. Southern Pine War Committee Press Release, November 30, 1943, SPA Records, Box 88b.

37. H. C. Berckes to Wright Patman, Nov. 29, 1943, SPA Records, Box 88b.

38. "Hearings before the Select Committee to Conduct a Study and Investigation of the National Defense Program in Its Relation to Small Business in the United States, House of Representatives, Seventy-Eighth Congress, First Session on H. Res. 18, a Resolution Authorizing an Investigation of the National Defense Program in Its Relation to Small Business, November 29 and 30, 1943, Part 30" (Washington, D.C.: Government Printing Office, 1943), pp. 2222-25, unrevised copy in SPA Records, Box 88a; Floyd B. Quigg, "Crossroads Listening Post," Chicago Journal of Commerce, Dec. 14, 1943.

39. U. S. Congress, House, Committee on Small Business, Current Lumber Industry Problems. Part I: "The National Lumber Situation as of January 1, 1944." Part II: "The Problems of the Southern Pine Industry as of January 1, 1944," 78th Congress., 2nd Sess., Rept. 987, pp. 5-9.

40. "Southern Pine at War," SPA Records, Box 81a, pp. 12-13; Collier, First Fifty Years, pp. 122-23, 125.

41. Hidy, Hill, and Nevins, Timber and Men, p. 465.

42. Southern Pine War Committee to Members of the Southern Pine Industry, Mar. 10, 1944, SPA Records, Box 75a.

43. J. Philip Boyd to Southern Pine Producers and Distributors, Mar. 6, 1944, SPA Records, Box 75a.

44. Hidy, Hill, and Nevins, Timber and Men, p. 465.

45. Southern Pine War Committee to Members of the Southern Pine Industry, July 1, 1944, Southern Pine War Committee to Members of the Southern Pine Industry, July 10, 1944, and J. Philip Boyd to the Lumber Industry, July 3, 1944, all in SPA Records, Box 75a.

46. "Proceedings of Meeting of the Southern Pine War Committee . . . October 26, 1944," SPA Records, Box 68a, p. 6.

47. Ibid., pp. 8, 10-11.

48. "Southern Pine Production And Stocks--Industry Totals," SPA Records, Box 12b.

49. "Southern Pine War Committee, New Orleans, Louisiana, Report on Operating Conditions in Southern Pine Industry, Analysis of Questionnaire Released by Southern Pine War Committee, January 29, 1945 . . .," mimeographed report, SPA Records, Box 76a, pp. 1, 2, 9.

50. Southern Pine Association Press Release, Aug. 31, 1944, SPA Records, Box 49a. The details of the award contest and the Southern Pine Association's presentation are included in "Southern Pine At War," SPA Records, Box 81a.

51. Hidy, Hill, and Nevins, Timber and Men, pp. 465-66.

52. "Southern Pine Production And Stocks--Industry Totals," SPA Records, Box 12b.

11

The End of an Era

During the 1950s the southern pine industry and the SPA continued to deal with their old perennial problems. They also encountered various kinds of changes which were to transform both the association and the industry before the decade was past its mid-point. In the more traditional areas, the industry continued to grapple with the problems of price ceilings and production controls, which were legacies of the World War II experience. Before these problems were resolved, the lumbermen and the SPA found themselves involved in another national defense mobilization effort, this time for the Korean War.

In the immediate postwar period, the continuation of ceilings on lumber prices was a matter of great concern in the industry. There was a tremendous demand for new housing, but the Truman administration, worried about inflation, was reluctant to remove price controls on lumber.[1] On August 18, 1945, President Truman issued an executive order providing that the Price Administrator could adjust price controls in order to eliminate inequities which would interfere with the transition to a peacetime economy. An industry advisory committee, composed of manufacturers, wholesalers, and commission men, and created by the SPA, had recommended in May, 1945, that southern pine price ceilings be adjusted upward, but the suggestion had been turned down by the Office of Price Administration.[2]

The new housing that was being constructed was very unsatisfactory, and the entire industry was being blamed. According to Eric Goldman, "Housing units kept going up . . . but rarely according to schedule and never enough.

369

The New South and the "New Competition"

Many new dwellings promptly started falling apart. They had been thrown together with green lumber, ersatz plumbing, slapdash carpentry, and a general air of who-cares."[3] The SPA was determined to shift the onus for insufficient and poorly manufactured lumber to the Office of Price Administration. In January, 1946, a special committee of manufacturers presented a statement to the Stabilization Administrator of the Office of War Mobilization and Reconversion, chronicling the industry's production and pricing problems, and blamed them on the OPA. The committee characterized recent OPA price adjustments in certain categories as inadequate and promised that "southern lumber operators can and will substantially increase production if given a price increase to justify their efforts and risks." It blamed the OPA's restrictions for the channeling of poorly manufactured and over-priced lumber into the black market.[4]

Finally in March, 1946, the OPA modified its ceilings on lumber prices, but its action failed to halt the booming black market. One Alabama manufacturer, in a typical complaint to the Southern Pine Association, reported "small mills . . . are utterly disregarding all OPA regulations and are selling lumber higher than our dress price even though the lumber is rough and green . . . OPA is simply making no effort in this territory to enforce the regulations. . . ."[5] At the SPA's annual meeting in May, the president of the National Retail Lumber Dealers' Association declared that black market operations were rampant, with individual truckers buying from mills for supposed intrastate delivery within a twenty-five mile radius and then driving the lumber as much as a thousand miles away and selling it at 25 to 100 percent above ceiling prices.[6] The chairman of the southern pine industry's Joint Emergency Committee charged that "OPA has wrecked our industry to the extent that there is only one answer—wipe the office of price administration off the books."[7]

A directive issued by Judge J. C. Collet in February, 1946, granting the industry a price increase was given credit for a rise in southern pine production, but the OPA's adjustments were characterized by the Southern Pine Industry Committee as "too little and too late." A press release made by the SPIC in September, 1946, accused the Office of Price Administration, National Housing Administration, and other government agencies of "placing false and 'foreign' philosophy [sic] of economics before

370

'American' needs," and said that "every experience of the
Southern Pine Industry with government agencies before,
during, and since the war has demonstrated that expediency,
politics, and promotion of 'foreign' ideals have had a
throttling effect upon the production of Southern Pine."[8]
Propaganda of this sort was accompanied by reprints of
newspaper and magazine editorials critical of the OPA and
other government agencies, which were widely distributed
by the SPIC.[9] When finally, in November, 1946, the Office
of Price Administration removed all price controls, the
price of lumber rose to the heights previously commanded
on the black market, and the SPIC turned its attention to
other matters.[10]

While deeply involved in domestic economic and
political matters, the SPA was also affected by developments in American foreign affairs. The Korean War, which
began in June, 1950, recreated the problems of organizing
the economy to meet both civilian and military needs. As
was true during both world wars, the southern pine
industry, the SPA, and the industry's committees were in
the forefront of the mobilization effort.

Actually, a defense program had been in operation
prior to 1950. The Southern Pine Association and the
Southern Pine Inspection Bureau had been working with the
office of the United States Corps of Engineers in St.
Louis on problems related to the procurement of lumber and
allied products by all of the armed forces. By the time
of the SPA's annual meeting in April, 1950, plans had been
made for mobilization of the industry in the event of
national emergency or war. Immediately after the meeting,
the SPIC appointed several technical committees to facilitate the defense effort. The most important of these were
a technical committee on lumber procurement, a timber
supply technical committee, and a price controls
committee.[11]

Shortly after the outbreak of war, Congress passed
the Defense Production Act, which authorized the freezing
of prices and stabilizing of wages, but, due to inadequate
enforcement mechanisms, it was not until early 1951 that
mandatory ceilings were imposed and the Office of Price
Stabilization established. However, the SPIC and its
technical committees began to swing into action shortly
after the North Korean invasion.[12] The committee on
lumber procurement maintained daily contact with the Corps
of Engineers in St. Louis and acted as a liaison between
the industry and military. It was responsible for the

preparation and dissemination of printed material outlining the government's lumber requirements and regulations.[13] The timber supply technical committee was authorized to make a survey of forest reserves, public and private, in the southern pine states and of the productive facilities of the southern pine industry. On April 16, 1951, it published a reasonably comprehensive statistical overview of the industry's productive facilities which could serve as a guide for both the industry and government.[14] The price controls committee considered the problems of stumpage prices and manufacturing costs in order to "aid in the establishment of equitable ceilings for Southern pine," but it was eventually disbanded because of the creation of an industry advisory committee by the OPA. The SPIC and its various specialized bodies also handled the normal range of wartime problems--dealing with the railroads and their regulatory agencies, publishing and interpreting the rapidly changing wage and salary stabilization regulations, and offering assistance to the industry on problems stemming from priorities on machinery and equipment.[15] Although the industry was ready and willing to undertake a mobilization and defense effort similar in organization and intensity to that of World War II, the military conflict in Korea was tailing off by the end of July, 1951, and despite inflation and the momentary dislocations spurred by the war, "the production and priorities problems of a full scale war were never seriously encountered."[16]

At the very time the SPA was mobilizing the defense effort, events within the industry were beginning to come to a head that would mark the end of one era and the beginning of another. Since the formation of the association in 1914, the industry had experienced a gradual evolution in nature and leadership. During the SPA's early days, it had been dominated by large producers and strong pioneering individuals. These men had handpicked their association leaders and supported them as long as they stayed within certain broadly defined lines. As the pioneers began to fade from the scene, they were replaced by a new type of men, the managers. They were corporate employees who, although they ran their operations from the mill offices, were thoroughly familiar with the industry from standing timber to finished lumber and sales. These men had often grown up in the industry and in some cases eventually became corporate officers or even partial owners of the firms whose operations they managed.

The managers began to come into prominence in the industry during the 1920s, sharing the spotlight with the pioneers until the 1930s, when they truly came into their own. Within the SPA itself somewhat the same change took place. John E. Rhodes, who had been handpicked by John Henry Kirby and other industry giants, died during the early 1920s and was replaced by H. C. Berckes, who moved into a position of leadership as a contemporary of the new managers. Berckes, however, had been with the association since the beginning and enjoyed the friendship and confidence of the older leaders as well. As secretary-manager, consequently, he acted in the knowledge that although he was just an employee, he could go to both the old pioneers and the new managers as an intimate and receive authorizations to act on decisions on important matters without delay. More important, knowing these men's views and having their confidence, he could act somewhat independently with the assurance that they would generally support him.

With the changes in leadership, the industry itself was changing. By the 1920s many of the large mills were cutting out and either ceasing operations altogether or moving their facilities to the West Coast. There were dire predictions that the industry and with it the association were dying. However, renewed hope came with the realization of the tremendous regenerative powers of the southern forests. About the same time, hundreds of small "peckerwood" mills began operations, cutting patches of southern pine in supposedly deforested areas the big mills had cut through. Although the Southern Pine Association acted to enlist many of these small producers as subscribers, it was not sufficiently successful to be able to presume to speak for the vast majority of producers in the industry. Within the SPA, then, to the old divisions between east and west, and longleaf and shortleaf producers, was joined that of large producers against small.

The changing nature of the industry required that the SPA secretary-manager exhibit great sensitivity to the currents and needs of subscribers and that he have the ability to mold its disparate elements together into a coherent whole. For nearly thirty years, H. C. Berckes exhibited those qualities and became the stabilizing force around which the SPA was maintained. Berckes came to be the personification of the Southern Pine Association. Despite occasional crises and personal resentments, to a remarkable degree Berckes kept the association intact from the 1920s until the end of World War II.

However, in the postwar period the industry and the SPA underwent significant changes in organization and personnel.[17] Many important firms and SPA subscribers were absorbed by, and became mere divisions of, larger diversified corporations. New managers frequently came with these mergers, and these men were frequently critical of practices and policies in both the industry and the association. Furthermore, they often had difficulty justifying association membership and activities to their superiors, and they had neither the power nor the inclination to give the SPA staff the support or quick decisions it had once so routinely relied upon. During this period, new leaders emerged even in many of the firms which remained independent. They not infrequently were the sons of the older pioneers and managers.

Berckes was, of course, affected by these changes although he claimed not to be fundamentally opposed to the emergence of new men within the industry or the association. Within the association he had prided himself upon training a capable corps of young men who would someday succeed him, just as he had succeeded John E. Rhodes. In fact, recognizing the changing nature of the industry, in 1950 Berckes was involved in the creation of a committee on study and planning which undertook a thorough survey of the SPA's background and development with the idea of modernizing and revamping it wherever necessary. In 1952 he helped organize a young men's conference in an effort to bring the new generation into a more meaningful role in the association. These efforts, although well intentioned, were largely negated by problems growing out of the Korean War and battles on the legislative and competitive fronts which absorbed much of the industry's attention, and, coincidentally, added to the growing split in the industry. The fact was that, despite his efforts, Berckes was not able to work effectively with the industry's new leaders. Not only did he disagree with them over policy matters, but they resented the independent and somewhat autocratic manner in which Berckes ran the association. Possibly some of the younger figures were beginning to find the secretary-manager's arch conservatism too strong for even the southern pine industry.

Increasingly in the 1950s one theme seemed to run through the publications and activities of the Southern Pine Industry Committee, a theme which stressed the need

for Americans to return to an older way of life, or as
H. C. Berckes saw it, to the principles on which the
United States had been founded and which had enabled it to
grow and prosper. With years of service behind him, the
secretary became bolder and more willing to explain his
personal views. In January, 1950, Berckes advised his
associates within and outside the industry to become
involved and warned that "our efforts will advance us
little if we do not get into the political battle in 1950
and '52."[18]

In 1950, the SPIC distributed an article published by
Berckes in a trade journal that revealed the direction in
which the Southern Pine Association leader was turning.
Entitled "Fight Fire with Fire," the piece warned that
"the great danger facing the American people today comes
from within. It is the trend toward Socialism." "For
twenty years," Berckes warned, "socialists, collectivists,
advocates of the welfare state, and other 'do-gooders'
have been propagandizing the American people and conditioning them to the acceptance of their theories. They
have made many converts." Berckes singled out "crack-
brained economists," "opportunists," and "demagogues
looking for power" as leaders of the movement, and
lamented the fact that businessmen and industrialists had
not taken the time or interest to fight them. He particularly urged that businessmen must "overcome our squeamish
attitude toward politics" and that "every business man
should contribute to the cause of sane government by supporting conservative candidates and by active propaganda
work for American business." "Learn the arguments against
socialized business," he counseled, "and discuss with
individuals the fallacy of Socialism. Make speeches, talk
over the radio, and send out persuasive anti-socialistic
literature."[19]

Although this philosophy, or at least open advocacy of
it, was not entirely accepted in the industry, it found
much powerful support. In a 1950 speech before the SPA's
annual meeting, for example, SPIC Chairman R. M. Eagle
noted that while his committee's "activities have been
restrained because the industry as a whole was not prepared to go the full distance some of its leaders thought
it should go . . . the Committee has been unwilling to
abandon the fight for old-fashioned ideals because of the
prediction in some quarters in the industry that the older
order of government and society in America had
disappeared." Eagle then went on to proclaim, "We are

battling all of these radically unsound and politically-
inspired, vote-getting proposals whether they take the
form of an FEPC, Social Security, Labor Relations Act,
forestry regulation, subsidized housing, Wage-Hour
measure, an extravagant budget, socialized medicine or
whatever must be fought."[20]

Berckes's political and economic views led him to
accept the philosophy of states rights and support the
Dixiecrats in the 1948 presidential campaign. Nominally,
Berckes was a lifelong Republican, but he was in general
political agreement with the SPA's dominantly Democratic
subscribers, at least during the greater part of his
employment by the association. As a Republican, the
secretary-manager enjoyed access to political circles not
open to many of his subscribers, thereby enhancing the
Southern Pine Industry Committee's lobbying efforts.[21]

Differences between Berckes and the lumber companies'
managers became increasingly apparent in the 1950s. The
first issue over which they divided had to do with the
inclusion of requirements for dry lumber in building
codes. Representing the West Coast lumbermen's interests,
the National Lumber Manufacturers' Association opposed
such a requirement. It also called upon the industry to
give greater support to a national advertising campaign.
Some of the new industry leaders supported both of these
positions while Berckes, believing they were detrimental
to the best interests of the SPA, opposed them. Berckes
and the SPIC, as has been related, had since the passage
of the original wages and hours legislation in 1938 fought
all efforts to raise the minimum wage levels. By the
1950s, however, some industry leaders voiced opposition
to the often blunt and always vigorous manner in which
Berckes conducted this fight; a number, in fact, stated
that the fight should be stopped entirely, thus under-
cutting Berckes's position in his own industry. In addition, there was a growing feeling in some quarters that
the SPA's activities had become too large and covered too
much territory. By cutting expenses and eliminating some
of the association's functions, it was argued, more money
could be channeled into advertising and trade promotion.

All of these criticisms and policy disagreements led
several large producers in the spring of 1953 to apply
pressure to SPA President J. R. Bemis to overhaul the
association's structure and change its emphasis. Bemis
appointed a new committee on study and planning, which
came up with recommendations for reorganization. The
SPA's board then created a special seven-man committee to

carry out those recommendations. Berckes and his staff were almost entirely excluded from these activities.

The changes which the SPA's seven-man committee ordered Berckes to implement were of major importance: they included the complete elimination of the forestry, labor information, and mechanical efficiency departments; the drastic curtailment of the activities of the traffic and the economics and statistics departments; and a major reduction in the SPA's contribution to the SPIC and the closing of the Washington, D.C., office. These changes required a drastic reduction in the association's office facilities and staff. The latter was cut from some forty employees to about twenty, and the savings of some $12,000 monthly were earmarked for advertising and trade promotion.

These changes were too much for Berckes to accept. In the spring of 1954, tired, ill, saddened, he returned one day to New Orleans from a meeting in Jacksonville, Florida. According to Berckes's account, with which, as noted, some industry figures disagree, "I walked in one day, the day I came in, the 15th of March, called my secretary in, dictated a wire to 'em, and walked out. I went fishin', literally and figuratively. That was the end of it." The telegrams went out to members of the board, who expressed varying degrees of shock and dismay and in some cases tried to reverse the decision, but nevertheless approved the resignation at their meeting on April 6, 1954. Berckes's departure marked the final step in the reorganization of the Southern Pine Association.[22]

An era had ended. For Berckes. For the southern pine industry. For the SPA. The industry was changing with the advent of new ownership patterns, leaders, and products. Plywood. Pulp and paper. Pressboard. The association would reflect this change and eventually become the Southern Forest Products Association. But the future was built upon the foundations of the past. Its successes, its failures, its lessons.

In reviewing this earlier era several things seem clear. The southern pine industry had provided a classic example of the New South experience in its origins, ownership patterns, and attitudes toward government, labor, and society. The advent of trade associations in the industry demonstrates a remarkable struggle between the classic concept of pure competition and the attraction of the "new competition" approach pioneered by Arthur

The New South and the "New Competition"

Jerome Eddy within the minds and among the ranks of lumber producers.

The Southern Pine Association became the major trade organization in the industry and one of the most important trade associations in the South and the nation. Its activities were built around the foundations of gathering and disseminating statistical information and establishing manufacturing quality standards. Both activities could lead to oligopoly or even monopoly, and thus on several occasions attracted the attention of government antitrust advocates. The SPA's experiences in these areas illustrate the troubles of trade associations generally with regard to the antitrust laws and also the nation's ambivalent antitrust attitudes.

The SPA was actively involved as a quasi-governmental agency during the mobilization efforts for both world wars and during the NRA's war against depression. Its experiences are reflective of the successes and failures of these endeavors and are a part of the story of the rise of what some call the "corporate state."

The association also led the southern pine industry's efforts in forestry and conservation. Motivated largely by self-interest, the lumbermen at first tried to unload "worthless" cut-over lands on unsuspecting World War I veterans and others for agricultural development (for which much of the land was unsuitable) and on the state or federal governments. Becoming aware of the fact that valuable second-growth timber could develop rapidly in the South, they then moved toward lobbying for favorable taxation and other governmental policies that would allow them to keep, reforest, and continually utilize their timber lands and developed a "sustained-yield" concept. The SPA represented the industry in these matters, and was in the vanguard of the development of more enlightened conservation attitudes. Its activities and attitudes are representative of the so-called "hard side" or practical, business-oriented, side of Progressivism which some students see in the conservation and other Progressive reform movements.

There was little that was enlightened, or progressive, in the southern pine industry's attitudes toward labor, black or white. Laborers were generally regarded as a commodity to be bought as cheaply and utilized as thoroughly as possible. At best, physical conditions in the woods and mill towns were generally poor, working conditions bad, wages low, and the attitudes of employers

378

paternalistic. Organized labor was anathema. In all of these ways the SPA and its subscribers and industry were representative of the views and practices of the "New South."

The southern pine industry was the South's largest industry by many standards, and the Southern Pine Association one of its most significant trade associations. Thus, their attitudes and activities provide important insights into and examples of the attitudes and activities of "New South" business leaders and to some extent of the nation in general.

NOTES TO CHAPTER 11

1. Ralph W. Hidy, Frank Ernest Hill, and Allan Nevins, Timber and Men: The Weyerhaeuser Story (New York: Macmillan, 1963), p. 466; Eric F. Goldman, The Crucial Decade—and After: America, 1945-1960 (New York: Vintage Books, 1956), pp. 19-21.

2. Untitled mimeographed report, Southern Pine Association Records, Box 11a (Louisiana State University Archives, Baton Rouge, La.). Collection hereafter cited as SPA Records.

3. Goldman, Crucial Decade, 26.

4. "Statement Presented to Judge J. C. Collet, Stabilization Administrator, Office of War Mobilization and Reconversion, Washington, D. C., January 7, 1946, by Tom DeWeese, Chairman, Special Committee of Southern Pine Lumber Manufacturers," SPA Records, Box 12b.

5. M. P. Tinsley to H. C. Berckes, Mar. 19, 1946, SPA Records, Box L.I.S. 42.

6. "Lumber Lack Is Blamed on OPA," Times-Picayune (New Orleans), May 9, 1946.

7. "Lays Black Mart To Regulations," Times-Picayune (New Orleans), May 9, 1946.

8. Southern Pine Industry Committee Press Release, Sept. 20, 1946, SPA Records, Box 52b.

9. Examples of this type of material are scattered throughout the SPA Records. For examples see Boxes 9a, 31, and 49b.

10. Hidy, Hill, and Nevins, Timber and Men, p. 467.

11. "Proceedings of Thirty-Seventh Annual Convention of the Southern Pine Association and Industry-Wide Meeting under the Auspices of Southern Pine Industry Committee . . . April 7, 8 and 9, 1952," SPA Records, Box 68a, pp. 136-37; H. C. Berckes to James G. McNary, Feb. 2, 1951, SPA Records, Box 68a, p. 1.

12. On July 19 the SPIC wired Chairman W. Stuart Symington of the National Security Resources Board that due to the "increasing seriousness of the international situation and because you and other responsible authorities desire to accelerate the preparedness program, Southern Pine manufacturers meeting here today feel that you should be informed of their eagerness to cooperate 100% in the preparedness program. . . ." "Minutes of a Meeting of the Executive Committee of the Southern Pine Association . . . July 19, 1950," SPA Records, Box 70a.

13. H. C. Berckes to James G. McNary, February 2, 1951, SPA Records, Box 1. An example of these publications is a pamphlet put out by the Southern Pine Industry Committee on July 17, 1950, entitled "U. S. Government Requirements in Lumber Purchasing. Taken from Specifications of U. S. Corps of Engineers" (copy in SPA Records, Box 12a).

14. "Proceedings of Thirty-Sixth Annual Convention of Southern Pine Association. Also Industry-Wide Meeting under the Auspices of Southern Pine Industry Committee . . . April 16-17-18, 1951," SPA Records, Box 12a.

15. "Proceedings of Thirty-Seventh Annual Convention of the Southern Pine Association and Industry-Wide Meeting under the Auspices of Southern Pine Industry Committee . . . April 7, 8 and 9, 1951," SPA Records, Box 68a, pp. 68-70.

16. H. C. Berckes, "The Pitch in Pine: A Story of the Traditions, Policies and Practices of the Southern Pine Industry and the Men Responsible for Them" (unpublished manuscript in the author's possession), p. 254. In fact

the only episode which gave a touch of urgency to the
southern pine industry's military program during this period
occurred in 1951, when speakers representing the material
control and materials development divisions of the U. S.
Navy's Bureau of Ships addressed the Southern Pine Association's annual meeting and announced a wooden-ship-building
program. At that time bidding was in process or contracts
had been awarded for the construction of some ninety-five
wooden minesweepers in three classes, ranging from 138
through 165 feet in length. "Proceedings of Thirty-Sixth
Annual Convention of Southern Pine Association. Also
Industry-Wide meeting under the Auspices of Southern Pine
Industry Committee . . . April 16-17-18, 1951," SPA
Records, Box 73a.

17. The following account is based primarily upon
correspondence, copies of official Southern Pine
Association minutes and reports, and other materials which
are in the possession of H. C. Berckes. While the author
has examined all of these materials, due to their sen-
sitive nature some will not be cited at this time. It is
hoped that in the future they will become available to
others interested in the history of the Southern Pine
Association and the southern pine industry through the
good offices of either Mr. Berckes or the Southern Forest
Products Association. The general outline of the text
which follows accurately reflects the materials examined.
However, the opportunity to cite these materials would
have made it possible to add detail and thus depth to the
account. It should also be noted that not all industry
and association figures agree with Berckes's views of the
industry and association during his last years or with his
version of the reasons for or circumstances of his own
resignation or departure. However, despite the author's
efforts to elicit further information, none of Berckes's
critics have been willing to state publicly or go on the
record with their versions of the story. Until they do,
the official records of the SPA and the Berckes account
are the only available sources. It should also be noted
that Berckes has had his defenders, although it is
possible they may not have known the entire inside story
or stories. In 1965, for example, after the publication
of the SPA-sponsored The First Fifty Years of the Southern
Pine Association, written by SPA employee John M. Collier,
which gave only passing notice to Berckes despite his
thirty-plus years of association leadership, one saddened

lumberman protested to Collier that "we can all have whatever personal feelings we have about any of these men, but when an outstanding job was done, as in the case of H. C. Berckes, certainly they are entitled to more consideration in a history of this kind than was given them, and I am only sorry that some of your associates didn't bring these things more strongly to your attention." F. W. Girdner to John Collier, May 3, 1965, SPA Records, Box 21.

18. Undated form letter from the Southern Pine Industry Committee, dictated by H. C. Berckes, sent out to several hundred interested groups. SPA Records, Box 12a.

19. H. C. Berckes, "Fight Fire with Fire," Southern Lumberman, Dec. 15, 1949 (copy of the reprint pamphlet published by the Southern Pine Industry Committee in SPA Records, Box 54a).

20. R. M. Eagle, "What's Good for Business Is Good for the Nation," SPA Records, Box 54a.

21. Interview with H. C. Berckes, Jan. 24, 1968. By 1968 Berckes's quest for a leader who would "lead me out of the wilderness" had brought him to contribute money to the campaign of Alabama's George Corley Wallace.

22. Interview with H. C. Berckes, Feb. 10, 1968. There is additional information on the problems of mergers, the situation surrounding the reorganization of the Southern Pine Association, and Berckes's departure in interviews conducted with the former secretary-manager, who incidentally had been named SPA executive vice-president in 1952, on January 24, August 10, and November 6, 1968; and in Berckes, "Pitch in Pine," pp. 257-302. There are letters concerning Berckes's resignation and the appointment of his successor, Stanley P. Deas, in SPA Records, Box 52a. For information on the problem of mergers and their impact on trade associations see H. C. Berckes "The Effect of Mergers on Trade Associations," American Society of Association Executives Journal, IX (Apr., 1957); and Raymond Moley, "Trade Associations," Newsweek (Jan. 13, 1958), p. 92.

12

Epilogue:
From the SPA to the SFPA

The southern pine industry continued to be dominated by corporate mergers, the development of new products, and stronger marketing during the 1950s and 1960s. The Southern Pine Association was led during this period by Stanley P. Deas, a native Louisianian who spent practically his entire professional career with the association. The organization generally continued the policies of earlier years, although there was stronger emphasis on advertising and public relations, particularly on efforts designed to emphasize the industry's conservation and reforestation activities as the general public became ever more conservation oriented. The industry's ecological consciousness and permanence were stressed through the "Third Forest" campaigns which got underway during these years. In 1970 Deas retired and was succeeded by William F. Ganser, who had come to the association in the mid-1960s from a career as staff engineer and director of public information for the American Institute of Timber Construction.

During Deas's tenure a number of important developments for the industry and association occurred. In 1954 efforts were implemented to reduce the costs of running the organization and to allow the members, through the board of directors, to maintain closer control over the financial activities of the staff. These included elimination of club memberships at association expense and the appointment of a new audit and salary committee which regularly and closely investigated the financial practices and expenditures of the staff organization. In 1957 the old Missouri charter was dissolved and the SPA was now reorganized as a Louisiana corporation which no longer described its members as "subscribers" to its services. In the early 1960s, as southern pine plywood came into increasing prominence, the association started to make its services available to the plywood industry. During this period the SPA was constantly at odds with the National Lumber Manufacturers' Association over the question of moisture-content provisions in building codes. The NLMA, dominated by western producers, wanted more lenient standards than did southern pine manufacturers, and after years of conflict the Southern Pine Association withdrew from the NLMA in 1965.

Concerned about its image and anxious to strengthen its efforts during the 1970s, the SPA commissioned an opinion survey by Marsteller Research of New York in an effort to determine "what the southern lumber industry wants from trade associations." The survey concluded that owners and managers of lumber companies in the South generally thought favorably of wood product associations and said they were satisfied with services, although a minority complained about overlapping functions, excessive numbers of meetings, and too many organizations. The study said that the SPA confronted three major problems: (1) convincing its members and the industry of its value, particularly since many complained that membership costs were too high and they did not use association services enough; (2) stressing popular services; and (3) appealing to the "little guy."

With regard to services, the report said that "almost nobody is interested in services like labor relations, group insurance, freight rates, films, or cost accounting." On the other hand, "the three biggest subjects of interest are: Specifications and standards, Federal legislating, and Forestry." The report noted that "there is current discussion within the SPA leadership on how to improve its forestry program." With regard to the "little guy," the report noted that "the bulk of non-members are smaller producers than the present membership. Many of them feel the SPA is run by the big mills, by "'western' interests." In its conclusion the report said that attracting new members for the SPA posed two significant problems. First was the difficulty of breaking through the indifference "because of past mistakes, confusion of SPA with the SPIB, and an equating by many of the SPA with the functions of the Southeast Lumber Manufacturers Association." It noted that four of every ten nonmembers belonged to SELMA. The second problem centered around the question of whether or not the SPA could launch a membership drive that would emphasize the "new" association and its values to new members, thus breaking through their indifference. Obviously, as the organization approached the 1970s, it was concerned about its future.

As the new decade started, the association began to implement some of the suggestions of the Marsteller Report. First were a reorganization of the association's structure and the creation of associate, as well as regular, memberships. The associate members were drawn from machinery manufacturers, laminators, treaters, wholesalers, financial institutions, and others sharing the objectives of the organization. Under the new structure dues were reduced and a one-member, one-vote policy introduced. There was also a significant name change to eliminate confusion with the Southern Pine Inspection Bureau, create a new image, and reflect more accurately the nature of the modern industry. The Southern Pine Association became the Southern Forest Products Association. The SFPA also reaffiliated with the NLMA, which had by now become the National Forest Products Association.

The SFPA's emphases in the 1970s were upon technical assistance for planners and builders and the "Third Forest" program, designed to double timber growth in the South through new incentives and increased assistance for nonindustrial private landowners who were estimated to hold some 70 percent of the South's forest land. The "Third Forest" program was billed as having broad environmental objectives, including greatly increased recreational opportunities for the general public; soil, water, and wildlife conservation; improvement of the rural economy; and help with the solution of air pollution problems.

In 1976, in order to determine how successful the SFPA had been in its efforts to respond to the changing needs of the industry, another study was undertaken by Marsteller Research. The study was conducted through 124 telephone interviews with active and associate members representing the 65 active member companies and 126 associate member companies in the SFPA. The researchers were particularly interested in determining whether the restructuring enacted as a result of the 1969 survey had been successful, what the members wanted from the association in the approaching years, how the members perceived the value of the SFPA's services, and the members' outlook on business for the next three to five years.

The conclusions of the 1976 Marsteller Report provide an excellent measuring stick of where the SFPA stood in the late 1970s. The majority of members described themselves as "very satisfied" with the association. There were no major complaints. Over three-fourths regarded the dues structure as equitable. The members also strongly endorsed the association's newsletter as an excellent means of communicating with the industry, praised the SFPA's field services and sponsorship of its machinery exposition, and were greatly concerned about "government influence," including particularly "increasing government control of timber land," which nearly half termed "the most important issue that the Southern Pine lumber industry will have to face in upcoming years." Two-thirds of the active members surveyed "suggested that government relations should be the activity most aggressively pursued by the Association in the future." Most of those surveyed reported difficulty in obtaining adequate trucks or rail cars for their shipments, and the majority of the members were negative toward the idea of incorporating new services into the current association programs.

During the early 1970s the board of directors approved a new government affairs division; the association's safety program was continued; a transportation program served by a traffic consultant and attorneys continued to work for the protection of members in freight rate and product shipment matters; statistical activities were continued, including publication of the Weekly Trade Barometer; marketing, technical, and mechanical efficiency programs continued to thrive; and the association did extensive public relations work, through direct contacts and the media, to emphasize the industry's forestry and conservation activities and to improve its image generally.

Southern Pine Association leaders of earlier decades would not have been greatly surprised by the problems, activities, and objectives of the Southern Forest Products Association in the 1970s.[1]

Epilogue: From the SPA to the SFPA

NOTE TO CHAPTER 12

1. The material in this brief epilogue is drawn from the following sources: interview with Stanley P. Deas, Jan. 7, 1971; "Notes By S. P. Deas, 1953-66," Southern Pine Association Records, Box 21 (Louisiana State University Archives, Baton Rouge, La.). Collection hereafter cited as SPA Records; "Introducing . . . the Southern Forest Products Association," Southern Building, June, 1970, p. 18; "Confidential, What the Southern Lumber Industry Wants from Trade Associations: An Opinion Survey Conducted for the Southern Pine Association, Project 69160, Marsteller Research, 866 Third Avenue, New York, New York, October, 1969," SPA Records, Box 20; "Annual Report, Southern Forest Products Association, Fiscal Year, 1972-1973," SPA Records, Box 20; "Southern Forest Products Association, Membership Survey, Prepared by Marsteller Research . . . Project 76298, September, 1976," SPA Records, Box 20.

Selected Bibliography

I. PRIMARY SOURCES

MANUSCRIPTS

H. C. Berckes Papers, University of Mississippi Library, Oxford.

Alexander Gilmer Collection, University of Texas Archives, Austin.

John Henry Kirby Papers, University of Houston Library, Houston.

Kurth Papers, Stephen F. Austin State University Library, Nacogdoches, Texas.

National Recovery Administration Records, National Archives, Washington, D.C.

Records of the Federal Trade Commission, Bureau of Corporations, National Archives, Washington, D.C.

Records of the United States Department of Justice, National Archives, Washington, D.C.

Records of the United States Shipping Board, National Archives, Washington, D.C.

Southern Pine Association Records, Department of Archives and Manuscripts, Louisiana State University, Baton Rouge.

Bibliography

Temple Industries Records, Stephen F. Austin State University Library, Nacogdoches, Texas.

GOVERNMENT PUBLICATIONS

Federal

Baruch, Bernard M. American Industry in the War, a Report of the War Industries Board. Washington, Government Printing Office, 1921.

Greeley, William B. Some Public and Economic Aspects of the Lumber Industry, Part I of Studies of the Lumber Industry, United States Department of Agriculture, Report No. 114. Washington, Government Printing Office, 1917.

Interstate Commerce Commission Reports, XXVII, XXXIII.

Marceron, L. W., and C. Judkins. Selected Trade Associations of the United States, National and Interstate, United States Department of Commerce, Foreign and Domestic Commerce Bureau, Market Research Series. Washington, Government Printing Office, 1937.

Report of the Federal Trade Commission on Lumber Manufacturers' Trade Associations. Washington, Government Printing Office, 1922.

Report of the Federal Trade Commission on War-Time Costs and Profits of Southern Pine Lumber Companies. Washington, Government Printing Office, 1922.

Stone, Peter A., et al. "Economic Problems of the Lumber and Timber Products Industry." Mimeographed, United States National Recovery Administration, Division of Review, 1936.

Tariff Problems of the South: Hearing of the Southern Tariff Association before the Committee on Ways and Means, House of Representatives, Sixty-seventh Congress, First Session, April 20, 1921. Washington, Government Printing Office, 1921.

U.S., Department of Commerce, Bureau of Corporations. Conditions in Production and Wholesale Distribution

Bibliography

Including Wholesale Prices, Part IV of The Lumber Industry. Washington, Government Printing Office, 1914.

U.S., Department of Commerce, Bureau of Standards. Lumber, Simplified Practice Recommendation R16-29. Washington, Government Printing Office, 1929.

_____. Fourteenth Annual Report of the Secretary of Commerce, 1926. Washington, Government Printing Office, 1926.

_____. Tenth Annual Report of the Secretary of Commerce, 1922. Washington, Government Printing Office, 1922.

_____. Thirteenth Annual Report of the Secretary of Commerce, 1925. Washington, Government Printing Office, 1925.

_____. Twelfth Annual Report of the Secretary of Commerce, 1924. Washington, Government Printing Office, 1924.

U.S., Department of Labor, Division of Negro Economics. Negro Migration in 1916-17. Washington, Government Printing Office, 1919.

U.S., House Committee on Small Business. "Current Lumber Industry Problems." Part I. "The National Lumber Situation as of January 1, 1944." Part II. "The Problems of the Southern Pine Industry as of January 1, 1944." 78th Congress, 2d Session, Report 987.

U.S., Senate, Hearings on S. 170, Building of Merchant Vessels under the Direction of the United States Shipping Board Emergency Fleet Corporation, 65th Cong., 2d sess., 1918.

_____. Open-Price Trade Associations. Document No. 226, 70th Congress, 2nd Session, 1929.

U.S. Statutes at Large, XL.

State

Rader, Perry S. Reports of Cases Determined by the

Bibliography

<u>Supreme Court of Missouri</u>. Columbia, E. W. Stephens
Publishing Company, 1915.

<u>The Revised Statutes of the State of Missouri</u>, 1909, III.

NEWSPAPERS

<u>Arkansas Democrat</u> (Little Rock), April 17, 1946.

<u>Baltimore Sun</u>, May 1, 1908.

<u>Beaumont Journal</u>, May 12, 1894.

<u>Business Week</u>, April 27, May 18, 1946; October 25, 1947.

<u>Commercial Appeal</u> (Memphis), June 29, 1918.

<u>Constitution</u> (Atlanta), March 20, March 22, 1946.

<u>Evening Star</u> (Washington), February 23, 1937.

<u>Globe and Commercial Advertiser</u> (New York), July 31, 1918.

<u>Houston Post</u>, June 3, 1918.

<u>International Woodworker</u>, October 2, 1946; June 18, 1947;
    August 22, September 12, 1951; February 25, 1953.

<u>Journal</u> (Atlanta), November 21, 1946.

<u>Monroe Morning World</u>, November 3, 1946.

<u>National Negro Voice</u> (New Orleans), October 3, 1925.

<u>New York Lumber Trade Journal</u>, May 15, July 15, 1908.

<u>New York Times</u>, May 12, 16, 1946.

<u>Star</u> (Washington), March 17, May 12, 1946.

<u>States</u> (New Orleans), May 27, 1946.

<u>St. Louis Times-Democrat</u>, April 29, 1908.

<u>The Kansas City Times</u>, October 10, 1945.

Bibliography

Times-Democrat (New Orleans), October 6, 1912.

Times-Picayune (New Orleans), March 31, 1933; September 21, 1940; August 15, 1943; April 26, May 9, September 29, 1946.

Wall Street Journal, January 22, 1947; May 11, 1949.

OTHERS

Interviews with H. C. Berckes, January 24, February 10, August 10, November 6, 1968.

Interviews with Stanley P. Deas, January 7, January 8, 1971.

II. SECONDARY WORKS

MANUSCRIPTS

Berckes, Herbert C. "The Pitch in Pine: A Story of the Traditions, Policies, and Activities of the Southern Pine Industry and the Men Responsible for Them." In the author's possession.

Boyd, James. "Cut-Over Lands." Southern Pine Association Records, Box 77a, Department of Archives, Louisiana State University, Baton Rouge.

_____. "Gross Darkness-Then Comes Dawn." Southern Pine Association Records, Box 77a, Department of Archives, Louisiana State University, Baton Rouge.

_____. "It Is War!" Southern Pine Association Records, Box 77a, Department of Archives, Louisiana State University, Baton Rouge.

_____. "On the Firing Line in the Inspection Department." Southern Pine Association Records, Box 77a, Department of Archives, Louisiana State University, Baton Rouge.

_____. "Trade Promotion." Southern Pine Association

Bibliography

Records, Box 77a, Department of Archives, Louisiana State University, Baton Rouge.

Carper, N. Gordon. "The Convict-Lease System in Florida, 1866-1923." Ph.D. dissertation, Florida State University, Tallahassee, 1964.

DeMouy, Max Lee. "Trade Associations and Price Policies." M.A. thesis, Louisiana State University, Baton Rouge, 1939.

Easton, Hamilton Pratt. "The History of the Texas Lumbering Industry." Ph.D. dissertation, University of Texas, Austin, 1947.

Fraunberger, R. C. "Lumber Trade Associations, Their Economic and Social Significance." M.A. thesis, Temple University, Philadelphia, 1951.

Grant, Harold Lafayette, Jr. "The Southern Paper Company, 1911-1928." M.A. thesis, University of Mississippi, University, 1958.

Green, George Norris. "The Far Right Wing in Texas Politics, 1930's-1960's." Ph.D. dissertation, Florida State University, Tallahassee, 1966.

Hall, Covington. "Labor Struggles in the Deep South." Unpublished manuscript in Special Collections Division, Howard Tilton Memorial Library, Tulane University of Louisiana, New Orleans.

"The History of the Weston Lumber Co." In the possession of H. C. Berckes, New Orleans, Louisiana.

Hodge, Jo Dent. "Lumbering in Laurel at the Turn of the Century." M.A. Thesis, University of Mississippi, University, 1966.

King, Helene. "The Economic History of the Long-Bell Lumber Company." M.A. thesis, Louisiana State University, Baton Rouge, 1936.

Latham, Huey, Jr. "A Comparison of Union Organization in Two Southern Paper Mills." M.A. thesis, Louisiana State University, Baton Rouge, 1962.

Bibliography

Lowry, Stanley Todd. "Henry Hardtner, Pioneer in Southern Forestry: An Analysis of the Economic Bases of His Reforestation Program." M.A. thesis, Louisiana State University, Baton Rouge, 1956.

McCord, Charles R. "A Brief History of the Brotherhood of Timberworkers." M.A. thesis, University of Texas, Austin, 1959.

McWhiney, H. Grady. "The Socialist Vote in Louisiana, 1912: An Historical Interpretation of Radical Sources." M.A. thesis, Louisiana State University, Baton Rouge, 1951.

Martin, James William. "History of Forest Conservation in Texas, 1900 to 1935." M.A. thesis, Stephen F. Austin State College, Nacogdoches, 1966.

Massey, Richard Walter, Jr. "A History of the Lumber Industry in Alabama and West Florida, 1880-1914." Ph.D. dissertation, Vanderbilt University, Nashville, 1960.

Morgan, George T., Jr. "No Compromise--No Recognition: John Henry Kirby, the Southern Lumber Operators' Association, and Unionism in the Piney Woods, 1906-1916." Paper read at the convention of the Southwestern Social Science Association, Dallas, Texas, 1967.

Nowlin, R. S. "Economic Development of the Kirby Lumber Company of Houston, Texas." M.A. thesis, George Peabody College for Teachers, Nashville, 1930.

Ready, Milton L. "The Southern Tariff Association." M.A. thesis, George Peabody College for Teachers, Nashville, 1930.

Scribner, Robert Leslie. "A Short History of Brewton, Alabama." M.A. thesis, University of Alabama, University, 1935.

Stokes, George Alwin. "Lumbering in Southwest Louisiana." Ph.D. dissertation, University of Wisconsin, Madison, 1954.

Bibliography

Tinsley, James A. "The Progressive Movement in Texas." Ph.D. dissertation, University of Wisconsin, Madison, 1954.

Weaver, Harry. "Labor Practices in the East Texas Lumber Industry to 1930." M.A. thesis, Stephen F. Austin State College, Nacogdoches, 1961.

BOOKS AND PAMPHLETS

Acheson, Sam Hanna. Joe Bailey, The Last Democrat. New York, Macmillan Company, 1932.

Allen, Ruth A. East Texas Lumber Workers, an Economic and Social Picture, 1870-1950. Austin, University of Texas Press, 1961.

Andreano, Ralph (ed.). The Economic Impact of the American Civil War. Cambridge, Mass., Schenkman Publishing Company, 1962.

Beaver, Daniel R. Newton D. Baker and the American War Effort, 1917-1919. Lincoln, University of Nebraska Press, 1966.

Bellush, Bernard. The Failure of the NRA. New York, W. W. Norton and Company, 1975.

Boerker, Richard H. D. Behold Our Green Mansions, a Book about American Forests. Chapel Hill, University of North Carolina Press, 1945.

Bontemps, Anna, and Jack Conroy. Anyplace but Here. New York, Hill and Wang, 1966.

Bradley, Joseph F. The Role of Trade Associations and Professional Business Societies in America. University Park, Pennsylvania State University Press, 1965.

Brissenden, Paul F. The I.W.W.: A Study of American Syndicalism. New York, Columbia University Press, 1920.

Brooks, John G. American Syndicalism: The I.W.W. New York, Macmillan Company, 1913.

396

Bibliography

Catton, Bruce. The War Lords of Washington. New York,
Harcourt, Brace and Company, 1948.

Chamberlain, John. The Enterprising Americans, a Business
History of the United States. New York, Harper & Row,
1963.

Clarkson, Grosvenor B. Industrial America in the World
War: The Strategy behind the Lines, 1917-1918.
Boston, Houghton Mifflin Company, 1923.

Cole, Wayne S. Senator Gerald P. Nye and American Foreign
Relations. Minneapolis, University of Minnesota
Press, 1962.

Collier, John M. The First Fifty Years of the Southern
Pine Association, 1915-1965. New Orleans, Southern
Pine Association, 1965.

Craven, Wesley Frank. The Southern Colonies in the
Seventeenth Century, 1607-1689. Baton Rouge,
Louisiana State University Press, 1949.

Cuff, Robert D. The War Industries Board, Business-
Government Relations during World War I. Baltimore,
Johns Hopkins University Press, 1973.

Dana, Samuel Trask. Forest and Range Policy, Its
Development in the United States. New York,
McGraw-Hill Book Company, 1956.

Dionne, Jack. A Brief Story of the Life of John Henry
Kirby. n.p., n.d.

Dorfman, Joseph. The Economic Mind in American
Civilization. Vols. IV and V, 1918-33. New York,
Viking Press, 1959.

Dubofsky, Melvin. We Shall Be All, History of the
Industrial Workers of the World. Chicago, Quadrangle
Press, 1969.

Eddy, Arthur Jerome. The New Competition. New York and
London, D. Appleton, 1912.

Bibliography

Fairchild, Byron, and Jonathan Grossman. The Army and Industrial Manpower. Washington, Department of the Army, 1959.

Faulkner, Harold U. The Decline of Laissez Faire, 1897-1917. New York, Holt, Rinehart and Winston, 1951.

Fine, Sidney. The Automobile under the Blue Eagle: Labor, Management, and the Automobile Manufacturing Code. Ann Arbor, University of Michigan Press, 1963.

Foth, Joseph Henry. Trade Associations, Their Services to Industry. New York, Ronald Press Company, 1930.

Galambos, Louis. Competition & Cooperation: The Emergence of a National Trade Association. Baltimore, Johns Hopkins University Press, 1966.

Gambs, John S. The Decline of the I.W.W. New York, Columbia University Press, 1932.

Gilb, Corinne Lathrop. Hidden Hierarchies: The Professions and Government. New York and London, Harper and Row, 1966.

Goldman, Eric F. The Crucial Decade--and After, America, 1945-1960. New York, Vintage Books, 1961.

_____. Rendezvous with Destiny, a History of Modern American Reform. New York, Vintage Books, 1956.

Greeley, William B. Forest Policy. New York, McGraw-Hill Book Company, Inc., 1953.

_____. Forests and Men. Garden City, N.Y., Doubleday & Company, 1951.

Hawley, Ellis W. The New Deal and the Problem of Monopoly: A Study in Economic Ambivalence. Princeton, N.J., Princeton University Press, 1966.

Hays, Samuel P. Conservation and the Gospel of Efficiency, the Progressive Conservation Movement, 1890-1920. Cambridge, Mass., Harvard University Press, 1959.

Bibliography

_____. The Response to Industrialism: 1885-1914.
Chicago, University of Chicago Press, 1957.

Haywood, William D. Bill Haywood's Book: The
Autobiography of William D. Haywood. New York,
International Publishers, 1929.

Hickman, Nollie. Mississippi Harvest: Lumbering in the
Longleaf Pine Belt, 1840-1915. University, University
of Mississippi Press, 1962.

Hidy, Ralph W., Frank Ernest Hill, and Allan Nevins.
Timber and Men: The Weyerhaeuser Story. New York,
Macmillan Company, 1963.

Himmelberg, Robert F. The Origins of the National
Recovery Administration: Business, Government, and the
Trade Association Issue, 1921-1933. New York, Fordham
University Press, 1976.

Horn, Stanley F. The Southern Pine Story. New Orleans,
Southern Pine Association, n.d.

_____. This Fascinating Lumber Business. New York,
Bobbs-Merrill Company, 1943.

Jensen, Vernon H. Lumber and Labor. New York, Farrar &
Rinehart, 1945.

Joubert, William H. Southern Freight Rates in Transition.
Gainesville, University of Florida Press, 1949.

Johnson, Hugh. The Blue Eagle from Egg to Earth. Garden
City, N.Y., Doubleday & Company, 1935.

Kaufman, Burton I. Efficiency and Expansion, Foreign
Trade Organization in the Wilson Administration,
1913-1921. Westport, Conn., Greenwood Press, 1974.

Kerr, Ed. History of Forestry in Louisiana. Baton Rouge,
Louisiana Forestry Commission, 1958.

King, John O. "The Early History of the Houston Oil
Company of Texas, 1901-1908," Texas Gulf Coast
Historical Association Publications, III (April,
1959).

Bibliography

Kirsh, Benjamin S., and Harold Roland Shapiro. Trade Associations in Law and Business. New York, Central Book Company, 1938.

Kolko, Gabriel. Railroads and Regulation, 1877-1916. Princeton, N.J., Princeton University Press, 1965.

_____. The Triumph of Conservatism, a Reinterpretation of American History. Chicago, Free Press of Glencoe, 1963.

Kornbluh, Joyce L. (ed.) Rebel Voices, an I.W.W. Anthology. Ann Arbor, University of Michigan Press, 1964.

Lasswell, Mary. John Henry Kirby, Prince of the Pines. Austin, Encino Press, 1967.

Leuchtenburg, William E. Franklin D. Roosevelt and the New Deal, 1932-1940. New York, Harper & Row, 1963.

Lewis, George G., and John Mewha. History of Prisoner of War Utilization by the United State Army, 1776-1945. Washington, Department of the Army, 1955.

Lillard, Richard G. The Great Forest. New York, Alfred A. Knopf, 1947.

Lively, Robert A. The South in Action: A Sectional Crusade against Freight Rate Discrimination. Chapel Hill, University of North Carolina Press, 1949.

Loehr, Rodney C. Forests for the Future: The Story of Sustained Yield As Told in the Diaries and Papers of David T. Mason, 1907-1950. St. Paul, The Forest Products History Foundation, 1952.

Lowitt, Richard. A Merchant Prince of the Nineteenth Century: William E. Dodge. New York, Columbia University Press, 1954.

Lucia, Ellis. Head Rig: Story of the West Coast Lumber Industry. Portland, Overland West Press, 1965.

Lyon, Leverett S., et al. The National Recovery Administration, an Analysis and Appraisal. Washington, Brookings Institution, 1935.

Bibliography

McGeary, Martin Nelson. *Gifford Pinchot, Forester-Politician.* Princeton, N.J., Princeton University Press, 1960.

Marshall, F. Ray. *Labor in the South.* Cambridge, Mass., Harvard University Press, 1967.

Maunder, Elwood C. (comp.). *James Greeley McGowin--South Alabama Lumberman: The Recollections of His Family.* Santa Cruz, Calif.: Forest History Society, 1972.

_____. *Voices from the South, Recollections of Four Foresters.* Santa Cruz, Calif.: Forest History Society, 1977.

Michie, Allan A., and Frank Rhylick. *Dixie Demagogues.* New York, Vanguard Press, 1939.

Mitchell, Broadus. *Depression Decade, from New Era through New Deal, 1929-1941.* New York, Holt, Rinehart and Winston, 1947.

Moore, John Hebron. *Andrew Brown and Cypress Lumbering in the Old Southwest.* Baton Rouge, Louisiana State University Press, 1967.

Morgan, George T., Jr. *William B. Greeley, a Practical Forester, 1879-1955.* St. Paul, Forest History Society, Inc., 1961.

Mowry, George E. *The Era of Theodore Roosevelt, 1900-1912.* New York, Harper & Brothers, 1958.

Myers, J. Walter, Jr. *Opportunities Unlimited, the Story of our Southern Forests.* Chicago, Illinois Central Railroad, 1950.

National Industrial Conference Board. *Trade Associations: Their Economic Significance and Legal Status.* New York, National Industrial Conference Board, 1925.

Patterson, James T. *Congressional Conservatism and the New Deal: The Growth of the Conservative Coalition in Congress, 1933-1939.* Lexington, University of Kentucky Press, 1967.

Bibliography

Renshaw, Patrick. The Wobblies: The Story of Syndicalism in the United States. Garden City, N.Y., Doubleday & Company, 1967.

Rollins, Alfred B., Jr. Franklin D. Roosevelt and the Age of Action. New York, Dell Publishing Company, 1960.

Scott, Emmett J. Negro Migration during the War. New York, Oxford University Press, 1920.

Sobel, Robert. The Age of the Giant Corporations, a Microeconomic History of American Business, 1914-1970. Westport, Conn., Greenwood Press, 1972.

Soule, George. Prosperity Decade, from War to Depression: 1917-1929. New York, Holt, Rinehart and Winston, 1947.

Steen, Harold K. The U.S. Forest Service, a History. Seattle, University of Washington Press, 1976.

Steigerwalt, Albert K. The National Association of Manufacturers, 1895-1914: A Study in Business Leadership. Ann Arbor, University of Michigan, Bureau of Business Research, Graduate School of Business Administration, 1964.

Thompson, Fred. The I.W.W.: Its First Fifty Years. Chicago, Industrial Workers of the World, 1955.

Tindall, George Brown. The Emergence of the New South, 1913-1945. Baton Rouge, Louisiana State University Press, 1967.

Todes, Charlotte. Labor and Lumber. New York, International Publishers, 1931.

Tuttle, William M., Jr. Race Riot, Chicago in the Red Summer of 1919. New York, Atheneum, 1970.

Wahlenberg, W. G. Longleaf Pine: Its Use, Ecology, Regeneration, Protection, Growth, and Management. Washington, Charles Lathrop Pack Forestry Foundation, 1946.

Bibliography

Whitney, Simon N. Trade Associations and Industrial Control, a Critique of the N.R.A. New York, Central Book Company, 1934.

Wiebe, Robert H. Businessmen and Reform: A Study of the Progressive Movement. Cambridge, Mass., Harvard University Press, 1962.

Wilson, Joan Hoff. American Business and Foreign Policy, 1920-1933. New York, Atheneum, 1970.

Woodward, C. Vann. Origins of the New South, 1877-1913. Baton Rouge, Louisiana State University Press, 1951.

Zaremba, Joseph. Economics of the American Lumber Industry. New York, Robert Speller & Sons, 1963.

ARTICLES

Alilunas, Leo. "Statutory Means of Impeding Emigration of the Negro," Journal of Negro History, XXII (April, 1937), 148-62.

Appleman, R. E. "Timber Empire from the Public Domain," Mississippi Valley Historical Review, XXVI (September, 1939), 193-208.

Barry, Richard. "Slavery in the South To-day," Cosmopolitan Magazine, XLII (March, 1907), 481-91.

Berckes, H. C. "The Effect of Mergers on Trade Associations," American Society of Association Executives Journal, IX (April, 1957).

Boisfontaine, A. S. "The Southern Pine Association in Retrospect: Seventeen Years of Trail Blazing in the Trade Association Field," Southern Lumberman, CLXIV (December, 1931), 109-14.

Boyd, James. "Fifty Years in the Southern Pine Industry," Southern Lumberman, CLXIV (December, 1931), 59-67.

Burns, Anna C. "Henry E. Hardtner, Louisiana's First Conservationist," Journal of Forest History, XXII (April, 1978), 78-85.

Bibliography

Carrott, H. Browning. "The Supreme Court and American Trade Associations, 1921-1925," Business History Review, XLIV (Autumn, 1970), 320-29.

Claiborne, John Francis Hamtramck. "A Trip through the Piney Woods," Publications of the Mississippi Historical Society, IX (1906), 487-538.

Clark, Thomas D. "The Impact of the Timber Industry on the South," Mississippi Quarterly, XXV (Spring, 1972), 141-64.

Compton, Wilson. "Lumber, an Old Industry and the New Competition," Harvard Business Review, X (January, 1932), 161-69.

Connolly, Frank A. "Lumber Organization Activity in the Half-Century," Southern Lumberman, CLXIV (December, 1931), 107.

Cooper, George. "Trade Associations before 1900," American Trade Association Executives Journal, VI (January, 1954), 13-21.

Creel, George. "The Feudal Towns of Texas," Harper's Weekly, LX (January 23, 1915), 76-78.

Cuff, Robert D. "A 'Dollar-a-Year Man' in Government: George N. Peek and the War Industries Board," Business History Review, XLI (Winter, 1967), 404-20.

_____. "Bernard Baruch: Symbol and Myth in Industrial Mobilization," Business History Review, XLIII (Summer, 1969), 115-33.

_____. "Herbert Hoover, the Ideology of Voluntarism and War Organization during the Great War," Journal of American History, LXIV (September, 1977), 358-72.

Demmon, E. L. "Henry E. Hardtner," Journal of Forestry, XXXIII (October, 1935), 885-6.

Donald, Henderson H. "The Negro Migration of 1916-1918," Journal of Negro History, VI (October, 1921), 383-498.

Bibliography

Doree, Bill. "Texas' First Steam-Powered Sawmill," Gulf Coast Lumberman, C (April, 1963), 13.

"European War and Its Result," Gulf Coast Lumberman, II (September 1, 1914), 7.

"European War and the Lumber Situation," Gulf Coast Lumberman, II (August 15, 1914), 4.

Fickle, James E. "The Louisiana-East Texas Lumber War of 1911-1912," Louisiana History, XVI (Winter, 1975), 59-85.

_____. "Management Looks at the 'Labor Problem': The Southern Pine Industry during World War I and the Postwar Era," Journal of Southern History, XL (February, 1974), 61-76.

Fleming, Walter L. "'Pap' Singleton, the Moses of the Colored Exodus," Louisiana State University Bulletin, VII (August, 1909), 61-82.

Foner, Philip S. "The I.W.W. and the Black Worker," Journal of Negro History, LV (January, 1970), 45-64.

"Forcing Ship Timber Production," Gulf Coast Lumberman, V (November 15, 1917), 22.

Gable, Richard W. "Birth of an Employers' Association," Business History Review, XXXIII (Winter, 1959), 535-45.

Galloway, John A. "John Barber White and the Conservation Dilemma," Forest History, V (Winter, 1962), 9-16.

Garvin, Roy. "Benjamin or 'Pap' Singleton and His Followers," Journal of Negro History, XXXIII (January, 1948), 7-23.

Gates, Paul Wallace. "Federal Land Policy in the South, 1866-1888," Journal of Southern History, VI (August, 1940), 303-30.

Glad, Paul W. "Progressives and the Business Culture of the 1920's," Journal of American History, LIII (June, 1966), 79-80.

Bibliography

"Government Conscripts All Lumber Over 2 Inches Thick," Gulf Coast Lumberman, V (November 15, 1917), 22.

"Government Takes All Long Leaf Timbers," Gulf Coast Lumberman, V (October 15, 1917), 30.

Grove, Nettie Thompson. "John Barber White, 1847-1923," Annals of Kansas City, I (December, 1923), 15-20.

Hall, Covington. "I Am Here for Labor," International Socialist Review, XIII (July, 1912), 223-26.

_____. "Revolt of the Southern Timber Workers," International Socialist Review, XIII (July, 1912), 51-52.

Hamilton, Lawrence S. "The Federal Forest Regulation Issue, Recapitulation," Forest History, IX (April, 1965), 2-11.

Hawley, Ellis W. "Herbert Hoover, the Commerce Secretariat, and the Vision of an 'Associative State,' 1921-1928," Journal of American History, LXI (June, 1974), 116-40.

Haywood, William D. "Timber Workers and Timber Wolves," International Socialist Review, XIII (August, 1912), 105-10.

Higgins, Billy D. "Negro Thought and the Exodus of 1879," Phylon, XXXII (Spring, 1971), 39-52.

Himmelberg, Robert F. "Business, Antitrust Policy, and the Industrial Board of the Department of Commerce, 1919," Business History Review, 42 (Spring, 1968), 1-23.

Hoole, W. Stanley. "Alabama's World War II Prisoner of War Camps," Alabama Review, XX (April, 1967), 83-114.

"Houston Oil Company Sold Their Cut-Over Land," Gulf Coast Lumberman, IV (September 1, 1916), 28.

Kane, Lucile. "Selling Cut-Over Lands in Wisconsin," Business History Review, XXVIII (September, 1954), 236-47.

Bibliography

Koistinen, Paul A. C. "The 'Industrial-Military Complex' in Historical Perspective: The Interwar Years," Journal of American History, LVI (March, 1970), 819-23.

_____. "The 'Industrial-Military Complex' in Historical Perspective: World War I," Business History Review, XLI (Winter, 1967), 378-82.

"Labor Troubles at Saw Mills," Gulf Coast Lumberman, V (October 15, 1917), 49.

LeDuc, Thomas. "The Historiography of Conservation," Forest History, IX (October, 1965), 23-28.

Lively, Robert. "The American System: A Review Article," Business History Review, XXIX (March, 1955), 81-96.

"Lumber Administrator Changes," Gulf Coast Lumberman, VI (August 1, 1918), 6.

McClendon, James H. "The Development of Mississippi Agriculture: A Survey," Journal of Mississippi History, XIII (April, 1951), 75-79.

MacKaye, Milton. "The CIO Invades Dixie," Saturday Evening Post, 219 (July 20, 1946), 12.

McWhiney, Grady. "Louisiana Socialists in the Early Twentieth Century: A Study in Rustic Radicalism," Journal of Southern History, XX (August, 1954), 315-36.

Mason, John Brown. "German Prisoners of War in the United States," American Journal of International Law, XXXIX (April, 1945), 198-215.

Maunder, Elwood R. "Ride The White Horse--Memories of a Southern Forester," Forest History, III (Winter, 1960), 3-14.

Maxwell, Robert S. "Lumbermen of the East Texas Frontier," Forest History, IX (April, 1965), 12-16.

_____. "The Impact of Forestry on the Gulf South," Forest History, XVII (April, 1973), 31-35.

Bibliography

_____. "One Man's Legacy: W. Goodrich Jones and Texas Conservation," _Southwestern Historical Quarterly_, LXXVII (January, 1974), 355-80.

Millet, Donald J. "The Lumbering Industry of 'Imperial' Calcasieu, 1865-1900," _Louisiana History_, VII (Winter, 1966), 51-69.

Moley, Raymond. "Trade Associations," _Newsweek_, LI (January 13, 1958), 92.

Moore, John Hebron. "William H. Mason, Southern Industrialist," _Journal of Southern History_, XXVII (May, 1961), 169-83.

Morgan, George T., Jr. "No Compromise--No Recognition: John Henry Kirby, the Southern Lumber Operator's Association, and Unionism in the Piney Woods, 1906-1916," _Labor History_, X (Spring, 1969), 193-204.

"Mr. Kirby and the Southern Pine Industry," _Gulf Coast Lumberman_, VI (August 15, 1918), 9.

Nash, Gerald. "Experiments in Industrial Mobilization: WIB and NRA," _Mid-America_, XLV (July, 1963), 157-74.

Nash, Gerald K. "Research Opportunities in the Economic History of the South after 1880," _Journal of Southern History_, XXXII (August, 1966), 308-24.

Nelson, Charles A. "Born and Raised in Madison, the Forest Products Laboratory," _Forest History_, XI (July, 1967), 6-14.

"Orange Will Celebrate," _Gulf Coast Lumberman_, IV (November 1, 1916), 30.

Palmer, Dewey H. "Moving North: Migration of Negroes during World War I," _Phylon_, XXVIII (Spring, 1967), 52-62.

Peoples, Morgan D. "'Kansas Fever' in North Louisiana," _Louisiana History_, XI (Spring, 1970), 121-35.

Persons, William. "Lumber Industry Investigations Made by the U.S. Bureau of Corporations," _The American Economic Review_, V (March, 1915), 153-56.

Bibliography

"Pine Men Oppose Bill to Restrict Hours of Labor," Four L Lumber News, XIII (April 15, 1931), 4.

Polenberg, Richard. "The Great Conservation Contest," Forest History, X (January, 1967), 13-23.

Potter, David M. "The Historical Development of Eastern-Southern Freight Rate Relationships," Law and Contemporary Problems, XII (1947), 416-88.

Reed, Merl E. "Lumberjacks and Longshoremen: The I.W.W. in Louisiana," Labor History, XIII (Winter, 1972), 41-59.

Sharfman, Isaiah Leo. "The Trade Association Movement," American Economic Review, XVI (March, 1926), 203-18.

Silver, James W. "Paul Bunyan Comes to Mississippi," Journal of Mississippi History, XIX (April, 1957), 93-119.

_____. "The Hardwood Producers Come of Age," Journal of Southern History, XXIII (November, 1957), 427-53.

Stevens, Walter B. "John Barber White," Missouri Historical Review, XVII (January, 1923), 221-22.

Terrell, Mary Church. "Peonage in the United States," Nineteenth Century and After, LXII (August, 1907), 306-22.

Van Deusen, John G. "The Exodus of 1879," Journal of Negro History, XXI (April, 1936), 111-29.

Wand, Richard Ben. "Lumber's Labor Problem," Southern Lumber Journal, LXIX (August 10, 1945).

Weaver, Robert C. "Negro Labor since 1929," Journal of Negro History, XXXV (January, 1950), 20-38.

Wells, Philip P. "Philip P. Wells in the Forest Service Law Office," Journal of Forest History, XXII (April, 1978), 78-85.

Westcott, Minita. "History of Trade Associations," American Trade Association Executives Journal, VIII (April, 1956), 31-39.

Bibliography

White, Roy R. "Austin Cary, the Father of Southern Forestry," _Forest History_, V (Spring, 1961), 2-5.

Wiebe, Robert H. "Business Disunity and the Progressive Movement, 1901-1914," _Mississippi Valley Historical Review_, XLIV (March, 1958), 664-85.

"Women for Sawmill Engineers," _Gulf Coast Lumberman_, V (March 15, 1918), 40.

"Yellow Pine Industry of 1916," _Gulf Coast Lumberman_, IV (January 1, 1917), 4.

Index